Using Norton Utilities® 6

ALAN C. ELLIOTT

Using Norton Utilities 6

Copyright © 1992 by Que® Corporation.

Library of Congress Catalog No.: 91-66193

ISBN: 0-88022-861-X

94 93 92 91   4 3 2

Interpretation of the printing code: the rightmost double-digit number is the year of the book's printing; the rightmost single-digit number, the number of the book's printing. For example, a printing code of 91-1 shows that the first printing of the book occurred in 1991.

Using Norton Utilities 6 is based on Norton Utilities 6.0.1, Norton Commander 3.0, and Norton Backup 1.1.

Publisher: Lloyd J. Short

Product Development Manager: Thomas H. Bennett

Managing Editor: Paul Boger

Book Designer: Scott Cook

Production Team: Michelle Cleary, Sandy Grieshop, Audra Hershman, Betty Kish, Phil Kitchel, Joe Ramon, Tad Ringo, Linda Seifert, Louise Shinault, Kevin Spear, Bruce Steed, Phil Worthington

CREDITS

Product Director
Shelley O'Hara

Production Editor
Fran Blauw

Editors
Kelly Currie
Cindy Morrow
Susan M. Shaw

Technical Editor
Thomas Neuburger

Composed in *Cheltenham* and *MCP Digital*
by Que Corporation

DEDICATION

To my ever-supportive wife, Annette

ALAN C. ELLIOTT

Alan C. Elliott is an assistant director of Academic Computing Services at the University of Texas Southwestern Medical Center in Dallas. He holds a master's degree (M.A.S.) in statistics from Southern Methodist University and an M.B.A. degree from the University of Texas at Arlington. He is the author of several books including the first edition of *Using Norton Utilities*, *Introduction to Microcomputing with Applications*, *A Daily Dose of the American Dream*, and *PC Programming Techniques*. He is the coauthor of Que's *Using PROCOMM PLUS* with Walt Bruce and is a coauthor of the 1985 and 1988 editions of the *Directory of Statistical Microcomputing Software*. He is also author of the software packages Kwikstat (Data Analysis), PC-CAI (Computer Assisted Instruction) and Information Please (Free-Form database), published by TexaSoft. His articles have appeared in professional and popular periodicals, including *PC Week*, *Collegiate Microcomputer Journal*, *Communications in Statistics*, and *American Statistician*.

TRADEMARK ACKNOWLEDGMENTS

ACKNOWLEDGMENTS

I want to thank Karen Bluestein for the opportunity to work on the second edition of this book. The entire staff at Que was very professional, helpful, and supportive throughout the project. Special thanks go to Fran Blauw, Shelley O'Hara, Susan Shaw, and Kelly Currie for their help in editing the manuscript and asking insightful questions to make the presentation better. Thomas Neuburger deserves thanks for his careful technical review of the manuscript.

This project could not have been finished without the support of my wife, Annette, and without some patience from my kids, Mary and William.

CONVENTIONS USED IN THIS BOOK

The conventions used in this book have been established to help you learn to use the program quickly and easily. As much as possible, the conventions correspond with those used in the Norton Utilities documentation.

Screen names, menu names, and menu options appear in headline-style format. For example, select the Time and Date option.

Words or commands that you must type appear in lowercase *italics*. For example, type *prompt*. Or, they appear on a separate line in uppercase letters. For example, type

    COPY REPORT:TXT C:REPORT.TXT

Prompts or messages that appear on-screen are in digital type. For example,

    Do you wish to continue or stop? (Y/N)

Guidelines for the command syntax used in this book follow:

- Items enclosed in [brackets] are optional.

- For words written in *italic*, substitute the appropriate parameter. To use the DISKREET [*switches*] syntax, for example, you may type

    DISKREET /ON

- The [*d:*] option is a designation for the disk drive name, such as drive A, B, C, or D.

- The [*filespec*] option is a designation for a file specification. Unless noted, this specification can include a path name. The file specification for a file named MYFILE.TXT in the \WP50 directory, for example, is \WP50\MYFILE.TXT.

- The [*color*] option refers to a selection of colors. A color designation in a command line, for example, could be WHITE ON BLUE.

CONTENTS AT A GLANCE

TABLE OF CONTENTS

II: Using Norton Utilities

6 Managing Your Computer's Resources 229

III: Using Norton NDOS

IV: Using Norton Commander

V: Using Norton Backup

Who Should Read Using Norton Utilities?

Using Norton Utilities is for anyone who uses an IBM or compatible personal computer with the PC DOS or MS-DOS operating system. Norton Utilities 6 and the companion programs, Norton Commander 3.0 and Norton Backup, give you capabilities to protect, recover, and manage your computer's resources beyond what is available from standard DOS commands. This book will help you get the most out of your computer and the Norton programs.

Norton Utilities, Commander, and Backup are known as the premier data recovery and disk management programs available for IBM PC and compatible computers. The goals of this book are to

> Help beginning computer users understand and learn how to use these programs.

> Help new and seasoned users gain insights into making information storage more reliable, safer, and better organized.

Computer users with some experience will tell you "It's not *if* you will lose information on your computer—it's *when!*" You are reading this book because you want to prevent that inevitable *when*, or you already have experienced it and are looking for a way to make sure that it doesn't happen again. Perhaps you are in the middle of a crisis and are looking for some way to recover information that may be lost. This book contains the information that, along with Norton Utilities, can give you the best chance of data recovery and can help you prevent many kinds of data loss in the future.

Hard disks can be a blessing and a curse. They are a blessing because they can store a great deal of information. They are a curse when you have hundreds of unorganized files and you can't find the one you need. The file-management commands in Norton Utilities and the organizational features in Norton Commander can help you manage your hard disk. This book will show you how to use these programs to organize your disk, find lost files, navigate through a maze of directories, and be more productive in the use of your hard disk.

What Is Covered in This Book?

This book covers Norton Utilities 6, with references to Norton Utilities 5.0 and Norton Advanced Utilities 4.5. This book also covers Norton Commander Version 3.0 and Norton Backup, Versions 1.0 and 1.1.

This book is divided into five parts and four appendixes. The following sections discuss the contents in more detail.

Part I: Taking Charge of Your Computer

Part I of this book provides an overview of Norton Utilities and Norton Commander. Because you may be using one or both of these programs, the overviews are separated into two brief chapters. If you are interested only in Norton Utilities, for example, you easily can skip the information concerning Commander. The book will at times explain how the two programs can work together to enhance your control and use of your computer, however.

Part II: Using Norton Utilities

Part II begins by introducing the most commonly used features of Norton Utilities. This part groups the various Norton commands into four major topics based on how you use the program. Chapter 3 describes ways to protect your information on disk—how to prevent accidental formatting, how to restore formatted disks, how to protect files from erasure, and how to get rid of important information safely. Chapter 4 discusses ways to recover lost information—information that you have erased or lost because your disk has been damaged.

Chapter 5 is devoted to showing you how the utilities can help take good care of your hard disk—increasing safety, speed, and efficiency. Chapter 6 brings together a number of other Norton commands to help you better manage the information in your computer.

Part II concludes with Chapter 7, a reference section that lists Norton Utilities commands alphabetically and gives a brief summary of the use of each command. This reference section will be helpful if you are comfortable with a command, but simply need a reminder about its syntax or options.

Part III: Using Norton NDOS

Part III, consisting of Chapter 8, introduces Norton NDOS, a program that replaces many DOS commands with enhanced versions of the commands, and introduces over 40 new commands. You continue using DOS commands like you have always used them, but with NDOS you suddenly have a more powerful DOS. Part III introduces you to the power of NDOS and contains a reference to its commands, including the enhanced DOS commands and the new NDOS commands.

Part IV: Using Norton Commander

Part IV begins with an explanation of how you can use Norton Commander as a supplement to DOS. Even if you are well versed in DOS, you can benefit from the enhanced power provided by Norton Commander. Commander operates like a super-DOS that is always available when you are at a DOS prompt. From the DOS prompt you still can enter a normal DOS command, or you can access a Commander feature. If you use a mouse, you can access Commander's features by pointing to an option on-screen and clicking the mouse button—just point and shoot.

Chapter 9 describes the basic DOS-enhancing features of Norton Commander. The disk-management features enable you to use menus and on-screen graphics which assist you in copying, renaming, erasing, finding files, and so on. With the directory-management features, you can make, remove, and change directories. The viewing feature enables you to examine Lotus 1-2-3 files, dBASE files, and a variety of other popular kinds of spreadsheet, database, word processing, graphics, or text files at any time—without having to use the program that created these special files.

Chapter 10 describes how you can create and use menus to make access to programs easier and more intuitive. With Commander and a modem, you can link to MCI Mail, which enables you to send and receive electronic mail and send paper mail and faxes. You can access other electronic messaging networks by using MCI Mail.

Part V: Using Norton Backup

Part V, consisting of Chapter 11, covers the use of the Norton Backup program. This program enables you to copy information from your hard disk to a number of floppy disks. Then, if your hard disk is damaged or you lose files that cannot be recovered, you can use the backup copies of your hard disk to retrieve that information. Chapter 11 covers Versions 1.0 and 1.1 of Norton Backup. The differences in these versions are minor. Version 1.1 is an update to provide compatibility with a larger number of computers than Version 1.0 provided.

The Appendixes

The several appendixes give you additional information and tips about using Norton Utilities and Commander. If you are a computer beginner, you will want to read the brief introduction to PC DOS and MS-DOS (Appendix A). This appendix contains information about the basic DOS commands that are referred to in this book.

Appendix B provides a comparison of DOS and Norton commands. If you already know and use some of these DOS commands, this comparison will show you which Norton commands you can substitute for DOS commands and what additional features the Norton commands offer.

Appendix C includes installation instructions for Norton Utilities, Norton Commander, and Norton Backup. You already may have installed these programs using the information in the original program manual. If not, Appendix C will lead you through the installation process. It also will give you some additional information not covered in the Norton program manuals.

If you have a problem with your disk and don't know which Norton command to use, see Appendix D. This troubleshooting guide is divided into two parts. The first part deals with common disk problems and solutions, including the following kinds of situations:

- The computer no longer boots from the hard disk.
- You cannot format the hard disk as a system disk.
- The computer has a virus infection.
- You have continuing read-and-write problems on your hard disk that you can solve only with a low-level format.

The second part of Appendix D discusses responses to common DOS error messages that deal with disk problems. The appendix refers to DOS and Norton commands that can help you solve the problem.

What You Need To Use This Book

To use this book you need to have an IBM PC-compatible computer that uses the MS-DOS or PC DOS operating system Version 2.0 or higher. Although many of the commands covered in this book will work on floppy disk systems, a significant amount of the book discusses hard disk management. You need copies of Norton Utilities, Norton Commander, or Norton Backup. Because the book contains three major sections covering these programs separately, you can use this book for information on one, two, or all three programs. Some examples require you to attach a printer to your computer. Also, you may need a blank diskette for some examples.

Before you read this book, you should familiarize yourself with a text-editing program such as DOS's Edlin editor or the DOS Editor, available in Version 5.0 of DOS. Edlin is described briefly in the introduction to DOS (Appendix A). Any editor or word processor that can save files in Text mode will do. If you already use a text-editing or word processing program that can save files in text mode, you can use that program for the small amount of editing used in the examples in this book. Most of the tutorials in the book do not require text editing. Even if you do not know how to use a text editor, most examples in this book include alternative ways of creating needed files.

6

How To Use This Book

This book explains how to use Norton Utilities from a topical viewpoint and on a command-by-command basis. If you are a new user of Norton Utilities (or want to refresh your knowledge of the programs), you will want to read Chapters 3 through 6 carefully. These chapters cover the use of Norton commands.

If you already know how to use a Norton command, but you need a refresher about the command syntax or options, refer to Chapter 7. This chapter lists the commands alphabetically and briefly explains all options. You may want to refer to Chapter 7 often, even after you learn the basics of Norton commands. To learn about using NDOS, refer to Chapter 8. You can use NDOS with or independent of the other Norton Utilities commands.

If you have a problem with a diskette or hard disk and don't know which commands are appropriate to fix the problem, refer to the troubleshooting guide in Appendix D. This appendix also is useful when you encounter a disk-related DOS error message. Appendix D contains a selection of alphabetically listed DOS error messages. Each message is described with possible causes and solutions.

What Is Not Covered in This Book

Some problems related to information on your computer are beyond the scope of this book. If you lose information by accidentally erasing a range of cells in a Lotus 1-2-3 worksheet before saving it, for example, this book (and Norton Utilities) cannot help you recover from the mistake. Also, if you turn off the computer or lose power before saving a file to disk, the information is lost. These are instances when information is stored in the electronic memory of the computer and has not been placed on disk.

At times, software programs may contain bugs that make the information in a file useless. The logical nature of the file may be fine—that is, the file is okay according to DOS, but the information in the file has been scrambled or overwritten by the program. This kind of problem cannot be solved with the Norton programs. If you overwrite a file on disk with a file having the same name, the original file cannot be recovered because its space on disk now is being used by different information. These are cases where the file is stored properly on disk, but the information in the file is wrong.

Although Norton Utilities may be helpful for recovering from damage caused by some computer virus programs, these dangerous programs are getting more and more sophisticated in their capability to destroy data on a computer. There are simply too many ways that a virus can destroy data to be covered in this book. Appendix D gives you some help on this topic, however.

Physical damage to a hard disk or diskette can make data unrecoverable by the methods covered in this book. In some cases, professional disk repair technicians can extract information from a physically damaged disk. Mechanical problems with a disk drive also can cause loss of information. These problems must be corrected by a technician before you can recover any information.

Taking Charge of Your Computer

An Overview of Norton Utilities

N orton Utilities 6.0 consists of a number of programs (often called *Norton commands*) that provide you with tools to manage information on disk. These tools include programs to protect information, recover information, make your hard disk work more efficiently, and manage your computer resources.

Although PC DOS and MS-DOS have a number of useful commands, they lack some of the elements necessary to give you vital control over the safety of your files. One of the purposes of Norton Utilities is to fill this gap left by DOS.

If you are familiar with how to use DOS commands, you will find that many of the Norton commands use a similar syntax and therefore will be simple to learn and use. You can use some of the Norton commands as replacements for DOS commands. The replacement commands generally contain significant improvements over the normal DOS commands. The Norton Safe Format command, for example, not only formats a disk, but also is designed to prevent you from accidentally formatting a disk. Also, you can use Norton commands by selecting options from a menu so you don't have to remember all the options to include in the command given at the DOS prompt.

If you have been using Norton Utilities 4.5 or 5.0, you will find that some of the Version 4.5 commands have been incorporated into the newer Version 5.0 and 6.0 commands. Some commands originally included in 4.5 were absent from 5.0, but have been reincorporated into 6.0. Chapter 7, which gives you an alphabetical listing of Norton commands, lists 4.5, 5.0, and 6.0 commands. NDOS, a Norton Utilities replacement program for COMMAND.COM, is described in Chapter 8.

The Norton Utilities commands fall into four basic categories:

Category	Function
Group 1	Protects the information on your disk.
Group 2	Helps you recover lost information.
Group 3	Helps you fine-tune and manage the resources on your hard disk.
Group 4	Helps you manage the information on your hard disk to make your work more efficient and productive.

This chapter provides an overview of the Norton Utilities commands and refers you to the chapters in which you can find more specific information about the commands.

Beginning with DOS 5.0, DOS contains several commands related to information recovery. The relationships between the Norton commands and the new DOS commands, particularly MIRROR, UNDELETE, and UNFORMAT, are covered as part of the descriptions of the Norton commands IMAGE, UNFORMAT (Chapter 3), and UNERASE (Chapter 4).

Protecting Your Files

The Norton Utilities programs probably are most famous for helping you to recover lost information. These programs also are useful in preventing the loss of information. In fact, the old adage "a stitch in time saves nine" has relevance here. If you can safeguard your information on disk from the beginning, so much the better. Specific details on protecting the information on your disk are provided in Chapter 3, "Protecting Your Files."

A number of bad things can happen to information on your disk. *Physical problems* involve damage to the storage media and the mechanics of the disk drive. *Logical damage* involves the loss of magnetically stored information on disk.

Physical damage to a floppy diskette can be the result of a coffee spill, a bent diskette, a diskette left in a car on a hot summer day, or any number of other misuses of the diskette. You should always store a floppy diskette in its protective envelope and never expose it to heat, dust, or liquids.

A hard disk can sustain physical damage if you move the computer or bump it while it is operating. Even if you drop the computer only an inch, you can damage the hard disk. Usually, only a technician can repair physical damage to a disk—and then not always. Problems related to misaligned disk drives also require technical help.

Because information on a disk is stored as a magnetic image, this image can weaken until information is difficult or impossible to read. Loss of information on disk often results from accidental deletion of files or accidental formatting of the disk. Logical damage to a disk occurs when DOS loses information about where the data is stored—that is, DOS "forgets" where a file is located on disk. With Norton Utilities, you may be able to fix (or prevent) damage related to logical problems, magnetic weaknesses, or accidental erasure or formatting of the disk.

Preventing Problems

One of the strengths of Norton Utilities is its capability to help you prevent problems. Probably the first thing you should do with Norton Utilities is to make sure that you are safe from the prospect of someone accidentally formatting your hard disk. Otherwise, you could lose weeks, months, or years of work in a matter of minutes. Prevent this disaster by using the Safe Format command, a Norton replacement for the DOS FORMAT command. Safe Format gives you an added layer of protection against accidental formatting because the user must go through a few more steps to initiate a format.

If you load Norton Utilities with the Install program that comes on disk, you can replace the DOS FORMAT command with the Norton Safe Format command (see Appendix C). If you do not choose this option during the installation, you still can perform that task manually (see Chapter 3). Even if you manage to format a disk accidentally, you still can recover all information by using the Norton Format Recover command (unlike DOS's FORMAT command).

Restoring Formatted Disks

Implementing the Image (Format Recovery) procedure protects you from the accidental formatting of your disk. Each time you boot your computer, the Image program stores information about your files (a duplicate copy of DOS directory information) on disk. Then, if your disk is formatted accidentally, the UnFormat program can use this duplicate information to restore the formatted disk. When a disk is formatted, the actual data on the disk is not disturbed. The format clears out the file information in the disk's directory. With a duplicate copy of the information on disk, the UnFormat program can reconstruct the information needed to unformat the disk and get all the files back.

Preventing Files from Being Changed or Erased

Individual files on disk can be lost if you accidentally overwrite them with another file or erase them. You also may have files that you want to protect from being used by the wrong person. The Norton Disk Monitor program enables you to protect information on your disk from unauthorized use. If you have a number of files that you want to protect from accidental change or use, the Disk Monitor program can help.

Keeping Erased Information Out of the Wrong Hands

Another way to protect information is to make sure that it does not fall into the wrong hands. As mentioned before, formatting a disk does not destroy the information on the disk but simply erases some of the information in the disk's directory. If you erase a file or format a disk, someone with a program such as Norton Utilities can recover that information, so the data is not safely destroyed. This problem is a potential one for anyone who places financial, personal, corporate, or other secret or valuable information on a disk. Norton provides alternatives to the DOS ERASE (DEL) and FORMAT commands. You can use the WipeInfo command to completely destroy information on a disk.

Recovering Damaged or Lost Files

Chapter 4, "Recovering Files," explains techniques for recovering information from lost or damaged files. No matter how many precautions you take, you still have a good chance of losing some information on your computer disk. You may enter the command DEL *.DAT, for example, rather than DIR *.DAT. This simple typographical error can mean the erasure of important information. Perhaps you erase a file because you think you have another copy of it elsewhere—only to find that the erased file was your only copy after all. Also, you may intentionally format your disk because you have a backup and then discover that the backup is no good. Before Norton Utilities arrived on the scene, you had little hope of recovering any of that information. Now you have a number of tools to give you more than a fighting chance to recover lost data. Beginning with Version 5.0, DOS contains the commands UNDELETE and UNFORMAT, which are similar to the Norton file-recovery commands.

Losing or Damaging Files

Files can be lost or damaged in a number of ways. You can format your disk accidentally. You can inadvertently or incorrectly enter the DEL or ERASE command and erase a whole batch of important files. Loss of information also can occur when the power shuts off for some reason before you save a file to your disk. Perhaps your program freezes, forcing you to perform a *warm boot* (pressing Ctrl-Alt-Del) before all information is written to a file. Your disk may become too full so that DOS loses information about where the contents of a file are located. Bugs in software, hardware failures, and human errors are all potential causes of damaged files.

Recovering Files

In many cases, Norton Utilities can help you recover all or portions of damaged or lost files. The primary programs for recovery include the UnErase, UnFormat, Norton Disk Doctor II (NDD), and Norton Disk Edit commands.

The UnErase command is useful for recovering files that you have erased. Norton Disk Doctor II is a powerful program that attempts to diagnose problems with your disk (such as those caused by fragmented files, unclosed files from power outages, and so on) and correct these problems automatically.

The Norton Disk Edit program enables you to "perform surgery" on the information on disk. By directly editing the inner workings of the disk, you can remove or replace bad or damaged information with good information. If the disk information that contains the addresses of files on disk is damaged, for example, you may be able to transplant a new copy of this information to disk—making the information usable again. The Disk Edit program is powerful *and* dangerous. Like the knife of a surgeon, Disk Edit can be helpful in the hands of someone who carefully and knowledgeably uses it. If you accidentally change important disk information, however, you can destroy access to all the data on your disk.

Taking Care of Your Hard Disk

Keeping information on your disk safe is vital. As with an automobile, a few maintenance tasks can keep your machine running smoothly and at top speed. Chapter 5 covers several Norton Utilities commands that you can use to perform these maintenance procedures.

Testing Your Computer

Problems relating to your hard disk can mount before you even realize that a problem exists. Norton Utilities includes commands that enable you to keep track of how your computer system and hard disk are performing. The Norton Disk Doctor closely examines all the information on your disk and determines whether problems exist that could cause information in a file to become lost. NDD optionally attempts to correct such problems when they are found.

Making Your Disk Run Faster

One of the problems with disks is that, after much use, files become overly entangled or fragmented. When DOS runs out of enough space to store a file in one contiguous area on the disk, the operating system resorts to storing a part of a file here, a part there, and so on. This problem can get bad enough to cause DOS to lose information on some files. Also, because DOS must look here and there to find a file, your access to the hard disk can be slowed considerably. The Norton Speed Disk (SPEEDISK) command can rearrange the files on your hard disk in such a way as to remove fragmentation and restore maximum speed to the disk. If you hear your disk grinding when a file is being read or saved, or if your disk seems to be slowing down, you may be able to regain speed by using the Speed Disk command.

Another command that can help your hard disk work more efficiently is the Calibrate (CALIBRAT) command. You can use this command to adjust how much information DOS reads from your hard disk in one pass. Fine-tuning this adjustment can give your hard disk more speed. Calibrate also can perform a nondestructive low-level format of your hard disk to check the disk for reliability without disturbing the information already on disk.

Have you ever spent time looking through a directory listing to find a particular file? Being able to list the files by the date they were created—or by size, name, or extension—would undoubtedly be helpful. With the Norton Directory Sort (DS) command, you can sort files in a number of ways, and then use the DIR command to list the sorted directories. This procedure enables you to search for files easier and faster. The Norton NDOS DIR command also enables you to display files in sorted order. For more information, see Chapter 8.

Other Norton commands that can make your disk more efficient are FileFind (FILEFIND) and File Size (FS). You can use these commands to determine how much of the disk is being used to store files and how much of the space is allocated for use but is not used.

Managing Your Computer's Resources

A number of commands in Norton Utilities can give you more control over your computer than you can have by using DOS commands alone. These Norton commands help you manage your hard disk more efficiently and enable you to choose certain setup parameters for your computer.

Because a hard disk can store many files, just keeping track of potentially thousands of files easily can become a management nightmare. Suppose that you created a report last month but now cannot remember which directory contains table 1.A or where that graphic about sales on the East Coast is located. Norton has the commands to enable you to find information quickly.

Are you tired of working on a monitor that displays black and white (or black and amber or black and green) when you are using DOS—even though you are using a color monitor? Would you like to display more that 25 lines on your EGA monitor? Would you like to create your own custom program menu? Chapter 6, "Managing Your Computer's Resources," describes how to control these items by using Norton Utilities. Norton's NDOS also includes a number of enhancements to DOS commands and some new commands that enable you to manage your hard disk better and more efficiently. These commands are described in Chapter 8.

Navigating Directories

As newer and more advanced hard disks come on the market, users must deal with keeping track of more information on disk. The Norton Change Directory (NCD) command enables you to navigate between directories much more easily than having to remember the full name of each directory on disk. The NCD command replaces the functions of the DOS commands Change Directory (CD), Remove Directory (RD), and Make Directory (MD)—and offers more. With NCD, you can display the directory on-screen in a tree-like graph that shows various relationships among the directories. Using the arrow keys or the mouse, you can highlight the directory you want to access. Not only can you make, change to, and remove directories as in DOS—in NCD, you also can rename directories.

Finding Information

Within each directory on disk, you may have hundreds of files. Finding a particular file can be a nightmare. Often you know you have a file on disk but you cannot remember where you saw it. The Norton FileFind and File Locate commands enable you to find a specific file no matter which directory holds it. The FileFind and Tool Search commands also can perform a text search to find a file by searching the text inside the file. FileFind and Tool Save can even search files that you have erased.

Controlling Your Computer's Settings

The Norton Control Center is a utility that enables you to make your computer do things you may never have thought possible. You can change the size of your cursor, for example. If you use a laptop with a hard-to-read monitor, making the cursor bigger makes it easier to find on-screen. Some PCs require that you use the DOS Setup program on the diagnostic disk to permanently set the date and time on the computer. You now can do that with the Norton Control Center. Other settings available include monitor colors, how fast characters repeat when you hold down a key for more than a few seconds, how many lines are displayed on-screen, and settings for serial ports.

Creating Better Batch Files

Batch files contain series of commands that you use repetitively. DOS has a number of commands that are used in batch files, such as the PAUSE command and the ECHO command. Norton Utilities supplies some additional commands, called the Batch Enhancer commands, that enable you to create more sophisticated batch files. Using these commands, you can draw boxes, prompt the user for input, branch according to the user's answer, and so on.

Issuing Norton Commands

You should be convinced by now that Norton Utilities has myriad commands that can help you use your computer more safely and more productively. This program has other helpful features, however. Unlike most DOS commands, which you can use only from the DOS prompt, Norton gives you two ways to use commands. First, if you are familiar with a command, you can type it at the DOS prompt just as you would use any DOS command. Second, you can access Norton commands from a menu—one that reminds you of the purpose of the command and the options that are available. The following sections discuss how to use Norton Utilities.

Giving Commands from the DOS Prompt

You can use Norton Utilities commands as if they were DOS commands. In fact, Norton designed commands so that they operate with a syntax similar to DOS commands. To format a disk in drive A with the system switch (make the disk a bootable disk), for example, you can enter the familiar DOS command

    FORMAT A:/S

To format a disk in drive A with the Norton Safe Format command and the same option, enter this command:

SFORMAT A:/S

Notice that the syntax of the two commands is identical; only the names of the commands are different. Also notice that a command consists of distinct parts—the command (SFORMAT, in this example), any parameters (the disk drive), and switches. In the discussion of each command, the appropriate syntax is explained.

Using the Norton Menu

If you do not remember how to enter a Norton command at the DOS prompt, you have another option. Norton Utilities provides you with an easy-to-use menu interface with which you can access the Norton commands. This interface is called the *Norton menu*. To use the Norton menu, you need to remember only one command: NORTON.

If you are not in the Norton directory, however, DOS cannot execute this command unless you have given a PATH command that includes the Norton directory (usually \NORTON) in the DOS search path. The DOS search path typically is set up in the AUTOEXEC.BAT file, in a line similar to this one:

PATH C:;\C:\DOS;C:\NORTON

With the \NORTON directory included in the path (in this example, the directory is on drive C), you can access the Norton menu (and all Norton commands) from any directory and drive on your computer.

The AUTOEXEC.BAT option in the configuration menu enables you to add your Norton directory to your path. Choose the AUTOEXEC.BAT option, and then choose the option to add the Norton Utilities directory to the PATH statement. See "Modifying the AUTOEXEC.BAT File," later in this chapter, for more information.

After you type *Norton* at the DOS prompt, you see a screen similar to the one in figure 1.1.

The Norton menu screen consists of two parts. On the left side of the screen is a box containing a list of the available Norton commands. In figure 1.1, the Disk Doctor command is highlighted on the list. At the bottom of the screen, notice the command NDD. This is the command name of the Norton Disk Doctor. To the right of the command list is a brief description of the highlighted command. In this case, a description of Norton Disk Doctor is given, including the syntax of the NDD command and available switches. Not all commands are visible at one time in the command list. In a list box such as this, you can use the up- and down-arrow keys to display the remaining commands. You can press Home to go to the top of the list and End to go to the bottom of the list.

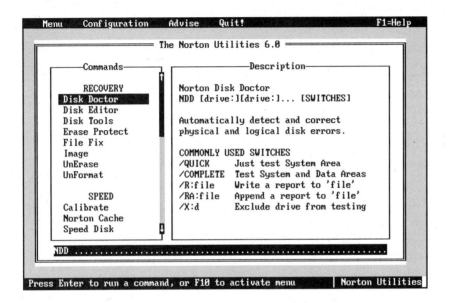

```
 Menu    Configuration    Advise    Quit!                    F1=Help
┌──────────────────────────────────────────────────────────────────┐
│              ═══════ The Norton Utilities 6.0 ═══════              │
│  ┌─Commands─────────┐  ┌─Description──────────────────────────┐   │
│  │                 ▲│  │                                      │   │
│  │     RECOVERY     │  │ Norton Disk Doctor                   │   │
│  │ ▓Disk Doctor▓▓▓▓ │  │ NDD [drive:][drive:]... [SWITCHES]   │   │
│  │  Disk Editor     │  │                                      │   │
│  │  Disk Tools      │  │ Automatically detect and correct     │   │
│  │  Erase Protect   │  │ physical and logical disk errors.    │   │
│  │  File Fix        │  │                                      │   │
│  │  Image           │  │ COMMONLY USED SWITCHES               │   │
│  │  UnErase         │  │ /QUICK      Just test System Area    │   │
│  │  UnFormat        │  │ /COMPLETE   Test System and Data Areas│  │
│  │                  │  │ /R:file     Write a report to 'file' │   │
│  │     SPEED        │  │ /RA:file    Append a report to 'file'│   │
│  │  Calibrate       │  │ /X:d        Exclude drive from testing│  │
│  │  Norton Cache    │  │                                      │   │
│  │  Speed Disk     ▼│  │                                      │   │
│  └──────────────────┘  └──────────────────────────────────────┘   │
│  ▌NDD ..............................................................│
├──────────────────────────────────────────────────────────────────┤
│ Press Enter to run a command, or F10 to activate menu │ Norton Utilities│
└──────────────────────────────────────────────────────────────────┘
```

FIG. 1.1.

Using the Norton menu to select other commands.

You can list the commands in the Norton menu by topic or alphabetically. See "Using the Menu Menu," later in this chapter, for more information.

Press Esc to end the Norton menu program and to return to the DOS prompt.

Using the Point-and-Shoot Method

With the Norton menu, you can point to the name of the command you want to use by using the arrow keys on the cursor keypad to move the highlight up or down in the command list. After you highlight (point to) the command you want to use, you can press Enter to run (shoot) the command. This point-and-shoot method enables you to choose and run a command easily without having to remember the exact command name or options.

At the bottom of the Norton menu is an input line that displays the selected command—the one to which you are pointing. Your cursor is positioned after the command on the input line. Here, you can type any options or switches before you press Enter to activate the command.

To run a command and enter switches, follow these steps:

1. Point to the command you want to use.

2. Type the appropriate switches or options.

3. Press Enter.

Using a Mouse

If your computer has a mouse attached, you also can use the mouse to point and shoot. When you move the mouse, you will see a pointer (a block or an arrow) on the Norton screen. To choose a command, point to the command and click the left or right mouse button once. The command appears at the bottom of the screen and you then can type any appropriate switches or options and press Enter to run the command.

To reveal commands that are not shown on the list, place the mouse pointer on the up or down arrow at the top or bottom right of the command box. You then can press the mouse button to move the command list up or down. The bar on the right of the command box is called a *scroll bar*. You can point to the highlighted rectangle, press and hold a mouse button, and moving the mouse pointer up and down, scroll through the list. Or, click on the top, middle, or bottom of the scroll bar to move to the top, middle, or bottom of the list.

On a two-button mouse, pressing both buttons together is the same as pressing Esc on the keyboard.

Editing the Command Line

Some command lines get complicated, and you may get to the end of a line before you realize that you have made an error at the beginning. You can use the Backspace key to erase all your work and start over, of course. If you use the built-in WordStar-like editing keys, however, you can save yourself some work. Table 1.1 lists these editing keys.

Viewing the Help Screens

At the top right of the Norton menu, F1=Help is displayed. This reminds you that you can press F1 to bring up a series of Norton Help screens that function like a minimanual for the Norton Utilities. You also can select Help by pointing to F1=Help with your mouse pointer and clicking once.

Table 1.1 Norton Menu Editing Keys

Key	Effect
→	Moves cursor to the right
←	Moves cursor to the left
Ctrl-D	Moves cursor right one character
Ctrl-S	Moves cursor left one character
Ctrl-→ or Ctrl-F	Moves cursor right one word
Ctrl-← or Ctrl-A	Moves cursor left one word
Ctrl-Home	Moves cursor to beginning of line
Ctrl-End	Moves cursor to end of line
Backspace	Deletes character to the left
Del or Ctrl-G	Deletes character at cursor
Ctrl-T	Deletes word to the right
Ctrl-W	Deletes word to the left
Ctrl-Y	Deletes the line

Using the Norton Menu Bar

On the top line (menu bar) of the Norton menu, the menu items Menu, Configuration, Advise, and Quit! appear. Menu, Configuration, and Advise are pull-down menus. The Quit! option ends the Norton menu program. The other menus contain options on using or configuring the program. These menus are explained in the next few sections of this chapter.

To open one of these menus, press F10 or point to the menu item with the mouse pointer and click once. After you extend a pull-down menu, you can move to one of the other menus by pressing the right- or left-arrow key or by pointing to the menu bar, pressing and holding the mouse button, and dragging the mouse to the left or right. Figure 1.2 shows the Menu pull-down menu.

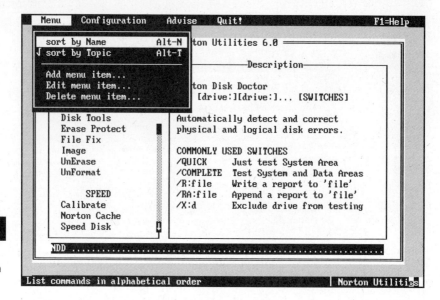

FIG. 1.2.

Accessing the
Menu pull-down
menu.

To choose an item on a pull-down menu, you can use the up- and down-arrow keys to highlight your choice and then press Enter. Alternatively, you can point to your choice with the mouse cursor and click. Notice that the Sort topics have Alt commands listed across from them, which you can use as shortcuts. The shortcut for Sort by Name is Alt-N, and the shortcut for Sort by Topic is Alt-T. When you see commands like these listed in a pull-down menu, it means that you can access these commands without pulling down the menu by pressing the key combination listed. Therefore, to sort commands by name even when the Configuration menu is not pulled down, you can enter the command Alt-N. (Hold down the Alt key and press the N key.)

Another way to choose an option from a pull-down menu is to press a *hot key*. A hot key enables you to use a shortcut to perform a function. Often, a hot key is the first letter of the menu choice. However, if there are two menu options that begin with the same letter, the hot key is the capitalized letter in the option. (In color mode, these hot keys are highlighted on-screen.) For the two Sort options, for example, the hot keys are N for Sort by Name and T for Sort by Topic. After you extend the Menu pull-down menu, you can press N to choose the Sort by Name option, T to sort by topic, and so on.

Using the Menu Menu

The Menu menu contains five options. The first set of options includes Sort by Name and Sort by Topic. These two options affect how commands are listed in the Commands box. The commands in the Commands box of the Norton Menu are listed by topic. The topics are Recovery, Speed, Security, and Tools. Because the list is longer than the box, you can only see the Recovery and Speed topics in the Commands box. Within the topics, the commands are listed alphabetically. If you choose the Sort by Name option from the Menu menu, the commands are listed in alphabetical order by name.

The next three options on the menu are Add Menu Item, Edit Menu Item, and Delete Menu Item. Each of these is followed by an ellipsis. When you see the ... indication after a command option, it means that after you choose that option you will need to select or enter additional information before the command performs a task.

You can use these three commands to customize the Norton menu. You can add your own commands to the list, edit how the commands are presented, or delete items from the menu. See Chapter 6 for information on how to change items on the Norton menu.

Using the Configuration Menu

When you choose the Configuration menu, it presents eight options (see fig. 1.3). These options are divided into four sections. The first option enables you to control video and mouse options. The second section, containing three options, enables you to choose options for the Norton Cache program and modify your AUTOEXEC.BAT and CONFIG.SYS files (see Chapter 5). The third section, containing two options, enables you to select alternate names for Norton programs and to expand programs from their original compressed format. The fourth section, consisting of two options, enables you to set passwords and enable or disable the Norton menu.

Setting Video and Mouse Options

The Video and Mouse option on the Configuration menu enables you to choose how the Norton menu (and other Norton menus) appears on your monitor. After you choose this option, a screen similar to the one in figure 1.4 appears. There are four types of settings in this dialog box: Screen Colors, Mouse Options, Graphics Options, and Screen Options.

FIG. 1.3.

Accessing the Configuration menu.

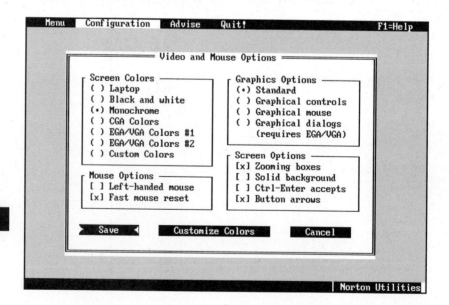

FIG. 1.4.

Setting video and mouse options in the Norton menu.

The Screen Colors and Graphics Options boxes contain radio buttons. These buttons are represented by parentheses (or circles on EGA or VGA monitors) with a dot in the middle of only one of the options per box. The term *radio button* comes from being able to choose only one radio station on your car radio by choosing one button. When you choose one button, all other buttons on the radio are turned off. In the same way, when you see a dialog box that contains radio buttons, you know that you can choose only one option in that box.

To select a radio button, use the arrow keys to highlight the button you want to choose, and then press the space bar to choose the button. This will turn off any other radio button in the box. If you have a mouse, point to the button you want to choose and click once. You also can select buttons by pressing the appropriate hot key. The hot key is the first letter of the option name or the capitalized letter of an option. You press L, for example, to select the Laptop option in the Screen Colors box.

In the Screen Colors box, you can choose from seven color combinations: Laptop, Black and White, Monochrome, CGA Colors, EGA/VGA Colors #1, EGA/VGA Colors #2, and Custom Colors. The Laptop, Black and White, and Monochrome options use combinations of black and different intensities of white. The color options use mostly blue, green, black, and white. If you don't like the color choices available, choose the Custom Colors option, which enables you to choose the colors to be used in the program.

In the Graphics Options box, the Standard option displays a square cursor-like mouse pointer and nongraphics radio and check buttons which use parentheses ( ) and brackets [ ] rather than circles and boxes. The Graphical Controls option displays round radio buttons but the mouse cursor is in the standard mode. In the Graphical Mouse option the controls are round and the mouse pointer is an arrow. For the Graphical Dialogs (requires EGA/VGA) option, the mouse pointer is an arrow and the dialog boxes contain graphical icons.

Two boxes in figure 1.4, Mouse Options and Screen Options, contain check boxes. Unlike radio buttons, you can choose any number of check boxes in an option box. Use arrow keys to point to the box you want and press the space bar to turn the option on or off (an X means the option is turned on). If you are using a mouse, point to an option and click. Also, you can press the option's hot key to choose an item.

In the Mouse Options box, the Left-Handed Mouse option enables you to choose your mouse for left-handed or right-handed use. This simply changes the meanings of the buttons on a two-button mouse. You should turn on the Fast Mouse Reset option if you are using PS/2 or COMPAQ mouse ports.

In the Screen Options box, you can select the Zooming Boxes option so that when dialog boxes appear on-screen, they look like they zoom into place—the boxes grow from a small square to the final size. The Solid Background option enables you to choose a solid or textured background on Norton menu screens.

The Ctrl-Enter Accepts option, when checked, enables you to press Ctrl-Enter as an equivalent to selecting OK in a dialog box, which accepts the current settings in the box and closes the box. When Ctrl-Enter is checked, you can use Enter to select items within the dialog box. When Ctrl-Enter is not selected (the default condition), pressing Enter in a dialog box selects OK and closes the box. The Button Arrows option enables you to turn on or off the active command markers (see the triangles in the Save box at the bottom of fig. 1.4.). In monochrome mode, these triangles always appear on the active button. In color mode, if the Button Arrows option is off, the active button appears in a different color.

After you set all the options you want in the Video and Mouse Options box, choose Save to save this information to disk. To choose Save, press Enter, press the S hot key, or point to the Save box with your mouse pointer and press Enter.

Setting the Norton Cache Options

The Norton Cache is normally initiated from the AUTOEXEC.BAT or CONFIG.SYS files. The third and fourth options in the Configuration menu enable you to set up the cache command. Before you use these options, you can choose settings for how the cache will be initiated by choosing settings in the Norton Cache menu option. The options you select here determine how the cache command is set up in the CONFIG.SYS or AUTOEXEC.BAT files. Before choosing your selections here, you should read more about the Norton Cache program, as described in Chapter 5.

The options you may choose from the Norton Cache dialog box include Loading, High Memory, Cache Options, and Memory Usage. The Loading option enables you to choose to load the Cache Program from CONFIG.SYS or AUTOEXEC.BAT or to choose not to load the cache program at all. Loading from AUTOEXEC.BAT makes it possible to unload the cache program from memory.

The High Memory option enables you to choose to load the cache program into high memory or conventional memory. If you have only 640K or less memory, you must choose the conventional memory option. If you have sufficient memory, choosing the high memory option reduces the amount of conventional memory used, which enables you to have more memory available for running application programs.

The Cache options enable you to use floppy drives for the cache and to choose the IntelliWrites option. Using floppies for cache is not recommended because they are slow. The IntelliWrites option reduces the amount of head movement used in writing to the disk cache, but it may slow down the execution of the program. By default it is set as on.

The Memory Usage option enables you to choose how much memory the cache will use for expanded, extended, and conventional memory for DOS or Windows. The maximum amount of memory available is listed, and a default size is indicated. Usually, you will want to avoid using any conventional memory, and you will use extended or expanded memory for the cache.

Select OK to accept the settings in the Norton Cache dialog box. Then go to the CONFIG.SYS or AUTOEXEC.BAT option on the Configuration menu to place the cache options in the appropriate start-up file.

Modifying the CONFIG.SYS File

The CONFIG.SYS option in the Configuration menu enables you to add (or change) the necessary information to your CONFIG.SYS file to support the Norton DISKREET and NDOS programs and to load the supporting device drivers PCSHADOW.SYS and KEYSTACK.SYS. Information on the setup and use of the DISKREET program is covered in Chapter 3. Information on the use and setup of NDOS can be found in Chapter 8. You should use the PCSHADOW driver when using COMPAQ shadow RAM and the KEYSTACK driver when using NDOS (see Chapter 8).

Modifying the AUTOEXEC.BAT File

The AUTOEXEC.BAT option in the Configuration menu enables you to add (or change) statements in your AUTOEXEC.BAT file. You may add or change commands in your AUTOEXEC.BAT file related to any of the following tasks:

- Adding Norton Utilities to your PATH statement
- Setting the NU environment variable
- Loading the DISKMON utility
- Loading the EP utility
- Running the IMAGE utility
- Running the NDD utility with the /QUICK option

Adding Norton to your PATH statement enables you to run Norton programs from any directory on your computer. The NU environment variable tells your computer where to find the Norton files on disk. The DISKMON (Disk Monitor) utility, the EP (Erase Protect) utility, and the IMAGE utility are discussed in Chapter 3. The NDD utility is discussed in Chapter 4.

Selecting Alternate Names

The Alternate Names option on the Configuration menu enables you to choose between two names for several Norton programs. You may, for example, prefer to use the short name for a program to save keystrokes or you may prefer the long name because it is easier to remember. The programs having alternate names follow:

Long Name	Short Name
DISKEDIT	DE
FILEFIND	FF
SFORMAT	SF or FORMAT
SPEEDISK	SD
SYSINFO	SI

When you choose Alternate Names, you are given the option to choose all short names, all long names, or to select the name you want to use for each program (see fig. 1.5). Use the arrow keys (or mouse) to point to one of the radio buttons in each option box. Then press the space bar or click the mouse button to make your selection. After you make all your choices, press Enter or click on OK.

Expanding Programs

The Norton programs on disk are in a compressed form to save disk space. This means that when a program loads into memory, it expands to regular size, and then begins to run. This process can take five to seven seconds on a slow (8088-based) computer. For faster machines, there is usually no detectable delay. If you are using a slow machine, you can choose Expand Programs from the Configuration menu to expand the program files so that there is less delay in running a program.

Expanded programs will occupy more of your disk space, however. To cause the programs to be expanded, choose OK from the Expand Program Files dialog box, or choose Cancel to not expand the programs. Once the programs are expanded, they cannot be compressed again.

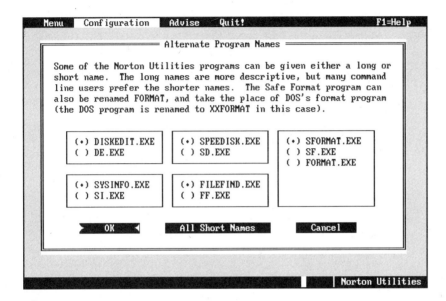

FIG. 1.5.

The Alternate Program Names dialog box.

Setting Passwords

Norton Utilities enables you to place password-protection on any of 11 Norton Utility programs to prevent the unauthorized use of these programs. When you choose the Passwords option from the Configuration menu, you may then choose to specify or remove the password for any of the following programs (see fig. 1.6):

Calibrate
Configuration
Disk Doctor
Disk Editor
Disk Tools
File Fix
Safe Format
Speed Disk
UnErase
UnFormat
WipeInfo

To specify that a program is to be password-protected, highlight the check box next to the command name and press the space bar to turn the check off or on. When you have checked all programs you want to protect, press Enter or click on Set Passwords.

FIG. 1.6.

The Password
Protection
dialog box.

There is one password that is applied to all programs you choose to password-protect. Once you specify a password and choose the programs that are protected, you will only be able to run those programs after entering the password. When you set the password, you must enter it a second time as a verification. Do not forget the password, because you will be unable to run the protected programs without it.

Choosing Menu Editing Options

The Menu Editing option on the Configuration menu enables you to enable or disable the editing of the Norton menu. Normally, you can add, delete, or change the contents of the Norton menu. If you are not careful, however, you can mess up the menu so that you can no longer access Norton programs from it. To prevent the menu from being changed, choose the Disable Editing option.

Using the Advise Menu

When you choose the Advise menu, five options are revealed
(see fig. 1.7):

> Common Disk Problems
> DOS Error Messages
> CHKDSK Error Messages
> Application Error Messages
> Search

These items give you advice on solutions to problems you may encounter. If you choose Common Disk Problems, for example, a screen such
as the one in figure 1.8 appears. The Common Disk Problems option
covers problems such as when your computer will no longer boot from
a disk, if you have formatted your hard disk, problems in copying files,
and other topics related to accessing information on your disk.

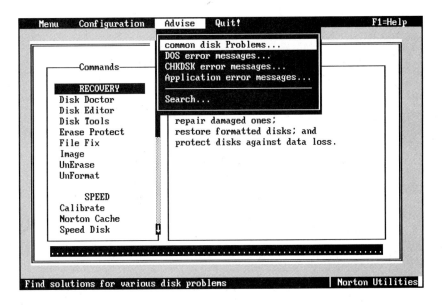

```
 Menu    Configuration    Advise    Quit!                    F1=Help

                              common disk Problems...
                              DOS error messages...
              Commands        CHKDSK error messages...
                              Application error messages...
             RECOVERY
          Disk Doctor         Search...
          Disk Editor
          Disk Tools                repair damaged ones;
          Erase Protect            restore formatted disks; and
          File Fix                 protect disks against data loss.
          Image
          UnErase
          UnFormat

             SPEED
          Calibrate
          Norton Cache
          Speed Disk


 .........................................................................
 Find solutions for various disk problems           | Norton Utilities
```

FIG. 1.7.

The Advise
menu.

The DOS Error Messages option gives explanations for DOS messages
that you get when you use a DOS command and it does not work properly (for example, Abort, Retry, or Fail).

The CHKDSK Error Messages option tells you what to do if the DOS
CHKDSK command finds problems on your disk, such as problems in
the File Allocation Table (FAT).

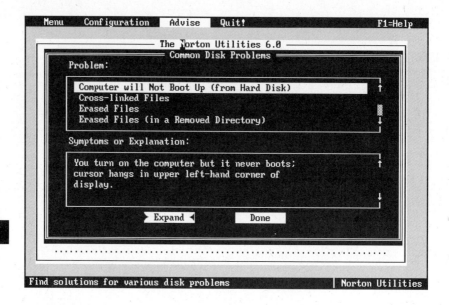

FIG. 1.8.

The Common
Disk Problems
dialog box.

The Application Error Messages option lists common messages found in popular software packages such as WordPerfect, Lotus 1-2-3, and dBASE and recommends solutions.

The Search option enables you to type an error message (or a portion of the error message) and then searches for that error message and displays advice concerning that message. For more information on the Advise menu topics, see Appendix D.

Getting Instant Help

In addition to the information provided about commands on the Norton menu screen, you have another way to get on-screen help about Norton commands. If you enter at the DOS prompt a Norton command followed by a question mark, a Help screen appears. This screen lists the command's possible options and switches and may give some sample uses of the command. To get information on the File Date (FD) command, for example, enter the following at the DOS prompt:

    FD ?

Remember to include a space between the command (FD) and the question mark (?). Figure 1.9 shows the help information that appears on-screen.

```
C:\NU>fd ?
File Date, Norton Utilities 6.0, Copyright 1991 by Symantec Corporation

Change the file time and date information.

FD pathname [/D[date]] [/T[time]] [/P] [/S]

    /D[mm-dd-yy]  Set the date to [mm-dd-yy]
    /T[hh:mm:ss]  Set the time to [hour:minute:second].
    /P            Pause after each screen.
    /S            Include Subdirectories.

Running FD without /D and /T will stamp the current
date and time on all files matching the file specified.

C:\NU>
```

FIG. 1.9.

A help screen for the Norton File Date (FD) command.

Chapter Summary

The information on your computer disk may not be safe. Accidental erasures, unintentional disk formatting, problems with computer programs, power outages, and other difficulties can compromise your data. Although DOS has a few options that can help you protect your data, more are needed. Norton Utilities gives you additional ways to build in preventive measures and protect the information on your computer disk. Then, if a loss occurs, you still may be able to recover some or all of your information by using Norton Utilities' recovery techniques.

Norton Utilities programs are not only for protection and recovery. The program also includes a number of commands that help you manage the information on your computer and make your disk run faster and safer.

This book helps you get the most out of Norton Utilities. It groups and explains the commands by the four basic ways you will use them: protection, recovery, maintenance, and management of information on your hard disk.

An Overview of Norton Commander

Norton Commander 3.0 is a program that makes your personal computer easier to use and gives you more control over your computer than you have with DOS alone. Commander offers you

- An easier way to perform many common DOS commands such as COPY, RENAME, DELETE, and others. Rather than forcing you to remember DOS syntax for these commands, Commander leads you through the command process with a series of menus and prompts.

- Commands that perform tasks that DOS cannot do. Commander enables you to rename directories, view sorted directories, compare directories, control hidden file attributes, and so on.

- A way to view spreadsheet, database, and word processing files without using the application program.

- A communication program for sending and receiving MCI mail.

- A communication link for sending information between two computers.

■ The option to choose between entering commands at the DOS prompt or accessing commands from a menu structure. You also can use a mouse to access menus in Commander.

This list of features is not exhaustive, but should give you an idea of the kinds of tasks you can perform with Commander. Using Norton Commander is like adding a "power package" to a plain automobile. DOS is that plain automobile that generally gets you where you want to go. With Commander added onto DOS, however, you have power windows (pull-down menus), extra horsepower (commands that can do more than DOS commands), a car phone (MCI Mail), and more. Commander makes using your computer more fun, and the program's array of features also can make you more productive.

This book guides you through the setup and use of Norton Commander to show you how to take advantage of its numerous features. You learn why you would use a Commander feature, when you would want to use a feature, and how to use the feature. This overview introduces you to Commander's capabilities and menu structure and tells you how to access menu choices. Details of the menu items are covered in Chapters 9 and 10.

Working with Basic Commander Features

Chapter 9 covers the basic features of Norton Commander. These include the ability to perform commands such as Copy, Rename, and Move from a menu interface. You also can view WordPerfect and other word processor files, Lotus 1-2-3 and other spreadsheet files, and dBASE and other database files directly from Commander without accessing another program. Chapter 9 also covers Commander's version of the Norton Change Directory command which is more extensive than the similar command in Norton Utilities.

Working with Advanced Commander Features

Chapter 10 covers several advanced features of Norton Commander. These include creating your own menus, specifying file extension meanings, and using Commander Mail and Commander Link.

Creating Menus

One of the ways you can customize Commander so that your computer works intuitively for you is to create and use your own menus. You can create menus to automate a series of commands that you perform regularly. You may create a menu that enables you to choose which application program to begin (WordPerfect, Lotus 1-2-3, Excel, and so on), for example. If you are familiar with batch files, you will find that these menus are created similarly and perform similar tasks. Rather than just use DOS batch commands, however, you can access Commander menu commands.

Specifying File Extensions

If Commander knows which application is associated with a file in a directory listing, you can choose that file and have Commander automatically load the application, using the file name you have highlighted on-screen. You first must define the file types you plan to use, however. You can specify that all files with the WP extension are WordPerfect files, for example. Then if you choose a file with a WP extension by selecting the file name on-screen, Commander loads WordPerfect with that file being edited.

Using Commander Mail

With Commander, you can access MCI Mail. To do so, you must have a modem attached to your computer and a phone line. You also must have an MCI account number and password. When you use MCI Mail, you can send and receive electronic mail, faxes, telexes, and paper mail.

If you do not have an MCI Mail account, you can arrange to get one by calling 1-800-444-6245. Normally, a fee is required to set up the account, but sometimes MCI waives the fee. (At the writing of this book, the fee was $35.) Ask the service representative whether MCI will waive the fee because you are using Norton Commander.

T I P

Using Commander Link

Commander Link enables you to move information quickly between two computers. To use Commander Link, you must have a serial cable connecting the two computers and Commander Link must be running on both computers. The cable between the computers must be a *null modem cable*—a special serial cable that acts as a modem link between two computers (for more information, see Chapter 9). You can purchase such a cable from your local computer shop. Commander Link is helpful for moving large numbers of files from one computer to another. You can use Link to copy your WordPerfect directory from one computer to another, for example.

Using Norton Commander

This book assumes that you already have installed Norton Commander on your hard disk. If you have not, refer to Appendix C for installation instructions. Be sure that you choose to place the \NC directory name in the PATH statement in your AUTOEXEC.BAT file (an option during installation). If you already have installed Commander but did not place \NC in your PATH statement, refer to Appendix A on how to use the DOS PATH command and how to edit an AUTOEXEC.BAT file.

To begin the Norton Commander program, type *nc* at the DOS prompt. A screen similar to the one in figure 2.1 appears. As you learn in Chapter 9, you can customize the way that Commander looks on your screen. Generally, the screen includes four areas of interest: a right panel, a left panel (not visible in fig. 2.1), a menu of function key commands at the bottom of the screen, and a menu bar at the top of the screen (not visible in fig. 2.1). You can control the visibility of the panels on-screen by pressing Ctrl-F1 for the left panel or Ctrl-F2 for the right panel or choosing these options from the Left or Right pull-down menus. Notice also that the normal DOS prompt appears just above the function key menu.

Using Menus and Commands

Commander gives you a choice in how you can access computer commands. You can enter a command at the DOS prompt or choose a command from one of Commander's menus. When Commander is running, the DOS prompt always appears on-screen. If you enter a DOS command, it works as it always has worked (although pressing F3 will not

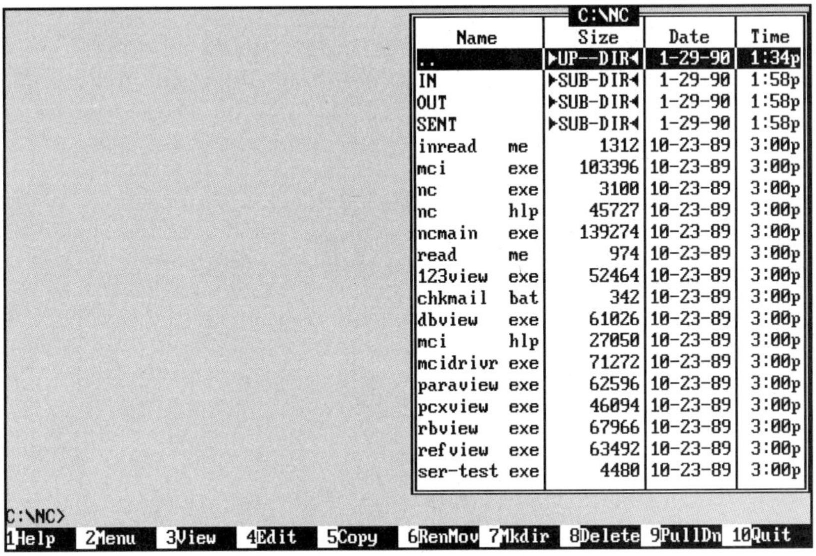

```
                              ┌──────────C:\NC──────────┐
                   │    Name     │  Size  │  Date  │ Time  │
                   │..           │▶UP--DIR◀│ 1-29-90│ 1:34p │
                   │IN           │▶SUB-DIR◀│ 1-29-90│ 1:58p │
                   │OUT          │▶SUB-DIR◀│ 1-29-90│ 1:58p │
                   │SENT         │▶SUB-DIR◀│ 1-29-90│ 1:58p │
                   │inread    me │    1312│10-23-89│ 3:00p │
                   │mci      exe │  103396│10-23-89│ 3:00p │
                   │nc       exe │    3100│10-23-89│ 3:00p │
                   │nc       hlp │   45727│10-23-89│ 3:00p │
                   │ncmain   exe │  139274│10-23-89│ 3:00p │
                   │read      me │     974│10-23-89│ 3:00p │
                   │123view  exe │   52464│10-23-89│ 3:00p │
                   │chkmail  bat │     342│10-23-89│ 3:00p │
                   │dbview   exe │   61026│10-23-89│ 3:00p │
                   │mci      hlp │   27050│10-23-89│ 3:00p │
                   │mcidrivr exe │   71272│10-23-89│ 3:00p │
                   │paraview exe │   62596│10-23-89│ 3:00p │
                   │pcxview  exe │   46094│10-23-89│ 3:00p │
                   │rbview   exe │   67966│10-23-89│ 3:00p │
                   │refview  exe │   63492│10-23-89│ 3:00p │
                   │ser-test exe │    4480│10-23-89│ 3:00p │
                   └─────────────┴────────┴────────┴───────┘
C:\NC>
1Help  2Menu  3View  4Edit  5Copy  6RenMov 7Mkdir  8Delete 9PullDn 10Quit
```

FIG. 2.1.

The Norton Commander opening screen.

recall the command). When the command's action is finished, you are returned to the Commander screen. If you enter at the DOS prompt a command to begin an application program—such as a word processor—the application runs normally, and you return to the Commander screen when you exit that program. If you want to access a Commander command rather than a DOS command, you must choose the command from a Commander menu or by using a hot key combination. (On the initial Commander screen, only one menu is present—the function key menu. See Chapter 9 for information on how to control which menus are displayed.)

Understanding the Selection Methods

To access Commander features such as menu commands, you may use a technique called *point and shoot*. When the Commander screen is displayed and you press the up- or down-arrow key on the cursor keypad, a highlight moves up or down in the list of files in the right panel of the screen. If you want to select a file to be used in some actions (such as when you're copying, renaming, and so on), you point to the file by highlighting it. Then, to choose what you want to do to the file (shoot), you press Enter or a menu key (such as one of the function keys). In many cases when using Commander, you point to an item by highlighting it and you choose it by pressing Enter.

If you are using a mouse, a small square cursor appears on-screen. You can move this cursor by moving the mouse. The point-and-shoot technique with a mouse is to move the mouse pointer to a menu item or file name (point) and then choose the item (shoot) by clicking the left or right mouse button. If you have a mouse, you can use the mouse or the arrow keys to point to a selection.

In most menus and dialog boxes, you also can choose an option by pressing the first letter of the option. In some menus, more than one option starts with the same letter. In that case, an option's name may have all lowercase letters except one character. To choose that option, you press the option's uppercase character, even if it is not the first character of the name. If you see the menu selection tiMe in a menu, for example, press M to choose that option.

Accessing the Function Key Menu and the Menu Bar

You access Commander's features through two types of menus: the Function Key menu and the menu bar.

The Function Key menu appears along the bottom of the Commander screen. To access the function key commands, you press the appropriate function key on the keyboard or point to the function key name on-screen and click the mouse button. Chapter 9 explains how to use the function keys. The F2 (Menu) function key, however, is covered in Chapter 10.

The menu bar consists of five menus: Left, Files, Commands, Options, and Right. To make the menu bar at the top of the screen visible, press F9 (PullDn). Then, to pull down one of the five menus, press the left- or right-arrow key to highlight the menu name and press Enter. If you are using a mouse, point to the menu you want and click the mouse button. When you select a menu, it appears on-screen. Figure 2.2 shows the Left menu selected.

To choose one of the options from a selected pull-down menu, use the up- and down-arrow keys to point to an option and then press Enter, press the uppercase letter associated with your menu choice, or point to a selection with the mouse. After one of the pull-down menus is in view, you also can use the right- and left-arrow keys to move between the five menu bar menus to choose other commands. With the mouse, you can point to the menu bar, click and hold the button, and drag the mouse pointer left or right to make one of the other menus appear. To close a pull-down menu, press Esc or click the mouse button while pointing outside the menu box. See Chapter 9 to learn more about using menu options.

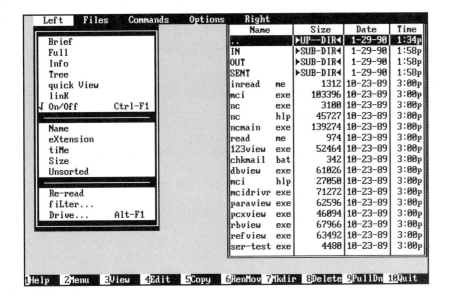

FIG. 2.2.

Displaying the
Left menu.

Getting Help

The Norton Help system is like a miniature manual on disk. After you
choose the Help option by pressing F1 or choosing Help from the Files
menu, you see the menu shown in figure 2.3. Choosing any of these
menu options displays helpful information. If you want to know about
the program's Find Files option, for example, you can choose Find Files
from the Help menu to display information about how to use that option. Choose one of the Help menu options by using the arrow keys to
highlight the option and then pressing Enter, or by pointing and clicking with the mouse. To exit the Help menu, press Esc or choose the
Cancel option at the bottom of the screen.

Quitting Norton Commander

When you press the F10 (Quit) function key to end Commander, the
dialog box in figure 2.4 appears.

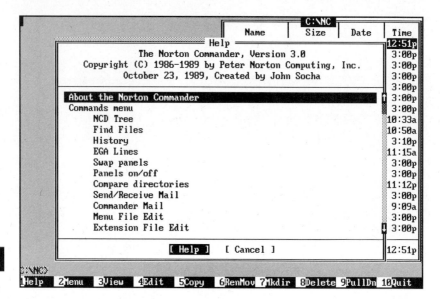

FIG. 2.3.

The Help menu.

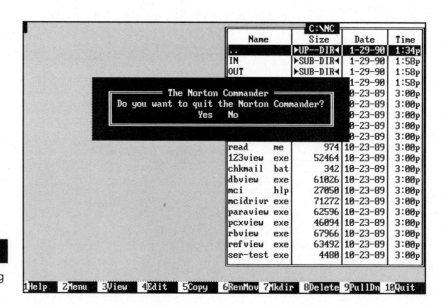

FIG. 2.4.

The Quit dialog box.

You have several ways to choose Yes or No:

- Use the right- and left-arrow keys to move the highlight to Yes or No, and press Enter to select the highlighted choice.

- Press the first letter of your choice—press the N key to choose No or press Y to choose Yes.

- Using the mouse, move the pointer to your choice and click the mouse button.

Chapter Summary

Norton Commander gives you power beyond DOS and gives you a more user-friendly environment for your computer. With Commander, you still can access DOS commands in the normal way, but you also can perform some DOS functions (and more) from menus. Commander enables you to pick and choose how to manage your files and how to control your computer setup. As a bonus, you also have access to PC-to-PC communications and MCI Mail.

Using Norton Utilities

PART

II

OUTLINE

Protecting Your Files

The information stored on your disk is subject to many potential dangers. As the computer operator and systems manager, you must protect your information in the following ways:

- Prevent information from being lost as a result of accidental formatting

- Prepare for possible accidental formatting

- Prevent important files from being erased or overwritten

- Permanently dispose of valuable or secret information

This chapter discusses the Norton Utilities commands that can help you protect the information on your disk in these ways. The Safe Format (SFORMAT) command gives you protection against accidental formatting and provides protection and speed beyond that available in the DOS FORMAT command. Just in case your disk is reformatted accidentally, Norton provides the Image and UnFormat commands. Using the Image command, you can prepare for an accidental format so that you can recover your files after the format by using the UnFormat command.

The Erase Protect command protects erased files by preserving the undestroyed information for a certain amount of time so that you can unerase files if necessary. The Disk Monitor command protects your files from being overwritten or erased.

The Diskreet command protects files from being used by an unauthorized person. The WipeInfo command enables you to get rid of secret or valuable information safely so that no program can recover it.

Preventing Accidental Formats

Formatting is the procedure that prepares a disk (a floppy or a hard disk) to store information. If you format a disk that contains information (files), the information on the disk is erased. This loss can be devastating if the disk contained important data that is hard to recover.

Computer users commonly call in their company's computer support people, for example, to help recover accidentally formatted hard disks. Sometimes the hard disk contained important research, financial, or organizational information and was not backed up regularly. In many cases, these people must reconstruct the information that had been on disk from letters, papers, and records dating back several years. This process may cost thousands of dollars in personnel time. In some cases, the original source of the information cannot be recovered. Few people are prepared in any way for this expensive problem.

 **NOTE**   Although Norton Utilities does not provide a backup procedure, backing up information on disk should be a standard practice and the first step in protecting your data. DOS provides a process for making backup copies of your hard disk by using the BACKUP command. You also can buy a backup program called Norton Backup. A number of other software programs also enable you to back up your hard disk onto floppy disks, tapes, or other media. Using the DOS BACKUP procedure is covered in Appendix A. See Chapter 11 for more information on using the Norton Backup program.

Depending on the version of DOS you are using, it is easy to reformat a disk accidentally. Versions of DOS before 3.3 enable you to format the hard disk (drive C) simply by entering the following command:

    FORMAT C:

(If you are at the C> prompt, you just use the FORMAT command.)
Then you press Enter in response to a prompt asking whether you are
sure that your disk is in place. Beginning with DOS Version 3.3, you also
must give a volume name to the disk before the format proceeds.

Whatever the cause, accidental formatting is a problem that continues
to occur, even with the recent DOS safeguard of requiring a volume
label in the FORMAT command. The Norton Utilities Safe Format command gives you additional levels of protection against accidental formatting. Safe Format displays on-screen, for example, information
about the impending format. Even after entering the Safe Format command, you must choose to begin the process by selecting an item from
the Safe Format menu. The menu also gives you easy access to a number of formatting options. If the disk already contains data, Safe Format
gives you a warning message.

Also, even if you choose to proceed with the format, Safe Format saves
a copy of the old file information to a place on disk that can be recovered. Because the formatting procedure essentially just wipes out all
information about where files are stored on disk, you can use the old
file information to recover the information on disk. Refer to "Restoring
Formatted Disks," later in this chapter, for a discussion of how file recovery works.

Installing Safe Format

You can install Safe Format in one of two ways. One method is to use
the Norton command SFORMAT rather than the DOS command FOR-
MAT. You may sometimes forget to type *sformat* in place of *format*, however, or someone who does not know the Norton command may be
using your computer. The second—and better—way to install Safe Format is to substitute the SFORMAT command for the DOS FORMAT command on disk. Suppose that your DOS commands are in a directory
named C:\DOS and the Norton commands are in a directory named
C:\NORTON. To replace DOS FORMAT with SFORMAT, follow these
steps:

1. Rename the old DOS FORMAT.COM command by using this
   command:

   RENAME C:\DOS\FORMAT.COM XXFORMAT.COM

2. Copy the Safe Format command (SFORMAT.EXE) from the
   \NORTON directory to the \DOS directory with this command:

   COPY C:\NORTON\SFORMAT.EXE C:\DOS\FORMAT.EXE

Your RENAME and COPY commands may differ slightly. If your DOS commands are in a directory other than the \DOS directory, substitute that directory name for \DOS in the preceding examples. Similarly, if your Norton commands are in a directory other than \NORTON, substitute that directory name for \NORTON. If your directories are on a drive other than drive C, substitute your drive name for C.

Renaming the old FORMAT.COM file as XXFORMAT.COM is important. If the FORMAT.COM (DOS version) and FORMAT.EXE (Norton version) files exist on disk, the FORMAT command accesses the COM version (old DOS), because DOS always chooses to run a COM-type program rather than an EXE-type program if both programs exist in the same directory.

Also, make sure that you do not have another FORMAT.COM located somewhere on your disk in a directory that is accessed (according to your path) before your DOS directory. If the PATH statement in your AUTOEXEC.BAT file begins with PATH C:\;C:\DOS, for example, DOS accesses the root directory (\) before the \DOS directory when looking for a command file. If the root directory contains a FORMAT.COM command, DOS uses that version of FORMAT and not the Norton Safe Format command.

Starting Safe Format from the DOS Prompt

The syntax of the SFORMAT command is

SFORMAT [*d:*][*switches*]

or

FORMAT [*d:*][*switches*]

where *d:* is the letter of the drive you want to format, and *switches* are the available switches you can use with Safe Format.

If you type the SFORMAT or FORMAT command without any options, the Safe Format menu screen appears so that you can select the options to use for the format.

You use switches in the command to select formatting options. In interactive mode, you can select these options from the Safe menu screen. Safe Format has the same switches as the DOS FORMAT command, in addition to a few added by Norton. The Norton Safe Format switches that are similar to DOS FORMAT switches are listed in table 3.1. The Norton Safe Format switches particular to Norton are listed in table 3.2.

NOTE When the syntax of a command is described throughout this book, optional parameters are listed in [*brackets*]. In the FORMAT command, therefore, the drive letter described as [*d:*] is an optional parameter. It does not have to appear when you use the command. When you use items listed in brackets in the description, do not type the brackets on the DOS command line. If parameters are included in the description of a command and are not enclosed in brackets, those parameters are required.

Table 3.1 Norton Safe Format Switches Similar to DOS FORMAT Switches

Switch	Effect
/B	Leaves space for system files
/S	Places system files on disk
/V:*label*	Places a volume label on disk
/1	Formats as single-sided
/4	Formats as 360K (in 1.2M drive)
/8	Formats 8 sectors per track
/N:*n*	Specifies number of sectors per track (*n* = 8, 9, 15, or 18)
/T:*n*	Specifies number of tracks (*n* = 40 or 80)
/F:*size*	Specifies size of floppy disk (*size* = 360, 720, 1.2, 1.44, or 2.88)

To format a disk in drive B as a system disk (copy system files to the disk) and place the volume label MYDISK on the disk, for example, use this command:

    FORMAT B:/S/V: MYDISK

Notice in the command that the drive name is represented as a single letter followed by a colon. If you provide no drive name, you must choose from the Safe Format disk list the drive letter of the disk to format. Using the up- and down-arrow keys, you can move the highlight to the drive of your choice and press Enter. Or, you can press the key on your keyboard that corresponds to the drive letter. To select drive B, for example, press B on the keyboard. If you are using a mouse, you can point to the drive letter and click.

Table 3.2 Unique Norton Safe Format Switches	
Switch	**Effect**
/A	Enables you to bypass choosing Begin Format from the Norton Safe Format menu. The format begins without any response required from you. This switch is primarily for use in batch files, where you perform the same kind of format repetitively and want to avoid having to answer prompts. You need to be careful when using this switch because it defeats some of the purposes of the Safe Format command. If you are sure that the format you want to perform is selected properly, however, the /A switch can save you some time.
/D	Enables you to revert to the DOS FORMAT procedure. With this switch, the format is performed as if it were performed by the DOS FORMAT command—the system information is not saved for possible recovery. You may want to use the DOS version of FORMAT if the disk contains files that you do not want to be recovered easily (for example, personnel records).
/Q	Enables you to perform a quick format. This switch is useful for formatting disks that you have formatted previously. Rather than check the entire disk for bad sectors, as in a normal format, the command in the quick format mode merely replaces the system area of the disk with a new system area. This process is essentially the same as erasing all the files on the disk.
/size	Specifies size of floppy disk (size = 360, 720, 1.2, 1.44, or 2.88).

If you have an old formatted diskette that you want to reformat, you don't have to wait 45 seconds (which is what a normal 360K disk takes). Entering the command

    FORMAT B:/Q

performs a quick format that takes only 10 to 15 seconds to perform. This version of FORMAT is only usable on previously formatted diskettes.

Starting Safe Format from the Norton Menu

You also may choose the Safe Format command from the Norton menu. To use this method, begin Norton Utilities by entering the command *norton* at the DOS prompt and pressing Enter. The Norton Utilities menu appears, as shown in figure 3.1. Use the down-arrow key or your mouse to scroll down the Commands list until the Safe Format option is highlighted. Then press Enter or click the mouse button twice to begin the SFORMAT program.

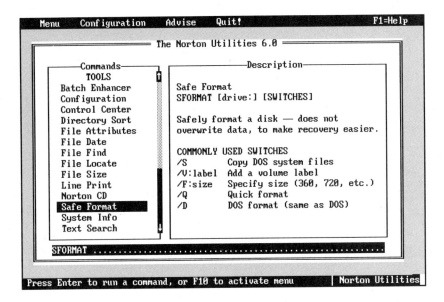

```
 Menu   Configuration   Advise   Quit!                      F1=Help
┌──────────────────── The Norton Utilities 6.0 ─────────────────────┐
│ ┌─Commands─────────┐  ┌────────────Description────────────────┐    │
│ │      TOOLS       │█ │                                       │    │
│ │ Batch Enhancer   │  │ Safe Format                           │    │
│ │ Configuration    │  │ SFORMAT [drive:] [SWITCHES]           │    │
│ │ Control Center   │  │                                       │    │
│ │ Directory Sort   │  │ Safely format a disk — does not       │    │
│ │ File Attributes  │  │ overwrite data, to make recovery easier.│  │
│ │ File Date        │  │                                       │    │
│ │ File Find        │  │ COMMONLY USED SWITCHES                 │    │
│ │ File Locate      │  │ /S       Copy DOS system files        │    │
│ │ File Size        │  │ /V:label Add a volume label           │    │
│ │ Line Print       │  │ /F:size  Specify size (360, 720, etc.)│    │
│ │ Norton CD        │  │ /Q       Quick format                 │    │
│ │ Safe Format      │  │ /D       DOS format (same as DOS)     │    │
│ │ System Info      │  │                                       │    │
│ │ Text Search      │▼ │                                       │    │
│ └──────────────────┘  └───────────────────────────────────────┘   │
│ SFORMAT ...........................................................│
└───────────────────────────────────────────────────────────────────┘
 Press Enter to run a command, or F10 to activate menu │ Norton Utilities
```

FIG. 3.1.

Choosing the Safe Format command from the main Norton menu.

From the Norton menu, you also may begin SFORMAT with one or more of the switch options described in tables 3.1 and 3.2. To use a switch from the menu, highlight the Safe Format option on the Commands list. Notice in figure 3.1 that the command SFORMAT appears toward the bottom of the screen. You can add switches to this command by typing them from the keyboard. What you type appears in this command line, just as if you were entering the command at the DOS prompt. After you enter the options you want to use, press Enter to begin the Safe Format command.

Selecting Options from the Safe Format Screen

After you issue the Safe Format command (and, if necessary, indicate the drive to format), the Safe Format screen appears (unless you used the /A switch at the DOS prompt). This screen enables you to choose from menus the same options that are available with switches (see fig. 3.2).

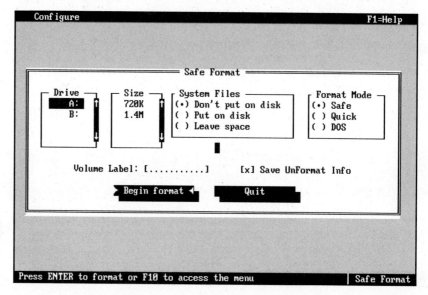

FIG. 3.2.

The Safe Format screen with menu selections.

The Safe Format screen consists of several option boxes and fields. To change some of the settings on the Safe Format screen, use the arrow keys or Tab to move from one option to another and select your choices. The Safe Format screen contains the following four option boxes:

- *Drive:* Tells you which disk is to be formatted. Depending on how you installed Norton Utilities, hard disk names may not appear in the list of drives to format.

- *Size:* Tells you the size of the disk—360K, 1.2M, and so on—about to be formatted. The program detects the sizes of disks your computer supports and lists them in the Size box. Norton Version 6 supports the new 2.88M disks that also are supported by DOS 5.0.

■ *System Files:* Tells you whether the disk to be formatted will contain the system files or whether space will be reserved for system files. (These settings relate to the /S and /B switches.) Notice that the System Files options are radio buttons, so you can choose only one option in the box at a time: Don't Put on Disk, Put on Disk, or Leave Space.

■ *Format Mode:* Tells you which format mode will be used—Safe, Quick, or DOS. (These settings are radio buttons and relate to the /Q and /D switches.) The format modes are described in table 3.3.

Table 3.3 Norton Utilities Format Modes

Mode	Effect
Safe	Formats the disk but keeps file information on disk so that you can recover files.
Quick	Creates a new system area and does not overwrite any data area. This mode is useful for formatting previously formatted floppy disks. By erasing the system area that contains the addresses of all files and directories on disk, this format is simply a quick way to erase all files and remove all directories from a disk.
DOS	Formats a disk, using the regular DOS procedure. No recovery information is written to disk, and Format Recover may not be able to recover any files.

The Volume Label option near the bottom of the Safe Format screen tells you which, if any, label will be given to the disk. To enter a volume label, press the Tab key until the highlight appears at the Volume Label option (or point to the option with the mouse and click once). Then, enter the label you want to place on the formatted disk. (You also can set this option by using the /V:*label* switch.)

The Save UnFormat Info option causes Safe Format to take a "snapshot" of the disk's system area so that you can unformat the disk if you discover that you formatted the wrong disk.

You can use the arrow keys, the Tab key, or your mouse to highlight the Quit option and then press Enter (or just press Q) to end Safe Format.

Starting the Format

The Begin Format option on the Safe Format screen initiates formatting with all the option settings chosen on the Safe Format screen. When all options are set as you want them, press Enter to choose Begin Format, or point to the Begin Format option with your mouse and click. After you select this option, the Safe Format command attempts to read the disk to see whether you are attempting to format a disk that already contains data. Figure 3.3 shows the warning that is given if information is found on a disk to be formatted. This safeguard prevents you from formatting a disk that contains important data.

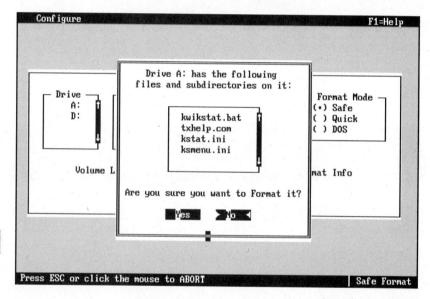

FIG. 3.3.

The Safe Format warning screen.

If the disk to be formatted contains information, you are given the option to stop the procedure before the formatting begins. You simply choose No. If you choose not to proceed, you are returned to the Safe Format screen with the menu selections offered. If you choose Yes on the warning screen, the format process begins.

After the format process begins, statistics and a display of progress appear on-screen (see fig. 3.4). The graph tells you how much of the disk has been formatted. Next to the graph are statistics with which you can track the progress of the format. This screen also shows you how much space is available on the disk and whether any bad sectors are found.

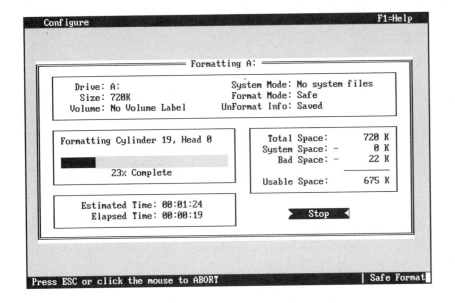

```
                        ══ Formatting A: ══
  ┌─────────────────────────────────────────────────────────┐
  │  Drive: A:               System Mode: No system files    │
  │   Size: 720K             Format Mode: Safe               │
  │ Volume: No Volume Label  UnFormat Info: Saved            │
  │                                                          │
  │ ┌──────────────────────┐   ┌──────────────────────────┐ │
  │ │ Formatting Cylinder   │   │  Total Space:    720 K   │ │
  │ │         19, Head 0     │   │ System Space: -    0 K   │ │
  │ │ ▓▓▓▓▓▓░░░░░░░░░░░░░░░   │   │   Bad Space: -    22 K   │ │
  │ │      23% Complete      │   │                          │ │
  │ │                        │   │ Usable Space:    675 K   │ │
  │ └──────────────────────┘   └──────────────────────────┘ │
  │ ┌──────────────────────┐                                │
  │ │ Estimated Time: 00:01:24 │      ►  Stop  ◄            │
  │ │ Elapsed  Time: 00:00:19  │                            │
  │ └──────────────────────┘                                │
  └─────────────────────────────────────────────────────────┘

 Press ESC or click the mouse to ABORT          | Safe Format|
```

FIG. 3.4.

Safe Format in progress.

If you press Esc during the format process, a dialog box appears, asking

Do you wish to cancel the current operation?

If you are using the Save UnFormat Info option or the Safe Format mode, you may as well let the format finish, even if you mistakenly format the wrong disk. Then you can recover the information with the UnFormat command. If you are using the DOS or complete format mode and discover that you are formatting the wrong disk, interrupt the format immediately and attempt to recover the original information on disk with the UnFormat command (see Chapter 4 and the next section, "Restoring Formatted Disks").

Restoring Formatted Disks

No matter how many precautions you take, you (or someone else) still may find a way to accidentally format a disk containing important information. With a little preventive medicine, however, you can handle this problem. The medicine is the Norton Utilities UnFormat command. This powerful command has two aspects. First, you can use it to plan for the possibility of an accidental format—you save the Image command store file information to a safe location on disk each time you boot. Second, if you ever need to recover a formatted disk, you can use the UnFormat command to access that file information to reconstruct your disk directories.

Preparing for an Accidental Format

Norton Utilities does its best to help you recover from a hard disk format. Before Norton Utilities, an accidental format was a disaster. The thoroughness of the work Norton can do, however, depends on how well you prepare your computer for this potential problem. There are three ways that you can protect your computer (and yourself) against accidental format of your hard disk. First, you should perform a periodic backup of your hard disk (you then can recover from the backup). Second, you should use the Norton Safe Format command on your computer rather than the standard DOS FORMAT command (this saves information to disk that helps Norton unformat the disk, if necessary). Third, you should use the Norton Image command.

The Image command creates a file on your hard disk named IMAGE.DAT. This file contains system and directory information about the files on your hard disk drive. When a hard disk is formatted, the system and directory information is changed to tell DOS that all file space is available on your disk. The actual contents of the files on disk are not changed. Therefore, the IMAGE.DAT file is able to provide an alternate copy of the information DOS needs to "find" your files on disk—that same information that was destroyed with the hard disk format. Norton can use this information to recover your system and directory information to its previous state, giving DOS back the information needed to access your files on disk—thus performing an unformat.

Because UnFormat can help recover only the files that were present the last time the Image command was run, you need to use Image periodically. For most people, a convenient method is to issue the command each time the computer is booted. The next section describes how to do that.

Running Image from the AUTOEXEC.BAT File

To run the Image command each time you boot your computer, you need to place the command in your AUTOEXEC.BAT file. (The *AUTOEXEC.BAT file* is a batch file containing a series of commands that execute each time you boot your computer.)

If you are familiar with the AUTOEXEC.BAT file and are comfortable using an ASCII editor, you simply can add the word *image* to your existing AUTOEXEC.BAT file. If you stored Norton Utilities in a directory other than the root directory (usually \NORTON), make sure that a PATH command precedes the IMAGE command in the AUTOEXEC.BAT file. Your AUTOEXEC.BAT file, for example, may contain the following lines:

```
PATH C:\;C:\DOS;C:\NORTON
IMAGE
```

The first command (PATH) sets up the DOS search path to look for commands first in the root directory, then in the DOS directory, and finally in the \NORTON directory. The next line issues the Norton Image command, which DOS now is able to find in the \NORTON directory.

If you are not familiar with your AUTOEXEC.BAT file or do not know how to use an ASCII editor to change the file, you can use the following alternative procedure. This example assumes that your Norton Utilities commands are in a directory named \NORTON, that you are booting from drive C, and that you already have an AUTOEXEC.BAT file in the root directory. Follow these steps to add the Image command to AUTOEXEC.BAT:

1. Make sure that you are in the root directory by typing this command:

    CD\

2. Rename the current AUTOEXEC.BAT file by using this command:

    RENAME AUTOEXEC.BAT AUTOEXEC.OLD

3. Create a temporary file that contains the Format Recover command. Type the following line and then press Enter:

    COPY CON TMP

    The cursor moves to the next line at the left margin, with no prompt displayed.

4. Enter the following line and then press Enter:

    \NORTON\IMAGE

5. Press Ctrl-Z.

    You have created a file named TMP. The regular DOS prompt now reappears.

6. Enter the following command at the DOS prompt:

    COPY TMP+AUTOEXEC.OLD AUTOEXEC.BAT

This command places the IMAGE command from the file named TMP in the first line of your AUTOEXEC.BAT file.

Now when you boot your computer, Norton issues the Image command and creates the file IMAGE.DAT. You can erase the TMP file. The AUTOEXEC.OLD file contains your old version of AUTOEXEC.BAT, in case you need it again.

If the IMAGE.DAT file is present, other Norton commands (Disk Edit and UnErase, for example) use that file automatically. These programs do not need the IMAGE.DAT file to work, but if the file is there, the programs work faster and better.

Running Image from the DOS Prompt

You do not have to run the Image command from the AUTOEXEC.BAT file. You can run the Image command at any time by entering the command at the DOS prompt. The syntax is

IMAGE [*switch*]

If IMAGE.DAT already exists, the old IMAGE.DAT is renamed IMAGE.BAK. The only switch for this command is /NOBACK. If you use the /NOBACK switch, the file IMAGE.BAK, which contains information from the preceding use of the IMAGE command, is not created.

If you enter the command with no switches, the program creates a new copy of the IMAGE.DAT file on disk.

NOTE As an added safety measure, in case you accidentally format your hard disk, make sure that you have a bootable floppy disk that contains the UnFormat program. Format a floppy disk in drive A, using the /S (System) switch. Place a copy of the UNFORMAT.EXE program from your \NORTON directory on the disk in drive A. Also keep on this disk important files such as AUTOEXEC.BAT, CONFIG.SYS, and any other files needed to boot your computer. Other commands to place on this floppy disk for emergency use include the DOS command DEBUG and the Norton commands NDD (Norton Disk Doctor II), Disk Edit, and Safe Format. Keep the disk nearby in case you need to use it.

DOS 5.0 contains a command called MIRROR that is similar in function to the NORTON Image command. When you enter the MIRROR command at the DOS prompt, information is written to a file that contains a duplicate copy of your disk's system and file directory. If you have used the MIRROR command and your disk has been format-ted, the Norton UnFormat command can read that information and use it to restore the formatted disk.

Recovering a Formatted Disk

You will have a much easier time recovering your data if you planned ahead and issued the Image command recently. Even if you formatted your hard disk and do not have an IMAGE.DAT file, however, you may be able to recover data.

If your hard disk has just been formatted, you need to proceed with some care. Do not write new information to the hard disk before at-tempting to perform a recovery. First boot the computer from a floppy disk, using the same version of DOS that was on the hard disk before it was formatted.

If your boot floppy disk does not contain the UnFormat command, place in the floppy disk drive a disk containing the UnFormat com-mand. From this drive (drive A, for example), enter this command:

UNFORMAT *d:*

where *d:* is the name of the disk to unformat. If you know that you have used the Image command to create a recovery information file, use the command

UNFORMAT *d:* /IMAGE

If you know that you have used the MIRROR command (a command similar to Norton's Image command and available in DOS 5.0) to create a recovery information file, use the command

UNFORMAT *d:* /MIRROR

An explanation of the UnFormat procedure appears on-screen (see fig. 3.5). If you choose to continue, you are prompted to select the drive to unformat (see fig. 3.6). Use the arrow keys or your mouse to select the drive and then choose OK to continue.

You then are asked if the disk to be unformatted had used the program IMAGE.EXE or MIRROR.COM to save recovery information (see fig. 3.7). Choose Yes if you know that the IMAGE.DAT or MIRROR.FIL file was saved or if you are not sure. Choose No if you know for sure that no IMAGE.DAT file is on the disk. If you choose No, refer to the next sec-tion, "Unformatting Disks without IMAGE.DAT or MIRROR.FIL."

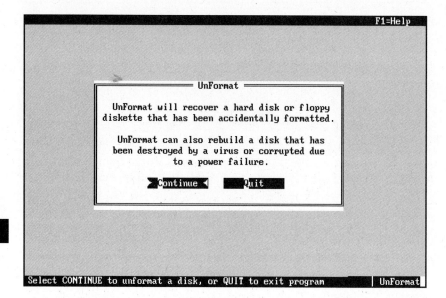

FIG. 3.5.

The UnFormat explanation screen.

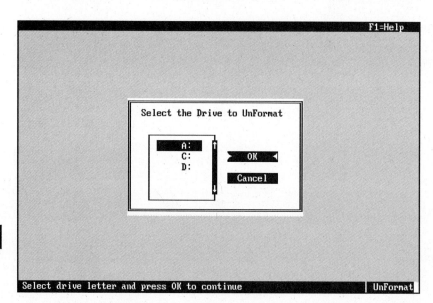

FIG. 3.6.

Selecting the drive to unformat.

Norton gives you one more chance to cancel the UnFormat command (see fig. 3.8). If you answer Yes in this dialog box, the unformatting process begins. The UnFormat program begins looking for the

IMAGE.DAT and IMAGE.BAK (or MIRROR.FIL or MIRROR.BAK) information on the disk. A graphic appears on-screen with a the message

```
Searching for IMAGE info...
```

When the IMAGE information is found, a screen like the one in figure 3.9 appears.

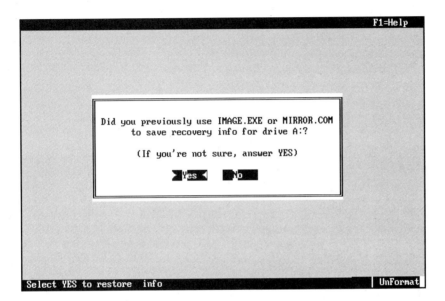

FIG. 3.7.

The UnFormat command prompt to search for IMAGE.DAT.

If two versions of the Image (or MIRROR) information (one named IMAGE.BAK or MIRROR.BAK) are found, a message tells you that two versions have been found, and you may choose to use the most recent version or the previous version. If the most recent IMAGE.DAT (or MIRROR) information is not usable (perhaps you ran the Image program after the disk had been formatted, for example) you may want to use the previous version—the IMAGE.BAK (or MIRROR.BAK) information.

After you select the Image version you want, still another screen asks whether you are sure that you want to restore the recovery information (see fig. 3.10). Answer Yes to continue. You then are prompted to choose between a full or partial restore. A partial restore restores only parts of the system area, including the boot record and the file allocation table. Usually, you will choose a full restore (see fig. 3.11).

Are you sure you want to
UnFormat drive A:?

> Yes <   No

Select YES to unformat, or NO to abort | UnFormat

FIG. 3.8.

The UnFormat
warning screen.

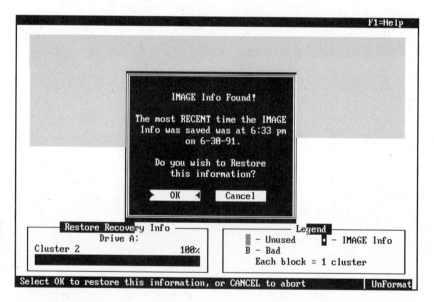

IMAGE Info Found!

The most RECENT time the IMAGE
Info was saved was at 6:33 pm
on 6-30-91.

Do you wish to Restore
this information?

> OK <   Cancel

Restore Recovery Info
        Drive A:
Cluster 2   100%

Legend
▓ - Unused   ▪ - IMAGE Info
B - Bad
Each block = 1 cluster

Select OK to restore this information, or CANCEL to abort | UnFormat

FIG. 3.9.

The UnFormat
IMAGE.DAT
screen.

CAUTION: Use the partial restore option only when you are using
the UnFormat command to restore a damaged portion of your
disk, such as the boot record. This is an uncommon option to use,
and is made available primarily for persons with a great deal of
experience with the disk structure.

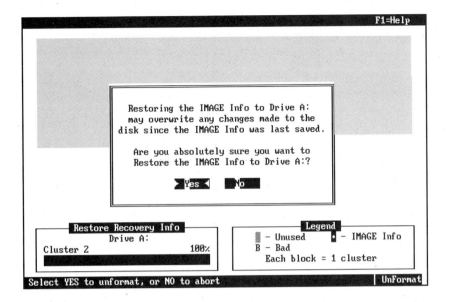

FIG. 3.10.

Choosing to restore the recovery information.

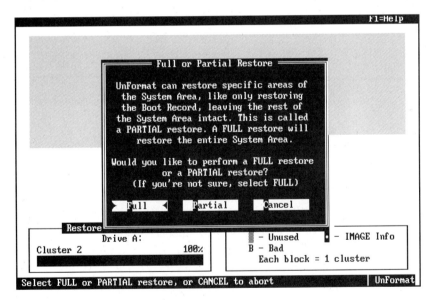

FIG. 3.11.

Selecting a full or partial unformat.

Finally, the restoration begins. You hear the drive churning as the information is recovered. The recovery process generally takes only a few minutes. When the recovery is finished, you see a message telling you that the drive has been restored successfully to its previous state.

After the recovery finishes, you still may have some problems with a few files—those that were changed since you gave the last Image command. Run the Norton Disk Doctor (the NDD command) to clear up any problems that may remain. These problems may be sectors that remain unallocated to files. The NDD command often can sort out these problems and recover the remaining files. To run the Norton Disk Doctor, enter this command at the DOS prompt:

NDD *d:* /QUICK

where *d:* is the drive name of the disk that was just restored. If the recovery was performed on the disk from which your computer boots, reboot your computer after running NDD. See Chapter 4 for more information on the NDD command.

The best way to learn how to use UnFormat is on a practice disk—when all you have to lose is some time. Format a disk and place several files on it. You even may want to include a few subdirectories. Now format the disk, using the Save UnFormat Info option from the Safe Format screen. After you format the test disk, run the UnFormat program and see how it can restore the disk. This procedure gives you some experience and confidence for the time when you may need to restore your disk in a real situation.

You can run the UnFormat command from a network to unformat a disk on your local machine. UnFormat does not work, however, on a network drive.

Unformatting Disks without IMAGE.DAT or MIRROR.FIL

If you did not prepare for the disk being formatted—you did not use Norton's Image command, the DOS MIRROR command, or Norton's Safe Format command—Norton Utilities may be able to help, but the recovery requires more work. The UnFormat command often can help you recover some files from a hard disk that has been formatted. You cannot, however, use UnFormat to restore a floppy disk that has been reformatted using a regular DOS format. When a hard disk is reformatted, only the system area is overwritten, not the entire disk. When a floppy disk is formatted in DOS format mode, the entire disk is overwritten.

Begin the UnFormat command, as described in "Restoring Formatted Disks," earlier in this chapter. If any chance exists that the IMAGE.DAT or MIRROR.FIL file is on disk, allow the UnFormat command to search for it. If you cannot find IMAGE.DAT or MIRROR.FIL, you must attempt to recover your data without them.

The UnFormat command attempts to recover as many files as possible. First, the program must search the disk, looking for directory and file names. This search may take some time.

UnFormat usually is able to recover all directories and all files in those directories except for the files in the root directory. Some versions of DOS (COMPAQ 3.1 and AT&T 2.11) overwrite information thoroughly with a format, and recovery is not possible.

When the UnFormat command finishes what it can do, your disk should contain directories named DIR0000, DIR0001, DIR0002, and so on. The original names of the directories are lost, but files are grouped in the new directories as they were in the original directories. All 1-2-3 files are in one directory, for example, and all WordPerfect files are in another directory.

You can retrieve the original names of the directories in one of two ways. If you are using a version of DOS earlier than 3.0, you need to make new directories, copy the files from each recovered directory into each new directory, and then delete the old directories and files.

You can use a second, much easier, method if you are working with DOS 3.0 or later versions. This technique uses the Norton Change Directory command. To rename a directory, enter the command

NCD /N

The /N switch tells NCD not to update the directory name information stored on disk in the TREEINFO.NCD file, because you do not want to keep the names DIR0000, DIR0001, and so on.

The NCD command brings up the Norton Change Directory screen. The screen includes a list of all the directories that have been recovered (DIR0000, DIR0001, and so on). To find out what the directories contain, you must examine the names of some of the files. If the directory DIR0001 contains WKS files, for example, it must be your Lotus 1-2-3 directory.

After you decide what the names of the directories should be (for example, DIR0000 is \WP50, DIR0001 is \LOTUS, and so on), you can change the directory names. Using the arrow keys, highlight the name of one of the directories. Press F6 (Rename) and type a new name for the directory. If you are using a mouse, point to the directory name you want to change and click once on that name to highlight it. Then, select the directory pull-down menu by clicking once on the Directory option on the menu bar, and then click on the Rename option. A dialog box appears where you can type a new name. Enter the new name for the directory, and then click on Okay. Continue this process until you have renamed all the directories. To exit the Norton Change Directory screen, press F10 (Quit).

After renaming the upper level directories on your disk, run the Norton Disk Doctor (NDD) program to clear up any problems with recovered files. These problems usually are unallocated sectors—portions of the disk that have not been assigned properly to a file or free space. The command to run the NDD program is

NDD C:/QUICK

The /QUICK switch tells NDD to test the system area of the disk only—not the entire disk. (The system area is where the unallocated sectors' information is located.)

If your disk is supposed to be bootable but is not, use the Norton Disk Doctor command to make a disk bootable. The Norton Change Directory (NCD) and Norton Disk Doctor (NDD) commands are covered in Chapter 4.

The UnFormat command is not perfect, but it restores all the information that was not erased during the formatting process. One of the major problems is that all the files in the root directory—AUTOEXEC.BAT, CONFIG.SYS, and others, for example—are lost. You must reconstruct these files. If you do not have backup copies of the files, you must rebuild them in a text editor.

Using UnFormat To Recover from a Virus Attack

The UnFormat command also may help you recover from some versions of destruction brought about by a computer virus. If your disk has become unusable because of a virus attack, use the UnFormat command to attempt recovery, just as if the disk had been formatted. If you have a recent copy of IMAGE.DAT (or MIRROR.FIL) on your disk, your chances of recovery are good.

Setting Attributes To Protect Files

The UnFormat procedure enables you to recover from a format, but there are other ways that files can be lost. Therefore, you need to be aware of other ways to protect your valuable information. One way of protecting your important files is to prevent them from being erased or overwritten. Suppose that you have a valuable Lotus 1-2-3 worksheet named ABLE.WKS. Overwriting that file from 1-2-3 is possible (and sometimes easy). If you overwrite the file, you cannot recover it with the UnErase command. Files that are particularly important to protect from erasure or change are COMMAND.COM, AUTOEXEC.BAT, and CONFIG.SYS.

A common problem occurs, for example, when one person gives a friend a floppy disk containing a program. The friend copies the program from the floppy disk to the hard disk with a command such as

COPY A:*.* C:

The problem with this command is that some files on the floppy disk may overwrite files on the hard disk, particularly COMMAND.COM. When you reboot the computer, the version of COMMAND.COM that was copied from the floppy disk may conflict with the other system files, and the computer therefore may refuse to reboot. Other important files such as AUTOEXEC.BAT and CONFIG.SYS also may have been overwritten.

Of course, copying a floppy disk onto the root directory of your hard disk without knowing much about what is on the floppy is ill-advised. To protect against this kind of problem if it does occur, however, you can set attributes for important files in the root directory on the hard disk. Then, if you copy a floppy disk that you do not know much about, you do not overwrite your original files.

Defining File Attributes

When you create a file on disk, DOS stores the name of the file as well as other pieces of vital information. You see some of this information when you enter the DOS DIR command—the size of the file, the date and time the file was created, and so on. DOS also stores four other pieces of information that you usually do not see. You can toggle these four pieces of information, called *attributes*, on or off. The attributes are listed in table 3.4.

With the Norton Utilities FA (File Attributes) and FileFind commands, you can control these attributes and protect important files from accidental change or erasure.

Using File Attributes as File Protection

You can use the FileFind command and file attributes to protect your files in several ways:

■ *You can make all important files read-only.* Be aware, however, that some files to which programs write should not be set to read-only. You should make at least the important files in the root directory (including COMMAND.COM, AUTOEXEC.BAT, and CONFIG.SYS) read-only. You can turn off the read-only attribute temporarily if you need to change any of these files.

■ *You can hide valuable files.* Hiding files can prevent other people from accessing your secret information. (This method is not foolproof. If other users know about the FileFind command, they can change the attribute back.)

■ *You can turn the archive attribute off for some important files for extra protection.* If you regularly back up your computer with *incremental backups* (backups of only those files that have changed since the last backup), the files that have been backed up already do not get backed up again. If you turn on the archive attribute for certain files, however, those files are included in the next backup, even if they have not changed since the last backup. You may want to take this step so that you have a duplicate copy of the backup in case one copy is damaged or lost.

Table 3.4 File Attributes

Attribute	Description
Archive	When the archive attribute is set (on), the file has not been backed up. When you create a file, DOS sets the archive attribute on. When you perform the backup procedure, the archive attribute is turned off.
Hidden	When the hidden attribute is set, the file does not appear in a directory when you perform the DIR command. On a bootable disk, the DOS files named IBMBIO.COM and IBMDOS.COM usually are hidden files. When you perform a CHKDSK command, you may notice a report of hidden files.
Read-only	When the read-only attribute is set, the information in a file can be read or used by a program, but DOS prevents the file from being changed or erased.
System	System files are similar to hidden files. When the system attribute is on, DOS considers the file a system file and does not display it in a directory when you issue a DIR command.

A number of other features of the FileFind command are not covered in this chapter. See Chapter 6, "Managing Your Computer's Resources," for more information.

Using the FA Command To Set Attributes from the DOS Prompt

Using Norton Utilities, you can set the file attributes by using the FA command or the FileFind command. To set attributes from the DOS prompt, use the FA command. The syntax for this command is

FA [*filespec*][*attribute switches*][*other switches*]

where *filespec* represents the specific files, *attribute switches* represents the attributes you want to change, and *other switches* represents the other available switches you can use with file attributes. The attribute switches include the following:

/A	Archive
/DIR	Hidden (for directories only)
/HID	Hidden
/R	Read-only
/SYS	System

To use the FA command to set an attribute, you follow the attribute switch with a plus (+) or minus (-) sign. A plus sign turns on the attribute and a minus sign turns off the attribute.

Other switches available for the FA command are

/CLEAR	Clears (removes) all attributes
/P	Pauses after each screen is displayed
/S	Includes files in subdirectories
/T	Reports totals only
/U	Reports unusual files (with at least one attribute set)

To display a list of all files in the current directory that have at least one attribute set, for example, enter the command

FA /U

To clear (turn off) all attribute settings for all files in a directory, use the command

FA /CLEAR

To set the file COMMAND.COM to read-only (thus, protecting it from being erased) use the command

FA COMMAND.COM /R+

To set all COM files to read-only, including those in subdirectories of the current directory, use the command

FA *.COM /R+/S

Changing Attributes Using the FileFind Command

Like the FA command, the FileFind command contains options to enable you to examine and change file attributes. FileFind enables you to set these attributes interactively from a menu. When you enter the command

FILEFIND

from the DOS prompt, the FileFind screen appears (see fig. 3.12). This screen contains several areas in which to enter information on setting file attributes. You enter the files you want to affect in the File Name entry area. If you want to set attributes for all files named *.COM, for example, enter the file specification

*.COM

in the File Name field. When setting file attributes, you do not place any information in the Containing field. Using the radio button options below the Containing field, you can specify if the files to be set are on the entire disk, the current directory and below, or on the current directory only. The Ignore Case option is not relevant for setting file attributes. To display the files that will be affected, use the Tab key to highlight the Start option and press Enter or click on the Start option.

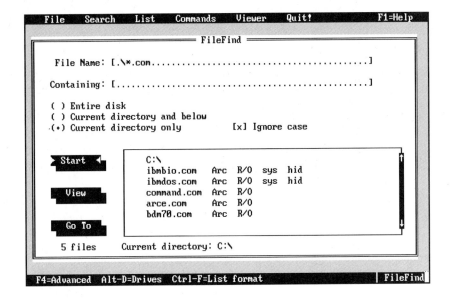

| File | Search | List | Commands | Viewer | Quit! | | F1=Help |

```
================================ FileFind ================================

  File Name: [.\*.com.........................................]

  Containing: [.............................................]

  ( ) Entire disk
  ( ) Current directory and below
 ·(•) Current directory only              [x] Ignore case


  ► Start ◄         C:\
                    ibmbio.com     Arc   R/0   sys   hid
                    ibmdos.com     Arc   R/0   sys   hid
    View            command.com    Arc   R/0
                    arce.com       Arc   R/0
                    bdm70.com      Arc   R/0
    Go To

    5 files      Current directory: C:\
```

F4=Advanced Alt-D=Drives Ctrl-F=List format | FileFind |

FIG. 3.12.

The FileFind screen.

NOTE The way the program displays the files in the list box of the FileFind screen is controlled by the Set List Display option, accessed from the List pull-down menu. To display the file names and attributes in the format shown in figure 3.12, choose the List option from the menu bar and then choose the Set List Display option (or press Ctrl-F). Use the mouse to select Name and Attributes. Or, use the up- and down-arrow keys to highlight Name and Attributes, press the space bar to lock in your choice, and press Esc to leave the option.

To specify attributes, press the F10 key to open the pull-down menus, and then use the right- and left-arrow keys to open the Commands pull-down menu. Choose the Change Attributes option on the Commands menu. If you are using a mouse, point to the Commands menu and click, and then point to the Change Attributes option and click. A dialog box like the one in figure 3.13 will appear. In this box, you can choose to set the attributes for the first file found to match the search criteria (in this example, COMMAND.COM) or set the attributes for the entire list of files that match the search criteria. Use the arrow keys to highlight the radio button beside the option you want; set the attributes for the single file listed or for the entire file list. Press the space bar to lock in your choice.

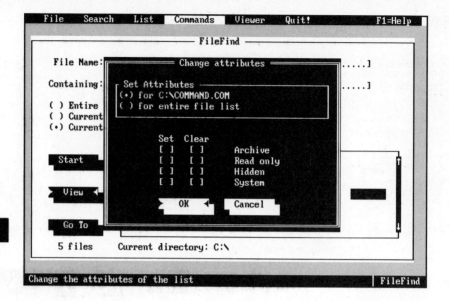

FIG. 3.13.

Changing file
attributes by
using FileFind.

Choose the attributes to set or clear by using the arrow keys to high-light your choice, and then press the space bar to lock in your choice. If you are using a mouse, point to the selection you want and click once. After you make all your selections in the Change Attributes dialog box, press Enter or click on the OK box. Another dialog box appears inform-ing you that the requested attributes have been set.

If you chose to set attributes only for the single matching file, and you choose the Change Attributes option again, the single file name listed in the Change Attributes dialog box will be the next file matching the search criteria.

To summarize how to set attributes using FileFind interactively, do the following:

1. Enter in the File Name field the file specification of the files you want to affect.

2. Choose one of the radio buttons indicating what portion of the disk FileFind should search: Entire disk, Current Directory and Below, or Current Directory Only.

3. Choose Start to list files that will be affected.

4. Press F10 to access the pull-down menus and use the right- or left-arrow keys to pull down the Commands menu. Or, point to the word Commands with the mouse pointer and click.

5. Choose Set Attributes. You should see a screen similar to figure 3.13.

6. Choose the option you want to set—for example, the read-only attribute. Use the arrow keys to move to the option; then press the space bar to turn it on or off. Or, click the option with your mouse. (An X should appear, indicating that the attribute is on.)

7. Press Enter to accept this setting.

Using Erase Protect

When you erase a file, DOS does not actually erase the contents of the file. DOS erases only some of the directory information about the file; this is why Norton can unerase a file. When you erase a file, however, DOS gets the message that the space on disk that the file used now is available for other files. After another file has written over the "erased" space, you no longer can unerase the erased file that occupied that space.

The Erase Protect command (called the File Save command in Norton Utilities Version 5.0) moves the contents of unerased files to a part of the disk that is not used as much. This process makes the files less likely to be overwritten, and the files remain unerasable longer. Erase Protect is able to manage this "erased" space on disk, and you can tell the command to stop protecting files after a certain number of days or after a certain amount of space is used for the erased information.

Erase Protect is a memory-resident program. When you begin the program, it stays in the computer's memory, monitoring what is going on while you run other programs. You can run the Erase Protect program interactively or as a DOS-type command. You need to run the program interactively at first to set your options for which drives you want to protect, how long you want to save files, and so on. Then you can activate the Erase Protect command by placing it in your AUTOEXEC.BAT file so that the protection is turned on each time you boot your computer.

Using Erase Protect Interactively

To use Erase Protect interactively, choose the Erase Protect option from the Norton menu or type *ep* at the DOS prompt. The Erase Protect screen appears (see fig. 3.14).

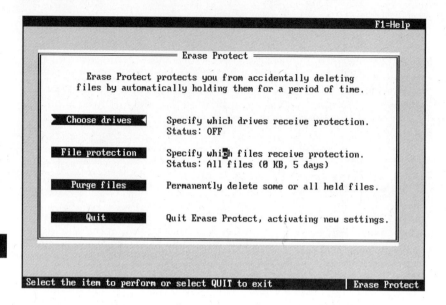

FIG. 3.14.

The Erase
Protect screen.

In this screen, you can specify the following options:

Option	Effect
Choose Drives	Specifies which drives to protect
File Protection	Specifies which files to protect
Purge Files	Removes files from protection
Quit	Quits Erase Protect

If you select Choose Drives, you are prompted to choose the disk
drives that you want to protect. Erase Protect monitors files being
erased only on the disks you specify.

If you select File Protection, you can choose which files you want Erase
Protect to protect when they are erased. From the File Protection
screen, you can instruct Erase Protect to monitor all files, a list of files,
or all files except those on a list (see fig. 3.15). Use the arrow keys to
highlight the option you want to choose on this menu, and then press
the space bar to lock in your selection. Or, point to the option with the
mouse pointer and click.

If you choose to protect files on a list or to exclude files on a list, you
must first make a list, of course. The Files box at the right of the File
Protection screen is where you enter your list. Notice that the Files list
has * . listed (no file names) a number of times. To place file specifications in this list, use the arrow keys, Tab, or the mouse to move to the

Files list box. Then enter extensions of the files you want to include or exclude. You may choose to exclude *.EXE and *.COM files, for example, because you probably have copies of these files on original disks. On the other hand, you may want to include *.DBF and *.WK1 files because these are important data files. You can choose to include or exclude; you cannot do both.

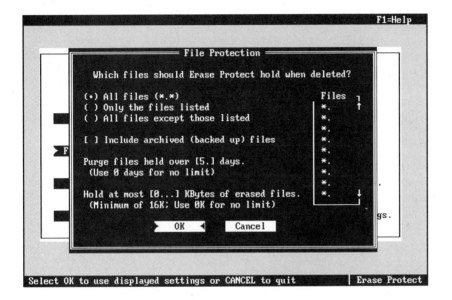

F1=Help

```
                        ═ File Protection ═
    Which files should Erase Protect hold when deleted?

    (•) All files (*.*)                          Files ┐
    ( ) Only the files listed                    *.      ↑
    ( ) All files except those listed            *.
                                                 *.
    [ ] Include archived (backed up) files       *.
                                                 *.
    Purge files held over [5.] days.             *.
    (Use 0 days for no limit)                    *.
                                                 *.
    Hold at most [0...] KBytes of erased files.  *.     ↓
    (Minimum of 16K; Use 0K for no limit)

              ► OK ◄      Cancel
```

Select OK to use displayed settings or CANCEL to quit | Erase Protect

FIG. 3.15.

The File Protection screen.

You also can choose to monitor or not monitor archived files by checking the Include Archived (Backed Up) Files option. Use the arrow keys to point to this check box and press the space bar, or click on the box using the mouse. Files that are archived—files that have the archive attribute off—already have been backed up, and you should have a copy of those files to recover if needed. Therefore, you may choose not to protect these files.

The Purge Files option on the File Protection screen enables you to choose how long a file is to be held before it is no longer protected. The default is five days. To change this length, use the arrow keys to move the cursor to the [5.] option or click on this option with the mouse pointer and type a new number. If you enter a zero here, it means that there is no limit to the length of time files will be protected. The Hold at Most option enables you to specify how much space on disk to use to hold erased files. To change this option, use the arrow keys to move to [0...] in this option (or click on the option with the mouse pointer) and enter a new number. The minimum you can enter is 16. If you enter a 0, it means there is no limit to the amount of space used to hold erased files.

Even if you don't use Erase Protect, you can recover an erased file by using the UnErase command as long as the file's space has not been used by another file.

When you quit Erase Protect, the options you chose are saved. Then, regardless of whether you begin the program from the DOS prompt or from your AUTOEXEC.BAT file, these settings are used.

Using Erase Protect from the DOS Prompt

The Erase Protect command usually is included in the AUTOEXEC.BAT file so that it is in effect when any files are deleted. The syntax of this command is

EP [*switches*]

The available switches for the Erase Protect command are listed in table 3.5.

Table 3.5 Erase Protect Switches

Switch	Effect
/OFF	Disables the Erase Protect command so that deleted files are not affected. The Erase Protect command remains in memory but does not function unless it is turned on by the /ON switch.
/ON	Enables the Erase Protect command to move deleted files to a safe area.
/SKIPHIGH	Indicates that you do not want Erase Protect loaded into high memory.
/STATUS	Displays the status of the Erase Protect command.
/UNINSTALL	Removes the Erase Protect command from memory if the command was the last memory-resident (TSR) command loaded.

The initial 640K RAM memory in your computer is referred to as *low memory*. Memory above 640K is called *high memory*. When a program is stored in high memory (as Erase Protect will be by default, if it is available), you have more low memory to be used by your applications programs. If you are using a memory manager (or DOS 5.0) that uses your high memory, use the /SKIPHIGH option to force the Erase Protect program to be stored in low memory.

Erase Protect enables you to protect erased files on a network. When you run the command the first time on a network, Erase Protect creates a directory named TRASHCAN branching off the root directory. The network manager should make this directory available to all users of the network. To run Erase Protect properly on a network, you should initiate the command after the network driver and shell are loaded.

Using Disk Monitor

You can use the Disk Monitor command to protect your information on disk from accidental or unauthorized destruction. Although setting attributes and using Erase Protect provide some protection, Norton's Disk Monitor command can give you an additional level of control over the use of files. Disk Monitor's file protection also can give you more safety against a virus infection.

Before you or another user can access a file (write to it, change it, or erase it), the Disk Monitor command protects the file by checking to see whether you have given permission for the file to be altered in this way. If the file is protected from change, Disk Monitor does not enable you or another user to alter the file. When a program that tries to alter a protected file is run—a spreadsheet program, for example—a message appears telling you that a protected file is about to be altered. You then can choose to allow the change to proceed, stop the change from happening, or cancel the protection.

Having such protection of important files can save you from virus programs that may try to alter critical files such as your COMMAND.COM, AUTOEXEC.BAT, and CONFIG.SYS files.

Setting Up Disk Monitor Interactively

The Disk Monitor command is a memory-resident program. When you begin the program, it stays in the computer's memory to monitor what is going on while you run other programs. You can use the Disk Monitor command interactively or from the DOS prompt. The first time you use Disk Monitor, however, you must use it interactively to select its initial settings. To begin Disk Monitor, choose Disk Monitor from the Norton menu or enter the following command at the DOS prompt:

DISKMON

A screen similar to the one in figure 3.16 appears.

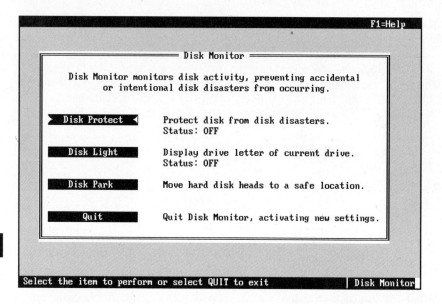

FIG. 3.16.

The Disk
Monitor screen.

The Disk Monitor screen contains the following four options:

Option	Effect
Disk Protect	Enables or disables protection for certain files
Disk Light	Turns on and off access light on-screen
Disk Park	Parks disk heads for moving computer
Quit	Quits and saves new settings

By using the arrow keys and Enter or the mouse pointer, you can choose one of these four selections. When you choose Quit, the settings you chose are stored in a file named DISKMON.INI. If you use Disk Monitor as a command from the DOS prompt, the settings in DISKMON.INI are used.

Choosing Disk Protect

The Disk Protect option on the Disk Monitor screen enables you to turn on and off protection and to specify which files you want to protect. After you choose the Disk Protect option, a screen similar to the one in figure 3.17 appears.

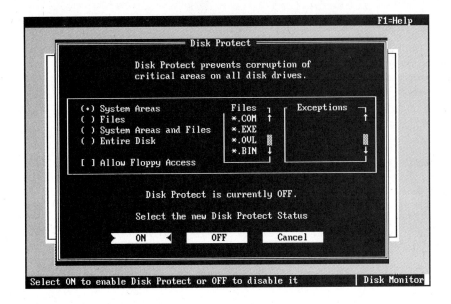

```
═══════════════ Disk Protect ═══════════════
      Disk Protect prevents corruption of
      critical areas on all disk drives.


   (•) System Areas        Files  ┐  ┌ Exceptions ┐
   ( ) Files               *.COM  ↑  │            ↑
   ( ) System Areas and Files  *.EXE  │            │
   ( ) Entire Disk         *.OVL  ▓  │            ▓
                           *.BIN  ↓  │            ↓
   [ ] Allow Floppy Access


      Disk Protect is currently OFF.

      Select the new Disk Protect Status

   ▶    ON    ◀     OFF          Cancel
```

Select ON to enable Disk Protect or OFF to disable it   Disk Monitor

FIG. 3.17.

The Disk Protect screen.

From the Disk Protect screen, you can choose one of the following options:

Option	Effect
System Areas	Specifies protection for the system area on your disk. This area includes the partition table, the boot record, and the system files.
Files	Specifies protection for files listed in the Files box, excluding all files listed in the Exceptions box.
System Areas and Files	Specifies protection of both system files and other files
Entire Disk	Specifies protection for entire disk

Another option on the Disk Protect screen is the Allow Floppy Access option. If you check this option, Disk Monitor enables you (or a program) to format floppy disks without asking for your permission.

To select any of the options on the Disk Protect screen, use the arrow keys to point to the option you want to select and press the space bar to lock in your selection. Or, point to a selection option with the mouse pointer and click.

To add file specifications to the Files or Exceptions list, use the arrow keys to move the cursor within one of the list boxes, and then type a file specification.

Choosing Disk Light

If you choose Disk Light from the Disk Monitor screen, a blinking light on your monitor tells you when your disk is being accessed. This light is helpful if you cannot easily see the disk light on your hard disk. Being able to see when your disk is being accessed is important so that you can monitor this activity visually. If you notice a program accessing a disk when it should not be using the disk, you may want to test that program for possible virus infection.

Choosing Disk Park

The Disk Park option on the Disk Monitor screen enables you to move the heads on your disk drive to a safe place so that you can move the computer without destroying data. On many new computers, the heads park automatically when you turn off the computer. If you do not know whether the heads park automatically, you should use Disk Park before you move your computer.

To select Disk Park, use the arrow keys to point to Disk Park and press Enter. Or, point to Disk Park with the mouse pointer and click once. Two beeps signal that the disk head has been parked.

Using Disk Monitor from the DOS Prompt

The syntax for using the Disk Monitor command from the DOS prompt is

DISKMON [*switches*]

The available switches for the Disk Monitor command are listed in table 3.6.

If you try to delete a file that is protected, the following message appears:

```
A delete operation was attempted on a protected file.
Do you wish to allow this operation?

Yes     No      Disable Protection
```

To enable the erase to take place, press Y (you do not need to press Enter). To cancel the delete, press N. To cancel the protection, press D.

Table 3.6 Disk Monitor Switches

Switch	Effect
/LIGHT+ or /LIGHT-	Turns the disk light feature on (+) or off (-).
/PARK	Parks all drives.
/PROTECT- or /PROTECT+	Turns the protect feature on (+) or off (-). When this feature is turned on, protection is set to your selections, which were stored in DISKMON.INI when you ran the command interactively.
	If you have not made previous selections (you do not have a DISKMON.INI file), the system files will be protected by default.
/SKIPHIGH	Tells the program that you do not want Disk Monitor loaded into high memory.
/STATUS	Displays a summary of the Disk Monitor status on-screen.
/UNINSTALL	Uninstalls the Disk Monitor program from memory if it was the last TSR loaded into memory.

Using Disk Monitor on a Network

Disk Monitor can work on a network to prevent the modification of some files on your local or network drives. The command is not designed, however, to protect the system area of a network server. Usually, the server contains its own protection capabilities. The Disk Light option of the Disk Monitor command enables you to "see" the network disk as it is accessed. This feature often gives you a better feel for network usage. Disk Park does not park network heads.

Encrypting Files with the Diskreet Command

The Norton Diskreet command enables you to protect files so that users cannot access the files without permission (the users must know a password). This command provides much more protection than using the Disk Monitor command or setting file attributes. Files stored by Diskreet are encrypted so that they are unreadable, even by the Disk Edit program. You can protect files individually or by group by using a pseudo-disk called an *ndisk*.

An ndisk operates like a disk drive, but files stored on this drive are encrypted automatically by Diskreet, and only users who know the password can access the files. If you try to access an ndisk, you are prompted to enter a password. If you do not know the password, you cannot type, read, or otherwise access the files on that "disk" successfully. After you open an ndisk by supplying the correct password, you may access these files, and they are decrypted as you access them. When you close the ndisk, the files again become inaccessible.

You can regulate access to an ndisk interactively or from a DOS prompt command. You can regulate the automatic closing of an ndisk after it has been inactive for a certain period, or you can create a hot key that quickly closes an ndisk. Also, you can audit access to an ndisk to determine whether someone has been trying to access your information without your permission.

You can choose two versions of ndisk encrypting called *quick encryption* (a Norton proprietary method) and *DES* (data encryption standard). The quick encryption option is fast and effective but not quite as secure as the DES method. That is, the quick method can be more easily deciphered than the DES method, because its algorithm for encoding is not as complex as the DES scheme. The DES method is slow but secure, and you probably will want to use it only if the information being protected is akin to the Manhattan Project (top secret).

When you store information in an ndisk, the data is secure. If you forget your password, not even Norton can help you unscramble your files.

Installing Diskreet

The Diskreet program is a memory-resident program (TSR), which means that when you load the program, it stays in memory and monitors the computer while you run other programs. Before you use the Diskreet program, however, you must include the following line in your CONFIG.SYS file:

DEVICE=*path*\DISKREET.SYS

where *path* is the name of the directory in which your Norton files are stored. If your Norton Utilities are stored in the directory named \NORTON, for example, you use this command:

    DEVICE=\NORTON\DISKREET.SYS

Options that you may use with DISKREET in this CONFIG.SYS command include the following switches:

Switch	Effect
/A20ON	If you are experiencing problems on a network drive or are losing characters during serial communication, use this switch. This causes communications to be handled differently and will usually solve the problem.
/NOHMA	Tells the command not to use the high memory area. Use this switch when you are running Windows.
/Q	Tells the command to operate in *quiet mode*; that is, it disables the warning message that appears when you run windows.
/SKIPHIGH	Tells the command not to load into an upper memory block. Use this switch when you are running Windows or when you are using a memory manager such as QEMM or 386 MAX.

When you boot the computer, the Diskreet DEVICE command tells DOS to make the Diskreet driver available for use. The first time you boot with the Diskreet device driver installed, you see a screen similar to figure 3.18. This screen gives you information about the Diskreet program, including all the default settings. Diskreet creates a file named DISKREET.INI that contains the settings for the program. When you boot again, you see only the copyright notice for Diskreet.

When you run Diskreet under Windows in standard or enhanced mode, a message appears when you initiate Windows, advising you that some Diskreet features (auto open, quick close, and auto close out) are disabled while you are in Windows. If you want to prevent this message from being displayed, place a /Q switch at the end of the DEVICE statement in your CONFIG.SYS file. For example, use this command:

    DEVICE=\NORTON\DISKREET.SYS /Q

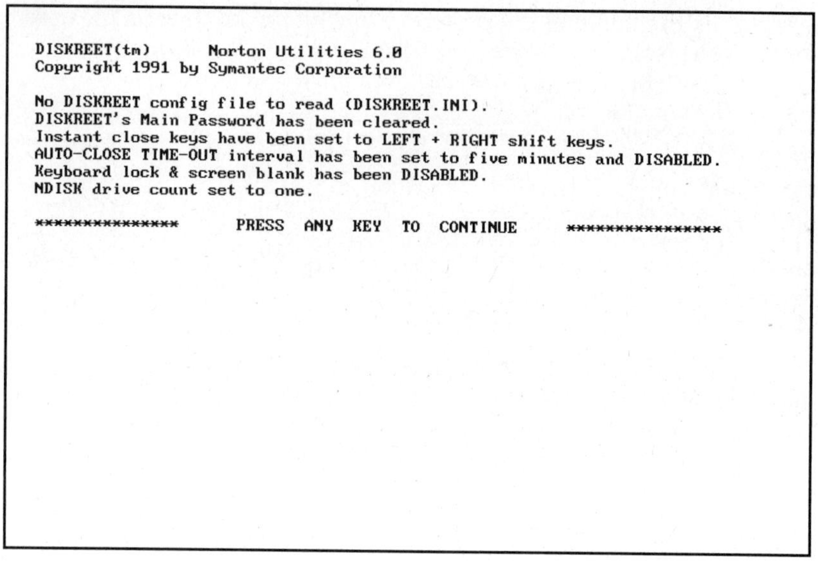

```
DISKREET(tm)        Norton Utilities 6.0
Copyright 1991 by Symantec Corporation

No DISKREET config file to read (DISKREET.INI).
DISKREET's Main Password has been cleared.
Instant close keys have been set to LEFT + RIGHT shift keys.
AUTO-CLOSE TIME-OUT interval has been set to five minutes and DISABLED.
Keyboard lock & screen blank has been DISABLED.
NDISK drive count set to one.

****************        PRESS  ANY  KEY  TO  CONTINUE        ****************
```

FIG. 3.18.

The initial Diskreet screen that appears the first time you boot.

The Diskreet driver takes up some of the RAM in your computer. If your computer has extended memory (over 640K), you can save some space for your program to use by placing the HIMEM.SYS driver (or PCSHADOW.SYS for COMPAQ computers) in your CONFIG.SYS file. To place the HIMEM.SYS driver (in the \NORTON directory) in the CONFIG.SYS file, for example, use the command

    DEVICE=\NORTON\HIMEM.SYS

Place the DEVICE command before the DEVICE=\NORTON\DISKREET.SYS command in your CONFIG.SYS file. If you are using an 80386-based computer, you can use an alternate memory manager such as QEMM or 386-to-the-max in place of HIMEM.SYS.

Using Passwords

Information stored with Diskreet is kept only as safe as your password. You should choose your password with care. The more important your information, the more careful you should be about choosing and protecting your password. Diskreet requires passwords of six or more characters.

Some ideas of passwords *not* to use are your name, names of relatives, names of pets, license plate numbers, or any other kind of name or number associated with you or your company. These combinations are the first things someone will try when attempting to get at your information.

The most effective passwords are random characters such as ZTLFEWBDD. But these are hard to remember. You could pick a strange word out of the dictionary, but a real hacker even may use some method of trying every word in the dictionary (spelled forward and backward) to get to your files. A compromise is to combine two words that are easy to remember but have no real meaning. Examples are LAUGH.BOOK, TREE/COMPUTER and WHITE:RING. If you choose to write down your password, place it in a protected area—a safe or a locked drawer, for example.

Three kinds of passwords are used in Diskreet. The *main* password is used to protect the Diskreet settings and affects all ndisks. The *disk* password protects a specific ndisk or group of files. The *file* password protects an individual file.

Using the Diskreet Command

To use the Diskreet command, you must travel through a series of setup screens that prompt you for information about how you want your file encryption to work. You need to answer questions about whether you want to encrypt files or disks, where to store information, which password to use, how much space to allocate to the disk, which method of encryption to use, and so on. The following paragraphs walk you through this setup procedure and explain the screens you see as you set up the Diskreet command.

To enter the Diskreet command, choose Diskreet from the Norton menu or enter the command DISKREET at the DOS prompt. The first screen you see is shown in figure 3.19. From this screen, you can choose to work with individual files or with a protected disk (an ndisk).

Encrypting and Decrypting Individual Files

If you choose the Files option from the Diskreet screen, a menu appears, enabling you to select from the following options:

    Encrypt
    Decrypt
    File Options

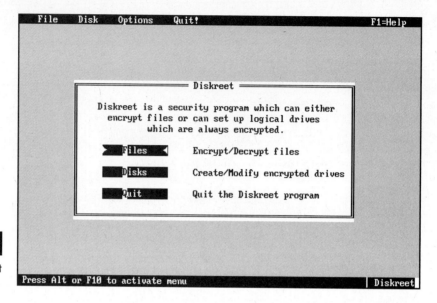

File   Disk   Options   Quit!   F1=Help

```
┌──────────────────── Diskreet ─────────────────────┐
│                                                    │
│      Diskreet is a security program which can      │
│      either encrypt files or can set up logical    │
│              drives which are always encrypted.    │
│                                                    │
│        ▶Files◀          Encrypt/Decrypt files      │
│                                                    │
│        ▶Disks           Create/Modify encrypted    │
│                         drives                     │
│                                                    │
│        ▶Quit            Quit the Diskreet program  │
│                                                    │
└────────────────────────────────────────────────────┘
```

Press Alt or F10 to activate menu | Diskreet |

FIG. 3.19.

The first Diskreet
screen.

If you choose Encrypt, a screen similar to the one in figure 3.20 appears. From this screen, you can choose which file to encrypt. Notice that the prompt File name appears. There you can enter the name of the file to encrypt. Using the three list boxes—Files, Dirs, and Drives—you can highlight the name of the specific file you want to encrypt. Use your arrow keys or Tab to move to the different prompts or list boxes on-screen, or point to a prompt or list box with your mouse and click. After you choose the file to encrypt, choose OK to continue (press Enter or point to OK and click).

Diskreet next prompts you to verify the file name. The encryption process creates the encrypted file with a different extension. If you encrypt the file named REPORT.WKS, for example, the file may be saved encrypted as REPORT.SEC (secret). You are prompted to enter a password to use; remember it. Passwords must contain a minimum of six characters and a maximum of 40 characters. Each encrypted file can be protected with a different password, or you can enter the same password for each file.

After the file is encrypted, it looks like gibberish if you try to read it. To get the file back to normal, you must decrypt it. To decrypt a file, choose the Files option from the Diskreet screen and then choose Decrypt. You see a file-selection screen like the one you use to choose a file to encrypt. After you choose the file to decrypt, you are asked for the password, and the file is decrypted.

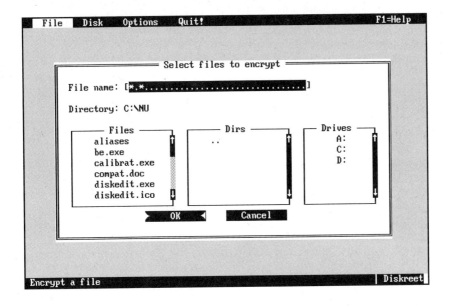

FIG. 3.20.

Choosing files
to encrypt.

To change the options for file encryption, choose File Options after you choose Files from the Diskreet screen. A screen like the one in figure 3.21 appears. From this screen, you can choose to encrypt by using the proprietary or the DES method. You also can tell Diskreet to get rid of an original file after it has been encrypted. If you do not choose this option, your old file remains unprotected on disk. You can set the attributes for the encrypted file to hidden and/or read-only, and you can choose to use the same password for as long as you are in Diskreet. That way, you do not have to enter a password each time to encrypt or decrypt a file. To select options on this screen, use the arrow keys to point to the option to set, and then press the space bar to lock in your selection. Or, point to the selection with the mouse pointer and click once.

After you choose settings on this screen, choose the Save option at the bottom of the screen to save this information to disk. Exit this screen by choosing OK.

Creating a Diskreet Ndisk

Unlike encrypting individual files, a Diskreet ndisk provides a method for automatically encrypting and decrypting all files that are written to or read. The following steps lead you through the creation of an ndisk:

```
┌─ File   Disk   Options   Quit!                          F1=Help ─┐
│                                                                  │
│         ╔═══════════ File Encryption Options ═══════════╗        │
│         ║ ┌─ Encryption Method ────────────────────────┐║        │
│         ║ │ (•) Fast proprietary method                │║        │
│         ║ │ ( ) DES (more secure but slower)            │║        │
│         ║ └────────────────────────────────────────────┘║        │
│         ║                                                ║        │
│         ║   [ ] Wipe/Delete original files after encryption      │
│         ║   [ ] Set Encrypted file to Hidden             ║        │
│         ║   [ ] Set Encrypted file to Read-Only          ║        │
│         ║   [ ] Use same password for entire session     ║        │
│         ║      ► Save ◄      ██ OK ██      Cancel         ║        │
│         ╚════════════════════════════════════════════════╝        │
│                                                                  │
│ File encryption/decryption options                    │ Diskreet │
└──────────────────────────────────────────────────────────────────┘
```

FIG. 3.21.

Choosing file-encryption options.

1. From the first Diskreet screen that appears after you enter the DISKREET command, choose the Disks option.

   The first time you choose this option, you see a screen like the one in figure 3.22.

```
┌─ File   Disk   Options   Quit!                          F1=Help ─┐
│                                                                  │
│                                                                  │
│           ╔═══════════ No NDisks Found ═══════════╗              │
│           ║                                        ║              │
│           ║        No Diskreet Drives Defined      ║              │
│           ║                                        ║              │
│           ║   Do you wish to define a new Diskreet Drive?        │
│           ║        ► Yes ◄        ██ No ██          ║              │
│           ╚════════════════════════════════════════╝              │
│                                                                  │
│                                                                  │
│ Press Alt or F10 to activate menu                     │ Diskreet │
└──────────────────────────────────────────────────────────────────┘
```

FIG. 3.22.

The No NDisks Found screen.

2. From this screen, choose Yes—you do want to create a new ndisk drive. The next screen you see asks where you want the ndisk information stored.

3. Choose where you want ndisk information stored. Usually, you choose your hard disk, although placing an ndisk on a floppy disk is possible.

   The next screen (which appears automatically) is shown in figure 3.23. It asks questions about how the disk is named, which encryption method to use, and which method of prompting for a password to use. Also, you can decide whether you want audit information shown when an ndisk is opened. This information shows you how many successful and unsuccessful attempts have been made to open your disk.

```
 File    Disk    Options    Quit!                         F1=Help


                      ═══ Make NDisk on Drive C: ═══
   ┌──────────────────────────────────────────────────────────────┐
   │ File Name: [░░░░░░░] Description: [..........................] │
   │ ┌ Audit ──────────────────┐  ┌ Password Prompting ──────────┐ │
   │ │ [x]  Show audit info when opened  ( )  Beep only          │ │
   │ │                             ( )  Pop-up prompt only        │ │
   │ ┌ Encryption ──────────────┐  (•)  Choose automatically     │ │
   │ │ (•)  Fast proprietary method  ( )  Manually open only     │ │
   │ │ ( )  DES (more secure but slower)                          │ │
   │ │          ► OK ◄        Cancel                               │ │
   └──────────────────────────────────────────────────────────────┘


 Press Alt or F10 to activate menu                        │ Diskreet│
```

FIG. 3.23.

The Diskreet screen for selecting options to create an ndisk.

4. Use your arrow keys and the space bar to choose the options you want, or point and click with a mouse.

   Enter a valid DOS file name at the File Name prompt. Press Tab (do not press Enter). The cursor moves to the Description field. Enter a description of the disk and press Tab. The cursor goes to the Audit check box. Press the space bar to turn the audit information on or off, and then press Tab.

   Using the up- and down-arrow keys (or mouse), point to the proprietary or DES encryption method and press the space bar to select the method you prefer. Then press the Tab key.

Using the up- and down-arrow keys and space bar (or mouse), choose one of the four password-prompting methods. The Beep Only option causes the computer to beep when you try to access a file on an ndisk. No prompt appears on-screen. You then must enter the password for the access to be successful. The Pop-up Prompt Only option causes a window to pop up on-screen, and you are prompted to enter the password. This method may not work in some programs that use high-resolution graphics screens. The Choose Automatically option enables Diskreet to choose the method of prompting that it thinks will work for the particular program being run. If you choose Manually Open Only, the only way to access the information is by first running the Diskreet program to open the disk.

5. After you choose your settings, choose OK (press Enter or click OK) to end this screen. If you choose Cancel (press Tab to highlight the Cancel option and press Enter, press Esc, or click on Cancel), all the settings revert to their previous states and the screen closes.

The Select NDisk Size screen next appears automatically, as shown in figure 3.24.

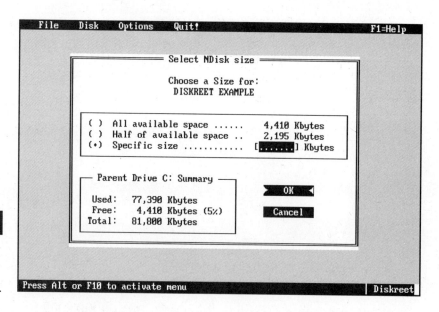

The Diskreet screen for choosing the size of an ndisk.

6. From this screen, select the size of your ndisk.

The All Available Space option uses all unused space on the disk. You probably will use this option only if you are making an entire floppy disk an ndisk. You can choose the Half of Available Space option if this is the amount of space you want to reserve. Usually, you need to use the Specific Size option. Choose the option and enter a reasonable amount of kilobytes according to how much information you expect to store on the disk. You can make the disk larger or smaller later. Because you can make the disk larger later, you don't need to go overboard by choosing a large amount of space. You may try selecting 360K initially (the size of a 5 1/4-inch floppy disk), to see if that is enough space for your needs. After you make your selection, choose OK.

7. In response to the prompts that appear, enter the same password twice as a verification. This is the *disk password*—not to be confused with the file passwords used when encrypting individual files. The password does not appear on-screen as you type it. Instead, a series of asterisks appears. Your password must contain at least six characters.

   The next screen warns you that you need to remember the password you just entered (see fig. 3.25). Information stored on an ndisk is worthless unless you know the password.

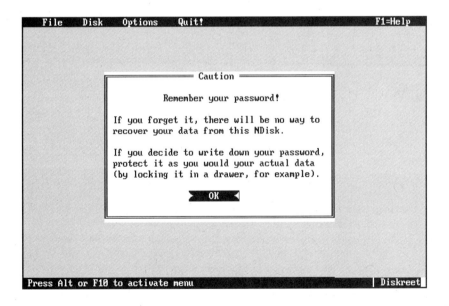

FIG. 3.25.

The Diskreet caution screen about the importance of remembering your password.

8. After you define your password, choose (or verify) the drive name of your new disk. Norton assigns an unused drive name (such as D or E) to your disk. Usually, you will have only one drive name (as in fig. 3.26), so you will choose OK to verify the drive letter. By

96

choosing System Settings on the Options menu, you can specify that more than one ndisk drive be created. (See "Using the Options Menu," later in the chapter.) If you have more than one drive, use the up- and down-arrow keys to select the drive to use. Choose OK to verify that the assigned drive name is acceptable.

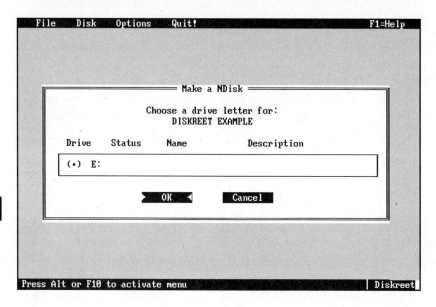

Make a NDisk

Choose a drive letter for:
DISKREET EXAMPLE

Drive   Status   Name   Description

(•) E:

OK ◄   Cancel

Press Alt or F10 to activate menu | Diskreet

FIG. 3.26.

The Diskreet selection screen for choosing the drive letter of an ndisk.

If you previously chose to show the audit information, an audit screen appears at this point, giving you information on when this disk was last opened, when the password was last changed, how many attempts have been made to open the disk, and how many of those attempts failed.

The creation of your ndisk is complete. Diskreet now shows a screen like the one in figure 3.27. This screen lists the one or more ndisks that are available to you. Using the arrow keys or mouse, you can select the disk you want to use or modify.

Modifying Diskreet Ndisk Options

After you begin the Diskreet program and choose the Disks option, you see a screen similar to the one in figure 3.27. From this screen, you can use the menu bar at the top of the screen to work with individual files (File), change selections concerning the ndisk (Disk), or change options related to how the ndisk works (Options). To open the pull-down menus, press F10 or point to one of the menu options (File, Disk, or Options) with the mouse pointer and click once.

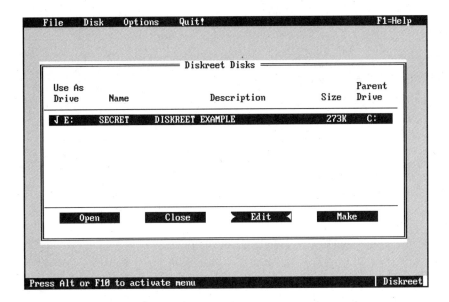

FIG. 3.27.

The Diskreet Disks screen with the menu bar.

Using the File Menu

The File menu enables you to encrypt or decrypt a file or change file options. For more information, see "Encrypting and Decrypting Individual Files," earlier in this chapter.

Using the Disk Menu

The Disk menu enables you to access, close, or delete ndisks and to modify their sizes and change disk passwords. When you pull down the Disk menu, you see the following selections:

Option	Effect
Search Floppies (Alt-S)	Tells Diskreet to search the floppy drives for ndisks. If you have just placed a floppy disk in a disk drive, Diskreet does not know that the disk is there until you choose the Search Floppies option. Notice that you can press Alt-S anytime the Diskreet program is running to choose this option.

Option	Effect
Close All (Alt-C)	Quickly closes all ndisks.
Adjust Size	Makes your ndisk larger or smaller. Norton prompts you to enter the new size for your disk.
Delete	Deletes an entire ndisk from your disk.
Change Disk Password	Changes the password used to access your ndisk. Backing up your ndisk before making a change in your password is important. If a power outage occurs during the change of passwords, you could lose all the information on your ndisk. You will be prompted to enter the old password. Then, you will be prompted to enter and verify a new password.

Using the Options Menu

After you choose Options from the Diskreet menu bar, you see the following selections:

■ *System Settings:* Displays a screen like the one in figure 3.28. This screen enables you to select the number of drives to allocate as ndisks and enables you to take the NDisk Manager out of memory. The NDisk Manager, which is loaded as a result of the DISKREET.SYS device driver in your CONFIG.SYS file, takes up about 50K of RAM. If you need that memory to run a program, you must choose the Do Not Load the NDisk Manager option and reboot your computer to reclaim that memory.

With the NDisk Manager not in memory, your ndisks do not function. To make your ndisks work again, you have to come back to this option, turn it off, and reboot.

■ *Startup NDisks:* Displays a screen like the one in figure 3.29. This screen enables you to indicate which disks should be opened for use when your computer is booted. To choose a disk for automatic opening, choose the Edit option. A list of available ndisks appears. Choose which ndisk to start up automatically; then choose whether it should open as soon as the computer is booted or the first time it is accessed.

If you choose to have an ndisk start automatically, you still are prompted to enter the password before the disk is opened. After you open the disk, the files in the disk are available until you close the disk.

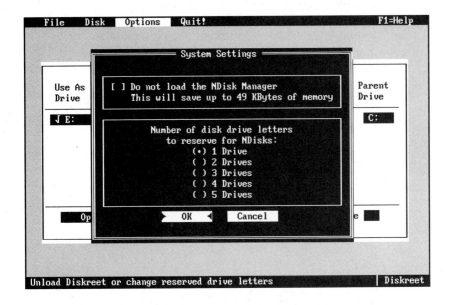

FIG. 3.28.

The System
Settings screen.

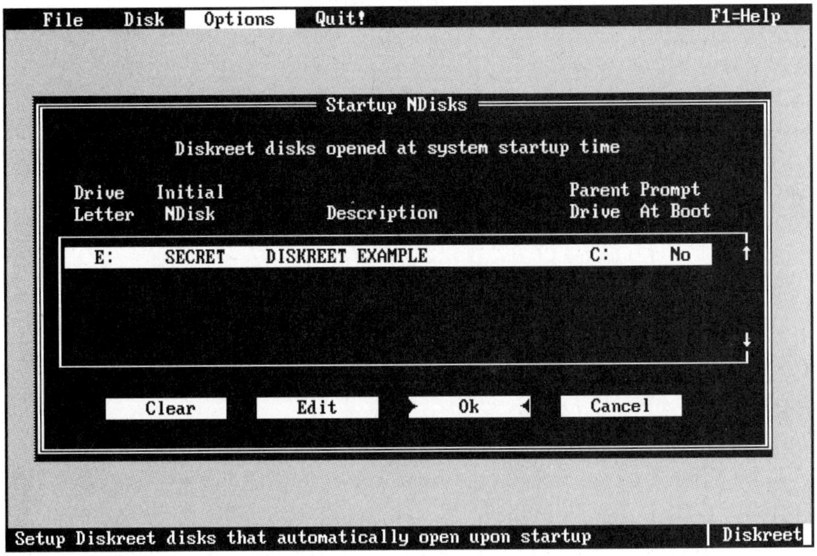

FIG. 3.29.

The Startup
NDisks screen.

■ *Auto Close Timeouts:* Displays a screen like the one in figure 3.30.
This setting tells Diskreet to close an ndisk if it has not been accessed for a certain amount of time. The default time is five minutes. When you choose this option, the cursor is in the check box.
To set this value, make sure that the Enable Auto Close setting is

marked by pressing the space bar (an X will appear in the box). Press Tab to move the cursor to the number of minutes and type the number you want. Press Enter to choose OK or click on OK with your mouse pointer.

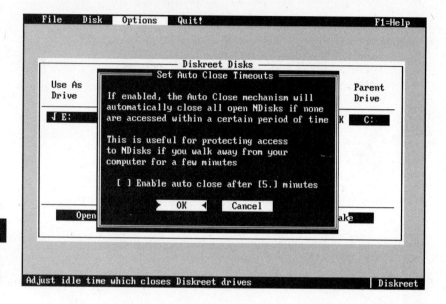

FIG. 3.30.

The Set Auto Close Timeouts screen.

- *Keyboard and Screen Lock:* Displays a screen similar to the one in figure 3.31. This screen enables you to choose a quick-close hot key and keyboard locking. Use the arrow keys or Tab to move the cursor to the check boxes and radio button you want to change. Press the space bar to lock in any selection. To choose the hot key, make sure that the Enable Quick-Close option is checked and then choose one of the hot-key combinations listed in the Quick Close/Lock Hot Key box. A quick-close hot key enables you to quickly close all ndisks.

  If you want the screen to clear and the keyboard to lock until the main password is entered, choose the Enable Locking option and then choose a hot key that you can use to turn on the locking. If you select both Enable Quick-Close and Enable Locking, the same hot key makes both take place at once.

- *Security:* Displays a screen similar to the one in figure 3.32. This screen enables you to choose what to do when an ndisk is modified. The Quick Clear option leaves encrypted information that is no longer used on disk (for example, an erased file). Therefore, the information can be restored and read (if someone knows the password). The Overwrite option writes over the data one time on the disk. This process usually is sufficient to destroy the data. If you really want security, however, choose the Security Wipe option, which writes over the data many times, using a Department of Defense procedure.

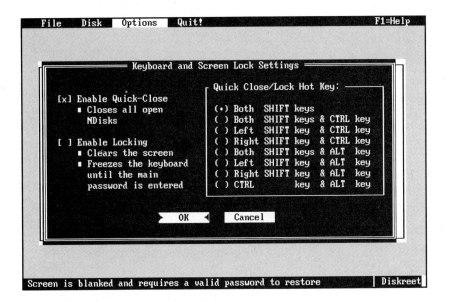

FIG. 3.31.

The Keyboard and Screen Lock Settings screen.

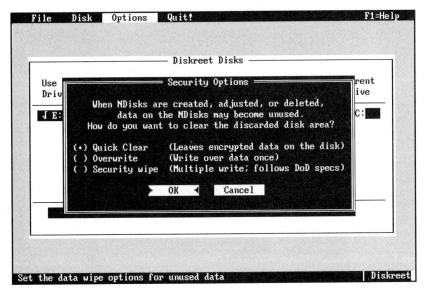

FIG. 3.32.

The Security Options screen.

■ *Change Main Password:* Enables you to specify a new main password. This password is needed to alter auto-close timeouts and keyboard locking. After you choose this option, you are prompted to enter a new main password, and then you are prompted to enter it again for verification.

Controlling Diskreet from the DOS Prompt

Many of the items that you can control through the series of Diskreet screens you also can control by using the Diskreet command at the DOS prompt. The syntax for using Diskreet from the DOS prompt is

DISKREET [*switches*]

The available switches for the Diskreet command are listed in table 3.8.

Table 3.8 Diskreet Switches

Switch	Effect
/CLOSE	Closes all ndisks
/DECRYPT:*filespec*	Decrypts specified file
/ENCRYPT:*filespec*	Encrypts specified file
/HIDE[:*d*]	Hides specified drive (ndisk)
/OFF	Disables use of Diskreet driver
/ON	Enables Diskreet driver
/PASSWORD:*your password*	Tells Diskreet which password to use for encryption or decryption of a file
/SHOW[:*d*]	Shows hidden drives (ndisks) being used to store files

You cannot use both /DECRYPT and /ENCRYPT in the same command. The switches /CLOSE, /HIDE, /ON, /OFF, and /SHOW can only be used alone, without any other options on the command line.

Using Diskreet on a Network

Diskreet ndisks are not designed to work as network drives. You can back up your ndisks, however, by copying them to a network drive. To read information from the disk, you need to copy the information back onto your local computer's drive. Using the Diskreet command, you can encrypt and decrypt individual files on a network drive. If you are on a Novell network, the Netware command MAP attempts to locate any ndisks on your computer and prompts you for a password. If you want to disable this prompting, enter the following three commands at the DOS prompt or create a batch file to issue these commands:

```
C:\NORTON\DISKREET /OFF
MAP
C:\NORTON\DISKREET /ON
```

Getting Rid of Files Permanently

With all this discussion about how to bring back files after disks have been formatted, you may be concerned about how to get rid of files permanently. The fact that some people do not even think about this problem (or did not know about it) is amazing. In a recent magazine story, a Fortune 100 company (a computer company, no less) auctioned off thousands of outdated PCs. Some were purchased by reporters who were able to unformat the hard disks and discover a great deal of important information.

After you erase a file by using the DOS ERASE or DELETE command, only one character in the disk directory is changed. This character tells DOS that the file is deleted. The contents of the file have not changed, and most of the information about the file still is intact. When you format a disk, the system information is erased, and information in the root directory is erased, but the contents of many files may be intact. For more information, see Chapter 4.

To give users a better way to prevent important information from being seen by unauthorized eyes, Norton Utilities provides the WipeInfo command. This command permanently deletes files and disks by physically overwriting the contents of the disk and not just modifying the directory information. If you have information that should not fall into the wrong hands, the WipeInfo command should be an essential part of your information protection plan.

Thoroughly understanding WipeInfo and how files are erased is important before you use the command to delete important files permanently.

WipeInfo overwrites the information on disk with several writes of random data. WipeInfo includes a government option that overwrites the information on a disk according to governmental Department of Defense (DoD) specifications. These specifications call for a 1/0 pattern (a pattern of 1s and 0s) to be written to the disk three times, a random number to be written to the disk, and then the last number written to the disk to be read back from the disk for verification (DoD 5220.22-M). The government has adopted these specifications because a single erasure of magnetic information may not be enough. A faint magnetic "fingerprint" may remain on a disk after a single erasure.

You can use WipeInfo interactively or as a command from the DOS prompt.

Using the WipeInfo Command Screen

To use WipeInfo from the command screen, enter the command

WIPEINFO

at the DOS prompt. A screen similar to the one in figure 3.33 appears.

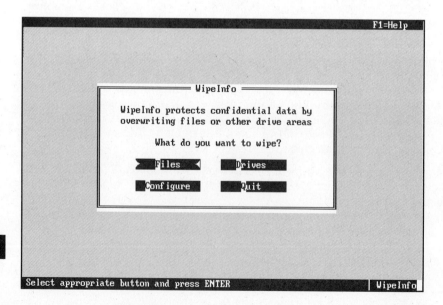

The WipeInfo screen gives you four options:

■ *Files:* Displays the Wipe Files screen (see fig. 3.34). On this screen, you can enter the names of the files to be wiped. Use the global characters * and ? to specify multiple files. By checking the appropriate boxes, you can choose to wipe files with matching file specifications in subdirectories, to have the program prompt you before wiping each file (confirm each file), and to wipe hidden files or read-only files that match the file specification. Also, you can choose to wipe the file or delete the file (like a regular DOS DELETE command). The Wipe Unused File Slack Only option causes WipeInfo to wipe only any portion of the disk that is allocated to a file but unused. This process does not affect the file itself but wipes out only the information in the slack space of the file. After you select your options, choose the Wipe option at the bottom of the screen to begin the wiping procedure; choose Cancel to cancel the wipe. The Directory option at the bottom of the screen enables you to change the current default directory.

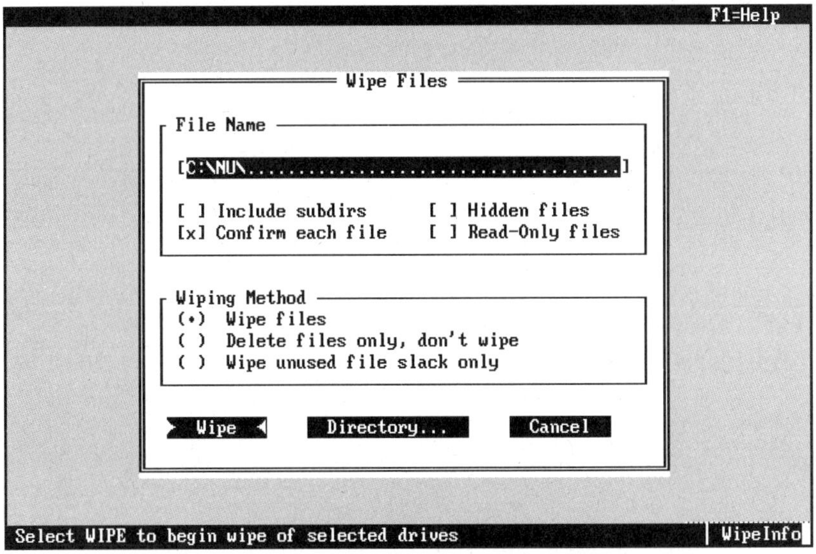

FIG. 3.34.

The Wipe Files screen.

■ *Drives:* Displays the Wipe Drives screen (see fig. 3.35). On this screen, you can select which drives to wipe. Also, you can choose to wipe the entire disk or only the unused portions of the disk. Wiping the unused portion of the disk gets rid of any erased files that someone could restore to see important information. After you select the options on this menu, choose Wipe to begin wiping or choose Cancel to cancel the wipe.

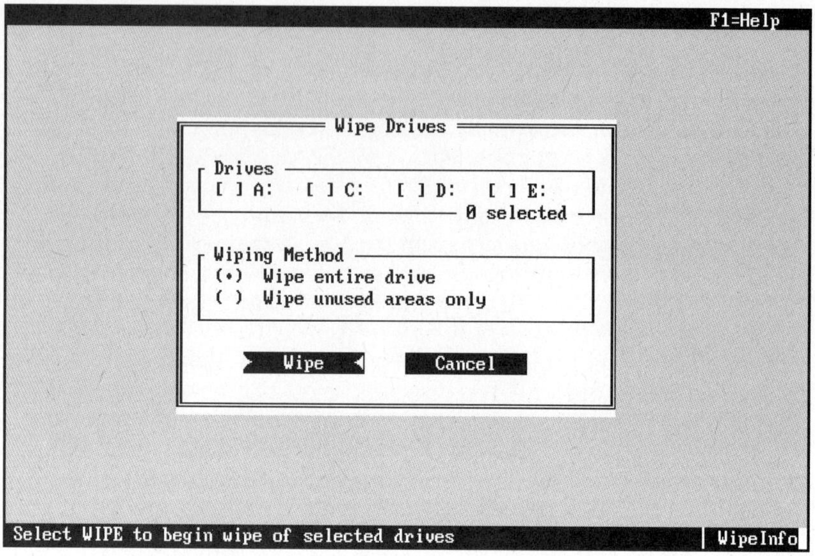

```
                                                           F1=Help

                    ╔══════════ Wipe Drives ══════════╗

                    ┌ Drives ──────────────────────────┐
                    │ [ ] A:   [ ] C:   [ ] D:   [ ] E: │
                    └──────────────────────── 0 selected ┘

                    ┌ Wiping Method ───────────────────┐
                    │ (•)  Wipe entire drive           │
                    │ ( )  Wipe unused areas only      │
                    └──────────────────────────────────┘

                          ▶  Wipe  ◀      Cancel

     Select WIPE to begin wipe of selected drives          WipeInfo
```

FIG. 3.35.

The Wipe
Drives screen.

■ *Configure:* Displays the Wipe Configuration screen, enabling you to decide how information is wiped from the disk (see fig. 3.36). From this screen, choose the Fast Wipe (default) or Government Wipe option. You can change several of the numbers within the options. For example, you can change the number of times 1s and 0s are written from 3 to another number (for example, 5) and change the final value written to disk from ASCII 246 to some other ASCII value (for example, 32). You use the arrow keys, Tab, or the mouse pointer to move to those fields to change the numbers.

For the Fast Wipe option, you can change the write value from 0 to another number from 1 to 255. For the Government Wipe option, you can change the number of times the write is repeated and the final value written (the default is 246). Also, you can change the Repeat Count setting from 1 to another number. After you choose these settings, choose the Save Settings option and then choose OK to return to the WipeInfo screen.

■ *Quit:* Exits the WipeInfo screen.

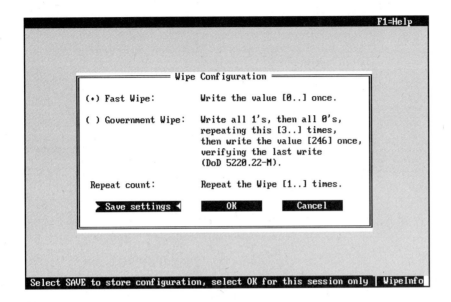

```
                                                    F1=Help

              ══════════ Wipe Configuration ══════════
            ║                                            ║
            ║  (•) Fast Wipe:      Write the value [0..] once.
            ║
            ║  ( ) Government Wipe:  Write all 1's, then all 0's,
            ║                       repeating this [3..] times,
            ║                       then write the value [246] once,
            ║                       verifying the last write
            ║                       (DoD 5220.22-M).
            ║
            ║  Repeat count:       Repeat the Wipe [1..] times.
            ║
            ║     ► Save settings ◄     █ OK █      █ Cancel █

 Select SAVE to store configuration, select OK for this session only | WipeInfo
```

FIG. 3.36.

The Wipe Configuration screen.

Using WipeInfo from the DOS Prompt

The WipeInfo command overwrites information on disk so that the information cannot be recovered. This process includes wiping files or the entire disk. The syntax for the WipeInfo command is

WIPEINFO d:[disk or file switches] [common switches]

The *disk switch* available for the WipeInfo command follows:

Switch	Effect
/E	Causes the command to overwrite only information that currently is unused or that is in "erased" files—files marked for erase by the DOS ERASE command but otherwise recoverable.

The *file switches* available for the WipeInfo command follow:

Switch	Effect
/K	Wipes out a file and any slack space allocated to a file. (See Chapter 4 for more information on slack space.)

Switch	Effect
/N	Uses "no-wipe" mode, which causes the WipeInfo command to behave like the ERASE command. The file is marked as erased but is not over-written.
/S	Wipes out files that match the file specification in the current directory and all subdirectories.

The *common switches* available for the WipeInfo command follow:

Switch	Effect
/G*n*	Uses a government-standard overwriting proce-dure. The default for *n* (number of overwrites) is 3. Value written to disk is ASCII value 246.
/R*n*	Overwrites the disk *n* times. The default is 1.
/V*n*	Selects the value that is to be used to overwrite information on the disk. The value can be from 0 to 255. Although the default is 0, the /G switch overrides this default.

To wipe disk D using the government standard, for example, enter the command

    WIPEINFO D:/G

When you begin WipeInfo from the DOS prompt with a file specification and switches, you skip the interactive WipeInfo screen and see the Wipe Files or Wipe Drives screen. From these screens, you can set or change options.

Even if you go ahead and begin WipeInfo and suddenly have a change of heart or discover that you are wiping out the wrong disk, you can interrupt the process by pressing Ctrl-Break. Some information on the disk still may be recoverable if the operation has not proceeded too far. In fact, Norton has designed WipeInfo to destroy the most unused part of the disk first, so if you stop the procedure quickly, you have a good chance of being able to use some of the information on disk.

A few software products store copy-protection information in the slack space of a file. If you wipe out the slack space with the /K option, you may cause a program to lose its capability to run. Although this storage practice is not common, if you use software with protection schemes, you may want to check with the software manufacturer to see whether wiping the slack space will affect the program's capability to run.

Use WipeInfo when you give a computer with a hard disk to another person and that computer contains information that should not be made available to the recipient. If you want to wipe out only data files but leave programs intact on a computer, first erase all the confidential files and then use WipeInfo with the /E switch to wipe out all the erased files. The programs are left intact.

Chapter Summary

Norton Utilities offers you a number of ways to protect your information on disk. Most of these safety measures, however, require that you do a little planning. Make sure that you set up your AUTOEXEC.BAT file to issue the Image command each time you boot. Also make sure that you are using the Safe Format command rather than the original DOS FORMAT command. If you accidentally do format a disk, you can recover it if you have taken these precautions.

Other safety precautions you can use include setting file attributes to read-only or hidden. Use Erase Protect, Disk Monitor, and Diskreet to monitor which files are used and changed on your disk. Finally, when protecting information means making sure that it does not get into the wrong hands, you can use WipeInfo to do a more thorough job of getting rid of information on disk than the DOS ERASE, DELETE, and FORMAT commands provide.

Recovering Files

Chapter 3 covers techniques for protecting the information on your disk by using preventive measures. At times, however, the best prevention does not work. You accidentally may use the command DEL when you meant to use DIR, for example. The consequences of these commands are quite different. The DIR command displays a list of files, and the DEL command deletes files.

Accidental erasure is probably the most common way that you can lose files. Accidental formatting is another common cause of information loss. Some information losses, however, are hard to control. You can lose files, for example, through excessive fragmentation on disk. Also, the magnetic image on your disk can be damaged if the magnetic field weakens.

This chapter shows how to recover lost information and describes the Norton UnErase command (unerases files or directories), the Norton Disk Doctor (searches for and corrects file problems on disk), Disk Tools (fixes various disk problems), File Fix (fixes dBASE, 1-2-3, and

Symphony files), and Disk Editor (examines and edits disk contents directly).

Before you learn how to use these Norton data-recovery commands, however, you must understand the basics of how disks work—valuable knowledge if you want to manage disks. If you already know how disks store information, you may want to skip the next section.

Understanding How Disks Work

This section describes how disks store information, how disks operate, and how DOS manages the information on disk. This information can give you a better understanding of what happens on your computer. Knowing how disks handle data can be particularly helpful if you use the Norton Disk Editor command to edit information on disk or recover erased files.

Computers have a *binary* thought process, meaning a computer's memory consists of 0s (zeros) and 1s (ones). A memory chip stores information in the computer's RAM (random-access memory) as an on or off signal, with the on signal being a 1 and the off signal a 0. Each RAM chip stores thousands of these signals. When you create a word processing document, for example, RAM stores the entire document as a series of 0s and 1s.

To store computer information, therefore, you must have a way to store these 0s and 1s. Early computers used *punch cards*. A hole punched in the card was interpreted as a 1; no hole meant 0. Today, the popular way to store computer information is on magnetic-sensitive media.

You may recall from elementary school when your science teacher placed some steel shavings on a sheet of paper and put a magnet under the paper. The shavings all pointed in one direction or another, according to the poles of the magnet. Recording media, such as that on a cassette recorder tape, a VCR tape, or a floppy diskette, is covered with a coat of iron oxide, which reacts to magnetism in a way similar to those steel shavings. On a cassette recorder, the recording head is an electric magnet that magnetizes the iron oxide on the tape as the tape goes by. The stronger the signal, the more the iron oxide reacts.

To store computer information to magnetic media, only two signals are needed: one strong and one weak. The computer interprets a strong magnetic signal as a 1 and a weak signal as a 0. Thus, a pattern of 1s and 0s can be written to and then read from magnetic media.

A computer disk is sort of a cross between a record and a cassette tape. Information on the disk is stored on magnetic tracks, which work like the magnetic coating on a cassette tape and the grooves on a record, except that you cannot see the tracks.

The magnetic media is coated on the top and bottom of floppy and hard disks. A small head similar to the recording head on a tape recorder rides just above the surface of the disk. This head places magnetic signals on the disk (patterns of 0s and 1s) and reads them back. The work of reading and writing to disk, however, is not done haphazardly, but is a precise bit of mechanical and software engineering.

How Floppy and Hard Disks Evolved

Disk media has improved over time. When the IBM PC first appeared in 1981, its only disk media was a single-sided diskette. The disk drive had a read/write head for only one side of the diskette. Soon, double-sided diskettes appeared for which the drive used a read/write head on both sides. This improvement to the drive was relatively straightforward. No new housing or motor was needed. The addition of a second head and some electronics doubled the disk's storage capacity.

Dust particles cause one problem with reading and writing information to a diskette. Dust in the air limits the precision (smallness) of the information storage area on the disk.

Another problem with diskettes is their floppiness. When they spin around in the disk drive, some up-and-down movement occurs. Because of this movement, keeping the read/write head close enough to work but not close enough to scratch the surface of the disk is difficult. In fact, some diskettes wear out because of contact with the read/write head.

Development of the hard disk solved the problems of dust and movement, as well as the problem of not having enough room on a disk to store information. A hard disk is housed in a dust-free compartment, so dust is not a problem. Also, the magnetic media is coated on a hard platter (hence the name *hard disk*). These two improvements enable the read/write head to be placed closer to the disk, to read and write with more precision, and to rotate faster, enabling data to be stored and retrieved more quickly than on a floppy diskette. Hard disks also have greater storage capacity than diskettes.

Most improvements to disk storage have involved the storage of more information with more precision on the magnetic surface of the disk. Mechanical and electrical improvements have given disks this capability, and DOS has responded with the capability to handle the added capacity.

How Disks Are Organized

DOS keeps track of the information stored on disk. When a floppy or hard disk is formatted, circular areas called *tracks* are written (magnetically) on the disk. A standard 360K floppy diskette (double-sided/double density) has 40 tracks, numbered 0 to 39. High-density (1.2M, 5 1/4-inch) and 3 1/2-inch (720K double-density and 1.44M high-density) diskettes use 80 tracks. Each track consists of a number of pieces called *sectors*. On a 360K diskette, each track has 9 sectors, numbered 1 through 9. Figure 4.1 illustrates the tracks and sectors on a typical 360K disk.

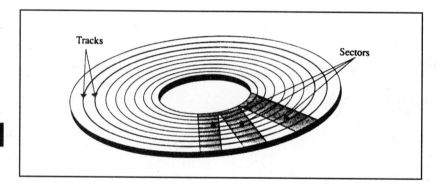

FIG. 4.1.

A disk's tracks and sectors.

Because disks are two-sided (numbered 0 and 1), the top and bottom of the disks contain tracks. A pair of matching tracks on a disk is called a *cylinder*. Some hard disks have more than one platter, or disk. When two disks are included, sides are numbered 0 and 1 on the first disk and 2 and 3 on the second disk. The set of four matching tracks on the two disks is the cylinder.

After the formatting process organizes a disk into tracks and sectors, DOS knows how to read and write information to the disk. The operating system now knows where to place the read/write head to read information from a particular track. In fact, DOS reads and writes information to the disk in a specific amount of bytes, called a *cluster*. A byte is eight 0 and 1 signals. Usually, each character stored on disk requires 1 byte of space. Thus, a byte often is referred to as one character of information. The number of sectors of information contained in a cluster depends on how many sectors per track are stored on disk. DOS uses two-sector clusters (1,024 bytes) on 360K and 720K diskettes, one-sector clusters (512 bytes) on 1.2M and 1.44M diskettes, and 4-, 8-, or 16-sector clusters on most hard disks.

How DOS Manages Information

Specific areas on a formatted disk hold particular kinds of information. The *system area* contains the boot record, the FAT (file allocation table), and the root directory. The system area is stored on track 0, the outermost track of the disk. Whenever DOS needs to know information about the files stored on a disk, DOS reads this information from the system area of the disk. When you enter a DIR command, for example, DOS first looks at the directory to get information on the files and displays this information on-screen.

The *data area*, where the actual information in files is stored, immediately follows the system information on disk. The system area controls the contents of this data area and how DOS knows how to read and write the data.

The Boot Record

DOS reserves the first sector of the first track of a disk as the DOS boot record. The *boot record* contains characteristics about the disk such as the DOS version used to format the disk, the number of bytes per sector on disk, the number of heads, and other information. The boot record is written to every formatted disk, even if the disk does not have booting capabilities. If the disk is a bootable disk, this record gives the computer information on where to find the start-up system information.

The File Allocation Table

The *file allocation table* (FAT) contains information about disk storage. The FAT tells DOS which clusters on the disk are in use, contain files, are available for use, or are bad and should not be used. When you must write a file to disk, DOS consults the FAT to find out where to store the information. If a file is large and cannot fit in one contiguous space on disk, DOS uses the FAT to find the next available space. The result is a *fragmented file*—a file that is stored in pieces on disk.

Also, because the FAT deals in clusters, a file may be allocated to a cluster that is not fully used. For example, if a cluster is 512 bytes, and a 200-byte file is stored, 312 bytes of unused space remain in the cluster. This space cannot be used by other files at the same time, so this area of disk space within this cluster is "wasted." This unused disk space is called *slack*. (You can determine the amount of slack on disk by using the Norton File Size command, discussed in Chapter 5.) Cluster sizes differ, so the slack space for a particular file on a floppy diskette may be different from the slack for the same file on a hard disk. Although a diskette may have a 512-byte cluster, for example, many hard disks have 2,048-byte clusters. The same 200-byte file has a slack space of 1,848 bytes on such a hard disk.

The Root Directory

The third part of the system information on disk is the *root directory*— the main directory (\) on any formatted disk. This disk space is allocated for storing information about the root directory's files. Subdirectories have their own areas where file information is stored. Subdirectories, like files, can be stored in the data area in no particular location. Table 4.1 shows the information that a directory reports for each file the directory contains.

Table 4.1 File Information Stored in the Root Directory

Item	Size in Bytes	Stored As
File name	8	ASCII characters
Extension	3	ASCII characters
Attributes	1	Bit values
Time	2	Coded time
Date	2	Coded date
Starting FAT entry	2	Word (a binary coded number)
File size	4	Long integer (size in bytes)

 NOTE The root directory reserves 10 bytes for future use in case something else about a file must be stored.

Notice that the file name storage is eight characters—the maximum length for a file name. The extension is allocated three characters. Attributes include read-only, archive, hidden, and system. (You can control the attributes with the Norton FileFind command, discussed in Chapter 3.) The starting FAT entry tells DOS where to look in the FAT to find where the file is stored on disk. The date and time entries tell DOS when this file was last changed, and the length entry tells DOS how much space the file takes in bytes. The information in the Stored As column specifies the method used to store this information.

How Files Are Erased

When you store a file on disk, the information the file contains is written to the disk's data area. The root directory (or a similar subdirectory) and the FAT stores the information about where the file data is. When you erase a file by using the DOS ERASE or DEL commands, the first character of the entry in the directory that contains the file name is replaced with the ASCII sigma character number 229 (Σ), and related entries in the FAT are zeroed out. DOS does not overwrite (unless you use the WipeInfo option, as explained in Chapters 3 and 7) or remove the information from the file. The ASCII character number 229 that DOS adds to the erased file's directory tells DOS that the file and the space the file occupied are now free to be used by other files.

If you erase a file named MYFILE, for example, the "erased" name becomes ΣYFILE in the DOS directory. The erased name does not appear when you use the DIR command, but you can view the name by using the Norton Utilities UnErase command.

Because the ERASE and DEL commands do not touch the real information in the file, you may be able to recover an erased file if you have written no other files (or few files) to disk since erasing the file. The rest of this chapter discusses ways to recover files.

Retrieving Erased Files and Directories

If the file space used by an erased file has not been used by a subsequent write to disk, you can recover the file by using the UnErase command. Because an erased file can have its contents overwritten at any time, you must decide as soon as possible that a file must be unerased.

You should have no problem unerasing a file immediately after the file has been erased. If you create one or more files after erasing a file, however, the original file may no longer be unerasable.

To issue the UnErase command, select the UnErase option from the Norton menu or enter the UNERASE command at the DOS prompt.

When you begin UnErase, the program searches for all unerasable files in the current directory. If the program finds erased files, the file names (as far as UnErase can figure out, without the first character) are displayed. If the file MARY.TXT has been erased, for example, the UnErase program reports that the file ?ARY.TXT can be recovered. Figure 4.2 shows a screen where a number of files are listed as candidates for unerasing.

```
  File     Search    Options    Quit!                        F1=Help
 ╔══════════════════════ Erased files in C:\KW ═══════════════════════╗
 ║     Name           Size       Date       Time     Prognosis        ║
 ║ ▓▓▓▓▓▓▓▓▓▓▓▓▓▓▓▓▓▓▓▓▓▓▓▓▓▓▓▓▓▓▓▓▓▓▓▓▓▓▓▓▓▓▓▓▓▓▓▓▓▓▓▓▓▓▓▓▓▓▓▓▓▓▓▓▓   ║
 ║     . .             DIR       3-04-91    7:37 pm   SUB-DIR          ║↑
 ║    ?ary    txt       387      7-18-91    6:22 pm   good             ║
 ║    ?ass    kw         12      7-18-91    6:22 pm   poor             ║
 ║    ?he     bak     2,288      5-10-91    6:04 pm   good             ║
 ║    ?ist    bak     1,308      4-27-91    3:28 pm   poor             ║
 ║    ?mp     bak     6,279      6-05-91    2:16 pm   good             ║
 ║    ?om.june bak    5,397      3-01-91    2:19 pm   good             ║
 ║    ?orn    bak       729      7-14-91    8:47 pm   good             ║
 ║    ?rof    bak     1,395      7-04-91   10:26 am   good             ║
 ║    ?ten    bak     1,269      6-18-91   12:33 pm   good             ║
 ║    ?upport bak     1,185      6-16-90    7:13 am   good             ║↓
 ║                                                                    ║
 ║        ┌───── Info ─────┐  ► ─── View ─── ◄  ┌─── UnErase ───┐      ║
 ╚════════════════════════════════════════════════════════════════════╝
  Select files to UnErase                                   │ UnErase
```

FIG. 4.2.

Viewing
potential files to
unerase.

UnErase provides a prognosis of the likelihood that these files can be unerased successfully. The possible prognoses are excellent, good, average, and poor.

To choose which file to unerase, use the cursor-movement keys to highlight the file name and press Enter to choose UnErase, or highlight a file name and click twice. If you choose to unerase the file ?ARY.TXT, for example, you see the screen in figure 4.3, which asks you for the first letter in the file's name.

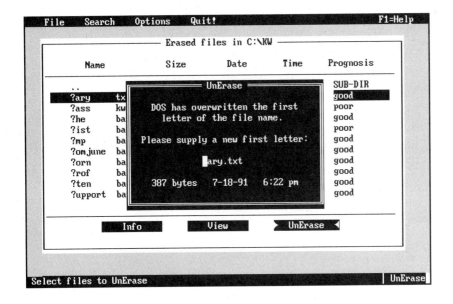

FIG. 4.3.

Supplying the first letter of an erased file's name.

To complete the process, press M to unerase the file MARY.TXT. You return to the screen shown in figure 4.2, where you can choose other files to unerase.

If a file cannot be unerased automatically, you see a message like the one in figure 4.4. In this case, you may use the Search for Lost Names option (see "Using the UnErase Search Menu," later in this chapter), or you may need to use the Manual UnErase procedure discussed in "Using Manual UnErase," later in this chapter.

To locate files in other directories, you can go to another directory from the current directory by using the following procedure. The top file name (highlighted in figure 4.2) is subdirectory information. If you highlight .. and press Enter or click twice, you go to the preceding directory—in this example, the root directory—where a list of all directories appears. Then you highlight another directory name, press Enter, and go to another directory to look for more files to unerase. As you see in the next section, you also can use the UnErase menu bar to change directories.

An erased directory appears in the list with other erased file names, but the word DIR appears in the Size column instead of a number. Figure 4.5, for example, contains information about an erased directory named TMP. Its name in the list is ?MP, and under the Size column the directory is listed as DIR. To unerase this directory, highlight its name and press Enter to choose the UnErase option. Or, you can highlight the entry with the mouse and click twice.

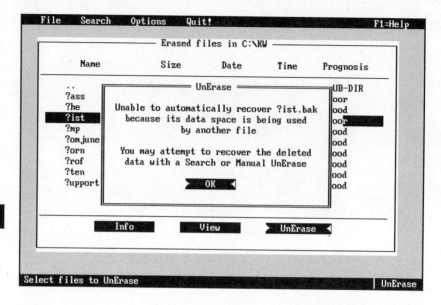

Erased files in C:\KW

Name	Size	Date	Time	Prognosis
..				UB-DIR
?ass				oor
?he				ood
?ist				oo
?mp				ood
?om,june				ood
?orn				ood
?rof				ood
?ten				ood
?upport				ood

UnErase

Unable to automatically recover ?ist.bak
because its data space is being used
by another file

You may attempt to recover the deleted
data with a Search or Manual UnErase

OK

Info   View   UnErase

Select files to UnErase   UnErase

FIG. 4.4.

A message
telling you that
a file cannot be
unerased.

Erased files in C:\

Name	Size	Date	Time	Prognosis
SCRATCH	DIR	4-17-91	7:46 pm	SUB-DIR
SPELL	DIR	6-18-91	7:30 pm	SUB-DIR
TEMP	DIR	4-28-91	8:54 pm	SUB-DIR
THINKER	DIR	4-27-91	2:00 pm	SUB-DIR
TWIN	DIR	3-04-91	4:48 pm	SUB-DIR
TYPESET	DIR	5-02-91	7:29 pm	SUB-DIR
VB	DIR	7-25-91	8:11 pm	SUB-DIR
VENTURA	DIR	5-02-91	7:29 pm	SUB-DIR
WINDOWS	DIR	4-11-91	7:16 pm	SUB-DIR
WP50	DIR	3-04-91	4:43 pm	SUB-DIR
?MP	DIR	3-04-91	8:02 pm	average
?utoexec bak	275	7-15-91	8:46 pm	excellent

Info   View   UnErase

Select files to UnErase   UnErase

FIG. 4.5.

Selecting a
directory to
unerase.

If the directory can be unerased, you are prompted to enter the first
letter of its name. After the directory is unerased, you can go to that
directory by clicking on its name to see whether the directory contains
any files that can be unerased. Unerasing the subdirectory does not
automatically unerase files that were in that directory. You must

specifically unerase files in the directory after you have unerased the directory itself.

If a file or directory cannot be unerased or is unerased only partially, you still may be able to recover portions of the file or directory by using the Norton Disk Editor (see "Using the Norton Disk Editor," later in this chapter). Always try to use UnErase to erase files and directories before resorting to the more complicated Disk Edit command. Your chance of successfully unerasing a directory or file depends mostly on whether you have created files that have overwritten the disk space used by the directory or file.

Notice the menu bar at the top of the UnErase screen. The menu items File, Search, and Options provide other choices for unerasing files. The Quit! selection ends the UnErase program.

Using the UnErase File Menu

The File menu at the top of the UnErase screen enables you to specify selections for listing, selecting, and naming files (see fig. 4.6). Notice the Alt commands beside some of the options. You can choose the corresponding option from the UnErase screen without opening the File menu. To choose the View Current Directory option, for example, press Alt-C.

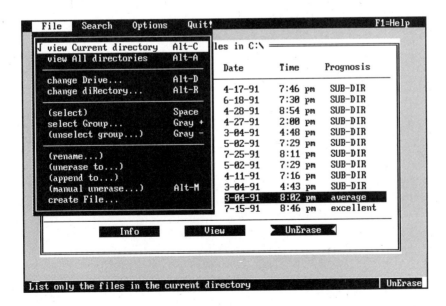

FIG. 4.6.

The File menu.

You cannot choose options when they appear in parentheses. In figure 4.6, for example, the option Rename appears in parentheses. This is because no file has yet been chosen to be unerased. If you highlight a file name for an unerased file, the option Rename becomes available and appears on the list without parentheses.

The File menu options follow:

- *View Current Directory:* Displays a list of all erased files in the current directory. This list includes the file name (with a question mark as the first character), date, time, and prognosis for recovery. Use this option when you want to find a file in the directory to unerase.

- *View All Directories:* Displays a list of all erased files in all directories on the current disk. Erased files are listed by directory in the UnErase box. You can highlight and unerase files in this list. Use this option if you want to unerase files in a number of directories, or when you are not sure which directory contains the files you want to unerase.

- *Change Drive:* Displays a list of erased files on another drive. Also displays a list of available drives, from which you can choose the drive to view.

- *Change Directory:* Displays erased files on another directory. Displays a list of directories, from which you can choose the directory you want to view.

- *Select:* Selects an individual file. Highlight that file name and choose the Select option from the File menu. You can choose the Select option only if a file name is highlighted in the UnErase list. The file name otherwise appears in parentheses, which means that you cannot choose the file then. Another way to select an individual file is to highlight the file name and press the space bar. After you select a file, arrowheads appear on both sides of the file name in the UnErase list of files.

- *Select Group:* Selects a group of files. You are prompted to enter a file specification for the files to select. If you type *.g*, for example, you select all files with extensions beginning with the letter g. Arrowheads appear on each side of each selected file name. You also may press the gray + (plus) key (on your number keypad) to invoke the Select Group option. After you select the files to unerase, choose the UnErase option. You then are prompted to enter the first character of each file name in your selection list.

- *Unselect Group:* Unselects the list of files to unerase. To unselect a group, choose Unselect Group from the File menu or press the gray - (minus) key. You then are prompted to enter a file specification. If you type *.gbk, for example, all files now selected with the extension GBK are unselected, and the arrows at the sides of those names disappear.

■ *Rename:* Renames files. If a file in the UnErase list is recovered, you can rename that file by highlighting its file name and choosing the Rename option. You are prompted to enter a new name for the file.

■ *UnErase To:* Unerases and saves files to another disk drive. After you choose UnErase, you are prompted to choose the drive name where you want the file to be copied as the file is unerased. To activate the UnErase To option, you must highlight a file name that can be unerased.

■ *Append To:* Appends the contents of the highlighted file to another file. You are prompted to enter the name of the file to which you want to append the highlighted file.

■ *Manual UnErase:* Unerases a file that you cannot unerase with the UnErase program. Usually, files with a poor prognosis cannot be recovered automatically. (See "Using Manual UnErase," later in this chapter.)

■ *Create File:* Creates a file by searching for erased clusters and building a file from unerased material on disk. This process is similar to a manual unerase. (See "Using Manual UnErase," later in this chapter.)

Using the UnErase Search Menu

With the UnErase Search menu, you can search for erased files, using certain criteria (see fig. 4.7). You can search for the kind of file (Text, dBASE, 1-2-3, Symphony, and so on), for files containing a text string, or for file names that may not appear on the UnErase list (files in erased subdirectories). You also may specify searches within a range of clusters on the disk.

The UnErase Search menu options follow:

■ *For Data Types:* Searches the disk for normal ASCII text files, dBASE-type files, Lotus 1-2-3-type files, or Symphony-type files. After you choose the Data Type option, you can select which file types to search for. After you finish the search, the files listed in the UnErase file list are those types you selected.

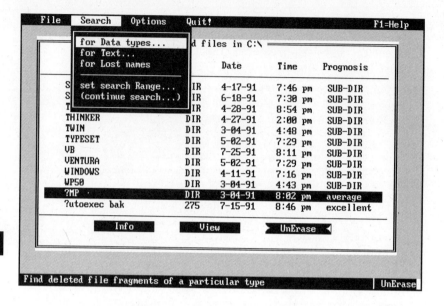

| File | Search | Options | Quit! | | | | F1=Help |

```
┌─────────────────────┐ d files in C:\
│ for Data types...   │
│ for Text...         │              Date      Time      Prognosis
│ for Lost names      │
│                     │  IR    4-17-91    7:46 pm    SUB-DIR
│ set search Range... │  IR    6-18-91    7:30 pm    SUB-DIR
│ (continue search...)│  IR    4-28-91    8:54 pm    SUB-DIR
└─────────────────────┘ DIR    4-27-91    2:00 pm    SUB-DIR
       TWIN             DIR    3-04-91    4:48 pm    SUB-DIR
       TYPESET          DIR    5-02-91    7:29 pm    SUB-DIR
       VB               DIR    7-25-91    8:11 pm    SUB-DIR
       VENTURA          DIR    5-02-91    7:29 pm    SUB-DIR
       WINDOWS          DIR    4-11-91    7:16 pm    SUB-DIR
       WP50             DIR    3-04-91    4:43 pm    SUB-DIR
       ?MP              DIR    3-04-91    8:02 pm    average
       ?utoexec bak     275    7-15-91    8:46 pm    excellent

         Info            View          ► UnErase ◄
```

Find deleted file fragments of a particular type   UnErase

FIG. 4.7.

The Search
menu.

- *For Text:* Searches for erased files that contain a certain string of text. If you choose this option, you are prompted to enter the text for which you want to search. If you are looking for files that contain information about the 1991 budget, for example, you may specify the text *1991 Budget* as your text string and press Enter. After the program finishes the search, the files listed in the UnErase file list are those that contain the text you specified.

- *For Lost Names:* Searches for file names that usually don't appear in the UnErase file list, such as erased files that have been part of an erased directory. If these lost file names are listed in the UnErase file list, you can unerase them like you can any other files.

- *Set Search Range:* Tells UnErase which clusters to search by specifying the Set Search Range criteria. You are asked to enter the beginning and ending cluster number. This procedure may save time if you have a large disk.

- *Continue Search:* Continues a search that was interrupted when you pressed Esc. If you want to continue the search from the point where the search stopped, choose this option.

Using the UnErase Options Menu

The Options menu enables you to choose a sort order to be used when listing file names in the UnErase file list. You also may choose to include nonerased (all) files in the list. Figure 4.8 shows the Options menu.

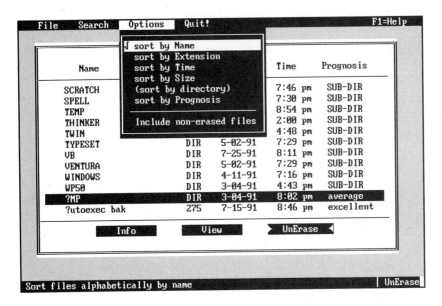

FIG. 4.8.

The Options menu.

From the list of options, you may choose to list files in sorted order: by file name (default), extension, time, size, or prognosis. You can use the Sort by Directory option if you earlier chose the View All Directories option from the File menu. You also may choose to include nonerased files in the list box. You may want to have these files listed to use the Rename or Append options from the File menu.

Using the Manual UnErase and Create File Options

Earlier, this chapter skipped descriptions of the Manual UnErase and Create File options in the UnErase File menu because these options require more knowledge about the way files are stored on disk. The descriptions here assume that you know how clusters are used to store files on disk. For more information on clusters, see "Understanding How Disks Work," earlier in this chapter, or refer to *Que's Guide to Data Recovery*, by Scott Mueller.

When you cannot unerase a file automatically with UnErase, you can try to assemble the file manually with the Manual UnErase procedure. The Create File procedure is the same as the Manual UnErase procedure, except that you start with a new file name instead of resurrecting an erased file name. If you start with an erased file name, the initial Manual UnErase screen contains information about the file's attributes, the first cluster in the file, the file size, and other information (see fig. 4.9). If you begin with a new file name, the screen is similar, but no attributes, no first cluster, and no known size for the file appear.

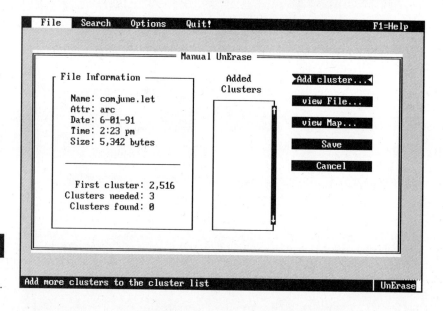

Use the options on the right side of the Manual UnErase screen to help you piece together the file to unerase. The Added Clusters box shows you which clusters to use to make up the file. If you know how many clusters are needed to make up the file, you know when you have completed the task of finding all of a file's clusters. Then you can save the file using the Save option and end the Manual UnErase procedure. Use the View File option to see the contents of the clusters that have been added to the list. The View Map option enables you to see a map of your hard disk and to see where the found clusters are located relative to one another. To cancel this procedure without saving, choose the Cancel option or press Esc.

Using Manual UnErase

To manually unerase a file, follow these steps:

1. Choose the name of the file you want to unerase from the UnErase screen. If UnErase cannot retrieve this file automatically, choose the Manual UnErase option from the File menu.

2. Select Manual Unerase from the File pull-down menu or press Alt-M. You will be prompted to enter the first letter of the file name.

3. Choose the Add Cluster option from the Manual UnErase screen. A menu appears with these options: All Clusters, Next Probable, Data Search, and Cluster Number options. Usually, you will first choose the All Clusters option. This adds all the file information. If all clusters are added, go to step 5. If all the clusters have not been found, use the Next Probable, Data Search, or Cluster Number option to locate the next cluster in the file (these options are explained in the next section).

4. Check that the clusters you have added belong to the file by choosing View File from the Manual UnErase screen. Move clusters, if necessary, so that the clusters are in the right order. (Moving clusters is covered in the next section.)

5. If all clusters have been found, stop and save the file to disk. If all clusters have not been found, return to step 2 and continue.

If you cannot recover the file by using Manual UnErase, you still may be able to recover all or parts of the file by using the Norton Disk Editor. See "Using the Norton Disk Editor," later in this chapter, for more information.

Adding Clusters to the File

If you choose the Add Cluster option from the Manual UnErase screen, the screen in figure 4.10 appears.

This screen lists four options that help you locate clusters for the file you are trying to unerase:

- *All Clusters:* Pieces together all of the most likely clusters that make up the erased file. When All Clusters cannot determine the next cluster, the option stops. The found clusters are listed in the Added Clusters box on the Manual UnErase main screen. If you locate all the clusters required to put together the erased file, you can choose the Save option to save the unerased file to disk as an unerased file. If all of the clusters have not been found, you must try one of the other three options.

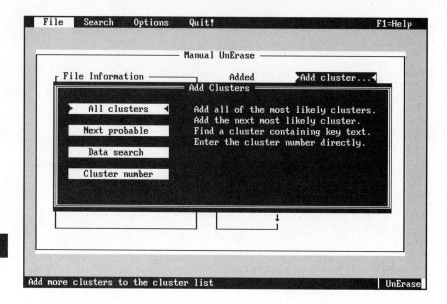

File   Search   Options   Quit!   F1=Help

─── Manual UnErase ───

┌ File Information ──────┐   Added   ►Add cluster...◄
                                ═ Add Clusters ═

►   All clusters   ◄   Add all of the most likely clusters.
                          Add the next most likely cluster.
    Next probable   Find a cluster containing key text.
                          Enter the cluster number directly.
    Data search

    Cluster number

Add more clusters to the cluster list   │ UnErase

FIG. 4.10.

The Add
Clusters menu.

■ *Next Probable:* Adds the cluster to the file that the program determines is the next probable cluster to the file. After you add such a
cluster, you then should choose the View File option to look at the
file's contents. If the file is a text file, you should be able to determine whether the pieces of the file are fitting together. If the cluster you added belongs to the file but is in the wrong order, you
can change the order of the clusters.

To move a cluster to another location in the cluster list, use the
cursor-movement keys or your mouse to highlight the cluster you
want to move. Press the space bar to pick up that cluster, and
then use the up and down cursor-movement keys to move that
cluster to a new location in the list. Press the space bar again to
anchor the cluster to the list.

If you add a cluster but then determine that the cluster does not
belong to the file you are trying to unerase, you can use the
cursor-movement keys (or mouse) and the space bar to select
that cluster. Then press the Del key to delete that cluster from the
Added Clusters list.

■ *Data Search:* Helps you find the next cluster in your file. Use this
option if Next Probable cannot locate the next cluster.

First, view the file and determine what is next in the file. Suppose
that you are unerasing a report. You find sections in the report
labeled I through VI. You therefore may want to search for the

text *VII* to find the next cluster. In other words, you must know enough about the contents of the file you are unerasing so that you know what text may be in the file. If you choose to search for text, you see a screen like the one in figure 4.11. You can enter the text in ASCII or hexadecimal code (Hex), but usually, you enter ASCII. If you enter search text in ASCII, the text also appears in Hex. If you want the search to be case-sensitive, unselect the Ignore Case option.

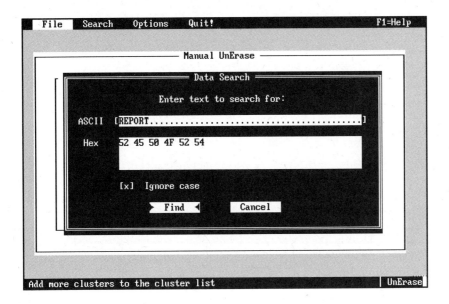

FIG. 4.11.

Specifying a search text string.

After you enter your search text and select Find, a search for the text begins. If the search text is found, a few lines of the cluster found appear on-screen. You can choose to do the following:

Option	Effect
Add Cluster	Adds this cluster to the list
Find Next	Continues search for next matching text
Hex	Displays the find in hexadecimal format (if text mode)
Text	Displays the find in text mode (if hexadecimal mode)
Done	Stops the search

The hexadecimal and text mode alternate. If the find is displayed in text mode, you optionally can choose hexadecimal mode. If the find is displayed in hexadecimal mode, you can change to text mode. Continue the search until you find the right cluster to add.

■ *Cluster Number:* Adds one or more clusters to the list. In some instances, you may know the cluster number of the cluster you want to add to your file. You intentionally may have placed clusters on the disk in particular locations, for example, to hide them for a special reason. Or, you may have located a cluster using a technique other than UnErase.

Doctoring Your Hard Disk

Besides losing information by erasing files and removing directories, you may lose information from flaws on the disk. Norton also provides a way to address this problem.

One of the most powerful programs in the Norton Utilities arsenal is the Norton Disk Doctor. Using detailed knowledge about the boot record, the file allocation table (FAT), and the system area, the Norton Disk Doctor often can figure out where problems exist on a disk and what can be done to eliminate the problems. Not all problems can be solved, but the Disk Doctor tries. You can begin NDD from the main Norton menu, or by entering the NDD command at the DOS prompt. To begin from the menu, use the up- and down-arrow keys to highlight Disk Doctor and press Enter, or point to Disk Doctor on the menu and click twice.

The syntax of the Norton Disk Doctor (NDD) command is

NDD [*d:*][*d:*][*switches*]

The *d:* designations are disk drive names; you can specify more than one drive. (Norton does not mention any limit.)

The available *switches* for the NDD command follow:

Switch	Description
/C	Complete test—tests for bad cylinders on the disk and the partition table, boot record, root directory, and lost clusters.

Switch	Description
/Q	Quick test—omits the test for bad cylinders but tests the partition table, boot record, root directory, and lost clusters.
/R:*file*	Instructs NDD to write a report about the results of its testing to the file named. Use with /QUICK or /COMPLETE.
/RA:*file*	Same as /R, but appends the report to the file instead of making a new file. Use with /QUICK or /COMPLETE.
/REBUILD	Tells NDD to try to rebuild the entire disk.
/X:*d*	Excludes drive *d* from examination.
/UNDELETE	Tells NDD to undelete a DOS partition detected by NDD in an earlier run but not undeleted. When you run NDD and find an old DOS partition, for example, NDD asks whether you want to undelete the partition. If you answer no, then the /UNDELETE switch enables you to try to undelete the partition later.

If you enter the NDD command with no switches, the command operates in interactive mode; you choose the options you want from a menu.

The Norton Disk Doctor main menu, shown in figure 4.12, contains four choices:

Option	Effect
Diagnose Disk	Examines your disk to check the integrity of the information stored on the disk.
Undo Changes	Undoes any changes made by NDD and returns your disk to its original state.
Options	Sets certain options for the program.
Quit	Ends the NDD program.

Details about the first three NDD options in this list are covered in the next few sections.

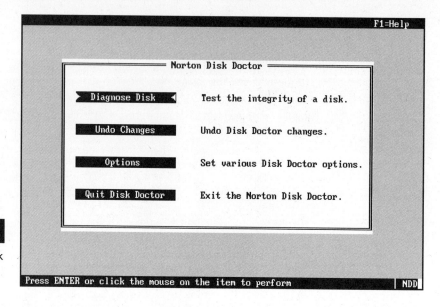

FIG. 4.12.

The Norton Disk Doctor main menu.

Diagnosing a Disk

The Norton Disk Doctor Diagnose Disk option performs various tests on your disk to check whether the stored information can be accessed properly. Use the Diagnose Disk option occasionally as preventive maintenance on your hard disk. Also, if your disk access becomes erratic—for example, you experience trouble trying to read a file or your computer no longer boots properly—use NDD to diagnose the problem.

If you have never used NDD on your hard disk, you may want to perform a full test so that you can find and resolve any problems or potential problems. Afterward, using the quick test (/Q) may be enough to find most file problems. NDD Diagnose Disk performs more than 100 tests to analyze your disk. Under normal disk operation, you probably should use the NDD diagnosis about once a month.

Problems on a disk usually result from corrupted information being placed on disk or bad spots on the disk that cause information to be unreadable. A bad spot, for example, can be caused by loss of the magnetic signal (image). NDD tries to read information from all parts of the disk. If part of the disk cannot be read and no file is using the bad part, the problem is simple to fix. NDD marks that area as bad, and from now on DOS knows not to use the area.

If the bad spot is located where a file is stored, however, NDD must try to read as much of the file as possible and move the file to a safe location on disk. Then the command marks the bad area so that the area never is used again.

NOTE Often, when NDD finds a problem on disk, a prompt asks whether you want the problem to be fixed or ignored. Unless you have a specific reason not to fix a problem, let NDD try to correct the problem on disk.

After you choose the Diagnose Disk option from the NDD menu, you see a list of possible disks to test (see fig. 4.13). Specify the disk or disks to test by using the cursor-movement keys to highlight the first disk of your choice and pressing the space bar. A check mark appears next to your choice. You then can choose any other disk to test. After you make your selections, press Enter to begin the test procedures.

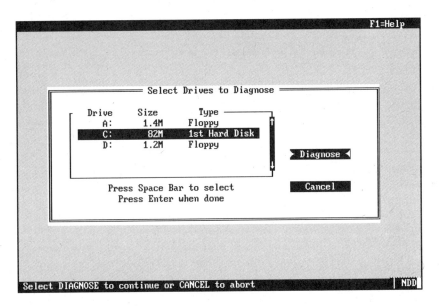

FIG. 4.13.

The Norton Disk Doctor's list of drives to diagnose.

Figure 4.14 shows the first test screen during a test of the hard disk. Notice the six-part test list at the top of the screen, titled Diagnosing Drive C:. As each part of the test progresses, the corresponding description for that test area is highlighted on-screen and a blinking dot appears before the description name. When a test for an area is complete, a check mark appears next to the test description.

Information about the progress of the current test being performed appears at the bottom of the screen. In figure 4.14, a test of the file allocation tables is in progress. You can stop the test at any time by pressing Esc.

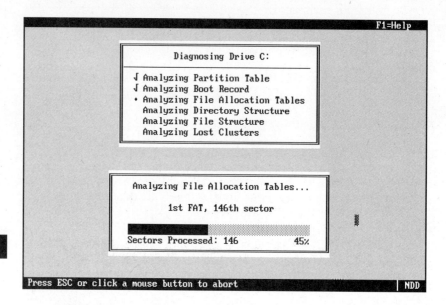

FIG. 4.14.

NDD lists tests
in progress.

The Norton Disk Doctor tests to see whether bad information is located
in the system areas or data areas of the disk. If your hard disk is partitioned into several disks (C and D, for example), the NDD partition
table checks to see whether the allocation of space is properly
accounted for.

The tests of the boot record, file allocation tables, and directory structure examine the integrity of the system information on disk. NDD determines whether the system information can be read from disk and
whether the system information makes sense. In the system area of the
disk, NDD reads the information and compares what has been read
from disk to what should be on the disk, just like you look at a manuscript to see whether all the parts—the title, the contents, the body,
and the index—are there. If NDD finds that something is missing,
wrong, or out of place, the program usually knows how to fix the
problem.

While NDD is going through the list of diagnostic tests, it may detect a
problem on the disk. Figure 4.15, for example, shows an example of the
kind of dialog box that appears if an error is found on the disk. In this
case, the error found is

        Boot Record Program is Invalid

A description is given of this error—

> A Bootable Disk contains a small program that loads the
> operating system.

and a recommendation is given,

> If you are unable to boot from this disk, but wish to
> do so, correct the situation.

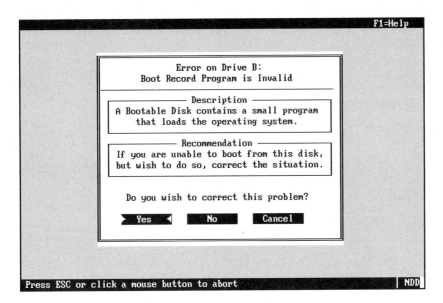

You have three choices to the prompt

> Do you wish to correct this problem?

Usually, if you are not sure what to do, it is best to take the recom-
mended course of action. In this case, it would be to have NDD fix the
problem. If you choose Yes, NDD fixes the problem. If you choose No,
NDD does not fix the problem, but continues with the diagnostic tests.
If you choose Cancel, the tests stop, and you are returned to the main
NDD menu.

When testing the file allocation table, NDD analyzes the FAT to see if
available space on disk is accounted for as space being used by a file,
sectors marked as bad spots on the disk, or free space. Space on a disk
may be unaccounted for when a file is not properly saved to disk. This

unaccounted space appears in the FAT as a lost cluster, a place on disk reserved for use by a file but never used. Lost clusters can occur when you turn off the computer, reboot the computer, or when the power fails while a file is open. A series of lost clusters related to one file is called a *chain*.

The file structure test examines how your files are stored on disk to make sure that the file allocation is okay. The lost clusters test looks for information about files not stored properly—a problem sometimes caused by programs that are abruptly stopped, as in a power outage. The surface test checks for physical defects on your disk.

When the list of diagnostic tests is completed, the Surface Test screen automatically appears, as shown in figure 4.16. From the Surface Test screen, you can choose several options about how to perform the test. Use the arrow keys or Tab to point to the options you want to set, and then press the space bar to lock in your selection. Or, point to an option with the mouse and click once. Press Enter to begin the test or click on the Begin Test option.

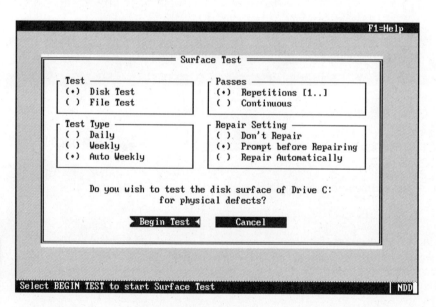

FIG. 4.16.

The Surface Test screen.

The Surface Test screen contains four boxes:

- *Test:* Tells the test to look at the surface of the entire disk (Disk Test) or to test only the portions of the disk occupied by files (File Test). File Test is faster, but Disk Test is more thorough.

■ *Test Type:* Enables you to select from three tests:

Daily	Performs a quick scan of the disk.
Weekly	Tests the disk more thoroughly than the daily test, but takes twice the time.
Auto Weekly	Combines elements of the two other tests and takes a little longer than the Daily test. This is the default test.

These option names may be confusing. You do not have to perform the Daily test daily or the Weekly test weekly. The names are meant only as a guide. The default test is the Auto Weekly test, which Norton recommends that you do every Friday.

■ *Passes:* Enables you to specify how often to repeat the test or to perform the test until you press Esc. Usually, one repetition (the default) is sufficient. If intermittent problems exist, however, you may want to run the test for a number of repetitions—up to 999 times—or continuously (continues testing indefinitely until you press Esc) to try to locate the problem.

■ *Repair Setting:* Tells NDD what to do if a problem is found during the Surface test. You can select from three options:

Don't Repair	Tells NDD not to try to repair the disk if a problem is located. Use if you want a report about your disk's problems but do not want to repair the disk.
Prompt Before Repairing	Tells NDD to ask whether you want a problem solved before trying to fix a disk problem. (This is the default setting.) Usually, you want NDD to tell whether a problem has been found so that you can decide whether you want to fix the problem.
Repair Automatically	Tells NDD to try to repair the problems as they are found, without prompting.

If the same fixes occur repeatedly, you may want to perform a low-level format of the disk (see Chapter 5).

Figure 4.17 shows a dialog box that can appear during a surface test. In this case, cluster 80 is found to contain a bad sector. You can choose to move the data in this cluster to a safe location, in which case the cluster no longer can be used, but the data in the file is now located in a good cluster. Notice the message that says

```
This cluster is in use by filename
```

If this cluster does not contain data used in a file, NDD marks rather than moves the cluster. Moving the data in the cluster places the file information in a new cluster that is good, which enables you to try to save the file information. Marking the cluster as bad prevents new information from being written to that cluster. If you choose the Skip option, the cluster is not affected. If you choose Auto, this and all subsequent bad sectors are marked or moved. Choose Cancel to end the test.

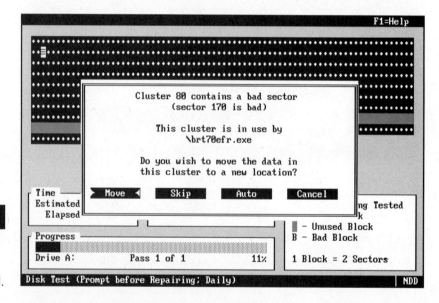

FIG. 4.17.

A message telling you that a bad sector has been found.

Creating a Report

When the disk analysis is complete, a brief summary appears on-screen (see fig. 4.18). You may want to produce a report about the disk test, particularly if disk problems are found. To produce a report, press Enter or click on the Report button. To end without producing a report, press Tab to move the cursor to the Done option and press Enter. Or, click on Done with the mouse. Figure 4.19 is a sample report. Keep these reports as a record of your disk problems.

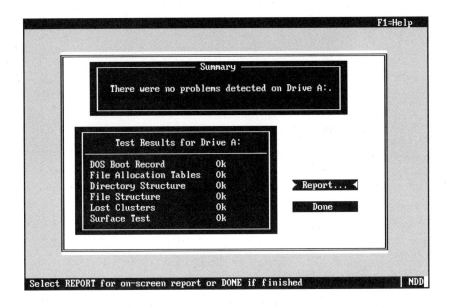

```
┌─────────────────── Summary ───────────────────┐
│                                                │
│  There were no problems detected on Drive A:.  │
│                                                │
└────────────────────────────────────────────────┘


┌──────── Test Results for Drive A: ────────┐
│                                           │
│  DOS Boot Record          Ok              │
│  File Allocation Tables   Ok       ┌──────────────┐
│  Directory Structure      Ok       │▶ Report... ◀ │
│  File Structure           Ok       └──────────────┘
│  Lost Clusters            Ok       ┌──────────────┐
│  Surface Test             Ok       │    Done      │
│                                    └──────────────┘
└───────────────────────────────────────────┘

Select REPORT for on-screen report or DONE if finished        NDD
```

FIG. 4.18.

The NDD summary screen after tests are complete.

The report's header provides the date and time of the analysis. The Disk Totals section tells about the disk's storage capacity. The *total disk space* is the number of bytes of information that the disk can hold. *Bad sectors* are places on disk that have been found (usually by the format procedure) to be unsuitable for storing information. If you subtract the number of bytes taken up by the user files and bad sectors from the total, you get the number of *bytes available on the disk*.

The Logical Disk Information section of the report describes the logical parameters used to store information on the disk. The media descriptor gives a code for what kind of disk is used. These codes are listed in table 4.2. In figure 4.19, the analyzed disk is a 160K, 5 1/4-inch diskette. The media descriptor of FE is a hexadecimal number code.

Table 4.2 System ID Codes Reported

Code	Designates
F0	1.4M, 3 1/2-inch disk
F8	Hard disk
F9	1.2M, 5 1/4-inch disk or 720K, 3 1/2-inch disk
FD	360K, 5 1/4-inch disk
FE	160K, 5 1/4-inch disk
FF	320K, 5 1/4-inch disk

```
                           NDD
                   Norton Utilities, 6.0
             Monday, September 30, 1991 4:09 pm

                 ***************************
                 *   Report for Drive B:   *
                 ***************************

                        DISK TOTALS
         _ _ _ _ _ _ _ _ _ _ _ _ _ _ _ _ _ _ _ _ _ _

           160,256 bytes Total Disk Space
           143,872 bytes in 42 User Files
            16,384 bytes Available on the Disk


                 LOGICAL DISK INFORMATION
         _ _ _ _ _ _ _ _ _ _ _ _ _ _ _ _ _ _ _ _ _ _
              Media Descriptor:  FE
               Large Partition:  No
                      FAT Type:  12-bit
                 Total Sectors:  320
                Total Clusters:  313
              Bytes Per Sector:  512
            Sectors Per Cluster:  1
             Bytes Per Cluster:  512
                Number of FATs:  2
             First Sector of FAT:  1
        Number of Sectors Per FAT:  1
         First Sector of Root Dir:  3
      Number of Sectors in Root Dir:  4
      Maximum Root Dir File Entries:  64
           First Sector of Data Area:  7


                PHYSICAL DISK INFORMATION
         _ _ _ _ _ _ _ _ _ _ _ _ _ _ _ _ _ _ _ _ _ _
                  Drive Number:  1
                         Heads:  1
                     Cylinders:  40
              Sectors Per Track:  8
                 Starting Head:  0
              Starting Cylinder:  0
               Starting Sector:  1
                   Ending Head:  0
               Ending Cylinder:  39
                 Ending Sector:  8


                  SYSTEM AREA STATUS
         _ _ _ _ _ _ _ _ _ _ _ _ _ _ _ _ _ _ _ _ _ _

            Boot Record Program is Invalid
                 Status: Corrected


                 FILE STRUCTURE STATUS
         _ _ _ _ _ _ _ _ _ _ _ _ _ _ _ _ _ _ _ _ _ _
           No Errors in the File Structure


                 SURFACE TEST STATUS
         _ _ _ _ _ _ _ _ _ _ _ _ _ _ _ _ _ _ _ _ _ _
                    Test Settings
                 _ _ _ _ _ _ _ _ _ _
                      Test:  Disk Test
                 Test Type:  Weekly
            Repair Setting:  Prompt before Repairing
          Passes Requested:  1
          Passes Completed:  1
              Elapsed Time:  21 seconds

            No Errors encountered in Surface Test
```

FIG. 4.19.

A summary report of NDD's tests.

The Physical Disk Information section includes information about how the data is physically on disk. The drive number tells you which drive the disk is in when analyzed. Drive numbers 0, 1, 2, and so on refer to drives A, B, C, and so on. In figure 4.19, therefore, the disk is analyzed in drive B (drive number 1).

The Norton Disk Doctor reports any problems found in the system area or the file structure, giving information about what problems exist and how (and whether) they are fixed. In the System Area Status section of the report, figure 4.19 shows that the boot record was invalid, but was corrected.

Problems that may be reported in the file structure area are fixes related to cleaning up files that are cross-linked or that contain lost chains. Both conditions refer to a misallocation of clusters to a file.

The material provided under the Surface Test Status section at the bottom of the report shows any problems found on the disk during the scan. Although the example in fig. 4.19 shows that no errors have been found, the section may include a message such as

```
Error reading Sector 15 in Cluster 3
Cluster 3 currently not in use
Status: Corrected; Marked as Unusable
```

In this case, a bad cluster is found, but no information exists in that area. The cluster, therefore, is marked as bad, and no file information is damaged. If the cluster contains information, NDD tries to move as much good information as possible to a good cluster and reports that the files are moved, but that they may not be fully recovered or usable.

If you discover by reading the report that NDD moved some of your files, you should examine those files to see whether they contain any damaged areas. You can examine word processing files in your word processor. If NDD moved program files (EXE or COM files, for example), you probably should recopy them from the original source to the disk to guarantee that the contents of the file are okay.

NDD will find problems with your disk relating to the reliability of the data stored on disk (tests for bad spots) and the correctness of the information in the boot record, the FAT, and the root directory. If problems are found in these areas, NDD will attempt to fix them.

Undoing Changes

You may want to reverse any changes made after running the NDD program on your disk. Perhaps a moved file no longer can be used, for example, and you want to try some other way, such as using the Norton Disk Editor, to recover the file. As NDD makes changes to your disk, the program stores the information about those changes to a file called NDDUNDO.DAT. If you choose the UnDo Changes option from the NDD menu, the disk is restored to its original condition.

Setting Options

If you choose the Options selection from the NDD menu, you see another menu that enables you to select settings for the surface test, a custom error message, and tests to skip (see fig. 4.20).

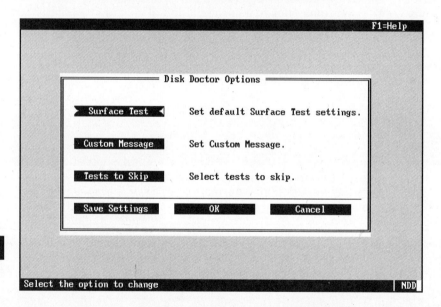

The NDD Options menu.

The options on the Disk Doctor Options screen follow:

- *Surface Test:* Displays a screen like the one in figure 4.16. You can choose options other than the normal defaults and save this information to disk. When NDD is used again interactively or as a command from the DOS prompt, your new defaults are used.

- *Custom Message:* Customizes the message that appears on-screen when NDD encounters an error in the system area test (see fig. 4.21). Suppose that you have placed the NDD command on several computers in your company but do not want inexperienced users to make corrections on their disks without the company computer-support team knowing about the problem. In this case, you can create a custom message like the one in figure 4.21:

Please Contact USER Support at ...

If NDD finds a system area problem, this message appears on-screen.

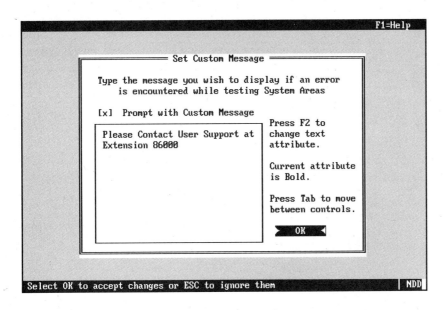

Set Custom Message

Type the message you wish to display if an error is encountered while testing System Areas

[x] Prompt with Custom Message

Please Contact User Support at Extension 86000

Press F2 to change text attribute.

Current attribute is Bold.

Press Tab to move between controls.

OK

Select OK to accept changes or ESC to ignore them | NDD

FIG. 4.21

The NDD Set Custom Message screen.

- *Tests to Skip:* Chooses tests for NDD to skip. You usually need this option if your computer is not 100-percent IBM PC-standard compatible. You may choose from four skip options, as shown in figure 4.22.

After you make selections in the Surface Test, Set Custom Message, and Tests to Skip screens, choose the Save Settings option from the Options menu to save this information to disk. Then, when the NDD program begins, these options take effect.

Using Disk Tools

Several options included in Norton Disk Doctor 4.5 are incorporated into Disk Tools for Versions 5.0 and 6, including the following:

Make a Disk Bootable
Recover from DOS's Recover
Revive a Defective Diskette

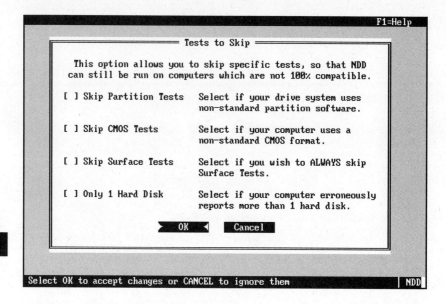

FIG. 4.22.

The NDD Tests
to Skip screen.

The Disk Tools command also contains the following options:

>   Mark a Cluster
>   Create Rescue Diskette
>   Restore Rescue Diskette

To begin Disk Tools, choose the Disk Tools option from the Norton
menu or enter the command

>   DISKTOOL

at the DOS prompt. A screen appears like the one in figure 4.23, which
contains the six menu options just mentioned. These options are
described in the following sections.

Making a Bootable Disk

Sometimes you may want to give an unbootable disk booting capabilities. This feature may be of particular importance for a hard disk. A
disk can lose its booting capability if the magnetic signal on the boot
record becomes weak or if the low-level format loses alignment with
the read/write head. Also, software programs accidentally may overwrite important system information required for booting. The NDD
command can place a fresh copy of the system information on the disk,
making the disk bootable again.

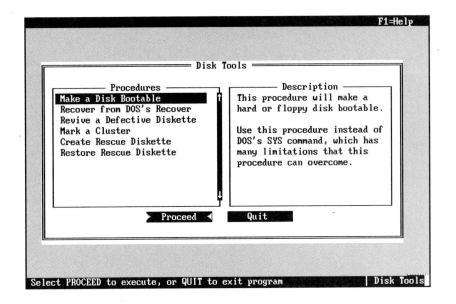

FIG. 4.23.

The Disk Tools
main menu.

Sometimes a disk may not have been set up properly as a bootable disk. If the disk is formatted originally as a nonbootable disk, DOS cannot make the disk bootable. Although DOS has a SYS command that should copy the system files to a nonbootable disk, the command works only if you told the format procedure to leave room on the disk to receive the system files. Otherwise, DOS writes data onto the area of the disk reserved for the system, so that the SYS command cannot work for that disk.

Disk Tools, however, can move files around, copy system information to the disk, and make the disk bootable. Using Disk Tools to make a disk bootable can save you a great deal of time. Without the Disk Tools command, you must copy all files off the disk, reformat the disk by using the /S switch, and copy files back to the disk. This process can take hours; the Disk Tools procedure takes only a few minutes.

If you choose the Make a Disk Bootable option from the Disk Tools menu, the program first prompts you to make sure that the correct disk is in the drive. Then the program moves any information in the system area to a free area and copies the appropriate system files and COMMAND.COM onto the disk.

In PC DOS, two system files that contain part of DOS are stored on the disk as hidden files and do not appear when you use the DIR command. If the disk does not have enough room to accept the system files, you see an error message. If you want to make this disk bootable, erase some non-DOS files and try the procedure again.

Recovering from DOS's RECOVER Command

Many people see the poorly named DOS RECOVER command and assume that the command can recover lost files or turn bad files into good files. You actually use the DOS RECOVER command to recover files with a defective sector. This DOS command is primitive, however, compared with what you can do in Norton Utilities.

The DOS manual states that the RECOVER command "recovers a disk with a bad sector." The recovery process used by DOS, however, eliminates all subdirectories on your disk and renames all your files to obscure names. Trying to find the contents of each file can take hours, and for some files the task may be nearly impossible. If you use Norton Utilities, you never should have a reason to use the DOS RECOVER command.

If you have used the RECOVER command accidentally or because you thought the command recovered damaged files, you can use the Norton Disk Doctor to place files back into their proper directories—as long as you have not written other files to the disk. You must rename files in the root directory and directories.

If you choose the Recover from DOS's Recover option from the Disk Tools menu, you are warned that you should use this procedure only if you have run the DOS RECOVER program or if the root directory on the disk has been destroyed. If you continue, you are prompted to choose the disk to recover. Select the drive name of the disk you want to recover.

If you choose to have the program proceed, a screen appears, showing you the progress of the recovery. You are told that Disk Tools has recovered the directories but names them DIR0000, DIR0001, and so on. All the files in the root directory are named FILE0000._DD, FILE0001._DD, and so on. Any files in directories other than the root directory are recovered with their full names intact.

Figure 4.24 summarizes what happens to a disk when you use Disk Tools to recover from the RECOVER command. The first part of the screen, listing (1), shows you the directory structure for a sample diskette. The root directory contains three directories and two files. Each directory (\WP, \123, and \DBF) contains two files. After the DOS RECOVER program runs, the result is listing (2). Now all directories are gone, and all files are in the root directory. All files have been renamed FILE0001.REC, FILE0002.REC, and so on. As noted in listing (3), the Recover from the RECOVER option recovers the directories (but not their names) and the files in the directories.

```
------------------------------------------------------------
RECOVERING FROM THE DOS RECOVER COMMAND
------------------------------------------------------------
(1) THE ORIGINAL DISK - Three directories each containing 2 files

COMMAND  COM     37637 06-17-88  12:00p
AUTOEXEC BAT       294 10-23-89  10:43a
WP          <DIR>        01-02-90  12:10p
___  LETTER  WP         294 10-23-89  10:43a
___  REPORT  WP         158 09-18-89  12:50p

123         <DIR>        01-02-90  12:10p
___  SALES   WK1        294 11-23-89  10:41a
___  BUDGET  WK2        158 05-16-89  12:20p

DB3         <DIR>        01-02-90  12:10p
___  SALES   DBF        298 11-23-89  10:47a
___  CUSTOM  DBF        158 11-18-89  12:33p

(2) After the DOS RECOVER program has been run - all files in root directory

FILE0001 REC      1024 01-01-80   4:17a
FILE0002 REC      1024 01-01-80   4:17a
FILE0003 REC      1024 01-01-80   4:17a
FILE0004 REC      1024 01-01-80   4:17a
FILE0005 REC      1024 01-01-80   4:17a
FILE0006 REC      1024 01-01-80   4:17a
FILE0007 REC      1024 01-01-80   4:17a
FILE0008 REC      1024 01-01-80   4:17a
FILE0009 REC      1024 01-01-80   4:17a
FILE0010 REC      1024 01-01-80   4:17a
FILE0011 REC     37888 01-01-80   4:17a

(3) After NDD has been run, 3 directories, two files each

DIR0000     <DIR>        01-02-90  12:10p
___  LETTER  WP         294 10-23-89  10:43a
___  REPORT  WP         158 09-18-89  12:50p
DIR0001     <DIR>        01-02-90  12:10p
___  SALES   WK1        294 11-23-89  10:41a
___  BUDGET  WK2        158 05-16-89  12:20p
DIR0002     <DIR>        01-02-90  12:10p
___  SALES   DBF        298 11-23-89  10:47a
___  CUSTOM  DBF        158 11-18-89  12:33p
FILE0003 _DD      1024 01-02-90  12:15p
FILE0004 COM     37888 01-02-90  12:15p
------------------------------------------------------------
```

FIG. 4.24.

Using Disk Tools to recover from DOS's RECOVER command.

To make all directory and file names what they were before using RECOVER, you must rename the files FILE0003._DD and FILE0004.COM, using the DOS RENAME command. You also must rename the directories by using the Norton Change Directory (NCD) command (see Chapter 6).

Reviving a Defective Disk

The next selection on the Disk Tools menu is the Revive a Defective Diskette option. This option mainly puts fresh format information on the disk. This procedure can be helpful if a diskette has become difficult or impossible to read, which may happen if you use a floppy diskette often. Sometimes the diskette begins to wear out, the software program overwrites the system area, the disk becomes scratched, or other problems cause the diskette to lose some information. If you have accessed the FAT so often that its information has begun to wear thin, the Revive a Defective Diskette process can place a new copy on disk.

During a normal format procedure, a disk is checked for bad spots. If found, these spots are marked and are not used to store information. A disk, however, can develop bad places after the original format has taken place. At times, the magnetic signal that stores information on disk may become weak and unreadable.

Also, on some parts of a hard disk, the magnetic coating may be thin in spots and may wear out over an extended period of use. If this problem occurs, you can use NDD to mark bad spots and move data to safe areas of the disk.

These bad areas in the magnetic media can limit access to data in a particular file or can sometimes make a disk completely unreadable. These problems often show up as read errors when you try to access information on a disk. You may get the message

```
Abort, Retry, Ignore, Fail?
```

when trying to read a disk that you know was readable earlier.

The Disk Tools program can try to recover information from this kind of disk. Disk Tools may perform a type of reformatting of certain areas of the disk. This formatting does not destroy information like normal formatting does, but instead re-creates certain vital parts of the disk to make the disk readable again. Disk Tools performs various tests on the disk to see whether the program can recover questionable information and rework defective areas to make the disk usable again.

After you choose the Revive a Defective Diskette option, the program first asks you to choose which floppy diskette to analyze. A screen reports the progress of the procedure. When the process is finished, you see a message that the diskette has been revived. You should diagnose the disk to check that the system information is not lost.

If you have problems with a diskette and have revived or recovered the disk by using Disk Tools, copy information from the original diskette to another diskette. If the first diskette is one that you use frequently and may be wearing out, copy the information to a new diskette and use the new one.

If you cannot revive a disk using NDD, the prognosis of recovery is bad. Your last possible choice is to use the Disk Editor to attempt to recover portions of the disk (see "Using the Norton Disk Editor," later in this chapter).

If you have problems with a hard disk, make sure that you keep backups. In fact, always keep backup copies of all important files even before you have problems with a hard disk.

Marking a Cluster

The Mark a Cluster option on the Disk Tools screen enables you to mark any cluster on a disk as bad or good. You may want to mark a cluster as bad, meaning that the cluster no longer can be used to store file information, if you discover that cluster has intermittent problems. By running NDD or other programs, you may find specific clusters that are bad—the cluster number is reported to you on-screen or in a report. You may run NDD, for example, to generate a list of bad clusters. Then, you can use Disk Tools to mark the clusters as bad. You also can mark a cluster as bad to hide and protect information; the information in that cluster is not overwritten as long as the cluster is marked as bad.

If you mark a cluster as bad that is being used by a file, the information in that cluster is copied to a safe location on disk so that the information in the file still is intact. Marking a cluster as good means that the cluster now is available for use to store file information. You also can use Mark a Cluster to bring back clusters that you have marked as bad. You mark a cluster as bad to protect new information from being written to that bad spot.

After you choose Mark a Cluster, you are prompted to tell which disk you plan to use (drive A, B, C, and so on). Then you are prompted to enter the number of the cluster to mark and whether you want to mark the cluster as bad or good.

Creating and Using a Rescue Disk

Options 5 and 6 on the Disk Tools menu are Create Rescue Diskette and Restore Rescue Diskette. After you choose Create Rescue Diskette, you see a screen like the one shown in figure 4.25. A rescue disk contains information about your disk, including information about your partition tables, your boot records, and your setup (CMOS) values. When you create a rescue disk, this information is written to a disk (usually a floppy disk) and stored in three files: PARTINFO.DAT, BOOTINFO.DAT, and CMOSINFO.DAT.

The partition information tells you how your hard disk was set up originally when you used the FDISK command to tell DOS how your disk was to be used (for example, one drive, two drives, the size of the drives, and so on). The boot information tells how your disk is formatted (under which version of DOS) and other system information.

The CMOS setup information stored in RAM is kept active by a battery. The PC-AT was the first computer to use this kind of setup. Many new computers no longer store information in CMOS. If you must run the setup program to configure your computer, then your computer has CMOS. If your battery dies, your computer loses its CMOS settings.

If your hard disk loses the partition, boot, or CMOS information, you can restore that data (except for date and time) to your disk by using the Restore Rescue Diskette option. After you choose this option, you can choose which of the three pieces of information to restore. You must have the floppy diskette containing the information to complete the restore successfully.

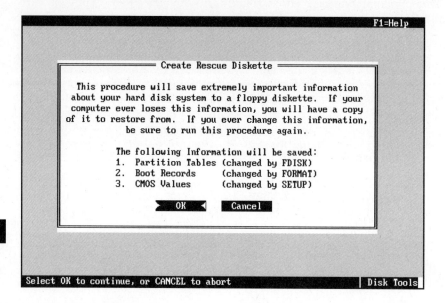

FIG. 4.25.

The Create Rescue Diskette screen.

Using File Fix

Use the File Fix command to recover corrupted dBASE, Lotus 1-2-3, or Symphony files. These files can become corrupted when the power is turned off abruptly, when a program accesses the file incorrectly, or when the information stored on disk is damaged because of a bad spot on the disk.

If you have erased all records in a dBASE database, the File Fix command often can recover those records. File Fix uses knowledge about how these files are created to try to recover the file information. Even if all information in the file cannot be recovered, File Fix may be capable of recovering some information.

Begin File Fix by choosing the File Fix option from the main Norton menu or entering the command

    FILEFIX

at the DOS prompt. Figure 4.26 shows the File Fix screen. From this menu, you can choose to fix Lotus 1-2-3, Symphony, or dBASE-type files. If you choose Quit from this menu, you return to the main Norton menu or to DOS, depending on where you originally began the program.

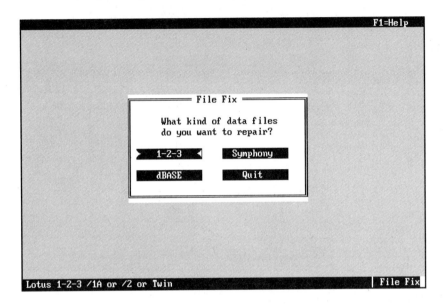

FIG. 4.26.

The File Fix screen.

Fixing dBASE Files

After you choose the dBASE option from the File Fix menu, you see the Choose File to Repair screen (see fig. 4.27). You can use the dBASE option to fix files created by programs that create and use dBASE-type files. These programs include dBASE II, III PLUS, and IV; FoxBASE; Clipper; Wampum; Kwikstat; and others.

From the Choose File to Repair menu, you can choose the file to fix. Use the cursor-movement keys to highlight the file to fix and press Enter. Or, highlight the file with a mouse and click. The Repair dBASE File screen appears.

The repair screen gives you several options for fixing the repair (see fig. 4.28). Before you choose a repair mode, notice the options at the bottom of the repair menu. To choose or unchoose an option (an x in the box means the option is chosen), use the Tab key or arrow keys to point to the option and then press the space bar to select or unselect the option. The first option, Use Clipper Field Limits, should be chosen if your DBF file was created by Clipper. The other two options, Fix Shifted Data Automatically and Strict Character Checking, are selected by default. If the repair is unable to work with these options selected, you may try the repair again with one or both options unselected.

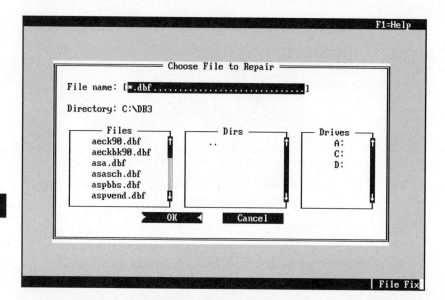

FIG. 4.27.

Using the Choose File to Repair Screen to select which file to fix.

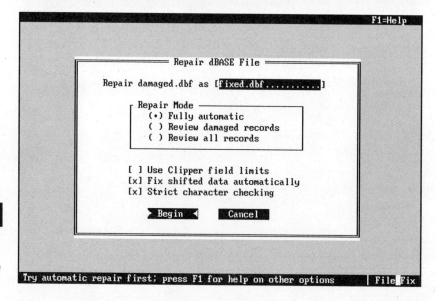

FIG. 4.28.

Selecting dBASE fix options from the File Fix menu.

Sometimes when dBASE files are damaged, the information in the database is shifted and is not aligned properly in the fields. In this case, choose Fix Shifted Data Automatically. If this option does not work, correct the shifting manually.

The Strict Character Checking option means that only characters that usually are allowed should be allowed in records. A few programs, such as the SBT Accounting series, enable special graphics characters in the record. If you use such a program, unselect the Strict Character Checking option.

After you set all the selections, choose Begin. To select a repair mode, use the Tab key or arrow key to point to the mode you prefer and then press the space bar to lock in your choice. Or, point to the mode with the mouse pointer and click once.

As your first pass at fixing the file, choose the Fully Automatic option. If this does not work, choose the Review Damaged Records option, which enables you to look at only those records that are corrupted. If the database is extremely corrupted, choose the Review All Records option.

If you choose the fully automatic mode, Norton proceeds with the repair without further prompts. If you choose to review the dBASE file (the Review Damaged Records or the Review All Records option), you see a screen like the one shown in figure 4.29. This screen lists the structure of the database as far as File Fix can determine. If this data has been corrupted, you can revise this information by choosing the Revise option. Otherwise, choose Accept.

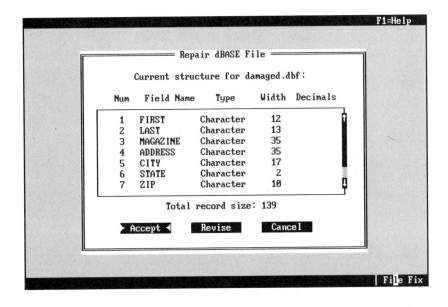

FIG. 4.29.

Using File Fix to display a dBASE database structure.

After accepting the database structure shown in figure 4.29, a second screen appears, as shown in figure 4.30. This screen displays the contents of a record. If the record looks okay, choose the Accept option, and the next record is displayed. If the data does not line up in the fields, you can shift the data by choosing the Shift option. If you want to reject a record, choose the Reject option. If you want to return to automatic mode for the rest of the records, choose the Mode option, and then Automatic. Select the Cancel option to cancel the fix.

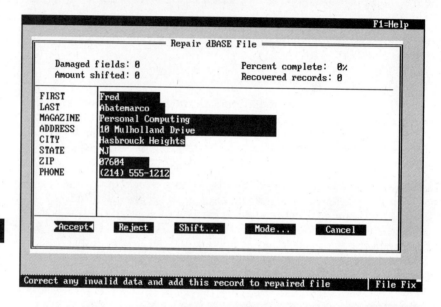

FIG. 4.30.

Viewing a
dBASE record
in File Fix.

After a file is fixed, a summary screen tells you how much of the file is accepted and how much is rejected. Always carefully examine the file in the program for which the file is intended before making a decision to recover the information fully.

Fixing 1-2-3 and Symphony Files

The 1-2-3 option on the File Fix screen enables you to fix spreadsheet files from the Lotus 1-2-3 program or similar programs, such as Twin. The Symphony option enables you to fix Symphony files.

The procedure for fixing 1-2-3 and Symphony files is similar. After you choose the 1-2-3 or Symphony option, you see a file list. Choose the file you want to fix.

The next screen that appears is similar to the one shown in figure 4.31. You may choose Attempt Recovery of All Data (including formulas, macros, and so on) or Recover Cell Data Only. Usually, you choose to recover all data. If this option does not work, choose to recover cell data only. After the recovery process is complete, File Fix gives you a summary screen listing how much of the file is recovered.

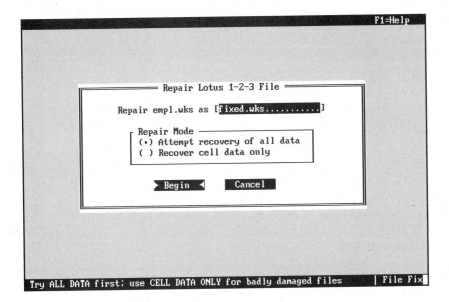

FIG. 4.31.

Selecting a 1-2-3 repair mode.

Using the Norton Disk Editor

UnErase and the Norton Disk Doctor are powerful programs, but sometimes even these programs cannot solve your problem. If you first tried UnErase and NDD to recover some information from a disk but still have important data to recover, your next step is the Norton Disk Editor option.

Disk Editor is a set of routines that enables you to explore the information on the disk down to the level of examining each individual byte. With Disk Editor, you can display and directly edit information on a disk, including system areas. You can search for lost data, try to fix problems in programs, and recover some or all portions of erased files.

Data recovery at this level is beyond the scope of this book. Only the essentials of the Disk Editor program are explained here.

> **WARNING:** Unless you are very knowledgeable about the structure of a disk, using Disk Editor for all but simple fixes can run the risk of making a disk unusable and unrecoverable. The discussion about Disk Editor assumes that you know disk storage terms such as *cluster, sector, partition table, FAT,* and so on. For more information, see "Understanding How Disks Work," earlier in this chapter, or *Que's Guide to Data Recovery,* by Scott Mueller.
>
> Using the Disk Editor program takes more knowledge about how the disk works and how information is stored than what the NDD and UnErase commands required. The Disk Editor program is not as easy to use or as automated as UnErase and NDD. Learning and using the Disk Editor program effectively may take a significant amount of time. If you try to recover some information that takes you only an hour to re-create, trying to use Disk Editor to get the data back may not be worth the trouble; you may just want to retype the information.
>
> Also, be aware that the Disk Editor program enables you to do good *and* bad. The program is powerful enough for you to destroy your entire disk.

Begin Disk Editor by choosing the Disk Editor option from the Norton menu or by entering the

   DISKEDIT

command. The syntax of the Disk Editor command follows:

   DISKEDIT [*d:*] [*path*] [*filespec*][*switches*]

The available *switches* for the Disk Editor program follow:

Switch	Description
/M	Selects maintenance mode, which means that Norton Utilities bypasses the DOS logical organization. You may need to use this mode if a disk is badly damaged. If Norton does not begin to analyze a disk when you run the command, you may want to try the /M switch to see whether that helps. You cannot work with files or unerase files in maintenance mode.

Switch	Description
/X:d	Excludes certain drives from absolute sector processing. Use this switch if you have nonexistent drives allocated.
	The letter *d* represents the list of drives to exclude. For example, DEF excludes drives D, E, and F from absolute sector processing.

When the Disk Editor program begins, you are told that you arc in read-only mode, which means that you can safely explore your disk without worrying about changing important information. You can change out of read-only mode by selecting the Configuration option from the Tools menu. The first screen that appears is shown in figure 4.32.

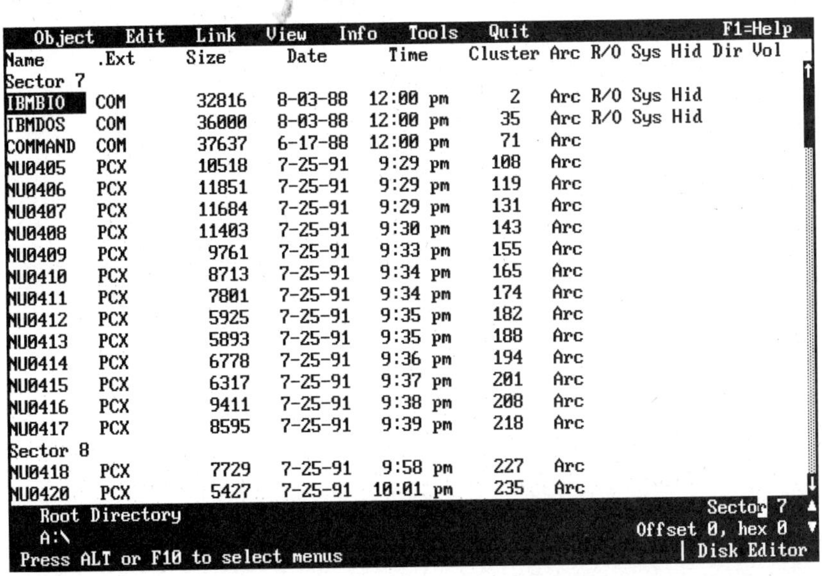

```
 Object   Edit   Link   View   Info   Tools   Quit              F1=Help
Name        .Ext    Size      Date      Time     Cluster Arc R/O Sys Hid Dir Vol
Sector 7
IBMBIO    COM      32816   8-03-88  12:00 pm        2   Arc R/O Sys Hid
IBMDOS    COM      36000   8-03-88  12:00 pm       35   Arc R/O Sys Hid
COMMAND   COM      37637   6-17-88  12:00 pm       71   Arc
NU0405    PCX      10518   7-25-91   9:29 pm      108   Arc
NU0406    PCX      11851   7-25-91   9:29 pm      119   Arc
NU0407    PCX      11684   7-25-91   9:29 pm      131   Arc
NU0408    PCX      11403   7-25-91   9:30 pm      143   Arc
NU0409    PCX       9761   7-25-91   9:33 pm      155   Arc
NU0410    PCX       8713   7-25-91   9:34 pm      165   Arc
NU0411    PCX       7801   7-25-91   9:34 pm      174   Arc
NU0412    PCX       5925   7-25-91   9:35 pm      182   Arc
NU0413    PCX       5893   7-25-91   9:35 pm      188   Arc
NU0414    PCX       6778   7-25-91   9:36 pm      194   Arc
NU0415    PCX       6317   7-25-91   9:37 pm      201   Arc
NU0416    PCX       9411   7-25-91   9:38 pm      208   Arc
NU0417    PCX       8595   7-25-91   9:39 pm      218   Arc
Sector 8
NU0418    PCX       7729   7-25-91   9:58 pm      227   Arc
NU0420    PCX       5427   7-25-91  10:01 pm      235   Arc
    Root Directory                                        Sector 7
    A:\                                           Offset 0, hex 0
Press ALT or F10 to select menus                        | Disk Editor
```

FIG. 4.32.

Viewing files in the current directory.

This screen displays the files found on the disk, listing file specification, size, date, time, the cluster where the file begins, and attributes now set. On the top bar of the screen is the Disk Editor menu bar containing seven menu selections: Object, Edit, Link, View, Info, Tools, and Quit. To open the pull-down menus, press F10, and then use the cursor-movement keys to select menus or items within menus. If you use a mouse, highlight a menu name and click.

Generally, use the options on this menu to find something on disk that you want to change, make the change, and then write the change back to disk. Suppose that you have a directory that cannot be erased with the DOS or Norton Remove Directory command. This situation can occur if a file or subdirectory has been corrupted and does not erase properly. DOS refuses to erase the directory because the operating system thinks the directory still contains information. You can erase this directory manually by replacing the first character of its name with the hexadecimal number E5, which is the symbol DOS uses to denote an erased file.

With Disk Edit, therefore, you can locate the directory name, change the first character, and then write the change back to disk. (In this example, you also run the CHKDSK/F command or NDD to clean up any lost clusters caused by the change.)

Using the Object Menu

You can choose the object that you want to edit by using the Object menu (see fig. 4.33). The objects that you can choose to use include the drive, the directory, the file, the cluster, the sector, or the physical sector. Select what you want to examine or edit on the disk. The next group of objects are the partition table, the boot record, and copies of the FAT. In this case, the Partition Table option appears in parentheses because the floppy diskette does not have partitions; you therefore cannot choose Partition Table now.

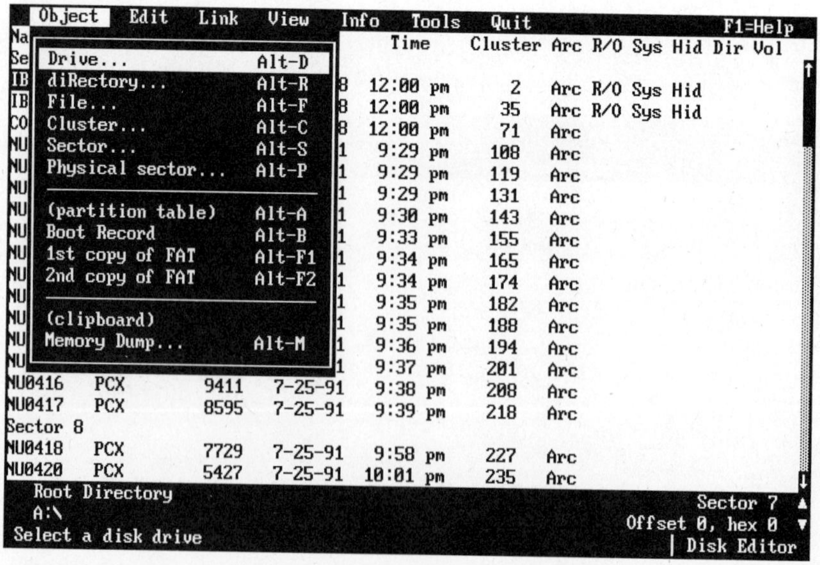

FIG. 4.33.

The Object menu.

The Clipboard option enables you to store a block of information from disk and to place that block elsewhere on disk. With the Memory Dump option, you can view, search, and copy information from your RAM memory. RAM may contain information not on disk if an application crashes before your information has been written to disk. Generally, before you do any editing on the disk, you choose which object to edit.

> **WARNING:** Use the Memory Dump option with care. Using the option may cause some computers to lock up, requiring a boot, which causes you to lose information in RAM memory (in this case, the information you currently have in the clipboard). This problem is particularly true of PS/2 machines.

Using the Edit Menu

The Edit menu enables you to edit information on disk (see fig. 4.34). The Undo option in the menu enables you to undo the last items you edited. Undo remembers 512 bytes of information and undoes items in the reverse order of how you did them. Undo, however, only undoes items within a sector boundary. If you have moved to another sector, Undo only undoes things in the current sector. If parentheses appear around the Undo command, you have nothing to undo.

```
  Object   Edit   Link   View   Info   Tools   Quit                    F1=Help
Name        .E                              Cluster Arc R/O Sys Hid Dir Vol
Sector 7         (undo)              Ctrl-U
IBMBIO    CO                                    2    Arc R/O Sys Hid
IBMDOS    CO  Mark                   Ctrl-B     35   Arc R/O Sys Hid
COMMAND   CO  (copy)                Ctrl-C     71   Arc
NU0405    PC  (paste over)          Ctrl-V    108   Arc
NU0406    PC  (fill...)                        119   Arc
NU0407    PC                                   131   Arc
NU0408    PC  (write changes...)    Ctrl-W    143   Arc
NU0409    PC  (discard changes...)             155   Arc
NU0410    PC                                   165   Arc
NU0411    PCX        7801   7-25-91   9:34 pm  174   Arc
NU0412    PCX        5925   7-25-91   9:35 pm  182   Arc
NU0413    PCX        5893   7-25-91   9:35 pm  188   Arc
NU0414    PCX        6778   7-25-91   9:36 pm  194   Arc
NU0415    PCX        6317   7-25-91   9:37 pm  201   Arc
NU0416    PCX        9411   7-25-91   9:38 pm  208   Arc
NU0417    PCX        8595   7-25-91   9:39 pm  218   Arc
Sector 8
NU0418    PCX        7729   7-25-91   9:58 pm  227   Arc
NU0420    PCX        5427   7-25-91  10:01 pm  235   Arc
     Root Directory                               Sector 7
     A:\                                     Offset 0, hex 0
  Begin/End marking a block                     | Disk Editor
```

FIG. 4.34.

The Edit menu.

The Mark, Copy, Paste Over, and Fill options enable you to manipulate information on the disk. You use the Mark option to capture information from the disk and place the data in the clipboard for copying elsewhere. To copy information, place your cursor at the beginning of the block you want to copy. Choose Mark from the Edit menu and move your cursor to the end of the block. The information between the beginning and end of the block is highlighted. If you use a mouse, set the mouse pointer at the beginning of the block, press the mouse button, and drag the mouse pointer to the end of the block. To place the information in the clipboard, select Copy from the Edit menu. The clipboard can hold up to 4,096 bytes (characters) of information.

The information remains in the clipboard until replaced with other information. To copy the information from the clipboard to somewhere else on the disk, go to that location, place your cursor where you want the information to begin, and choose Paste Over from the Edit menu.

 The Paste Over procedure overwrites information now in that location; no Insert mode is available.

Use the Fill option to fill a block of space with a single character. Mark a block, as described in the copy procedure. After you choose the Fill option from the Edit menu, you are prompted to select the character with which to fill the block. You can choose an ASCII character from a list box, and that character fills the entire marked region. This method erases sensitive information from disks.

After you make changes to a disk by copying or filling, these changes are not actually written to the disk until you choose the Write Changes option from the Edit menu. To choose not to make these changes, select Disregard Changes.

Using the Link Menu

The Link menu enables you to travel back and forth to areas related on a particular file (see fig. 4.35). Each file on disk is related to a directory and a FAT entry. When you are editing the contents of the file, you may need to reference information in the directory or FAT. How can you locate the directory on disk related to the file, or how can you locate the information in the FAT table associated with the file? The answer is the Link menu. If you choose the Directory option from the Link menu (while examining a file), the disk editor takes you to the place on disk containing the directory entry related to that file and places you in the appropriate directory viewer. Similarly, choosing the cluster chain

(FAT) option takes you to the place in the file allocation table (FAT) related to that file. Choosing the File option takes you back to the actual contents of the file.

```
 Object    Edit   Link   View   Info   Tools   Quit              F1=Help
Name      .Ext                                  ter Arc R/O Sys Hid Dir Vol
Sector 7          ┌─────────────────────────────┐                            ↑
IBMBIO    COM     │ File              Ctrl-F     │2   Arc R/O Sys Hid
IBMDOS    COM     │ (directory)       Ctrl-D     │5   Arc R/O Sys Hid
COMMAND   COM     │ Cluster chain (FAT) Ctrl-T   │1   Arc
NU0405    PCX     │ (partition)                  │8   Arc
NU0406    PCX     │                              │9   Arc
NU0407    PCX     │ (window)                     │1   Arc
NU0408    PCX   11403  7-25-91   9:30 pm    143   Arc
NU0409    PCX    9761  7-25-91   9:33 pm    155   Arc
NU0410    PCX    8713  7-25-91   9:34 pm    165   Arc
NU0411    PCX    7801  7-25-91   9:34 pm    174   Arc
NU0412    PCX    5925  7-25-91   9:35 pm    182   Arc
NU0413    PCX    5893  7-25-91   9:35 pm    188   Arc
NU0414    PCX    6778  7-25-91   9:36 pm    194   Arc
NU0415    PCX    6317  7-25-91   9:37 pm    201   Arc
NU0416    PCX    9411  7-25-91   9:38 pm    208   Arc
NU0417    PCX    8595  7-25-91   9:39 pm    218   Arc
Sector 8
NU0418    PCX    7729  7-25-91   9:58 pm    227   Arc
NU0420    PCX    5427  7-25-91  10:01 pm    235   Arc
   Root Directory                              Sector 7  ▲
   A:\                                   Offset 0, hex 0 ▼
View file's contents                         | Disk Editor
```

FIG. 4.35.

The Link menu.

If you are editing a partition rather than a file, the Link menu enables you to link to the partition table or boot record. In each case, the allowable links are noted by options in the Link menu not surrounded by parentheses.

The Window option on the Link menu enables you to look at the FAT table on one half of the screen while examining the contents of a file on the other half. In order to use this option, you must first be viewing a copy of the FAT. To view the FAT, choose the FAT option from the Objects pull-down menu. Then, to split the screen, press Shift-F5 (or choose Split Window from the View menu). To link the screens, choose the Windows option from the Link pull-down menu. You will then see a screen similar to the one in figure 4.36.

Using the View Menu

The View menu enables you to choose various options when viewing information on disk (see fig. 4.37). The As Hex and As Text options enable you to see the information on-screen in hexadecimal code or as ASCII text. Text files usually are viewed in text mode. Programs or coded files may be viewed in Hex format. The other modes enable you to view data appropriate to what you are looking at. If you look at the FAT, for example, you usually choose the As FAT option.

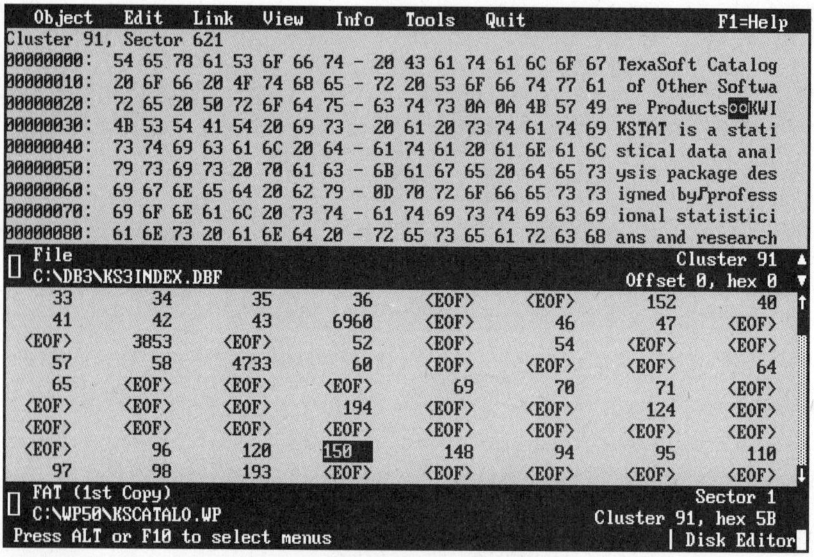

FIG. 4.36.

The screen showing sectors and clusters.

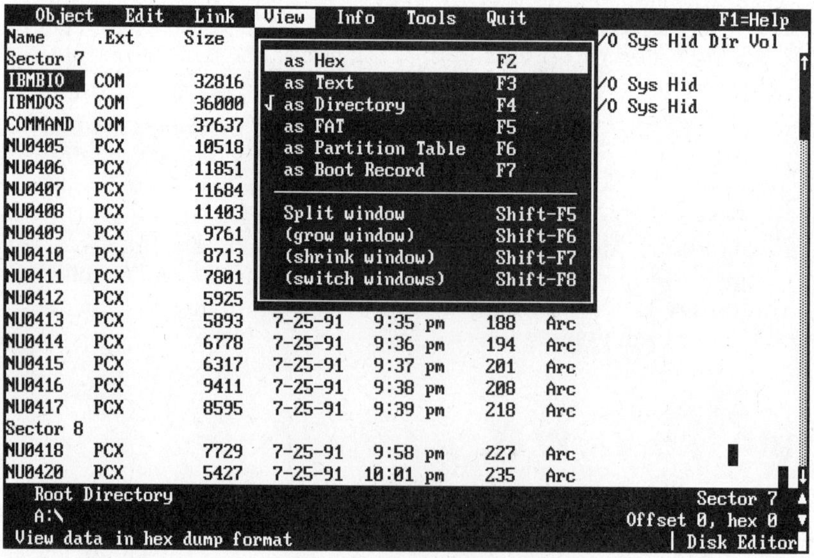

FIG. 4.37.

The View menu.

The Window options in the View menu enable you to split the screen and view two items simultaneously. You can split the screen by using the Split Window (Shift-F5) option, switch from window to window by using the Switch Window (Shift-F8) option, and adjust the size of the window by using the Grow Window or Shrink Window option.

Using the Info Menu

The Info menu enables you to display information about the object or drive you are viewing, or to look at a map (a graphic display) of the object in relation to all the clusters on disk. The Info menu is shown in figure 4.38. To look at a map of the IMAGE.DAT file created by the Norton Image program, for example, select the File option from the Object pull-down menu, and then select the file IMAGE.DAT from the list of files. Choose the Map of Object option from the Info pull-down menu, and a screen similar to the one in figure 4.39 appears. Notice the Fs on the map. These Fs show where within the disk space the selected object is stored.

```
   Object   Edit    Link    View   Info   Tools   Quit              F1=Help
 Name       .Ext    Size    Date               Arc R/O Sys Hid Dir Vol
 Sector 7                     Object info...
 IBMBIO    COM     32816    8-03-  Drive info...    Arc R/O Sys Hid
 IBMDOS    COM     36000    8-03-  (map of object...) Arc R/O Sys Hid
 COMMAND   COM     37637    6-17-                Arc
 NU0405    PCX     10518    7-25-91   9:29 pm   108   Arc
 NU0406    PCX     11851    7-25-91   9:29 pm   119   Arc
 NU0407    PCX     11684    7-25-91   9:29 pm   131   Arc
 NU0408    PCX     11403    7-25-91   9:30 pm   143   Arc
 NU0409    PCX      9761    7-25-91   9:33 pm   155   Arc
 NU0410    PCX      8713    7-25-91   9:34 pm   165   Arc
 NU0411    PCX      7801    7-25-91   9:34 pm   174   Arc
 NU0412    PCX      5925    7-25-91   9:35 pm   182   Arc
 NU0413    PCX      5893    7-25-91   9:35 pm   188   Arc
 NU0414    PCX      6778    7-25-91   9:36 pm   194   Arc
 NU0415    PCX      6317    7-25-91   9:37 pm   201   Arc
 NU0416    PCX      9411    7-25-91   9:38 pm   208   Arc
 NU0417    PCX      8595    7-25-91   9:39 pm   218   Arc
 Sector 8
 NU0418    PCX      7729    7-25-91   9:58 pm   227   Arc
 NU0420    PCX      5427    7-25-91  10:01 pm   235   Arc
    Root Directory                             Sector 7
    A:\                                  Offset 0, hex 0
 Get more information on the selected object      | Disk Editor
```

FIG. 4.38.

The Info menu.

Using the Tools Menu

The Tools menu gives you several tools for exploring the contents of a disk (see fig. 4.40).

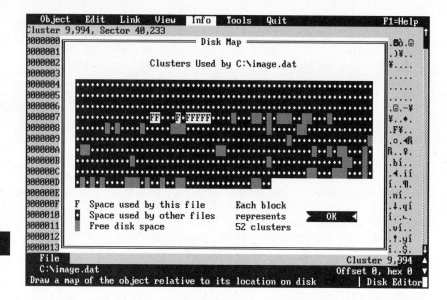

FIG. 4.39.

The Disk Map screen.

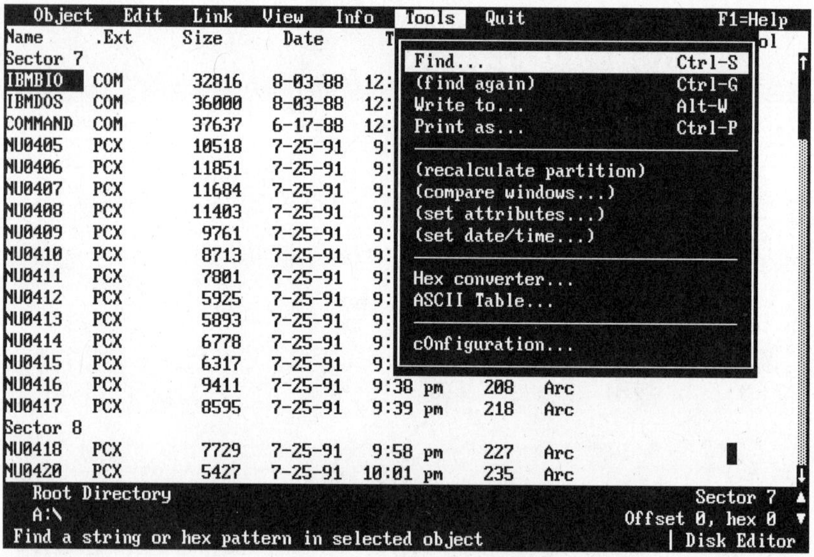

FIG. 4.40.

The Tools menu.

The Tools options follow:

Option	Effect
Find	Searches for a string of text on a disk. Find can be helpful if you are looking for information on disk but do not know which file (or erased space) contains the information.
Find Again	Repeats the last Find command.
Write To	Writes the current object you are editing to disk. You are asked to specify a file name, starting cluster number, or sector number for the Write To option. With Write To, you can find pieces of an erased file and write out the information to disk. The Write To option is a way to recover information that you cannot recover by using UnErase or Disk Tools.
Print as	Prints the current object you are editing to the printer. You can choose to print the information in hexadecimal, directory, FAT, boot sector, or partition table format.
Recalculate Partition	Calculates two items (available when you are in partition table view mode):
	The relative sector number from the starting sector coordinates
	The number of sectors from the starting and ending sector coordinates
Compare Windows	Compares two windows and places the cursor at the first point where the information in the windows disagrees.
Set Attributes	Changes the attributes for a group of files (available when you are in directory view mode).
Set Date/Time	Changes the date and time for a group of files (available when you are in directory mode).
Hex Converter	Converts a hexadecimal value to a decimal value, or vice versa. Also displays the ASCII character associated with the decimal value.
ASCII Table	Displays the ASCII character set and gives the decimal and hexadecimal value for each character.
Configuration	Sets several options for using the Disk Editor (see fig. 4.41).

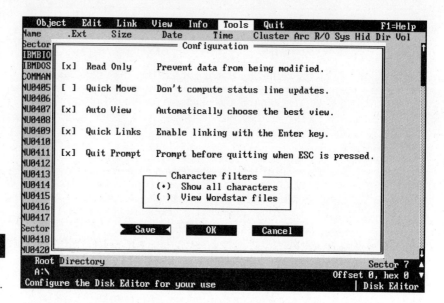

FIG. 4.41.

The Configuration dialog box.

The Configuration options that you can set follow:

Option	Description
Read-Only	Prevents you from writing changed information to disk. You can change the default setting for read-only to enable users to write changed information to disk.
Quick Move	Speeds up response time by omitting the rewriting of file names in the status bar.
Auto View	Tells Disk Editor to choose the most appropriate view to be used.
Quick Links	Links from one object to a related object when you press Enter or click the mouse button.
Quit Prompt	Tells Disk Editor to display a warning prompt when you press Esc to exit the program.
Show All Characters	Shows all characters as stored in the object. (This is a character filter that tells the program how to display text.)
View WordStar Files	Specifies that the text being viewed is stored in WordStar format. Thus, the characters shown are converted from WordStar codes to readable characters.
Save	Saves configuration selections to the file NU.INI.

Option	Description
OK	Ends the selection, but does not save changes to disk.
Cancel	Ends the Configuration option menu.

Chapter Summary

This chapter covered the core of Norton Utilities' file-recovery options, beginning with the easiest and quickest way to unerase a file: the UnErase command. This command should always be your first choice when trying to unerase a file. If your disk has other problems, such as not enabling you to read files from a disk that used to work, try the Norton Disk Doctor to cure what ails the disk. To recover a defective disk or to make a disk bootable, use Disk Tools. To recover a dBASE, Lotus 1-2-3, or Symphony file, use the File Fix command.

Finally, if you want to do some real surgery, you can resort to the Norton Disk Editor program and explore and edit the disk or manually unerase files. Try to use the most automated recovery programs first, and then progress to those commands in which you can do all the work yourself. Be warned, however, that the more power you are given, the more potential you have to mess things up. Practice on a floppy disk where your results do not matter before doing surgery on a "live" disk.

Making Your Hard Disk Work Efficiently

Previous chapters discuss using Norton Utilities to protect and recover files. You should perform other maintenance tasks on your hard disk to help prevent disk problems and to make your disk run smoothly and at top speed.

Just as an automobile needs occasional tuning, a hard disk needs to be adjusted to keep it running at its full potential. A little preventive maintenance goes a long way toward keeping your hard disk running well. When your hard disk gets out of shape (is too full, has too many fragmented files, develops unreadable sectors), it has to work harder to get information, which puts a strain on the hard disk's mechanisms and may cause them to wear out sooner. If the disk fails mechanically, an expert must rebuild it in a dust-free, clean room (a hospital operating room, for example) to get your information off the disk. If the plate of your hard disk is damaged, the potential for data recovery is slim.

Disk maintenance also is a productivity issue. When the disk is not running well, it slows down, which means that your work on the computer slows down.

Many computer users are in such a hurry that they do not take the time to do preventive maintenance. Spending a little time now, however, can save you from spending a great deal of time later. Norton Utilities gives you some easy-to-use tools that make the disk-maintenance chore as simple and efficient as possible.

Four Norton utilities that deal with making your hard disk work more efficiently are covered in this chapter (three Speed utilities and one Tool utility), as follows:

Utility	Effect
Calibrate	Enables you to tune the way that you read and write information to and from your hard disk.
Norton Cache	Enables you to adjust how information is read and written to and from your hard disk.
Speed Disk	Enables you to rearrange the files on your disk so that you can read and write to them faster.
System Information	Gives you information about your hard disk and produces important information about the current condition of your disk.

You can use all of these commands to make your hard disk access faster and more efficient. This not only gives you faster working programs; it also reduces wear and tear on your hard disk and may prolong its life.

Examining System Information

With the System Information (SYSINFO) command, you can compare your computer system with other computers in terms of processing and disk speeds. You also can examine the current status and use of the space on your hard disk and learn how your hard disk and RAM memory are being used. The System Information test compares the performance of your computer with the following:

- A standard IBM PC XT, using the Intel 8088 microprocessor, running at 4.77 MHz

- The IBM PC AT, using the Intel 80286 microprocessor, running at 8 MHz

- The COMPAQ 386 computer, using the Intel 80386 microprocessor, running at 33 MHz

The System Information command also is a good way to learn vital information about a computer quickly. If you help other people with their computers (as a user support technician, for example), the System Information command can help you discover information about a computer you have never used before. You may be interested in the existence of a math coprocessor, the type of video display being used, the existence of parallel and serial ports, the amount of memory available and used, and other items described by the System Information command.

When you run the System Information command from the Norton menu or from the DOS prompt with no switches, the program presents about 15 different screens, one following the other, of information about your computer. These screens and their contents are described in this chapter.

Starting System Information

You may begin the System Information command by choosing it from the Norton menu or by entering the command SYSINFO at the DOS prompt. The syntax for using the System Information command at the DOS prompt follows:

SYSINFO [*d:*][*switches*]

Where *d:* is the letter of the hard disk drive you want to test. The available *switches* for the System Information command follow:

Switch	Effect
/AUTO:*n*	Tells the command to operate in automatic mode. The *n* parameter specifies a delay of *n* seconds between screens. In this mode, the system information is shown screen by screen with a pause of *n* seconds between screens. The *n* is specified in the switch. If you do not specify an *n* in the switch, the pause between screens is 5 seconds.
/DEMO	Operates in Demo mode. Causes System Information to scroll continuously through four screens: System Summary, CPU Benchmarks, Disk Speed Benchmarks, and Overall Performance. You can use this switch to see how the performance of the computer measures up to other well-known computers (the XT, the AT, and the COMPAQ 386/33, for example).

Switch	Effect
/DI	Produces the Drive Information summary screen only.
/N	Skips the live memory probe. On some computers, the live memory probe forces you to reboot after the SI test. Use the /N switch to get around this problem. This is a necessary switch on some computers that are not 100-percent compatible clone computers. If the System Information command causes your computer to freeze (it does not respond to the keyboard anymore), use the /N switch to prevent this problem in the future.
/SOUND	Beeps between CPU tests.
/SUMMARY	Produces the System Information summary screen only.
/TSR	Shows all TSR (terminate-and-stay resident) programs in memory.

Viewing Summary Information

A System Information test on drive C of an IBM PS/2 Model 30/289 with an 80M hard disk was used to create these screens. The first screen reported—the System Summary screen—is shown in figure 5.1. Notice the four options at the bottom of the screen: Next, Previous, Print, and Cancel. To scroll through the screens, you can use your mouse or arrow keys to choose Next or Previous. Choose Print to print a summary of the screen to the printer. Choose Cancel to exit the current screen and go to the pull-down menu mode.

The System Summary screen contains system information about the computer being tested. The Computer box tells you the date of the BIOS (basic input/output system). This date can be important because some new programs will not run on older versions of the BIOS—your software should tell you if this is a problem.

Also reported in the Computer box are the microprocessors being used (in this case, an Intel 80286 running at 10 MHz). The various Intel microprocessors that can be reported are listed in table 5.1. Also reported in this box is the mouse type (if any) being used. The type of video adapter (monitor) in use is also reported. For this report, the adapter is listed as a Video Graphics (VGA) type adapter.

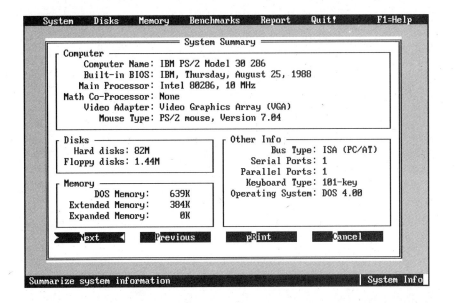

FIG. 5.1.

The System Summary screen for an IBM PS/2 Model 30/286.

Table 5.1 Intel Microprocessor Chips and Math Coprocessors

Chip Name	Computer	Math Coprocessor
80C88	Usually laptops	8087
80286	IBM AT class computer	80287
80C286	Usually laptops	80C287
80386	Wide variety	80387
80386SX	Wide variety	80387SX
80486	Wide variety	80487

The Disks box tells you the size of your hard disk(s) and floppy disk(s). The Memory box tells you how much DOS memory you have, and how much (if any) extended or expanded memory you have (the various kinds of memory are discussed in "Viewing the Memory Summary Screen," later in this chapter). The Other Info box reports the bus type, the number of serial and parallel ports, the keyboard being used, and the version of DOS being used. The bus type refers to one of the following busses:

Bus	Description
ISA	Standard bus for IBM PC and AT-type computers
MCA	Microchannel bus used on most IBM PS/2s
EISA	Extended Industry Standard Architecture bus. Similar in capability to the newer MCA bus, but retains compatibility with the older ISA bus.

The type of bus used determines what kind of expansion cards you can use for your computer. The ISA bus accepts only standard PC/AT-type expansion cards. The MCA bus accepts only MCA cards. The EISA bus accepts EISA or ISA cards.

The serial ports generally are used for communications—for example, a hookup to a modem. You usually use parallel ports to communicate with a printer.

Viewing the Video Summary Screen

When you press Enter while viewing the System Summary screen or click on Next, the Video Summary screen appears. The Video Summary screen in System Information gives you information about the type of monitor you are using (see fig. 5.2). The Display box on this screen tells you which type of display adapter is attached to the computer, the monitor type, and the current video mode.

A summary of several kinds of video adapters is given in table 5.2. The resolution column lists the number of dots, or pixels, that are on-screen. The larger the number of pixels, the greater the clarity of the screen's image.

Table 5.2 Common Video Adapters for IBM-Compatible Computers

Adapter Type	Resolution
Monochrome (text only)	640 x 350
CGA Composite	620 x 200
CGA Color	320 x 200 color mode 640 x 200 B&W mode
Enhanced Graphics (EGA)	640 x 350
Multicolor Graphics (MGA)	640 x 480, 16 colors
Vector Graphics (VGA)	640 x 480, 256 colors
Super VGA	800 x 600

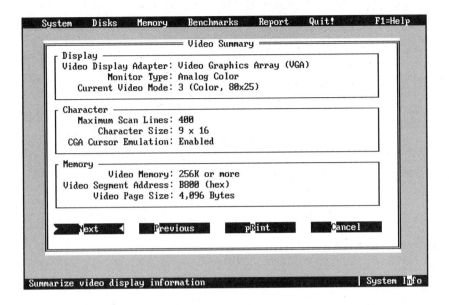

FIG. 5.2.

The Video
Summary
screen.

The Character box tells you the number of scan lines on-screen and
the number of pixels used to create a character on-screen (in this case
9 x 16 pixels). The more scan lines, the better the clarity of the picture.
The larger the number of pixels used to display a character on-screen,
the better the clarity of text.

If CGA Cursor Emulation is enabled, EGA or VGA monitors are able
to respond to cursor sizing calls in the same manner used by CGA
monitors.

The Memory box contains information about how much memory
is allocated to your display and how that memory is used. The Video
Segment Address tells where the video memory begins. This information may be important if you are programming to a video adapter or if
you have a program that requires a particular level of video features.

Viewing the Hardware Interrupts Screen

Pressing Enter or clicking on Next from the Video Summary screen
brings you to the Hardware Interrupts screen, which tells you the
"owner" of the interrupts in your system (see fig. 5.3). A *hardware
interrupt* is a way for hardware devices to request service from
the computer. Notice that the list of names includes items such as the
keyboard, communication ports, disks, and so on. When one of these
items wants to convey information to the computer or request service

from DOS, it sends an interrupt signal to the computer. Each device is assigned a unique interrupt signal, so the computer knows who is "talking."

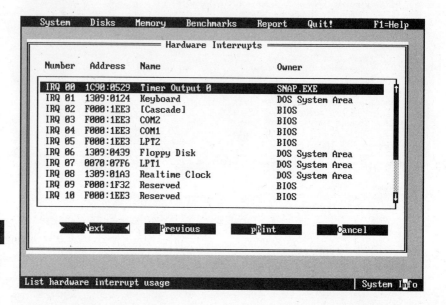

FIG. 5.3.

The Hardware Interrupts screen.

Occasionally, when you add a new device to the computer, you are asked to set its interrupt to one that is currently unused. Use this screen to find out which interrupt is unused. Look under the Number, Name, and Owner columns, to see which interrupts are unused. These columns are available for new devices that you add to your computer.

Viewing the Software Interrupts Screen

Software interrupts are similar to hardware interrupts, except that instead of a hardware device such as a disk drive requesting information from the computer, a software program requests action (see fig. 5.4). The interrupts listed on this screen may be useful for persons writing software programs that must take advantage of these interrupts.

Viewing the CMOS Values Screen

Pressing Enter or clicking on Next from the Software Interrupts screen brings you to the CMOS Values screen, which contains information about how your computer is configured (see fig. 5.5). An important piece of information on this screen is found in the CMOS Battery field. If your computer begins to operate erratically, losing time and date information and having problems finding your disks, you can check this screen to see if the battery is operational. If the battery is not operational, the computer may have lost information about its configuration. (See Chapter 4 for information on the Disk Tools Rescue Disk option.)

The Hard Disks box reports the drive types for your hard disks. On many newer PCs, this information is not needed. The Floppy Disks box reports the sizes of your floppy disk drives. The Installed Memory box reports the CMOS values for base and extended memory. The CMOS Status box tells you if your current values are okay. If any of these fields show the word Error, you may need to run your computer's Setup program and/or replace your battery.

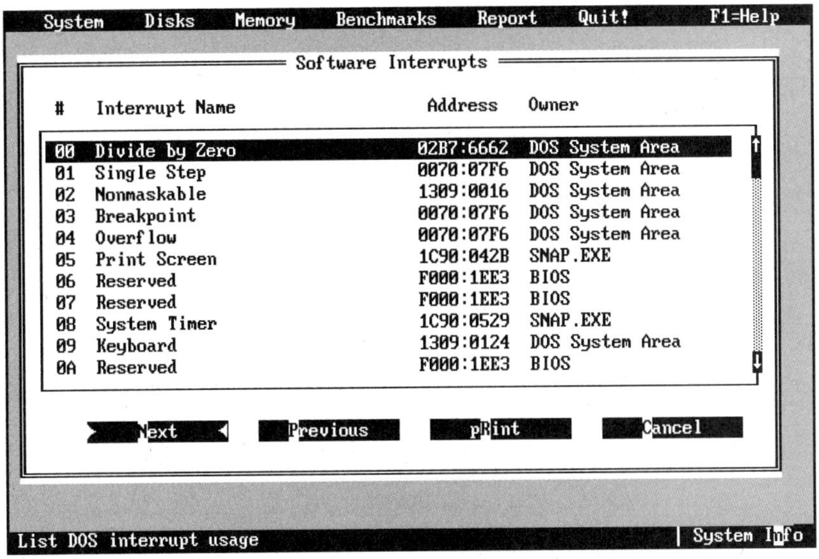

FIG. 5.4.

The Software Interrupts screen.

Viewing the Disk Summary Screen

You press Enter or click on Next from the CMOS Values screen to go to the Disk Summary screen. The Disk Summary screen tells you how many and which disk drives the computer has available for use. In figure 5.6, drives A, B, C, and D are available for use. Drives A, B, and D are floppy disk drives, and drive C is a hard disk. The hard disk drive C currently is using the directory \NU. The other disks, listed as Available, currently are not being used.

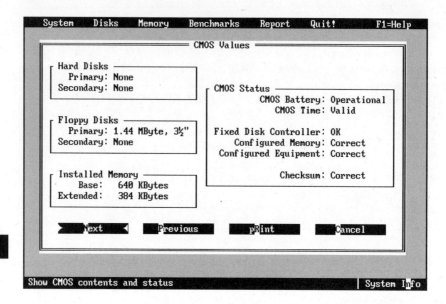

FIG. 5.5.

The CMOS
Values screen.

Viewing the Disk Characteristics Screen

Pressing Enter or clicking on Next from the Disk Summary screen
brings you to the Disk Characteristics screen, which gives you information about the current disk (see fig. 5.7). A list of available disks is
located in the box at the upper right of the screen. You can change to
another disk to see information about that disk. Use the up- and down-
arrow keys to change disks or point to a disk name (A:, for example) in
the list with the mouse pointer and click.

The Logical Characteristics box contains information about how the
magnetic information is stored on the disk. As discussed in Chapter 4,
the number of bytes per sector usually is 512. That is, when a track on
a disk is broken up into sectors, each sector holds 512 bytes of information. This number may change, however, with newer versions of DOS.

When reading information from a disk, DOS reads a certain minimum
amount of information at a time. That amount is called a *cluster*. The
number of sectors per cluster usually is two for floppy diskettes and
four or more for hard disks. The size of the cluster often determines
how much wasted space (slack space) is on disk, as discussed in
Chapter 3.

The media descriptor tells you what kind or size of disk has been formatted. Table 5.3 interprets the media descriptor codes displayed on
the report. Thus, the disk shown here is a hard disk (code F8).

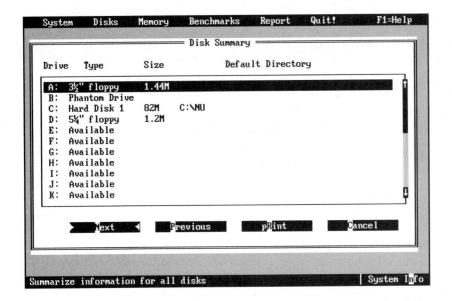

FIG. 5.6.

The Disk
Summary
screen.

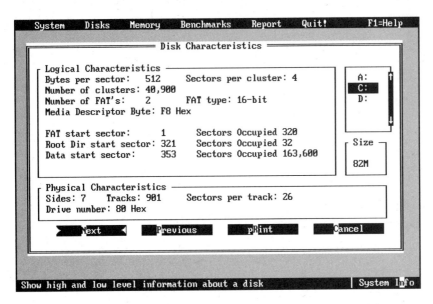

FIG. 5.7.

The Disk
Characteristics
screen.

The Logical Characteristics box also reports the number of file allocation tables on the disk. This usually is two, except in the case of RAM disks (memory disks), which may have only one copy of the FAT.

Table 5.3 Media Descriptor Codes

Reported Code	Disk Represented
F0	1.4M, 3 1/2-inch diskette
F8	Hard disk
F9	1.2M, 5 1/4-inch diskette or 720K, 3 1/2-inch diskette
FD	360K, 5 1/4-inch diskette
FE	160K, 5 1/4-inch diskette
FF	320K, 5 1/4-inch diskette

The remaining technical information given on the report is of little real use to most computer users. To a technical support person, however, some of this data can be helpful in editing the system information on a disk, using the Norton Disk Editor.

Viewing the Partition Tables Screen

Pressing Enter or clicking on Next from the Disk Characteristics screen brings you to the Partition Tables screen, which gives you information about the partitions on your hard disk (see fig. 5.8). In this case, there is only one hard disk. If you partition your hard disk into more than one drive by using the FDISK command (for example, drives C and D), each drive shows up as a partition. As a diagnostic tool, you can use this information to determine the number and size of partitions on the hard disk(s) and find out where they start and end on disk.

Viewing the Memory Summary Screen

Pressing Enter or clicking on Next from the Partition Tables screen brings you to the Memory Summary screen, which reports information about how your RAM memory is being used by your computer (see fig. 5.9). The Norton SYSINFO command looks at the computer's RAM (random-access memory) in two ways. The first section of the screen is the Dos Usage box. In this box, DOS reports 639K of available RAM memory, which is broken down into two parts. 212K of the memory is being used by DOS and resident programs. The rest is available for use by application programs.

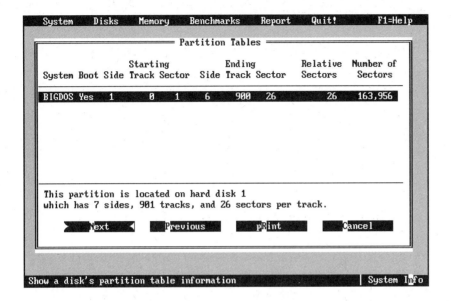

FIG. 5.8.

The Partition
Tables screen.

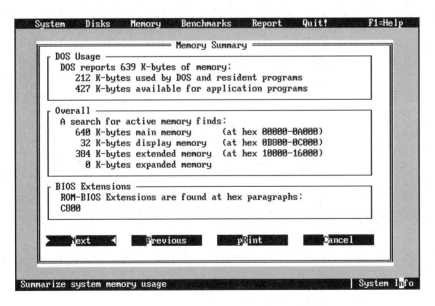

FIG. 5.9.

The Memory
Summary
screen.

The reason for the split is that when you boot your computer, it reads
DOS information on the boot disk and moves some of that information
into RAM so that the information is ready when needed. DOS information therefore takes up some of your RAM. If you have loaded any RAM-
resident programs (pop-up, terminate-and-stay resident, and so on),

they, too, are loaded into a portion of the RAM, like DOS. If too much of your RAM is taken up with memory-resident programs, you may have a hard time running large application programs such as Microsoft Windows or Aldus PageMaker.

The second box on the Memory Summary screen contains an overall report of the computer's memory locations. This box locates five kinds of memory, as follows:

Memory	Description
Main memory	About the same as the total memory reported by the DOS method.
Display memory	RAM located on the monitor display adapter card and used by the monitor.
Extended memory	Memory above 1M.
	Notice that in figure 5.9, more memory was found by SYSINFO's search for memory than by the DOS method because DOS only "sees" the first 640K.
Expanded memory	Add-on memory that can be accessed by certain programs that subscribe to a special way of using memory developed by Lotus, Microsoft, Intel, and AST companies. Many programs, such as Lotus 1-2-3, use this memory to be able to work with larger amounts of data (spreadsheets, databases, and so on) at one time.
Extra Memory	Any read/write memory above 640K and below 1M. (Although not shown in figure 5.9, Extra Memory may also be reported on this screen.)

The ROM-BIOS extended memory, if present, is memory located on add-in boards such as video display boards or hard disks, but is not a part of the normal RAM memory (this is reported in the BIOS Extensions box). The allocation of memory is important in running application programs (such as Lotus 1-2-3) and in networking. There are programs (such as QEMM) that enable you to re-allocate memory among these areas for the purpose of providing enough memory for certain applications to run.

Viewing the Extended Memory (XMS) Screen

Pressing Enter or clicking on Next from the Memory Summary screen brings you to the Extended Memory screen (see fig. 5.10). If you are using an extended memory manager, the details of the manager's allocation of memory are reviewed in this screen. An extended memory manager enables you to allocate a block of memory for use by an application. On this screen, the amount of allocated memory is 0, and is displayed in the Memory Usage box. The Upper Memory Blocks box reports on the use of Upper Memory Blocks (UMB) used by your system. Usually, this is only used on '386 class machines, and is managed by programs such as QEMM/386. With a memory manager program, you can mix extended and expanded memory to meet your application needs.

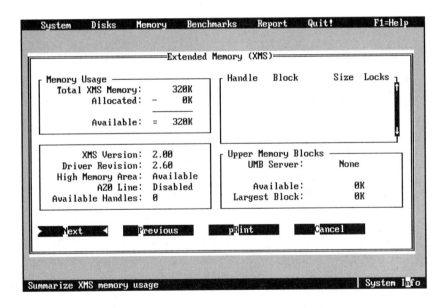

FIG. 5.10.

The Extended Memory (XMS) screen.

Viewing the TSR Programs Screen

Pressing Enter or clicking on Next from the Extended Memory screen brings you to the TSR Programs screen. *TSR programs* (terminate-and-stay resident)—also called *memory-resident programs*—are programs that, when begun, stay in the computer's RAM memory while other programs are running. By staying in memory, these programs are using some of the RAM memory, making it unusable for other programs. Therefore, you may need to be aware of how much space is being used by these programs. The TSR Programs screen lists the TSR programs and their sizes (see fig. 5.11).

By using the up- and down-arrow keys (or pointing and clicking with the mouse), you can highlight the TSRs listed. The fields Path, Command Line, and Memory Allocation Blocks at the bottom of the screen reflect the values for the highlighted TSR. The Path field indicates the location (directory) of the TSR on disk. The Command Line field indicates any command line options that were used when the TSR was begun. The Memory Allocation Blocks field shows how many blocks of memory are used by this TSR.

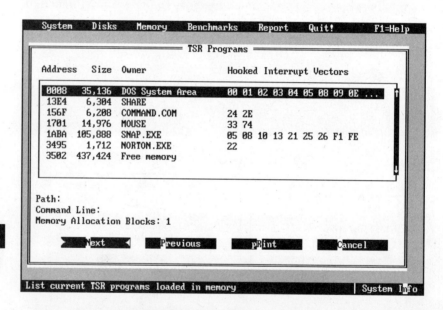

FIG. 5.11.

The TSR Programs screen.

You also may be interested in the order of these memory-resident programs because some programs can be uninstalled only if they are the last program loaded into memory. With the /TSR switch, you can see which programs are in memory, as well as the order of the programs.

If you use the Norton Disk Monitor command, for example, which is a TSR program, and then want to uninstall the program, you can enter the Norton Command

DISKMON/UNINSTALL

This takes the program out of memory only if it is the last TSR program in the list. Therefore, you need to uninstall these programs in the reverse order from how they were listed. (See Chapter 3 for more information.)

Another reason to be interested in TSRs is to know how much RAM they are using. Some large programs may require almost all of your available RAM in order to run. You may have to uninstall some TSR programs in order to run large application programs. Most TSR programs enable you to uninstall them—you must check each program's documentation. If you load a TSR program as a result of a command in your AUTOEXEC.BAT file, you also can remove that program from this batch file and reboot.

Viewing the DOS Memory Blocks and Device Drivers Screens

Pressing Enter or clicking on Next from the TSR Programs screen brings you to the DOS Memory Blocks screen (see fig. 5.12). Pressing Enter or clicking on Next from this screen brings you to the Device Drivers screen (see fig. 5.13). These screens display the addresses in memory-resident programs and device drivers. This information may be useful to programmers or technicians.

Viewing the CPU Speed Screen

Pressing on Enter or clicking on Next from the Device Drivers screen brings you to the CPU Speed screen, which shows a graphic comparison of the speed of the current computer—*This Computer*—with three other popular computers (see fig. 5.14). This screen gives you an idea of how fast your microprocessor works when compared to these other machines. The original IBM/XT running at 4.77 MHz is used as the base (1.0). The microprocessor in *This Computer* is running about 5.6 times faster than in an XT computer. Keep in mind that this test may be somewhat misleading because the processing speed of a computer has much to do with what you are processing. One computer may be better at processing numbers, for example, while another is adept at processing text fields.

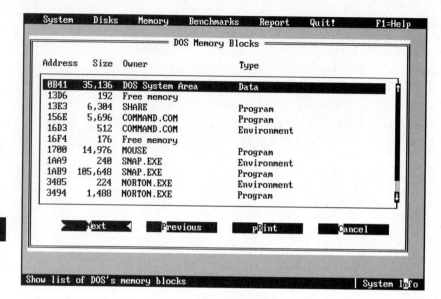

FIG. 5.12.

The DOS Memory Blocks screen.

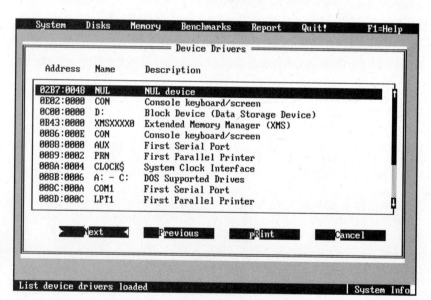

FIG. 5.13.

The Device Drivers screen.

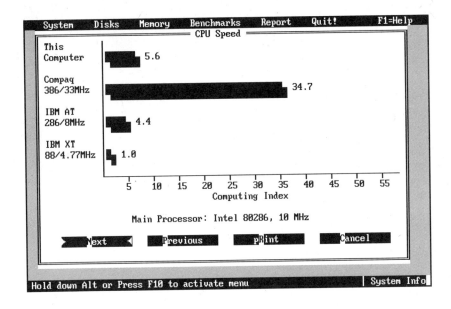

FIG. 5.14.

The CPU
Speed screen.

Viewing the Disk Speed Screen

Pressing Enter or clicking on Next from the CPU Speed screen brings
you to the Disk Speed screen, which displays a graphic comparison of
the speed of your hard disk when compared to three other popular
computers (see fig. 5.15). The hard disk in an IBM/XT computer is used
as the base line value (1.0). The hard disk in *This Computer* can access
information about 5.8 times as fast as the hard disk in the XT computer.
You should note, however, that hard disk access also is affected by
how much information is on the disk and whether the files on disk are
fragmented. Cache programs such as Norton Cache and Norton Calibrate can affect the efficiency of data access on your hard disk (see
"Using Calibrate" and "Using Norton Disk Cache" later in this chapter).

Viewing the Overall Performance
Index Screen

Pressing Enter or clicking on Next from the Disk Speed screen brings
you to the Overall Performance Index screen, which is a weighted combination of disk and CPU indexes, and gives you an overall comparison

of your computer with an IBM XT (see fig. 5.16). You should look at these indexes in the same way that you look at the reported miles per gallon on automobiles. The numbers are for comparison only, and your actual "mileage" may vary.

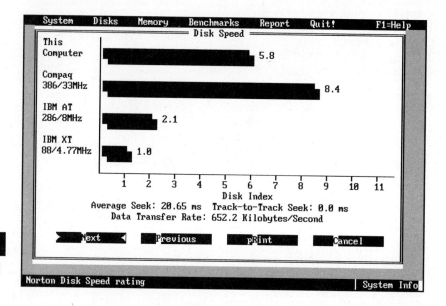

FIG. 5.15.

The Disk Speed screen.

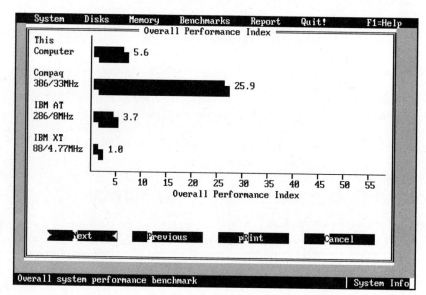

FIG. 5.16.

The Overall Performance Index screen.

Viewing the Network Drive Benchmark Screen

If you are connected to a network, there is an additional screen that is presented. When you press Enter or select Next from the Overall Performance Index screen, and if you are connected to a network, a screen listing network drives appears with the prompt

```
Select Network Drive
```

Use the up- and down-arrow keys to point to a drive name and press Enter. Or, point to a drive name with the mouse pointer and click.

In order for a benchmark test to be performed on a network drive, you must have read and write privileges for that drive. If you do not, a warning message will tell you that the benchmark test cannot be run. Otherwise, you will see a screen similar to figure 5.17. This screen graphically shows the average access times for this network drive for reading and writing information to the drive. You may want to compare this to the results of the Disk Speed screen (see fig. 5.15). Usually, network drives will have slower access times than your computer's hard disk.

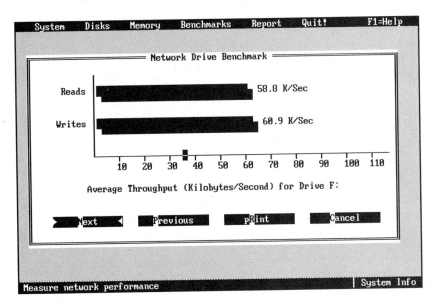

FIG. 5.17.

Viewing the Network Drive Benchmark screen.

Viewing Your CONFIG.SYS and AUTOEXEC.BAT Files

The last two screens shown in the System Information report are listings of your CONFIG.SYS and AUTOEXEC.BAT files (see figs. 5.18 and 5.19). You may want to look at the CONFIG.SYS file screen to check which device drivers you have installed; you can check the AUTOEXEC.BAT screen to see which TSR programs you begin at boot time.

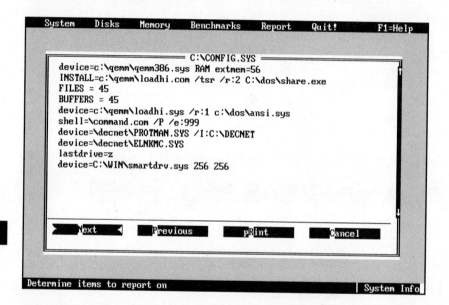

FIG. 5.18.

Viewing the CONFIG.SYS file.

Using the System Information Menu Bar

You can view all of the screens described in the previous sections one at a time by choosing the appropriate options from the menu bar at the top of the System Information screen. The options on the menu are System, Disks, Memory, Benchmarks, Report, and Quit! To open these pull-down menus, press F10 or point to a menu with the mouse and click. After you extend the menus, you can use the right- and left-arrow keys to move from menu to menu and the up- and down-arrow keys to select options within the menus.

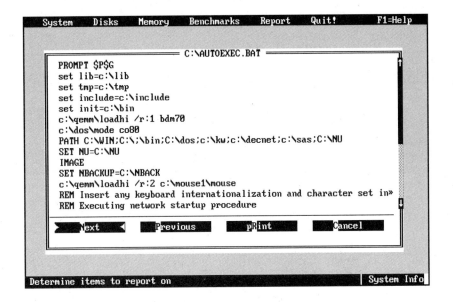

FIG. 5.19.

Viewing the
AUTOEXEC.BAT
file.

From the System menu (see fig. 5.20), you can choose any one of the
following screens to view:

> System Summary
> Video Summary
> Hardware Interrupts
> Software Interrupts
> CMOS Values (if available)

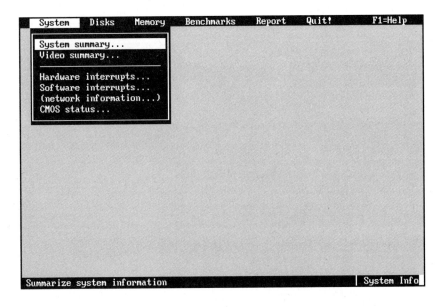

FIG. 5.20.

The System
menu.

From the Disks menu (see fig. 5.21), you can choose any one of the following screens to view:

    Disk Summary
    Disk Characteristics
    Partition Tables

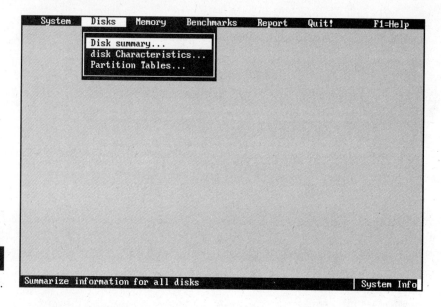

FIG. 5.21.

The Disks menu.

From the Memory menu (see fig. 5.22), you can choose any one of the following screens to view:

    Memory Summary
    Extended Memory (XMS)
    DOS Memory Blocks
    TSR Programs
    Device Drivers

From the Benchmarks menu (see fig. 5.23), you can choose any of the following screens to view:

    CPU Speed
    Disk Speed
    Overall Performance Index
    Network Performance Speed (if available)

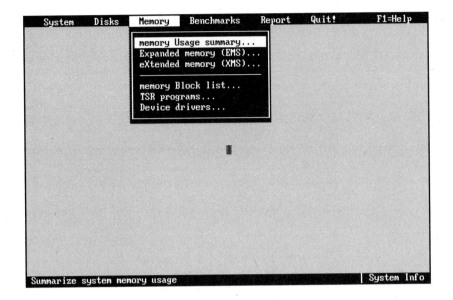

FIG. 5.22.

The Memory
menu.

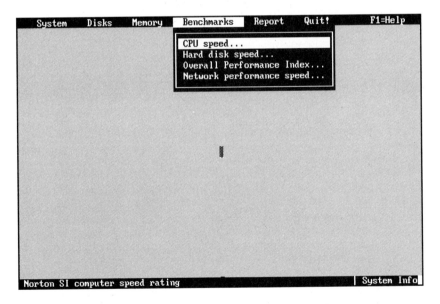

FIG. 5.23.

The Benchmarks
menu.

From the Report menu (see fig. 5.24), you can choose any of the following screens to view:

    View CONFIG.SYS
    View AUTOEXEC.BAT
    Print Report

194

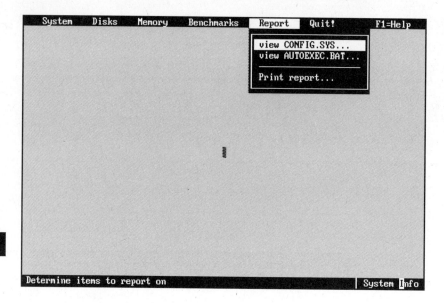

FIG. 5.24.

The Report
menu.

Choose Quit! from the menu bar or press Esc to end the System Information program.

Making Your Disk Run Faster with Speed Disk

Much already has been said about problems that can arise when the information in files stored on disk is fragmented. As you may recall from discussions in previous chapters, when DOS looks for a place to store a file, the system uses the first available cluster. If the file is too large to be stored in one cluster, DOS places part of the file in the first cluster and the next part of the file in the next available cluster. If a contiguous cluster is not available, DOS finds the next free cluster. Thus, one part of the file may be stored in one cluster, the next part stored in a cluster on another part of the disk, and so on.

When many files begin to be fragmented, as will happen over time, your disk access time may increase, because DOS must look in several places to read or write to a file. If the problem becomes too severe, you may even lose some information. Because the problem is so common, Norton Utilities offers a solution: the Speed Disk (SPEEDISK) command.

The Speed Disk command can rearrange the files on your disk so that each file is stored contiguously. You can use Speed Disk, for example, to enable DOS to save a word processing file to an optimized disk in five seconds, rather than in 30 seconds on a fragmented disk.

Trimming the time necessary to save files is not the Speed Disk command's only contribution. A number of programs access your disk many times while you are using them—Aldus PageMaker and Ventura Publisher, for example. The use of these programs can be slowed to a crawl if you have a slow hard disk. The Speed Disk command can have some beneficial productivity advantages when you use it periodically.

Speed Disk physically rearranges the files on your disk. You can use Speed Disk periodically to eliminate any file fragmentation that may have accumulated by repeated use of your disk, particularly a hard disk. You also can run Speed Disk whenever you notice that your disk has been slower than usual. The version of Speed Disk in Norton Version 6 is significantly faster than the Speed Disk programs in earlier versions of Norton Utilities.

Because of the drastic reorganization of your disk that occurs, you should take some precautions. First of all, make sure that no memory-resident programs are running. (You can use the System Information command to check this out.) Some programs may be accessing particular places on disk that will be moved by the disk reorganization. If you have a complicated AUTOEXEC.BAT file that loads several programs into memory, you may want to boot from a floppy diskette that contains only DOS and the Speed Disk program. This way, you ensure that no memory-resident programs are being used.

Second, although the Speed Disk command generally is safe, having a backup of your hard disk always is advisable before you do anything that alters your disk significantly.

Before running the Speed Disk command, another task you can do to help speed up your disk is to get rid of unnecessary files, such as un-needed backup (BAK) files. The fuller your disk is, the greater the likelihood of disk fragmentation. One way to eliminate unneeded files is to use the WipeInfo command in "nonwiping" or DOS ERASE mode across directories (use the /N switch). For example, if you want to erase all BAK files on disk, use the command

WIPEINFO C:*.BAK /N/S

The /N switch tells the command to erase files like a DOS ERASE command does, and the /S command tells the command to search for all files (in all subdirectories) that match the *.BAK specification. Because your initial search is in the root directory, this command erases all *.BAK files on disk.

Using Speed Disk's Recommendations.

Although there are a number of choices you can make when using the Speed Disk program, the easiest way to use the program is to enable it to make a recommendation about how to optimize your disk and then follow that recommendation. The following sections tell you how to use Speed Disk, how to follow its recommendations, and how to choose options to optimize your disk.

You can begin the Speed Disk program by choosing it from the Norton menu or by entering the command SPEEDISK at the DOS prompt. When you begin the Speed Disk program, the program reads information from system memory. You then see a screen like the one in figure 5.25. The drives that appear on your screen may be different, according to what drives you have available on your computer.

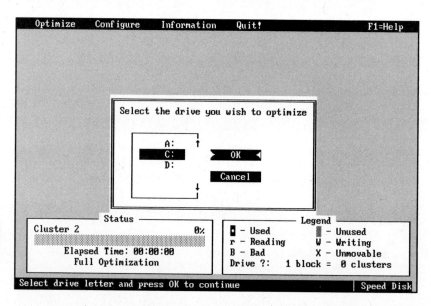

FIG. 5.25.

Choosing the disk drive to optimize.

From this box, you may choose which disk to optimize. Highlight the drive name of the disk you want to optimize and press Enter or point to the drive with your mouse and double-click.

After you choose the drive to optimize, Speed Disk analyzes the information on the drive and produces a Recommendation dialog box (see fig. 5.26). This box contains a recommended course of action. On this screen, for example, the Unfragment Files Only Optimization is recommended. To accept this recommendation, press Enter to choose the

Optimize option. To manually choose another optimization method, choose Configure. To end the program, press Esc.

FIG. 5.26.

The Speed Disk Recommenda-tion dialog box.

After you choose to accept the recommended optimization method, the optimization begins immediately. Once optimization has begun, do not turn off your computer. If you need to stop the program, press Esc.

> **T I P**
>
> If you have never optimized your disk, it is likely that full optimiza-tion will be recommended the first time you use Speed Disk. This method is the most thorough, and takes the longest time—maybe an hour, depending on your hard disk size. After you have fully optimized your disk, you may want to use the recommended approach on a weekly basis. Subsequent recommended optimiza-tion methods may be one of the faster approaches that takes only a few minutes.

The various optimization methods are described in table 5.3. If you want to manually choose one of these optimization methods or you want to choose other Speed Disk options, use the pull-down menus on the menu bar, as described in subsequent sections.

Table 5.3 Speed Disk Optimization Methods

Method	Effect
Full Optimization	Optimizes your disk by unfragmenting all files. It does not reorder your directories, however. It will reorder files if you have specified which files should go first. When finished, there are no holes in the directory structure.
Full with DIRs First	Moves directories to the front of the disk space, making their access faster. Also does everything the Full method does. This method offers the best overall gain in performance.
Full with File Reorder	Reorders files by directory, and does everything the Full method does. Files associated with directories that are placed first are also placed first in the file list. This method takes the longest amount of time to run.
Unfragment Files Only	Attempts to unfragment as many files as possible without removing all of the holes in the directory as with the Full method. This is a fast sort, and Norton recommends that you run this about twice a week.
Unfragment Free Space	Moves data forward on the disk to fill in any free space. It does not unfragment any files. This method may not provide significant speed for old files, but it provides space for new files to be stored as unfragmented files.

Manually Choosing Speed Disk Options

When you begin the Speed Disk program, you may want to choose not to accept the recommended optimization method. If this is the case, choose the Configure option from the Recommendation dialog box. This places you in the pull-down menu mode. The pull-down menus enable you to manually specify Speed Disk options. The menu bar choices are Optimize, Configure, Information, and Quit!. Use the right- and left-arrow keys to highlight the menu you want and press Enter. Alternatively, point to the menu with the mouse pointer and click. This extends the pull-down menu so that you can choose an option from the menu.

Using the Speed Disk Optimize Menu

The Speed Disk Optimize menu is shown in figure 5.27.

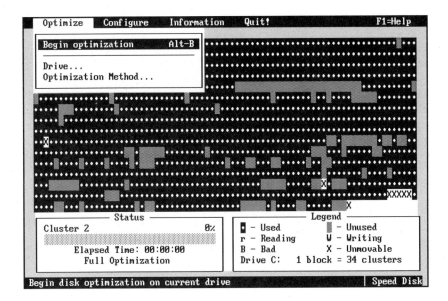

FIG. 5.27.

The Optimize
menu.

The options on the Optimize menu follow:

Option	Effect
Begin Optimization	Begins the optimization process. Before choosing this item, set all options on the other menus to your choice. Notice that you also can press Alt-B to begin optimization, even if you are not in this menu.
Drive	Enables you to choose which drive to optimize.
Optimization Method	Brings up the Select Optimization Method menu (see fig. 5.28). From this menu, you can choose which of the five optimization methods to use (see table 5.3). Use the up- and down-arrow keys to highlight the radio button of the method you want and press the space bar to select the option. Press Enter to lock in the option or Esc to cancel this menu.

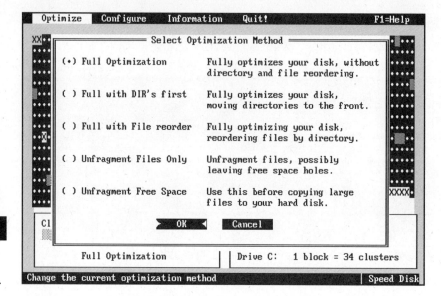

The Select
Optimization
Method screen.

Using the Speed Disk Configure Menu

The Configure menu enables you to choose options concerning
how files and directories are ordered in the optimization process
(see fig. 5.29).

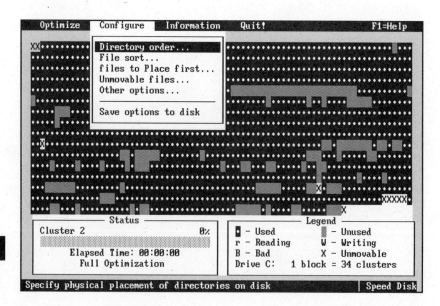

The Configure
menu.

The options in this menu follow:

> Directory Order
> File Sort
> Files To Place First
> Unmovable Files
> Other Options
> Save Options to Disk

The following sections describe these options.

Changing Directory Order

The Directory Order option accesses the Select Directory Order screen, which enables you to specify the order in which directories are placed on the disk (see fig. 5.30). The directories at the beginning of the disk will have the fastest access time. The order Speed Disk uses by default is the order you specified in your PATH statement, which usually is found in your AUTOEXEC.BAT file. The Directory Order box contains the list of directories that are ordered on your disk during optimization.

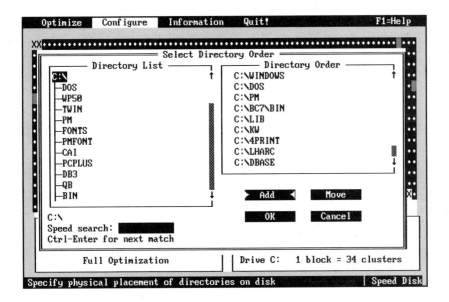

FIG. 5.30.

The Select Directory Order screen.

To specify a customized directory order, you can perform any of the following three actions:

- Move the files already in the list to new locations in the list.

- Add new directories to the Directory Order list.

- Delete directories from the Directory Order list.

To move a name in the Directory Order list, follow these steps:

1. If your cursor is not in the Directory Order box, press Tab to move it there.

2. Use your arrow keys or mouse to point to a directory name in the Directory Order list (not the Directory list). Press M or the space bar, or double-click the mouse button to select the directory name to move.

3. Using the up- and down-arrow keys, move the directory name to its new place in the list. Anchor the directory name in the list by pressing Enter (or double-clicking again).

If you have no more changes to make, use the right- and left-arrow keys to highlight the OK option and press Enter.

To add a new name to the Directory Order list, you must copy the name of a directory from the Directory List box on the left side of the screen to the Directory Order box on the right side of the screen. You move between the right and left sides by pressing the Tab key.

To add a directory to the Directory Order box, perform these steps:

1. If your cursor is not in the Directory List box, press the Tab key to place it there.

2. In the Directory List box, highlight the directory you want by using the up- and down-arrow keys.

3. Press Enter to add the selected directory to the end of the list in the Directory Order box. (Alternatively, double-click the mouse button.)

4. If you want to move the directory name to another location in the list, see the preceding steps on moving a directory.

To add other directories, repeat this procedure. If you have no more changes to make, use the right- and left-arrow keys to highlight the OK option and press Enter.

If you often change the files in a directory, you may not want this directory in the Directory Order box. To delete a directory from the Directory Order box, follow these steps:

1. Use the Tab key to place your cursor in the Directory Order box.

2. In the Directory Order box, highlight the directory name to delete, or point to it with the mouse pointer.

3. Use the right- and left-arrow keys to highlight the Delete option in the lower right corner of the screen. (When the cursor is in the Directory Order list box, the Add option changes to Delete.) Then press Enter or double-click with the mouse. (This step does not delete the directory from the disk.)

To delete additional directories, repeat this procedure. If you have no more changes to make, use the right- and left-arrow keys to highlight the OK option and then press Enter (or point to OK with the mouse pointer and click).

Selecting File Sort

The File Sort option enables you to specify how files are sorted within directories (see fig. 5.31). Choose Sort Criterion and Sort Order options from the File Sort box. A benefit to sorting files is that this reorganizes file names so that you can find the files quickly in a directory of names. When you create a file, DOS locates an empty spot in the disk directory and places the name and information about that file in the directory.

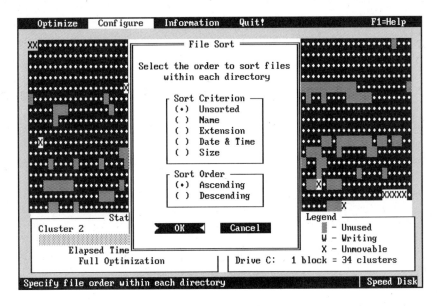

FIG. 5.31.

The File Sort box.

Usually, but not always, files in the directory are listed in the order in which they were created. Sorting enables you to place these files in the order that you choose. This feature can help you find certain files faster and determine easily which files are smallest or largest, which files were created last or first, and so on.

Placing Files First

Files placed at the beginning of the disk are accessed faster than those placed later on the disk. Therefore, you may want to place your most commonly used files at the beginning of the disk. Usually, this includes program files—files with the EXE or COM extension. Figure 5.32 shows the Files To Place First box, where you can place the file specifications for those files that you want to place at the beginning of the disk during optimization.

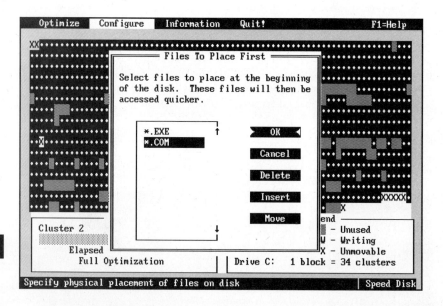

FIG. 5.32.

The Files To
Place First box.

To add a new file to the end of the list, use the up- and down-arrow keys to move the highlight to a blank line and enter a new file specification. You can use the global file characters ? and * in your filespec. To insert a new file within the list, move the cursor to a filespec and choose the Insert option from the Files To Place First box. Insert adds a blank line above the highlighted filespec so that you can enter a new filespec.

To move a file specification, highlight the filespec you want to move, and then press Tab until the cursor is on the Move option. (Alternatively, point with a mouse to Move and click). Then move the filespec up or down by using the arrow keys or by dragging it with the mouse.

To delete a file from the list, highlight the filespec and then choose Delete from the Files To Place First box.

Selecting Unmovable Files

Unmovable files will not be physically moved on disk during an optimization. Speed Disk will analyze your disk and mark all hidden files and files related to copy-protection schemes as unmovable. However, if you have other files that are not recognized by Norton as needing to remain unmovable, you can specify the file names manually in the Unmovable Files box (see fig. 5.33). Other files that should not be used are those used in copy-protection schemes. This type of file is becoming rarer, but if you have a copy-protected program, you may want to specify any files used in the protection scheme as unmovable.

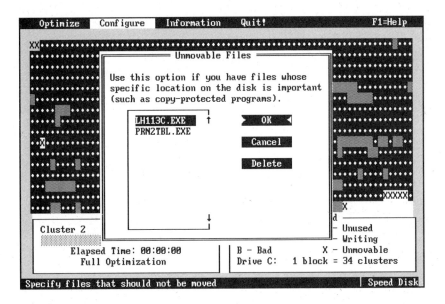

FIG. 5.33.

The Unmovable Files box.

To add a new file to this list, press the down arrow to go to a blank line and enter the new name. To delete a file from the Unmovable Files box, highlight the file name and choose Delete.

Selecting Other Options

The Other Options box from the Configure menu brings up the screen shown in figure 5.34. The Read-after-Write option causes Speed Disk to verify that information moved to different locations on the disk during optimization matches the original information. You also can choose the Clear Unused Space option. This option blanks out unused file space on disk so that old file information cannot be recovered from the disk. Use Clear Unused Space if you need to protect your old data from discovery by others. The Beep when Done option causes a beep to sound when the optimization is complete.

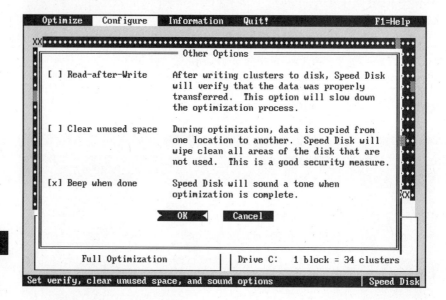

FIG. 5.34.

The Other Options box.

Saving Options to Disk

After you select options from the various Configure menu items, you can save your selections to disk by choosing Save Options to Disk from the Configure menu. Then, when you begin Speed Disk again, these options will still be in effect.

Using the Speed Disk Information Menu

The Speed Disk Information menu enables you to look at a number of pieces of information related to how your disk is optimized. The Information menu is shown in figure 5.35.

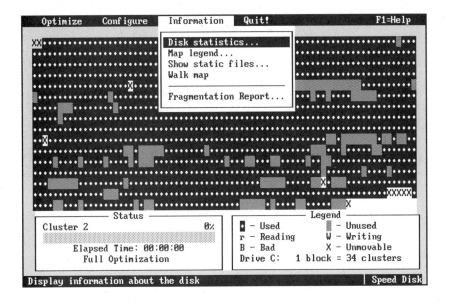

FIG. 5.35.

The Information menu.

The Disk Statistics option gives you information on the disk about to be optimized (see fig. 5.36). The most important information on the Disk Statistics for Drive C: screen is the Percentage of Unfragmented Files field. If this number is 95 percent or more, you have little fragmentation. If the number is about 90 percent, you probably should perform an optimization. If it is under 90 percent, you need a full optimization.

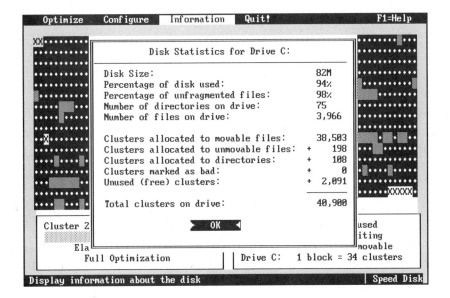

FIG. 5.36.

The Speed Disk statistics screen.

The Map Legend option gives you a key for the symbols used on the disk map in view during the optimization (see fig. 5.37).

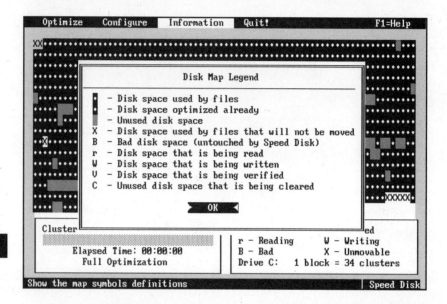

The Disk Map Legend screen.

The Show Static Files option gives you a list of files that the program has determined should not be moved (see fig. 5.38).

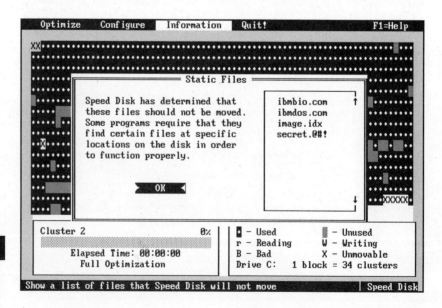

The Static Files box.

The Walk Map option displays the disk map and enables you to use the arrow keys to highlight blocks on the map. When you highlight a block, a cluster range is displayed. If you want to know where a bad block is located on disk, for example, you can use the Walk Map option to determine the location of the bad cluster. You may want to examine this cluster by using Disk Editor.

The Fragmentation Report option enables you to examine the amount of fragmentation of individual files (see fig. 5.39). In this figure, the left side of the screen is a directory tree. The NC directory is highlighted, which causes the files for that directory to appear in the list box on the right side of the screen. Notice that eight files have dots in front of their names. These files are fragmented. The percent of fragmentation is listed under the % column. Files that have 100% listed are completely unfragmented. Any file with 90% or less is considered highly fragmented. The lower this number, the more fragmentation of the file there is.

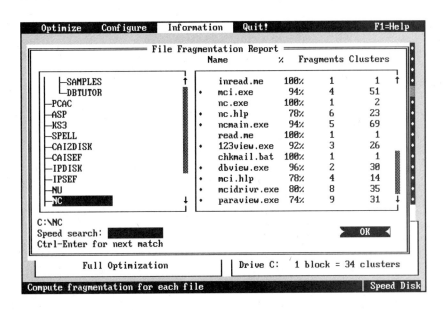

FIG. 5.39.

The File Fragmentation Report box.

Using Speed Disk from the DOS Prompt

You can use the Speed Disk command from the DOS prompt to bypass the menu interface by using the following syntax:

SPEEDISK [*d:*][*switches*]

The available *switches* for the SD command follow:

Switch	Effect
/B	Reboots after the command finishes.
/F	Performs a full optimization of the disk.
/FD	Performs a full optimization with directories first.
/FF	Performs a full optimization with file reorder.
/Q	Performs a quick compress optimization.
/SD[-]	Sorts files by date. If the minus (-) parameter is included, the sort will be from latest to oldest.
/SE[-]	Sorts files by extension. If the minus (-) parameter is included, the sort will be in descending alphabetical order.
/SN[-]	Sorts by file name. If the minus (-) parameter is included, the sort will be in descending alphabetical order.
/SS[-]	Sorts by file size. If the minus (-) parameter is included, the sort will be from largest to smallest.
/U	Attempts to unfragment as many files as possible without moving parts of the directory structure. Some damaged files may not get unfragmented.
/V	Uses verify-after-write data verification.

To perform an optimization of the directories in drive C, for example, you enter the command

    SPEEDISK C:/D

The directory optimization takes place automatically. When optimization is finished, you will be in the Configure menu. Press Esc to return to the DOS prompt. If you include the /B switch, your computer reboots after the optimization finishes. The Speed disk program cannot be used on a network drive.

Using Calibrate

You use the Calibrate command to optimize the speed and reliability of reading and writing information to and from your hard disk. In order for Calibrate to know how to optimize your hard disk, it runs a series of tests to determine some of the logical and physical characteristics of your hard disk. Calibrate is specifically for use on your hard disk. It is not intended to work on floppy disks, network disks, RAM disks, assigned disks (DOS ASSIGN command), or substitute disks (DOS SUBST command).

There are two reasons to use the Calibrate command. First, you use it to check your interleave factor (described later) to see if your disk is working efficiently. You need to test the disk only once. Next, if your hard disk is beginning to give intermittent errors when reading and writing files, you need to run Calibrate to evaluate and solve the problem. Norton recommends that you run Calibrate every three months to test your hard disk for problems.

Calibrate can improve the speed at which data is read from your hard disk by adjusting the disk's interleave factor. The interleave factor has to do with the way DOS reads and writes information from your hard disk. Because the hard disk is spinning at a rapid speed, the read/write head cannot always get information off the disk in one long stream. Often, information is read and written from the disk in 512K spurts of information (a sector). As the head is reading information from the disk, for example, it may read one 512K sector, then skip the next sector on the disk while the first sector of information is being sent to the computer, then read the next sector, skip the next, read the next, and so on.

The number of sectors skipped between reads is called the *interleave factor*. In this example, the interleave factor is 2 (sometimes called 2:1). Each hard disk has an optimum interleave factor—one that makes reading information from the hard disk as fast as possible. Some hard disks, however, may have been formatted at a less than optimum interleave factor. If your hard disk is running at a less than optimum interleave factor, the Calibrate command can adjust your disk to make it work faster.

Calibrate adjusts your interleave factor by performing a low-level format. This kind of format does not destroy the data on your disk. It simply adjusts how the information is stored on disk, and tests the reliability of information storage on the disk. A *low-level format*, unlike the normal high-level format (FORMAT command) of a hard disk actually reads and writes information to every area of the disk to verify its viability to store magnetic information. A high-level format does not do this kind of thorough testing of the disk.

There are some disks on which Calibrate cannot adjust the interleave factor; in other words, it cannot perform a low-level format. In this case, it still can perform some valuable tests, but will not be able to adjust the interleave. When you run the Calibrate program, it informs you if you have a hard disk that cannot be adjusted. Some of the disk types on which Calibrate cannot adjust the interleave include the following:

Drives with SCSI or IDE-type controllers
Drives that are not 100-percent IBM compatible
Drives with controllers that perform a sector translation
Drives with on-board disk caching
Iomega Bernoulli Box drives
Novell file servers
Any hard disk with a sector size other than 512K

In addition to the optimization of the speed of your hard disk, Calibrate can perform some tests to improve the reliability of information reading and writing to your hard disk. Calibrate can test each byte of your hard disk for reliability and will move any data that is in danger to a reliable portion of the disk.

Before you run Calibrate the first time, you should back up your hard disk. Although Calibrate is safe and reliable, you may run into problems on drives that are not 100-percent IBM compatible. After you run Calibrate on your computer and verify that your disks are compatible, you no longer need to back up each time you use the program.

Also, before you run Calibrate, you should remove all TSR programs from memory and have only essential device drivers (in your CONFIG.SYS file) in use when you use the Calibrate command. Many times, the easiest way to do this is to boot with your original DOS floppy disk in drive A.

You can run the Calibrate command by choosing it from the Norton menu or by entering the command CALIBRAT at the DOS prompt. If you run Calibrate without any switches, you see an opening screen like the one in figure 5.40. This Calibrate screen gives you a brief description of what Calibrate is about to do. The easiest way to use the program from this point simply is to continue to follow the directions on-screen, which lead you through a standard Calibrate session.

If you have more than one hard disk, Calibrate prompts you to choose which hard disk to analyze. If you have only one hard disk, you are not prompted; you go directly to the next screen. This screen lists the preliminary tests that will be performed on your hard disk (see fig. 5.41). These preliminary tests tell Calibrate what it needs to know about the logical and physical characteristics of your disk. Select the Continue option from this screen to go to the next screen.

Interpreting the System Integrity Test

When you continue to the System Integrity Testing screen, the System Integrity test begins (see fig. 5.42). As each test is progressing, a blinking dot appears to the left of the test name. When the test is finished, a check appears beside the name. If the tests determine that your disk is one in which the interleave cannot be adjusted, you see a warning screen like the one in figure 5.43. You still can continue with the other valuable tests, but the interleave options will be skipped.

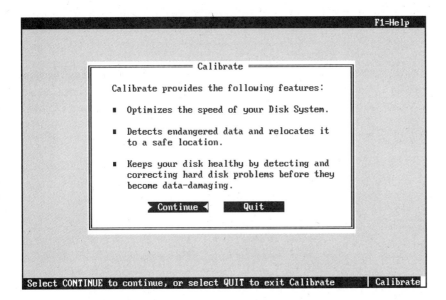

FIG. 5.40.

The Calibrate screen.

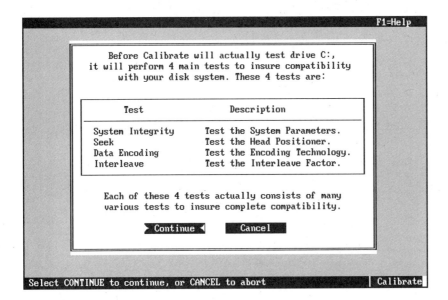

FIG. 5.41.

The Calibrate list of tests to be performed.

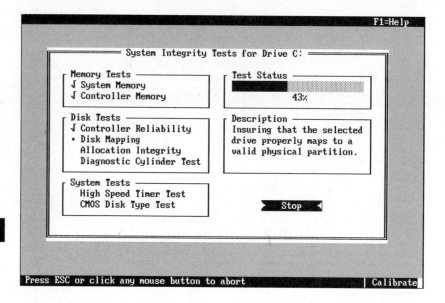

FIG. 5.42.

The System Integrity Testing screen.

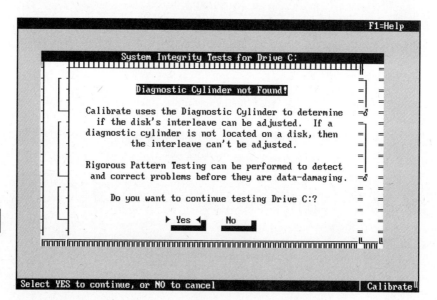

FIG. 5.43.

Calibrate warns you if it is unable to adjust the interleaving.

Interpreting the Interleave Test

If calibration is possible, Calibrate tests your disk using a number of possible interleaves. This takes several minutes. When this test finishes, a screen like the one in figure 5.44 appears. This screen is a graphic representation of the results of the Interleave test. Your disk will work optimally at the interleave that is lowest on the graph. This interleave number is designated with the caption *Optimal* on the graph. Your current interleave also will be captioned.

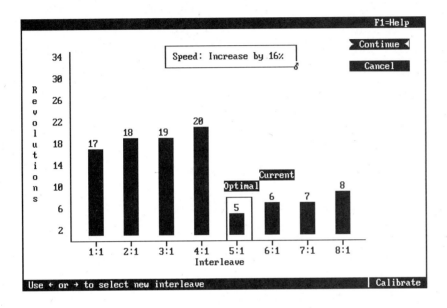

FIG. 5.44.

A Calibrate screen display-ing the results of the interleave test.

Notice the box around the optimal bar (5:1) on the graph in figure 5.44. This box indicates that the interleave will be set to the 5:1 setting dur-ing pattern testing. Also note at the top of the screen the message `Increase by 16%`. This means that if the interleave is changed to 5:1, you will get this kind of increase in the access to your hard disk. If you do not want to reset your interleave to the setting indicated by the box, you can use your right- and left-arrow keys to move the box to another setting. Choose Continue to continue with the program or Cancel to end Calibrate.

Interpreting the Seek Tests

If you continue with the calibration tests, you see the Seek Test screen (see fig. 5.45). This test examines how fast your read/write head on your hard disk can seek out information on your disk. As the tests are in progress, the movement of the head is animated on-screen, moving back and forth on the picture of the drive in the middle of the screen. Seek performs four tests. The Value column gives you the time it takes to perform these four tasks (in milliseconds).

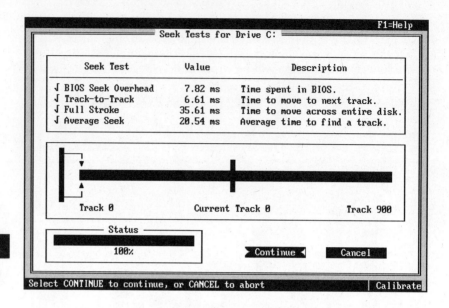

FIG. 5.45.

The Seek Tests
screen.

The four tests that the Seek test performs follow:

Test	Result
BIOS Seek Overhead	Tests the time spent getting ready to read information from the disk.
Track-to-Track	Tests how long it takes the head to move to the next track on disk.
Full Stroke	Measures how long it takes to move from one track to another track on the other side of the disk.
Average Seek	Determines how long, on the average, it takes to find and read information from the disk. The Average Seek is the number you most often see quoted in advertisements for hard disks. A fast disk will have an average seek time of less than 20ms. A slow hard disk will have an average seek of from 60ms to 80ms. If you are using disk-intensive application programs on your computer, the average seek time can be a major factor in how efficiently your computer works.

When you begin the Calibrate command from the DOS prompt, you can cause it to skip the Seek test by using the option /NOSEEK in the command line.

Interpreting the Data Encoding Test

The Calibrate Data Encoding Tests screen, shown in figure 5.46, appears when you choose the Continue option from the Seek Test screen. This test analyzes the physical characteristics of the hard disk. The information is useful so that the Calibrate program can do further testing, and may be of interest to a technician who is examining a hard disk for problems.

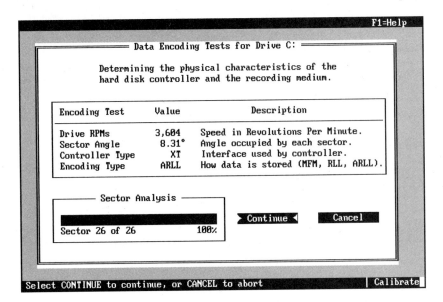

```
                                                              F1=Help
  ┌────────────────────────────────────────────────────────────────┐
  │  ┌════════════ Data Encoding Tests for Drive C: ════════════┐    │
  │  │                                                          │    │
  │  │     Determining the physical characteristics of the      │    │
  │  │     hard disk controller and the recording medium.       │    │
  │  │                                                          │    │
  │  │   ┌────────────────────────────────────────────────┐     │    │
  │  │   │ Encoding Test    Value         Description       │     │    │
  │  │   │                                                  │     │    │
  │  │   │ Drive RPMs       3,604   Speed in Revolutions Per Minute. │   │
  │  │   │ Sector Angle     8.31°   Angle occupied by each sector.   │   │
  │  │   │ Controller Type    XT    Interface used by controller.    │   │
  │  │   │ Encoding Type    ARLL    How data is stored (MFM, RLL, ARLL). │ │
  │  │   └────────────────────────────────────────────────┘     │    │
  │  │                                                          │    │
  │  │      ┌── Sector Analysis ──┐                              │    │
  │  │      │ ████████████████████ │  ► Continue ◄   Cancel     │    │
  │  │      │ Sector 26 of 26  100%│                            │    │
  │  │      └─────────────────────┘                             │    │
  │  └──────────────────────────────────────────────────────────┘    │
  │  Select CONTINUE to continue, or CANCEL to abort    │ Calibrate  │
  └────────────────────────────────────────────────────────────────┘
```

FIG. 5.46.

The Data Encoding Tests screen.

Interpreting the Pattern Testing

When you choose Continue from the Data Encoding screen, the Pattern Testing screen appears (see fig. 5.47). You use calibrate pattern testing to test your hard disk for defects. You can choose the thoroughness of this test on the Pattern Testing screen. The options run from No Pattern Testing to Rigorous Pattern Testing. The higher the level of testing, the more time is required. The No Pattern Testing option may take 5 to 10 minutes, and the Rigorous Pattern Testing option may last overnight, depending on the size of your hard disk.

You use pattern testing to test the disk for its read/write capabilities. A pattern of magnetic signals, such as 101010101, is written to the disk and then read back. Pattern testing uses the alternating 1 and 0 pattern, which is the most difficult pattern to read. If you did not receive a warning that Calibrate could not perform a low-level format, then the pattern testing also performs a low-level format as it tests the disk. This is a non-destructive, safe format (not like a regular format that clears information from the disk).

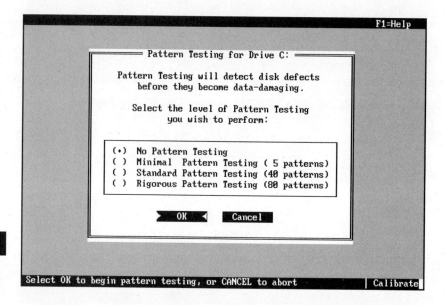

FIG. 5.47.

The Pattern
Testing screen.

Use the No Pattern Testing option if you indicated a new interleave factor in the previous Interleave test. This option is the quickest way to update your interleave factor. Use one of the other pattern-testing options if you have had some problems with your disk, such as losing information or files becoming unreadable.

When the pattern test begins, you see a disk map similar to the Speed Disk map that shows the progress of the test. You can interrupt the test safely by pressing Esc. If you stop the pattern-testing/low-level format in the middle of its run, Calibrate takes up where it left off when you begin it again.

Because pattern testing can take some time, Norton has a built-in screen-blanking routine which enables you to blank your screen so that the image will not become burned into your screen. During the pattern testing, press the space bar to blank the screen. While the screen is blank, a floating message appears occasionally to tell you that the testing is still in progress. Press the space bar again to bring the screen back.

Interpreting the Calibrate Report

After all of the Calibrate tests are complete, you see a report screen like the one in figure 5.48. This report summarizes all of the findings of the Calibrate tests. Notice that the report is in a box, so you can use the up- and down-arrow keys to view parts of the report not shown on-screen. It is a good idea to choose the Print option on the report screen so that you can keep a folder of these reports about your hard disk. These may become important if a technician needs to diagnose problems with your disk in the future. Optionally, you can choose the Save As option to save the report to a file. Choosing Done ends the report screen and returns you to the beginning of the Calibrate program, which displays an option screen for you to choose which disk to test. If you do not want to do further testing, press Esc to return to DOS or to the Norton menu.

Using the Calibrate Command from the DOS Prompt

If you begin the Calibrate command from the DOS prompt, you have several switches that you can choose. The syntax of the Calibrate command is

CALIBRAT [*d:*] [*switches*]

The available *switches* for the Calibrate command follow:

Switch	Effect
/BATCH	Does not prompt for any input from the user; returns to DOS when finished. This automates the entire test procedure. If you choose this option, you probably will want to choose one of the /R options as well to create a report of the test findings.
/BLANK	Blanks the screen while performing the tests.
/NOCOPY	Does not make a duplicate copy of the track being tested.
/NOFORMAT	Performs pattern testing only and skips the low-level format.

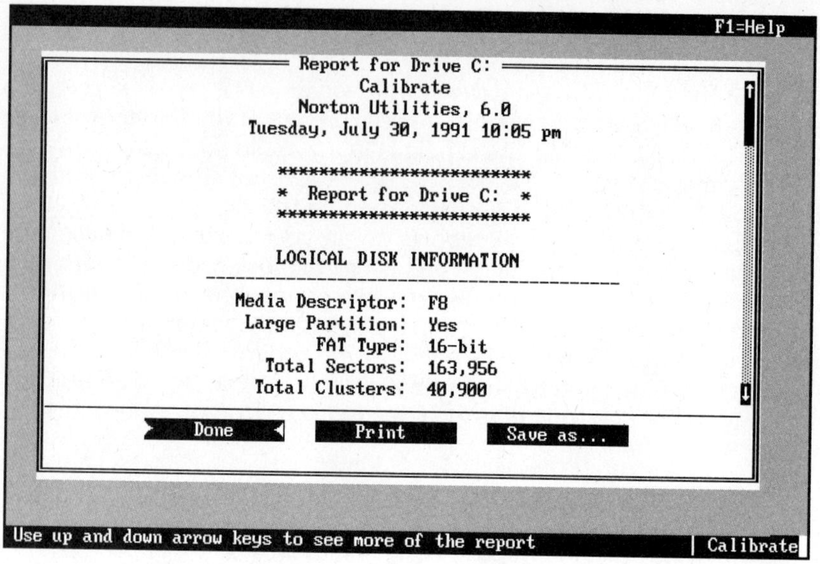

```
                                                          F1=Help
┌──────────────────────────────────────────────────────┐
│         ══════ Report for Drive C: ══════         ▲  │
│                    Calibrate                         │
│               Norton Utilities, 6.0                  │
│          Tuesday, July 30, 1991 10:05 pm             │
│                                                      │
│         ****************************                 │
│         *   Report for Drive C:  *                  │
│         ****************************                 │
│                                                      │
│         LOGICAL DISK INFORMATION                    │
│         ─────────────────────────────────────       │
│           Media Descriptor:  F8                     │
│            Large Partition:  Yes                    │
│                  FAT Type:   16-bit                 │
│              Total Sectors:  163,956                │
│             Total Clusters:  40,900            ▼    │
│  ┌──────────┐   ┌──────────┐   ┌──────────────┐    │
│  │   Done   ◄│   │  Print   │   │  Save as...  │    │
│  └──────────┘   └──────────┘   └──────────────┘    │
└──────────────────────────────────────────────────────┘
 Use up and down arrow keys to see more of the report    │ Calibrate
```

FIG. 5.48.

The Calibrate
report screen.

Switch	Effect
/NOSEEK	Skips the seek tests. Use this when you do not want Calibrate to test the head-positioning mechanism of the disk. Usually, you need to use Calibrate once without this switch to test the mechanism. Thereafter, use this switch.
/PATTERN:*n*	Tells Calibrate which testing level (*n*) to use. The parameter *n* can be 0, 5, 40, or 80. The higher the number, the more thorough the test, but the longer Calibrate takes to test the disk.
/R:*file*	Generates a report and writes it to the file name specified in the switch. You also must use the /BATCH switch when you use this option.
/RA:*file*	This switch is the same as the /R:*file* switch, but the information is appended to the file rather than becoming a new file.
/X:*drives*	Excludes named drives from the test. /X:DE, for example, would exclude disks D and E from testing.

Using Norton Disk Cache

The flow of information from the disk into a computer program is often the source of an information bottleneck. Although you can access information in the computer's RAM almost instantaneously, getting information from a disk can be very, very slow by comparison. If you are using disk-intensive programs, slow disk access can bring your program speed down to a crawl.

A solution to slow disk access is for the computer to read more information from the disk than is needed and place the extra information into RAM memory—hoping that the next piece of information requested by the program will then be in RAM and therefore accessed faster. Figure 5.49 shows how the information is read from the disk and stored in a buffer, waiting for the program to request the information. The disk buffer is called a *cache*.

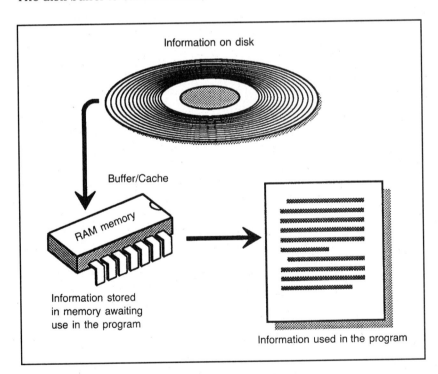

Information on disk

Buffer/Cache

RAM memory

Information stored
in memory awaiting
use in the program

Information used in the program

FIG. 5.49.

How caching
works.

If your computer has 1M of memory, for example, and your software programs can access only 640K of that memory at any one time, then you have extra memory that you can use as a disk cache. The more extra memory you can use as a disk cache, the more potential speed you can experience in disk access.

Extra memory is any memory above what your programs normally need. This can be regular DOS memory, which goes up to 640K. If all of your programs in memory (including DOS) use only 320K, then you have some extra memory that you can use as a cache. Other kinds of extra memory are extended and expanded memory. *Extended memory* is memory above 1M. *Expanded memory* is add-on memory that can be accessed by certain programs that subscribe to a special way to use memory developed by Lotus, Microsoft, Intel, and AST companies (LIM standard).

A disk cache can provide speed and extend battery life in laptop computers (by making the laptop use the motor on the hard disk less), as well as give your programs an enormous boot in speed. For comparison, reading information from a floppy disk can take around 200ms, while reading information from a hard disk can take 18ms to 80ms. Getting information from RAM takes less than 1ms.

The Norton NCACHE program does more than just create an information buffer. By using two features—IntelliWrites and SmartReads—NCACHE tries to guess which data you will read or write from the disk next in order to make the cache contain the information you are most likely to need. NCACHE does this by analyzing the pattern of past disk access to predict future disk access.

Beginning NCACHE from CONFIG.SYS or AUTOEXEC.BAT

You can use the NCACHE program in one of two ways. You can include the program as a line in your AUTOEXEC.BAT file, or you can include the program as a device driver in your CONFIG.SYS file. If you requested that the NCACHE program be installed in the Norton Install program, it was installed as a device driver in your CONFIG.SYS file. The benefit of installing NCACHE in your AUTOEXEC.BAT file is that if you installed it as the last TSR program, you can uninstall it from memory if you need to use the memory to run a large program. The advantage of placing the command in your CONFIG.SYS file is that it will have compatibility with more computers when used in this way.

In order to use NCACHE, your computer must be using DOS 3.0 or higher and have 256K of conventional (RAM) memory or more. However, NCACHE is not recommended unless you have some extended memory or you are using NCACHE on a laptop to help prevent excessive use of the hard disk.

To place the NCACHE program in your AUTOEXEC.BAT file, you can use the following syntax:

> *path*\\NCACHE [*parameters*]

Path refers to the directory name where the NCACHE file is stored. To place the program in your CONFIG.SYS file, you can use the following syntax:

> DEVICE=*path*\\NCACHE [*parameters*]

Either of these commands causes the disk cache to be in effect when you boot your computer. (Do not use both commands—use one or the other.) As with the AUTOEXEC.BAT file, you can enter this command from the DOS prompt at any time to begin or end the NCACHE program, using the parameters described later.

A wide variety of optional parameters is explained later in this chapter. You usually can use NCACHE with most default conditions on many computers. You should have to refer to the parameters only if you are having problems getting your cache to work correctly. Some ways in which you can use NCACHE follow. The commands listed are what you place in your AUTOEXEC.BAT file, although you can do the same thing by placing DEVICE= in front of the command and placing it in your CONFIG.SYS file.

The following command is used on an IBM PS/2 Model 30/286 computer (80286). Because programs used on this computer never use above 640K, the NCACHE is set to use 304K of the memory as a cache. The NCACHE program is in the \\NU directory

> \\NU\\NCACHE /INSTALL

The INSTALL parameter causes the NCACHE program to be installed using a default cache size which is equal to all available expanded memory plus all available extended memory. If you do not have any extended or expanded memory, the INSTALL option causes 128K of memory to be allocated to cache. After you enter this command, you see a screen like the one in figure 5.50. Notice that 304K is assigned as cache memory.

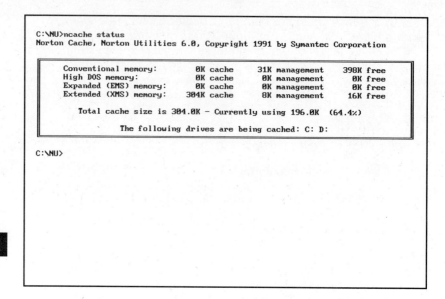

```
C:\NU>ncache status
Norton Cache, Norton Utilities 6.0, Copyright 1991 by Symantec Corporation

┌─────────────────────────────────────────────────────────────────────┐
│    Conventional memory:        0K cache    31K management    398K free│
│    High DOS memory:            0K cache     0K management      0K free│
│    Expanded (EMS) memory:      0K cache     0K management      0K free│
│    Extended (XMS) memory:    304K cache     8K management     16K free│
│                                                                       │
│       Total cache size is 304.0K - Currently using 196.0K  (64.4%)    │
│                                                                       │
│         The following drives are being cached: C: D:                  │
└─────────────────────────────────────────────────────────────────────┘

C:\NU>
```

FIG. 5.50.

The Norton
Cache screen.

You can use the /DOS, /EXT and /EXP options to allocate some other amount of conventional (DOS), extended (EXT) or expanded (EXP) memory for cache. Suppose that you want to create a small cache of 20K conventional memory. You would use the command

\NORTON\NCACHE DOS=20

The examples in this section are typical ways of using the NCACHE program. If you use one of these versions of the command, replace the DOS=20 with the amount of extra DOS memory you are willing to use as a cache. The most common command options you may want to use are the +S and +I options. The +S option enables SmartReads and +I enables Intelliwrites. These options can provide additional speed for some applications such as word processors, spreadsheets, and other programs. These options may not provide additional speed for use with database programs. You may have to experiment with these options to see which combination gives you the best disk access for the type of application programs you run.

Another option that you may use is the USEHIGH=YES option. If you are using an advanced memory manager on your computer such as QEMM or 386-to-the-Max, using this option enables NCACHE to use less of your initial 640K DOS memory, and may provide more memory for use in your application programs. If you need further options to make the program run to your needs, see the additional parameters described in the following section.

Using NCACHE Parameters and Options

A variety of parameters are available to specify how the NCACHE program creates and uses a disk buffer. The parameters available for both versions of NCACHE follow:

Parameter	Effect
[-]I	Enables or disables IntelliWrites. When on, this accelerates disk writes and returns control back to the application before the write is finished.
[-]A	Activates or deactivates caching. Use this if you need to deactivate caching in order to run a program in which you do not want caching to be used.
[-]C	Enables or disables caching of additional information. No new information is cached when this is disabled.
[-]P	Enables or disables write protection for drives.
[-]W	Enables or disables write-through caching. When write-through caching is disabled, writes are written directly to the disk, bypassing the cache.
BLOCK=*n*	Sets the size of the cache blocks. The *n* is a number in kilobytes. Use large blocks if you are accessing large files and your disk is unfragmented. Use smaller blocks if you access small files or if your disk is fragmented. Valid sizes are 512, 1024, 2048, 4096, or 8192 bytes.
DELAY=*ss.hh*	Delays writes to the disk in seconds or hundredths of a second (for example, 00.10 is one hundredth of a second). The default is 00.00. Slight writing delays can improve the speed of write-intensive programs.
DOS=*n* or DOS=*-n*	Specifies how much DOS (conventional) memory is to be used by the cache. Use this only when you do not have any expanded or extended memory. f a negative value is used, it means to leave that much memory free for other programs to use.
EXP=*n* or EXP=*-n*	Specifies how much expanded memory in kilobytes is to be used by the cache. If a negative value is used, it means to leave that much memory free for other programs to use.
	EXP=750, for example, means to use 750K of expanded memory for the disk cache. Any expanded memory used must be LIM 4.0 compatible.

Parameter	Effect
EXT=*n* or EXT=-*n*	Specifies how much extended memory in kilobytes is to be used by the cache. If a negative value is used, it means to leave that much memory free for use by other programs. The *n* is in kilobytes. EXT=256, for example, means to use 256K of extended memory for the cache.
F	Flushes the cache (empties it). This causes all writes to disk to be finished.
G=*n*	Specifies a group sector size (the default is 128). Specify a group size smaller than 128 if you are reading small pieces of information from a random file, such as in a database with small records.
INI=*path*	Tells the command where to look for the file that contains installation options. If your installation options are in your \NORTON directory, for example, you use the parameter INI=\NORTON.
INSTALL	Causes NCACHE to install using all default values. This includes using all available expanded and extended memory for the cache. This switch is often the easiest and quickest way to implement NCACHE.
OPTIMIZE=[S,E,M]	Tells NCACHE to optimize for speed, efficiency or memory.

The S (Speed) option sets the following parameters:

    /BLOCK=8K

    /DELAY=1.0

    /READ=8K

    /WRITE=*x* where *x* is the largest track (in K) of all tracks being cached.

The E (Efficiency) option sets the following parameters:

    /BLOCK=*s* where *s* is the smallest block size for the current cache size (usually 512K to 1M)

    /DELAY=1.0

    /READ=8K

    /WRITE=8K

Parameter	Effect
	The M (Memory) option sets the following parameters: /BLOCK=8K /DELAY=0.0 /READ=0 (disables the read-ahead feature) /WRITE=0 (disables IntelliWrites)
QUICK=ON/OFF	Displays the DOS prompt even when information still is being written to the disk.
R=Dn	Specifies how may sectors ahead it should read. A specification of R=0 or R=D0 disables read-aheads. R=n always causes read-aheads and a specification of R=Dn causes read-aheads only when the file being read is not a random file. The number of sectors that can be specified is from 0 to 15.
READ=n	Sets the maximum size for read-aheads. Use sizes of 8K to 64K in 1K-increments.
REPORT=[ON,OFF]	Tells command whether to display status information.
RESET	Resets the cache statistics, which are viewable on the NCACHE status screen.
SAVE	Saves current cache settings in the file specified by the /INI switch (or NCACHE.INI).
STATUS	Displays a number of statistics showing you how effectively the cache is working. Figure 5.50, for example, summarizes all of the options you have set.
UNINSTALL	Removes the command from memory. This command will not work unless the NCACHE program was the last memory-resident (TSR) program loaded into memory.
USEHMA=YES/NO	Uses the XMS high-memory area (HMA) to reduce the use of DOS RAM (if set to Yes). This is available only if you have an extended memory manager.
USEHIGH=YES/NO	Minimizes the use of conventional (low) DOS memory, if high memory is available (if set to Yes). The default for this command is No.
WRITE=n	Sets maximum size for IntelliWrites buffer. Use from 8K to 64K in increments of 1K.

Using Batch Files To Simplify NCACHE Options

Because there are so many options in the NCACHE programs, you may consider creating a few batch files to issue versions of the command that you use often. You can place the line

NCACHE /UNINSTALL

in a batch file called UNI.BAT, for example, and make the uninstall procedure easier. Suppose that you want to deactivate NCACHE during the use of a program. You can place the command

NCACHE -A

in a batch file called DEACTIVE.BAT. Then, to reactivate the command, you can have a batch file called ACTIVE.BAT which contains the command

NCACHE +A

If you use a complicated NCACHE command from the DOS prompt, you can place the command line

NCACHE USEHIGH=YES EXT=920 +S +I

in a file called CACHE.BAT. Then you only have to enter the command CACHE to begin the NCACHE program. Assigning these batch file names to tasks such as these makes working with long commands with difficult-to-remember options much easier.

Chapter Summary

This chapter covered Norton Utilities commands that are useful for getting the most out of your hard disk, including commands that make you knowledgeable about your system (System Information). To keep your disk running at top speed, you need to use the Speed Disk command. You also can use Speed Disk to arrange your files (sort file names) in an order that is convenient and easy for you to use. The Calibrate command enables you to fine-tune your disk access, and the NCACHE programs help you make disk access more efficient. These Norton commands give you much more information about the condition of your disks and the data they hold than the limited DOS disk-analysis commands can provide.

Managing Your Computer's Resources

So far, this book has concentrated on issues of safety and maintenance. This chapter introduces various Norton Utilities commands that make using your computer easier and more fun. The commands covered here include the Norton Control Center (NCC), Norton Change Directory (NCD), and Batch Enhancer (BE).

These commands enable you to navigate around your computer faster and with fewer keystrokes than you can with DOS. With these commands, you can modify some of your computer's environmental settings—such as colors, cursor size, and keyboard rate—and create better batch files.

Using Norton Control Center

With the Norton Control Center (NCC) utility, you can change a number of settings on your computer, such as the size of your cursor, your monitor's colors, the number of lines displayed, and the date and time. The Time Mark (TM) command that you may have used in Norton 4.5 is now in the NCC command for Versions 5.0 and 6.0.

You can use the Norton Control Center in command-line or interactive mode. This chapter first describes interactive mode, and then the options available from the command line.

Using NCC in Interactive Mode

If you enter the command NCC with no quick switches, you enter interactive mode, and the Norton Control Center menu appears (see fig. 6.1).

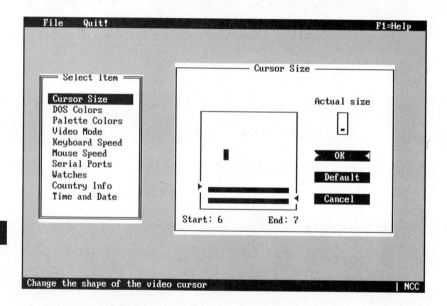

FIG. 6.1.

The Norton Control Center main menu.

Notice the list of items on the left side of the menu. These options represent the settings you can change in the Norton Control Center. The first option, Cursor Size, is highlighted when you enter the NCC command. With the up and down cursor-movement keys or the mouse, you can highlight one of these menu items. Then, when you press Enter or click, the highlight moves to the right side of the screen, where you can find information on the item you want to set. You also can use the right and left cursor-movement keys, Tab, or the mouse to move to the right or left portion of the screen.

After you choose your settings, press F10 to pull down the File menu at the top of the screen. This menu has two options:

Option	Effect
Save Settings	Saves the settings you choose to a file. You must save the settings so that you can activate the settings at any time from the DOS prompt by entering the NCC command with the /SETALL switch. See the command-line options described later.
Load Settings	Loads previously set NCC options that have been saved in a file.

To end the NCC program, choose the Quit! option from the menu bar or press Esc.

Setting Cursor Size

You can see the initial screen for setting cursor size on the right side of the screen in figure 6.1. Notice the two lines at the bottom of the rectangle and the fields labeled Start and End. For this particular video mode, the cursor consists of lines 6 and 7. (In higher resolution modes, you may have as many as 14 cursor lines.) This combination of lines 6 and 7 creates a cursor that looks like a small underline—the normal setting for most computers. For some computers in which the cursor may be hard to find—like on some laptops with hard-to-read displays—you may want to create a bigger cursor.

The possible cursor lines range from 1 to 7. If you want the cursor to be bigger, press the up-arrow key to add more lines. Figure 6.2 shows a selection that makes the cursor appear as a square rather than an underline. (The new version appears in the square in the upper right corner of the screen.)

After you size your cursor, press Enter to select OK and return to the NCC menu, where you can change another setting, or press Esc to end the NCC command.

Setting Monitor Colors

With the DOS Colors option, you can choose color settings for your computer. These settings, however, depend on the kind of monitor you have. Some computers support only a few colors, whereas others support hundreds. If you tire of the black and white you normally see when using DOS, you can use DOS Colors to choose colors that better fit your mood or decor.

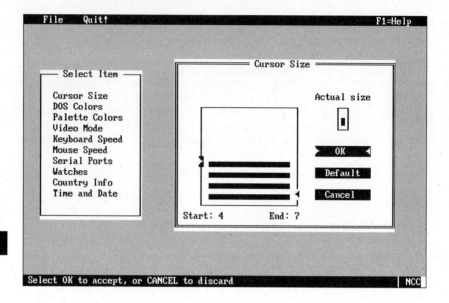

Cursor Size

Select Item

Cursor Size
DOS Colors
Palette Colors
Video Mode
Keyboard Speed
Mouse Speed
Serial Ports
Watches
Country Info
Time and Date

Actual size

OK

Default

Cancel

Start: 4   End: 7

Select OK to accept, or CANCEL to discard   NCC

FIG. 6.2.

Changing
cursor size.

After you choose DOS Colors, a screen similar to figure 6.3 appears.
You have three settings: Text Color, Background, and Border Color.
You can move among these settings by using the cursor-movement
keys. The Text Color box contains examples of how text appears with
various colors. A sample of the currently selected color combination
appears at the lower right of the screen in the message beginning

        This is an example of how...

The list contains white on black, yellow on black, white on blue, red on
blue, and dozens of other color combinations. To choose a color combination, scroll through this list. Arrows on the right and left point to
the color currently chosen.

The Background box contains two options: Blink and Bright. You may
want to use the Blink option to draw a user's attention to an important
screen. You probably would use this option from a batch file by using
the NCC command in command-line mode. See "Using NCC in
Command-Line Mode," later in this chapter.

After you choose the color options you want, choose OK at the bottom
of the box to return to the Select Item menu. If you want to revert to the
default colors, choose Default. If you want to revert to the previously
set colors and return to the Select Item menu, choose Cancel.

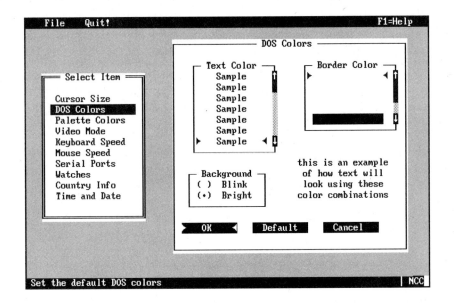

FIG. 6.3.

Changing the
DOS color
settings.

Setting Palette Colors

Notice that the NCC menu has Palette Colors, another color option
available for EGA and VGA monitors only. In the DOS colors option, you
can use only 16 colors at once, even if your monitor can display more
colors. You use the Palette option to choose which 16 colors you want
to use and the DOS Colors option to select how those 16 colors are
used (for example, which one is text, which is background, and so on).
If your monitor supports more than 16 colors, you can use the Palette
Colors option to select alternative colors to be used as the 16 DOS colors. You can change the normal DOS blue to a lighter shade of blue, for
example. Some computers have as many as 256 possible colors that
you can use as your 16 DOS colors. The colors that are available depend on the capabilities of your monitor.

After you choose the Palette Colors option, a screen similar to figure 6.4
appears, giving a list of 16 colors, including black. Although you cannot
see the actual colors in this black and white figure, you can see the
names of the colors to the left of the black box. When you first call up
this option, the colors are the 16 standard DOS colors. Using this
screen, for example, green is green. You can change the color to any
other supported color. You can change the color named green, for example, to purple. It still will be named green, but whenever a program
displays a color named green, it will actually appear as purple.

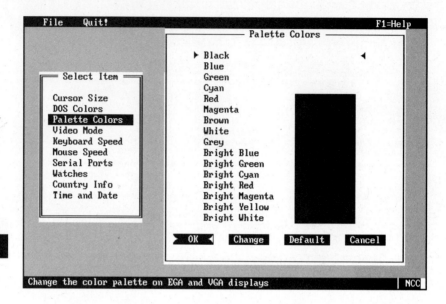

FIG. 6.4.

The Palette
Colors screen.

To choose an alternate color for one of these original DOS colors, highlight the original DOS color you want to change and choose the Change
option from the four options at the bottom of the Palette Colors screen.

Another color menu listing many alternate colors appears. You can
scroll through this list to find a new color and press Enter to choose
the color as the replacement for the original DOS color. Then you return to the screen in figure 6.4. If you choose a blue-green to replace
DOS's original blue, therefore, DOS displays a blue-green color where
the program usually displays blue.

After you select the colors you want, choose OK from the Palette Colors screen. If you want all the colors to revert to the normal DOS colors, choose Default. If you want to cancel this option and revert to the
colors as they were when you began NCC, choose Cancel.

Setting the Video Mode

Although the normal DOS monitor displays 25 lines per screen, some
monitors—EGA and VGA in particular—can display more. Using the
Video Mode option from the NCC menu, you can choose a new video
display for your computer (see fig. 6.5). Note that the available options
on the Video Mode menu include 25-line color, 40-line color, and 50-line
color. A filled radio button appears beside the current video setting.
You also can choose black and white or color mode from this screen.

Use the up or down cursor-movement keys to highlight the option you want, and then press the space bar to lock in the option. Or, point to the option you want with the mouse pointer and click. Then, press Enter to exit or click on OK with the mouse. Select Cancel to cause the video mode to revert to its earlier state.

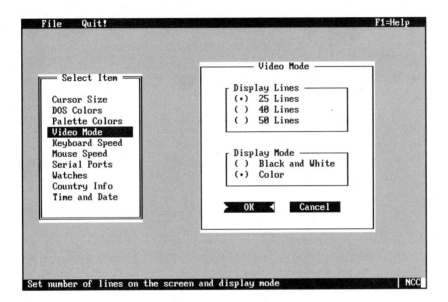

FIG. 6.5.

Choosing a video mode.

Setting Keyboard Speed

The IBM PC keyboard has several settings that you can change with the NCC command to suit your tastes. If you are a speed typist, for example, you may want to make the keyboard more responsive. If you select the Keyboard Speed option from the NCC main menu, you see a screen similar to figure 6.6. (The Keyboard Speed option is not available on some early versions of the PC.) If your computer does not support a change in keyboard speeds, Norton displays a message telling you that this option does not work on your computer.

The Keyboard Speed screen has two areas to set keyboard options. Use the top area to set the keyboard rate; use the bottom area to set the delay before auto repeat. *Keyboard rate* refers to how quickly a letter repeats when you hold down that letter's key. *Delay* refers to the length of pause after you press a key before that key begins repeating.

To set either parameter, use the cursor-movement keys to move the bar to the corresponding graphic control pictured on-screen: use the up and down keys to move between the two settings; use the right and left keys to set the rates. Or, point to a slide graph with your mouse pointer and, pressing the button, drag the setting to the desired spot. To choose the Fast settings for the keyboard speed and repeat, select the Fast button at the bottom of the Keyboard Speed screen.

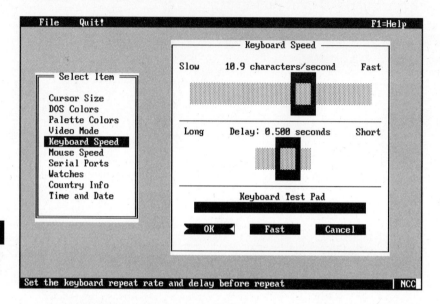

FIG. 6.6.

Controlling keyboard settings.

The normal delay rate before repeating is .5 second. You can change this delay to a minimum of .25 second or a maximum of 1 second. The normal repeat speed is 10.9 characters per second (cps). You can change this speed to a minimum of 2 cps or a maximum of 30 cps.

You can experiment with these settings by typing information on the Keyboard Test Pad to see how your new settings affect the keyboard rate. Press and hold down the A key, for example, and notice how much delay occurs before the letter starts repeating and how fast the letter repeats. When you are satisfied with your settings, choose OK to return to the Select Item menu. Choose Cancel to revert to the previous speed settings.

Setting Your Mouse Speed

If you use a mouse, you may want to adjust the device's *sensitivity*, or how the movement of the mouse corresponds to the movement of the mouse pointer on-screen. *Slow sensitivity* means that you must move the mouse more to see movement on-screen. *Fast sensitivity* means that a small movement of the mouse on your mouse pad translates to a big movement on-screen. If you select the Mouse Speed option from the Select Item box, you see a screen like the one in figure 6.7. The default sensitivity setting is 50 but may be set from 0 to 100.

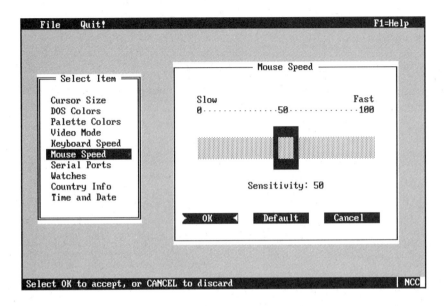

FIG. 6.7.

Setting the mouse speed.

Set the sensitivity by using the right and left cursor-movement keys. Or, point to the setting with your mouse pointer and click and drag the mouse to reach the setting you want.

Choosing Serial Port Settings

With NCC, you can choose the settings for your serial ports—a required task if you have a printer or other device that requires such settings working through your serial port. Devices such as printers, modems, plotters, and so on attached to a serial port may require a setting of 2400 baud, no parity, 8 data bits, and 1 stop bit. Usually, if you must choose serial settings for communications to a peripheral device (such as a printer) or to another computer, these settings are specified in your peripheral device's manual or by the computer to which you are connecting.

If you choose Serial Ports from the NCC main menu, the Serial Ports screen appears (see fig. 6.8). On this screen, you can set the baud setting, stop bits, parity, and data bits for up to four COM (serial) ports.

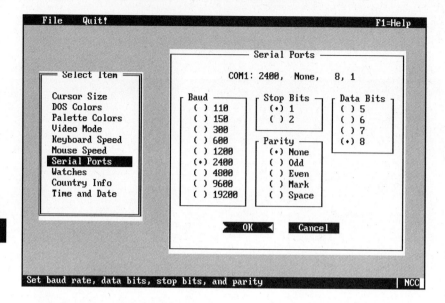

FIG. 6.8.

Selecting
settings for
serial ports.

These settings on the Serial Ports screen define how data communications take place through the serial ports:

Setting	Defines
Baud	Speed of the communications. Common baud settings are 110, 150, 300, 600, 1200, 2400, 4800, 9600, and 19200. The higher the baud setting, the faster the communication.
Stop Bits	Number of stop-bit signals sent with each pulse of information. Stop bits are usually set at 1 or 2.
Parity	Type of error-checking protocol to be used: None, Odd, Even, Mark, or Space. The most common setting is None.
Data Bits	Number of bits of information included in each communication pulse. This number is 5, 6, 7, or 8.

Use the cursor-movement keys to highlight the settings you want and press the space bar to lock in a setting in each option box. Or, select the settings with your mouse and click. Choose OK to lock in all selections or choose Cancel to revert to the previous settings.

Setting Stopwatches

Norton Utilities provides four stopwatches to enable you to time certain events. You can use the Watches option on the NCC menu to observe and reset these clocks. When you use the NCC command with the /START or /STOP options, the elapsed times appear on-screen. If the results of a /START or /STOP scroll off screen, you can view the time by using the NCC Watches option. You also can use the Watches option to reset the clocks before timing something (see fig. 6.9). An example of using these switches might be comparing the run time for two different software products—such as the amount of time an accounting package takes to perform its end-of-month report.

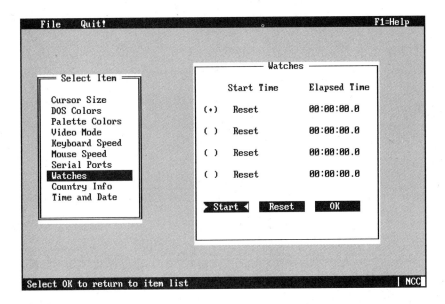

FIG. 6.9.

The Watches settings.

You can choose which watch to use by selecting one of the four radio buttons. Then you can reset or start the watch by choosing Start or Reset at the bottom of the screen. Choose OK to return to the Select Item menu. The stopwatches normally will be used in interactive mode, where the NCC command is issued from the DOS prompt. See "Using NCC in Command-Line Mode," later in this chapter.

Setting Country Info

Because a number of countries use PCs, a formatting standard is needed for certain items so that those items match the generally used standard of a country. In the United States, for example, dates usually are written in the month-day-year format; Europeans, however, write dates in the day-month-year format. Other formats that vary from country to country are time, currency (£ compared to $), lists (some countries use commas in lists, while some use semi-colons), and numbers (some countries use the form $1,000, while others use 1.000). The Country Info item enables you to set these items for your computer. If you are preparing a report to be sent to Europe, for example, you temporarily may change the date format so that Europeans can understand the report.

For the Country Info option to work, you must have the COUNTRY.SYS driver in your CONFIG.SYS file. If the COUNTRY.SYS driver is not in the file, a screen appears, giving you your current settings, but you cannot make any changes. If you can make changes, you see a screen like figure 6.10.

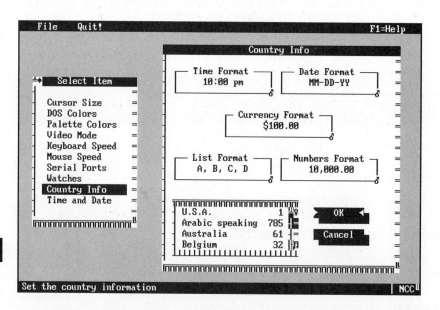

FIG. 6.10.

The Country Info settings.

If you want to be able to change your country settings, place a line like the following in your CONFIG.SYS file:

COUNTRY=001,850 C:\DOS\COUNTRY.SYS

The *001* specifies US and *850* is a selection for a character set. The other common character set used in the US is *437*. (See your DOS manual for more information on country settings.) Also, you must enter the following command from the DOS prompt (or in AUTOEXEC.BAT):

NLSFUNC \DOS\COUNTRY.SYS

assuming that you have stored the COUNTRY.SYS driver in a directory named \DOS. After you include the proper COUNTRY.SYS driver in your CONFIG.SYS file, reboot, and enter the NLSFUNC command, you can change your country settings in NCC.

On the Country Info screen, you see a list box at the bottom left listing a number of countries, including U.S.A., Arabic Speaking, Australia, and so on. If you choose a country from this list, the country info information changes to match that country's normal usage. After selecting a country, choose OK to lock in the formats. Choose Cancel to revert to the original setting.

Setting Time and Date

If your clock battery has failed, the date and time settings for your machine will not be correct. On some computers, particularly the AT, you must use the diagnostics disk to reset the date and time so that the computer remembers the settings. With the NCC Time and Date option, however, you can set these parameters without booting up with the diagnostics disk (see fig. 6.11). You can use the Time and Date option to set the date and time for a number of DOS computers, but some computers may not respond to your setting. You just have to experiment to see whether this NCC option works for your computer.

To set the date or time, use the cursor-movement keys to highlight the number that you want to change in the Date or Time box. Then use the plus (+) or minus (-) key to change the number up or down. (Or, you can enter the numbers.) Choose OK to lock in the change or choose Cancel to return the date and time to their previous settings.

Saving NCC Settings to Disk

After you select from the NCC menu, you can save the new settings to a file. Press F10 from the NCC menu to pull down the File menu, and then choose the Save Settings option. When prompted for a file name, type the name and press Enter. The settings you changed in NCC are saved to that file.

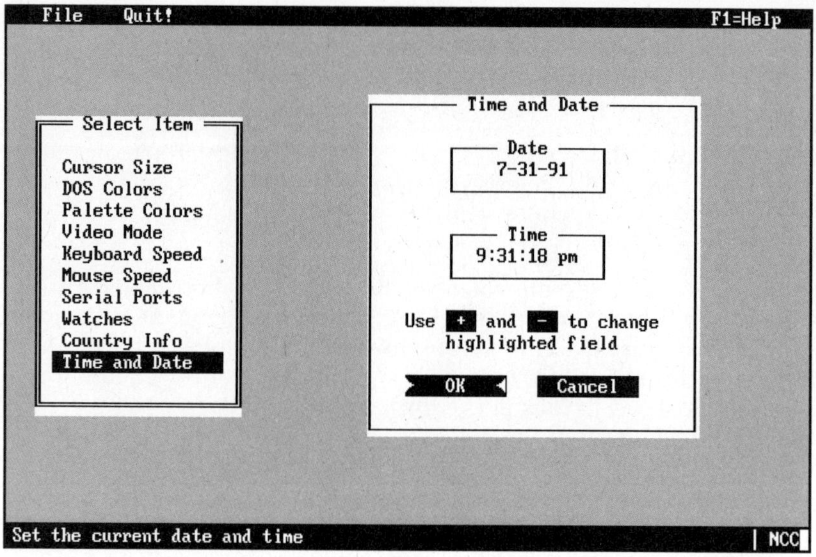

FIG. 6.11.

The Time and
Date settings.

After you save the information to a file, you can use command-line
switches to reset NCC to the settings you saved. Suppose that you
chose certain colors and other settings that you want to use all the
time and saved this information to a file named SETTINGS.NCC. You
can place the NCC command in your AUTOEXEC.BAT file with the
/SETALL switch, using the following command:

        NCC \NORTON\SETTINGS.NCC /SETALL

This command reactivates all settings (color choices, cursor size, and
so on) that you saved in NCC.

In this case, the SETTINGS.NCC file is in the \NORTON directory, so the
path name is necessary. The file otherwise is activated from the root
(\) directory. If you do not want to include the command in your
AUTOEXEC.BAT file, you can enter the same NCC command from the
DOS prompt.

Using NCC in Command-Line Mode

Several settings that you can choose interactively in the Norton Command Center also can be set from the DOS prompt by using NCC
command-line options. The syntax for the NCC command in command-
line mode is

NCC [*filespec*] [*switches*]

or

NCC [*switches*]

The *filespec* in the first version of the command refers to a file that contains system information specifications. Before you use this version of the command, you must create this file by using NCC in interactive mode to choose the settings you want and then save the information to a file. (See "Saving NCC Settings to Disk," earlier in this chapter.)

The available switches for the NCC command follow:

Switch	Effect
/25	Places the monitor in 25-line mode (same as /CO80).
/35	Places the monitor in 35-line mode (an option supported by EGA monitors only).
/40	Places the monitor in 40-line mode (an option supported by VGA monitors only).
/43	Places the monitor in 43-line mode (an option supported by EGA monitors only).
/50	Places the monitor in 50-line mode (an option supported by VGA monitors only).
/BW80	Places the monitor in black-and-white mode with 25 lines and 80 columns.
/CO80	Places the monitor in color mode with 25 lines and 80 columns.
/C:comment	Displays the text string *comment* when the command is executed. This option is useful for documenting what timer is being reported. If the comment contains any spaces, you must put quotation marks on both sides of the comment.
/CURSOR	Reads the information in the file named by filespec but sets only the cursor size.
/DOSCOLOR	Reads the information in the file named by filespec but sets only the previously chosen DOS colors for foreground, background, and border.
/FAST	Sets the keyboard rate at its fastest possible value.
/L	Displays the time and date on the left side of the monitor.

Switch	Effect
/N	Displays the current time and date.
/PALETTE	Reads the information in the file named by filespec but sets only the palette colors.
/SET	Reads the information in the file named by filespec and sets all parameters.
/START:*n*	Begins the stopwatch number *n*, where *n* can be from 1 to 4.
/STOP:*n*	Stops the stopwatch number *n*, where *n* can be from 1 to 4.

To set your VGA computer so that 50 lines are displayed on-screen and the keyboard rate is the fastest value, use this command:

NCC /50/FAST

Using Norton Change Directory

You use the NCC command to manage the hardware settings on your computer. You use the Norton Change Directory (NCD) command, on the other hand, to manage your software—the files on disk. With NCD, you can efficiently manage your directories on disk and navigate easily between directories.

NCD, one of the most useful commands from Norton Utilities, really is two commands in one. When used in a command-line mode, NCD substitutes for the DOS CD, MD, and RD commands, which you use to change, make, and remove directories. When used in interactive mode, NCD is a directory-management tool.

Using NCD in Interactive Mode

If you enter the NCD command with no parameters, you are placed in interactive mode, and a graphic representation of your directory structure appears on-screen (see fig. 6.12). The disk in this figure has four levels of directories. You can see that directory ONE-A has a subdirectory called TWO-A, which has a subdirectory called THREE-A, which has a subdirectory called FOUR-A. ONE-B has a subdirectory named TWO-B, but directory ONE-C has no subdirectories.

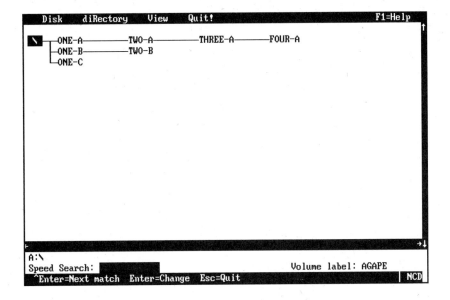

FIG. 6.12.

Using NCD in interactive mode.

To move to any directory on disk, use the cursor-movement keys to highlight the directory you want and press Enter. You exit from the NCD command and end up in the directory of your choice at the DOS prompt.

You can do much more than just change directories on this screen. Notice the menu bar at the top of the screen with the menu options Disk, Directory, View, and Quit!. Press F10 to open the menu bar or highlight one of the options with your mouse pointer.

The Disk menu contains the following options (see fig. 6.13):

Option	Shortcut Key	Function
Change Disk	F3	Selects from a list the disk for which you want to display the directory tree.
Rescan Disk	F2	Updates NCD's file TREEINFO.NCD that contains the names of all of the directories. If you have added or removed a directory without using the NCD command, you must select this option to ensure that the directory tree on-screen is accurate.

Option	Shortcut Key	Function
Volume Label	Alt-V	Changes the volume label on the disk or adds a volume label if one is not present. This function replaces the old VL command in Norton 4.5.
Free Space	Ctrl-F	Displays disk size, amount of space used, and amount of free space.

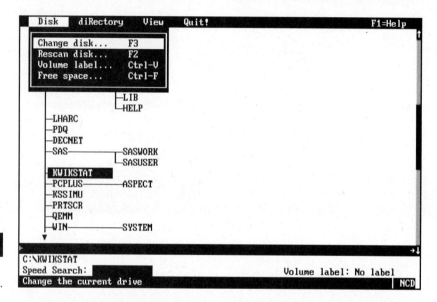

FIG. 6.13.

The NCD Disk pull-down menu.

Notice that each option has a command key. You can access the Change Disk option by pressing F3, for example, even if the Disk menu is not pulled down.

The Directory menu contains the following options (see fig. 6.14):

Option	Shortcut Key	Function
Print Tree	Alt-P	Prints a copy of the directory tree. This option is especially handy if your directory tree is too big to fit on-screen.
Rename	F6	Renames a directory. Highlight the directory you want to rename, press F6, or choose the Rename option. Then type the new name

Option	Shortcut Key	Function
		and press Enter. Remember that you cannot rename a directory in DOS, so this feature is particularly useful.
		In fact, if you have had to recover from the DOS RECOVER command or if you have unformatted a disk without the use of the IMAGE.DAT file, all directories named in the root directory are changed into obscure machine-generated names. (See Chapter 4 for more information.) The only way to retrieve the original names is to rename the directories with the NCD Rename feature.
Make	F7	Makes a new directory. Highlight the directory you want to add a subdirectory to and press F7 or choose the Make option. A new directory then appears on the graph. Enter a name for the new directory and press Enter.
Delete	F8	Removes a directory. Highlight the directory (which must not contain any files or subdirectories) and press F8 (Delete).
Tree Size		Displays the total size of all files in the currently selected directory and the total allocated disk space for the files.
Copy Tree	Alt-F5	Copies a directory to a new location on the tree. You also may choose to delete the files in the old position, which makes this command like a Move command. Because this option is potentially dangerous, it is turned off by default. You must turn the option on in the Configure option before using it.
		To use the Copy Tree command, use the arrow keys to highlight the directory to copy (or point with the mouse pointer and click).

Option	Shortcut Key	Function
		Then choose Copy Tree from the Directory pull-down menu (or press Alt-F5). You are prompted to enter the name of the directory to copy to. Enter the name and press Enter. The copy now takes place. See the following section, "Using NCD in Command-Line Mode."
Remove Tree	Alt-F8	Deletes a directory and all its subdirectories. By default this potentially dangerous option is turned off. You must turn the option on in the Configure option before using it.
		To remove a directory and all of its contents, use the arrow keys to highlight the directory or point to the directory with the mouse and click. Then choose the Remove Tree option from the Directory pull-down menu or press Alt-F8. You are prompted to verify that you want to remove the directory. See "Using the RMTREE Command," later in this chapter.
Prune and Graft	Alt-G	Moves a directory in the directory tree to another location. This enables you to rearrange your directory tree. Like the Remove Tree option, this option by default is disabled and must be enabled in the configure option.
		To interactively prune and graft a directory on the tree, first choose Prune and Graft from the directory pull-down menu (or press Alt-G). First, you must *prune* a directory (cut it off the tree). To do this, use your arrow keys to point to the directory you want to *pick up* and press Enter (or point to the directory with the mouse and click). Next, you must indicate where to *graft* the directory into the existing directory tree. By pressing

Option	Shortcut Key	Function
		the up- and down-arrow keys, you will see the pruned directory move up and down the tree. After you place the directory on the tree where you want it, press Enter to graft. Or, using the mouse, point to the location on the tree where you want to place the directory and click. A dialog box prompts you to confirm the graft.
Configure		Enables or disables the Copy Tree, Remove Tree, and Prune and Graft options.

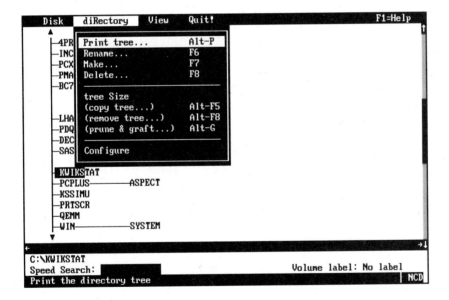

FIG. 6.14.

The NCD Directory pull-down menu.

Large directories may not fit entirely on the Norton Change Directory screen. The View menu enables you to choose to display more lines on-screen, if your monitor type supports that many. EGA screens can display 40 lines; VGA screens can display 50 lines.

The View menu contains the following items (see fig. 6.15):

    25 lines
    40 lines
    50 lines

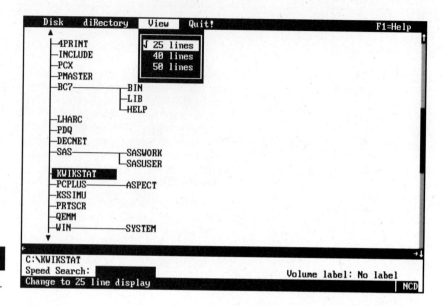

FIG. 6.15.

The View menu.

A check mark appears at the front of the selection being used (usually 25 lines).

You can quit NCD by choosing Quit or pressing Esc.

Using NCD in Command-Line Mode

In command-line mode, enter the NCD command at the DOS prompt and include options to define what you want to do. The syntax for the Norton Change Directory (NCD) command can be any of the following:

- NCD [*dirname*] [*switches*]

- NCD [*drive:*] /V:*label*

- NCD [*drive:*] /L[:OUTPUT [/A][/G[/N]][/T][/P]

- NCD MD [*dirname*]

- NCD RD [*dirname*]

- NCD SIZE [*dirname*]

- NCD COPY *source destination* [/DELETE]

- NCD GRAFT *source destination* [/NET]

- NCD RMTREE *dirname* [/BATCH]

The *dirname* is the name of the directory you want to change to, make, remove, or display size. The switches associated with the NCD command include /R and /N. The /R switch updates the file TREEINFO.NCD, which contains information about your directory tree structure. The /N switch instructs the NCD command not to write the file TREEINFO.NCD. If you use NCD on a write-protected disk, you must use the /N switch.

The /V:*label* option enables you to change the volume label on the disk. To change the volume label on the disk in drive A to MYDISK, for example, you can use the command

> NCD A: /V:MYDISK

The switches associated with displaying or printing the directory tree follow:

Switch	Effect
/L:*filespec*	Outputs the directory tree to the file specified in *filespec*. If the file name used here is LPT1, the tree will be output to the printer using line printer port 1. For example,
	NCD /L:LPT1
/A	Displays a tree for each nonfloppy disk drive.
/G	Displays the tree graphically.
/NG	Displays the tree using nongraphical characters (best in printing to a printer that does not support graphical characters).
/T	Displays the total number of files and their sizes.
/P	Pauses after each screenful of information is displayed. Press Enter to continue with the display.

To record a nongraphics version of your tree structure of all hard disks to a file named MYDIRS, for example, you can use the command

> NCD /L:MYDIRS /A /NG

To change directories by using the NCD command, enter NCD plus the name of the directory to which you want to change. Suppose that you want to change to a directory on disk named \ONE-A\TWO-A\THREE-A\FOUR-A. With the DOS CD command, you must enter the entire path name to go to that directory:

> CD \ONE-A\TWO-A\THREE-A\FOUR-A

Using the NCD command, you enter only the name of the destination directory, as in

NCD FOUR-A

In fact, you must enter only enough characters in the name to make the name unique, so you can enter the command

NCD FOUR

or maybe even

NCD F

If you have more than one directory beginning with the letter F, the NCD command switches to the first directory beginning with that letter. If you enter the command again (press F3 and Enter), NCD switches to the next directory beginning with the letter F. As you name your directories, you may want to choose unique names to make the NCD command that much faster to use. The more complicated your directory structure, the easier changing directories becomes with the NCD command.

You also can use the NCD command rather than the DOS MD and RD commands to make and remove directories. To make a directory, such as \FIRST\SECOND, enter the command

NCD MD \FIRST\SECOND

To delete that directory, enter

NCD RD \FIRST\SECOND

You may be tempted to pass up the NCD command for MD and RD, but a good reason exists for using NCD instead. The first time you run the NCD command, Norton analyzes and stores your entire directory structure in a file (TREEINFO.NCD) for quick access. If you use the DOS versions of RD and MD, the Norton file is not updated. If you use the NCD versions of MD and RD, the Norton file is updated, and changing directories continues to be quick and easy.

If you accidentally use the RD or MD command, you can update the Norton file TREEINFO.NCD by using the /R switch with the NCD command.

With the NCD COPY command, you can copy an entire directory to a new location. For example, to copy the directory named \MYDIR to the new location as a subdirectory of \YOURDIR, use the command

NCD COPY \MYDIR \YOURDIR

To delete the old directory (\MYDIR) after the copy, use the command

    NCD COPY \MYDIR \YOURDIR /DELETE

The result of this copy is that a directory named \MYDIR and all its contents is now a subdirectory of the \YOURDIR directory.

If you include the \DELETE switch, the old directory is deleted in the process. Before using the command the first time, you must enable the NCD COPY command from the Configure option on the Directory pull-down menu on the NCD screen.

Using the GRAFT Command

The NCD GRAFT command, similar to the NCD COPY command, doesn't just copy; it moves the source directory and all subdirectories to the destination location.

You may need to use the /NET switch if you use this command on a network. Normally, you do not need this switch.

The NCD GRAFT command, which is by default disabled, must be enabled by choosing Configure from NCD's Directory menu.

Using the RMTREE Command

The NCD RMTREE command removes a directory—including all files in that directory—from your directory tree. The command prompts you for confirmation before actually deleting the information. If you use the /BATCH switch, the prompt for confirmation is skipped. This poten-tially dangerous command, which is by default disabled, must be enabled by choosing Configure from NCD's Directory menu.

Creating Batch Files

The Norton Batch Enhancer (BE) is a powerful set of commands in its own right. Batch Enhancer gives you more flexibility in creating batch files.

Batch files normally consist of several DOS commands listed one after another. When a batch file is executed, DOS acts on these commands. The DOS language, however, has a few holes when you need to create useful batch files. You may want to prompt for input in a batch file and branch according to the user's response. Also, the capability to set colors, draw windows or boxes, and print text anywhere on-screen from a batch file is helpful. Norton's Batch Enhancer fulfills these needs.

The syntax for the Batch Enhancer command is

> BE *subcommand* [/DEBUG]

or

> BE *filespec*

The available subcommands for BE follow:

> ASK
> BEEP
> BOX
> CLS
> DELAY
> EXIT
> GOTO
> JUMP
> MONTHDAY
> PRINTCHAR
> REBOOT
> ROWCOL
> SA
> SHIFTSTATE
> TRIGGER
> WEEKDAY
> WINDOW

You can use the BE command at the DOS prompt, but the command generally is used in a batch file. The following command, for example, produces a standard system beep:

> BE BEEP

In a batch file, you may want to include this command at the end to signal when a process is finished.

Each BE subcommand has its own parameters, which are described in the following sections.

NOTE Some of the BE commands also are implemented in NDOS, which is described in Chapter 8. These commands include the following:

ASK
BEEP
BOX
CLS
DELAY
MONTHDAY
PRINTCHAR
REBOOT
ROWCOL
SA
SHIFTSTATE
TRIGGER
WEEKDAY
WINDOW

Using Script Files

A script file is similar to a batch file except that it uses the Norton BE program to execute the commands instead of DOS. A script file can contain any of the Norton BE commands; however, DOS commands are ignored. The advantage of writing a "batch" script file instead of a normal DOS batch file is that it runs faster and enables you to use the features of the BE commands not available in DOS. The syntax of the BE script command is

BE SCRIPT*filename* [[GOTO]*label*]

For example, you may create a file (script) named *setcolor* containing the command

SA Bright White on Blue

(Note that you do not have to include a BE in front of a subcommand when it is in a script. See "Using the SA Subcommand," later in this chapter.)

To run this script, enter the command

BE setcolor

at the DOS prompt. A script may contain a number of labels, and you can tell the command to begin executing at a particular label by entering that label name on the command line. Suppose that your file (script) named setcolor contained the following commands:

```
:blue
sa bright white on blue
exit
:green
sa bright white on green
exit
:red
sa bright white on red
```

Then, when you enter the command

BE SETCOLOR GREEN

The program will begin at the label :GREEN, perform the SA command, and then EXIT. (See "Using the Exit Subcommand," later in this chapter.) BE commands that may only be used in script files and not in regular DOS batch files include GOTO, JUMP, and EXIT.

Using the ASK Subcommand

The ASK subcommand enables you to capture a user's response and to act on that response. You can use the ASK command to create menus. If you use the ASK command in your AUTOEXEC.BAT file, you can control the way your computer is booted. Sometimes you may want to load memory-resident programs such as Sidekick at boot time, for example, and sometimes you may not.

The syntax of the ASK subcommand is

BE ASK *prompt*[*keys*][DEFAULT=*key*]
[TIMEOUT=*n*][ADJUST=*n*][*color*][/DEBUG]

The *prompt* is a text string that you want to display on-screen. (You must enclose the string in double quotation marks.) The cursor is placed after the prompt to anticipate a single-character user response.

A simple example of the BE ASK command follows. Suppose that you want your AUTOEXEC.BAT file to give you the option of booting with no memory-resident programs. You want the computer to ask the question:

```
Skip memory resident programs(Y/N)
```

If you press Y, you want to skip loading memory-resident programs. If you press N, you want the computer to go ahead and load those programs. Use the ASK command

BE ASK "Skip memory resident programs (Y/N)", YN

Notice that the expected responses are listed as the keys Y and N. The next few lines use the DOS IF ERRORLEVEL commands to tell the computer what to do when the user makes one of the choices. For example,

```
IF ERRORLEVEL 2 GOTO DOMEMORY
IF ERRORLEVEL 1 GOTO SKIP
```

If you press N, an errorlevel code 2 is generated and these commands send the flow of the batch file to a label named DOMEMORY. If you press Y, an errorlevel code 1 is generated and the flow of the batch file is sent to a label named SKIP. If you press any key, the computer beeps and the ASK command continues to wait for a Y or an N. A listing of how the complete batch file may look using the ASK command follows:

```
ECHO OFF
CLS
BE ASK "Skip memory resident programs(Y/N)",YN
IF ERRORLEVEL 2 GOTO DOMEMORY
IF ERRORLEVEL 1 GOTO SKIP
:DOMEMORY
REM place commands for memory resident programs here
:SKIP
REM place the rest of the AUTOEXEC.BAT command here
```

The REM lines are remarks about where to place the commands that load memory-resident programs and where to place other AUTOEXEC.BAT commands.

With the ASK subcommand's DEFAULT=*key* parameter, you can specify what Enter means. DEFAULT=Y, for example, means that pressing Enter is the same as choosing Yes.

With the TIMEOUT=*n* parameter, you can specify how long the ASK command waits for an answer before taking the default answer (*n* denotes the number of seconds to wait).

Using the /DEBUG switch causes the errorlevel of a command to be displayed. This switch helps you to figure out what the various errorlevel codes mean because you cannot find out in DOS.

If one menu will not hold all the options you want to use, you may have to use a multipart menu. You may have a two-layer menu, for example, with the first layer having 10 options. When BE returns an errorlevel in the second layer, you can adjust the errorlevel by 10 by including the option ADJUST=10 so that the level matches your IF...GOTO statements. If you did not adjust, the errorlevels on the second menu would be 1, 2, 3, and so on. With the adjustment, they become 11, 12, 13, and so on. This enables you to tell the difference between option 1, menu 1 (has an errorlevel=1) and option 1, menu 2 (has an errorlevel=11).

ADJUST= enables you to make the errorlevel numbers higher so that they do not conflict with some used already. If your first menu has four options, for example, the menu can end up with an errorlevel value of 1 to 4. Then, on a subsequent menu, you include an ADJUST=4 command to make your next menu begin with errorlevel values of 5, 6, and so on. You then use the resulting errorlevel number to branch to the proper location in the batch file.

You also can set colors in the ASK statement. The color options are described in "Using the SA Subcommand," later in this chapter. Including WHITE ON BLUE in the BE ASK command line, for example, causes the prompt to appear as white letters on a blue background. The color selection is in effect only for the ASK prompt.

Using the BEEP Subcommand

The BEEP subcommand produces a tone or series of tones. This command can come in handy if you create a batch file that performs a lengthy operation. You can use Beep to tell you audibly that the batch file is finished or is at a certain stage of the process.

The syntax for this subcommand is

> BE BEEP [*switches*]

or

> BE BEEP [*filespec*][/E]

If you include a *filespec*, the file specified should contain a list of tones to play. When used with a file specification, the /E switch instructs the BE BEEP command to echo the text in the file to the screen.

If you do not include a *filespec*, use switches to specify the tones to play. The switches available for the BE BEEP command follow:

Switch	Effect
/D*n*	Specifies the duration of a tone in measurements of 1/18th of a second. Thus, D3 specifies that the tone be sounded for 3/18th of a second.
/E	Echoes (displays) to the screen quoted text in comments in the Beep script file.
/F*n*	Specifies the frequency of a tone, where *n* is hertz (Hz), or cycles per second. The switch /F440, for example, plays a tone at 440 Hz. The larger the value of *n*, the higher pitched the tone.
/R*n*	Specifies that the tone be repeated *n* times.
/W*n*	Specifies a wait in durations of 1/18th of a second. The switch /W3, for example, causes a wait of 3/18th of a second. You usually use this switch as a wait between beeps.

The following command plays a tone at 440 Hz for one second (18/18), waits half a second (9/18), and then repeats the tone:

    BE BEEP /F440 /D18 /R2 /W9

To place this command in a file named TONE, leaving off the BE BEEP, just enter

    IF440 /D18 /R2 /W9

and enter the command

    BE BEEP TONE

at the DOS prompt to sound the tone.

Using the BOX Subcommand

The BOX subcommand enables you to draw rectangular boxes on-screen. Boxes are helpful for emphasizing on-screen messages and for creating menus.

The syntax for the BOX subcommand is

    BE BOX *top,left,bottom,right*[SINGLE|DOUBLE][*color*]

The top and left parameters specify the row number and column number, respectively, of the upper left corner of the box. Likewise, the bottom and right parameters specify the row number and column number of the lower right corner of the box.

The SINGLE or DOUBLE parameter specifies whether the edges of the box should have a single or double line. *Color* specifies color choices (see "Using the SA Subcommand," later in this chapter).

An example of using the BOX subcommand is

    BE BOX 2,10,10,70 SINGLE

This command draws a single-line box beginning at the 2nd row, 10th column and extending to the 10th row, 70th column of the screen.

Using the DELAY Subcommand

The DELAY subcommand enables you to cause a batch file to suspend operation for a period of time. Suppose that your batch file is displaying information on-screen. You may want to build in a delay so that you can read the information before some other information appears on-screen. The syntax for the DELAY subcommand is

    BE DELAY [*time*]

where *time* is measured in 1/18 of a second. Thus, the command

    BE DELAY 18

causes a one-second delay.

Using the EXIT Subcommand

The EXIT subcommand causes a script file to end (see "Using Script Files," earlier in this chapter). This subcommand, which has no options, can be used to stop a script at any point. The syntax is

    BE EXIT

This command should be used only in a script file. It has meaning in a regular DOS batch file.

Using the GOTO Subcommand

With the GOTO subcommand, you can control the starting point of a
script. This command can be used only in script files. It does not work
in DOS batch files. The syntax for the GOTO command is

BE *pathname* [[GOTO] *label*]

where *pathname* is a script file and *label* is a label in the script file. A
label is a statement in the file that begins with a colon. For example

:THISISALABEL

is a label. (See the example in "Using Script Files," earlier in this
chapter.)

Using the JUMP Subcommand

With the JUMP subcommand, you can do conditional branching in a
script. This command can be used only in script files. It does not work
in DOS batch files. Unlike GOTO, which always branches to a specified
label, JUMP enables you to branch to one of several labels based on the
current value of the exit code. The syntax of the JUMP subcommand is

JUMP *label1*,[*label2*[,...*labeln*]] [/DEFAULT:*label*]

where the first label is the name of the label where the flow of
the script is sent if the exit code is 1, the second label is the name of the
label where the flow is sent if the exit code is 2, and so on. If no label
matches the exit code, the flow goes to the label specified by the
label in the /DEFAULT switch. If no match to an exit code and no
default label exist, execution continues with the command following
the JUMP command.

For example, the following script file, named WHATDAY displays the
name of the day of the week:

```
be cls
be weekday
be jump su,m,tu,w,th,f,s
:m
be rowcol 1,1 "Today is Monday"
be jump /default:last
:tu
be rowcol 1,1 "Today is Tuesday"
be jump /default:last
```

```
:w
be rowcol 1,1 "Today is Wednesday"
be jump /default:last
:th
be rowcol 1,1 "Today is Thursday"
be jump /default:last
:f
be rowcol 1,1 "Today is Friday"
be jump /default:last
:s
be rowcol 1,1 "Today is Saturday"
:last
```

The BE CLS command clears the screen. The BE WEEKDAY command returns a 1, 2, 3, 4, 5, 6, or 7 (see "Using the WEEKDAY Subcommand," later in this chapter). The BE JUMP command branches to the correct day-of-week display. (The BE ROWCOL command prints the message at the top of the screen.) Then the JUMP /DEFAULT:LAST command branches to the :LAST label and ends the program.

Using the MONTHDAY Subcommand

The MONTHDAY subcommand returns the day of the month as an exit code, which then can be used in a JUMP subcommand or in an IF ERRORLEVEL command. The syntax for the MONTHDAY subcommand is

BE MONTHDAY [/DEBUG]

The /DEBUG option causes the exit code to be displayed on-screen.

This example shows how the BE MONTHDAY command could be used in a DOS batch file. The batch file (WHATDATE.BAT) clears the screen, and if today is the first day of the month, an important message is displayed on-screen:

```
echo off
cls
be monthday
if errorlevel 1 goto first
goto last
:first
echo TODAY IS FIRST DAY OF MONTH!
echo BE SURE TO MAIL YOUR HOUSE PAYMENT!
:last
```

You may compare this example with the example in the preceding section "Using the JUMP Subcommand" to see the difference in writing a batch file and writing a script file. This example used the DOS ERRORLEVEL command to branch, and the preceding section's example used the NORTON BE JUMP command to branch.

Using the PRINTCHAR Subcommand

The PRINTCHAR subcommand enables you to print a character a specified number of times. The command can come in handy if you are drawing images on-screen—perhaps highlighting a message, making a menu look fancy, and so on.

The syntax of the PRINTCHAR subcommand is

BE PRINTCHAR *character,repeats* [*color*]

The *character* can be any ASCII character. You can specify a number of *repeats* up to 80. The *color* parameter is described in "Using the SA Subcommand," later in this chapter.

> **T I P**
>
> In the BE PRINTCHAR command, you can use characters from the extended IBM character list—ASCII characters from 128 to 255—if your program can access them. (Some editors, such as WordStar, may not be capable of accessing the IBM-extended characters.) To use the Greek letter beta (ß) in the BE PRINTCHAR command, for example, hold down the Alt key, type the ASCII code 225 on the numeric keypad, and release the Alt key. (The ASCII codes for the extended character set are listed in the back of most DOS or BASIC manuals.) The letter ß should appear on-screen. To print the character 20 times, enter the command
>
> BE PRINTCHAR ß,20

Using the REBOOT Subcommand

The REBOOT subcommand enables you to perform a warm boot of the computer. The syntax of this command is

BE REBOOT [/VERIFY]

When you include the /VERIFY switch in the command, you are prompted to confirm whether the reboot should take place. This command may be useful if you change or replace your AUTOEXEC.BAT or CONFIG.SYS file within a batch file. Causing a reboot then resets your computer to the new values within these files.

Using the ROWCOL Subcommand

You use the Row Column (ROWCOL) subcommand to place the cursor somewhere on-screen before writing a message to the screen. With the ROWCOL command, you can place information anywhere on-screen and be creative in designing menus or messages.

The syntax for the Row Column subcommand is

> BE ROWCOL *row,col*[*,text*][*color*]

The *row* parameter represents the number of the on-screen row where you want the cursor to appear (normally, 1 to 25). The *col* is the number of the column on-screen (normally 1 to 80). The *text* is a message, enclosed in double quotation marks, that you want to display at the location specified. The *color* parameter is described in the next section.

Suppose that you are designing a menu screen and you want the text *ABC Company, Inc.* to appear on the top line of the screen. You can use this command:

> BE ROWCOL 1,33,"ABC Company, Inc."

The 1 specifies the top line of the screen and the 33 specifies that the message begins in the 33rd column. This specification centers the message on-screen.

Using the SA Subcommand

The Screen Attributes (SA) subcommand enables you to specify colors and other features of the screen. Using screen attributes, you can design your screen by highlighting text in different colors, boldness, and blinking. This feature can help to bring attention to messages on-screen or make your menus look more colorful.

The syntax for the Screen Attributes subcommand is

BE SA *main-setting* [*switches*]

or

BE SA [*intensity*][*foreground*][ON *background*][*switches*]

The options for *main-setting* are Normal, Reverse, or Underline. Choices for *intensity* are Bright, Bold, or Blinking. (Bright and Bold are identical.) Choices for *foreground* or *background* colors are white, black, red, magenta, blue, green, cyan, or yellow. The available switches follow:

Switch	Effect
/CLS	Clears the screen after setting the screen attributes. Enables you to see the effects of the Screen Attributes command immediately on-screen.
/N	Instructs the Screen Attributes subcommand not to set border color.

The Screen Attributes subcommand is helpful not only as a command in Batch Enhancer but also directly from DOS. To set your monitor to a blue background with white letters, for example, use the command

BE SA WHITE ON BLUE

This setting sets the color for the entire screen and stays in effect until you change the setting with another command.

Using the SHIFTSTATE Subcommand

The SHIFTSTATE subcommand reports the status of the Shift, Alt, and Ctrl keys. The command returns an exit code according to the state of the left shift, right shift, Alt, and Ctrl keys. You then can use the exit code to cause the script to branch with the JUMP command or DOS ERRORLEVEL command. The syntax of the SHIFTSTATE subcommand is

BE SHIFTSTATE [/DEBUG]

The /DEBUG switch causes the exit code to be displayed on-screen.

The exit codes returned by SHIFTSTATE follow:

Whether this key is in Shift state	Returned Code
Alt key (left or right)	8
Ctrl key (left or right)	4
Left Shift key	2
Right Shift key	1

For example, hold down the left Shift key and enter the following command at the DOS prompt:

    BE SHIFTSTATE /DEBUG

The response will be the message ERRORLEVEL:1. You can use SHIFTSTATE to create commands that do different tasks according to whether one of these keys is depressed when the command is invoked.

Using the TRIGGER Subcommand

The TRIGGER subcommand halts the execution of a script until a specified time. This command enables you to cause your script to wait until a specified time to continue execution. Suppose that you have a communications program set up to send data to a distant location. You can use this command to cause the program to begin execution early in the morning when telephone rates are lowest. The syntax for the TRIGGER subcommand is

    BE TRIGGER *hh:mm* [AM] [PM]

where *hh:mm* is hours and minutes in military (24-hour clock) time. Thus, 14:00 is 2 p.m. You also can use the AM or PM designation to specify a 12-hour clock time. Thus, 2:00 p.m. is the same as 14:00. In this designation, 12:00 a.m. is the same as 0:00 (midnight) and 12:00 p.m. is noon.

Using the WEEKDAY Subcommand

The WEEKDAY subcommand returns the day of the week as an exit code, similar to the MONTHDAY subcommand. You can use the

WEEKDAY command in a JUMP subcommand or in an IF ERRORLEVEL command. The syntax for the WEEKDAY subcommand is

BE WEEKDAY [/DEBUG]

The /DEBUG switch causes the exit code to be displayed on-screen.

Using the WINDOW Subcommand

Like the BOX subcommand, the WINDOW subcommand draws rectangular boxes. WINDOW also gives you the option to draw the rectangle with a shadow and to zoom the box onto the screen. You can use the WINDOW command to create menus or to highlight messages on-screen.

The syntax for the WINDOW subcommand is

BE WINDOW *top,left,bottom,right* [*color*] [SHADOW] [ZOOM]

The *top* and *left* parameters specify the row number and column number, respectively, of the upper left corner of the box. The *bottom* and *right* parameters specify the row number and column number of the lower right corner of the box.

The SHADOW parameter adds a shadow to the right and bottom edges of the window, which gives the window a standout effect on-screen. ZOOM makes the window appear to grow from a small rectangle to a rectangle that fits into the size indicated by the top, left, bottom, and right parameters. The *color* options are described in the section "Using the SA Subcommand," earlier in this chapter.

For example, the command

BE WINDOW 2,10,10,70

creates a rectangle on-screen.

Combining DOS and Batch Enhancer Commands

By combining DOS batch commands and Norton batch enhancer commands, you can create neat programs out of batch files. Figure 6.16 shows a batch file that uses DOS batch commands and several batch enhancer commands to create a menu system for your computer. This file is named MENU.BAT.

```
                echo off
                :begin
                cd\nu
                be sa white on blue
                cls
                be window 2,10,12,65 white on red shadow zoom
                be rowcol 3,30 "My Special Menu"
                be rowcol 5,16 "Exit to DOS......................D"
                be rowcol 6,16 "Begin Norton Utilities.............N"
                be rowcol 7,16 "Begin WORDPERFECT.................W"
                be rowcol 8,16 "Begin KWIKSTAT....................K"
                be rowcol 10,16
                be ask "Choose an option letter:",dnwk default=D
                if errorlevel 4 goto kwikstat
                if errorlevel 3 goto word
                if errorlevel 2 goto norton
                if errorlevel 1 goto thatsall

                :kwikstat
                cls
                cd\kwikstat
                KS
                goto begin

                :word
                cls
                cd\wp50
                wp
                goto begin

                :norton
                cls
                cd\nu
                norton

                :thatsall
                be sa white on blue
                cls
```

FIG. 6.16.

The batch file
MENU.BAT.

After you create the batch file MENU.BAT and issue the MENU command from the DOS prompt, a screen like the one in figure 6.17 appears. As you can see in lines 6 through 12 of the batch file in figure 6.16, the menu is made by first drawing a box with the WINDOW subcommand, and then using the ROWCOL subcommand to give the menu a heading and to locate the items for the menu. The ASK command captures the user's response, which is evaluated by the IF ERRORLEVEL commands. Each menu choice points to a label in the batch file, which begins a program or exits to DOS. If you choose a program by pressing N, W, or K, the program associated with that selection begins. After the program returns to DOS, the batch file continues to operate and displays the menu again.

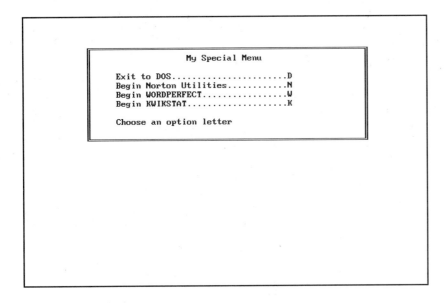

```
                    My Special Menu
      Exit to DOS.......................D
      Begin Norton Utilities...........N
      Begin WORDPERFECT................W
      Begin KWIKSTAT...................K

      Choose an option letter
```

FIG. 6.17.

The screen
displayed by
the batch file
MENU.BAT.

T I P

Notice in figure 6.16 that the MENU.BAT program is created to run
from the \NU directory. Because the BE command is located in this
directory, the program runs the fastest. If you use a menu program
like this one, be sure that you put the program in the directory that
contains the NORTON BE.EXE batch enhancer program. If you use
the BE command in another directory, DOS searches the directories
defined in your DOS path for the BE.EXE program. If the \NU directory is early in the path, the execution of the BE command goes
faster than if the \NU directory is later in the path.

Setting the Date and Time
Stamp on Files

There are two Norton commands that enable you to set the date and
time stamp (the date and time that appear when you do a DIR command) on files. The File Date (FD) Command is convenient to use from
the DOS prompt and the FileFind command enables you to set date and
time interactively.

You may want to control these dates when you are preparing a disk to be distributed. Knowing the file date and time enables you to easily catalog different versions of disks. When software is released, for example, the date and time often are set by the software producer according to what release and version number are on the disks. A time of 1:00 may mean that the program is Version 1. A time of 1:02 would mean Version 1.02, and so on. Then, if someone calls for help concerning the disk you sent them, knowing the date and time associated with the files on the disk could tell you precisely when the disk was distributed and what version of the program or data the person is using.

Setting File Date and Time with the File Date Command

The File Date (FD) command enables you to change the date and time stamp on a file. The syntax for the FD command is

FD [*filespec*] [/*switches*]

The available switches for the command follow:

Switch	Effect
/D	Sets dates on file in subdirectories
/D[:]*date*	Sets date (*mm-dd-yy*)
/P	Pauses after each screen is displayed
/T[:]*time*	Sets time (*hh:mm*)

For example, to set the date and time on all files on drive A to 1-1-93 at 12:00, you use the command

FD A:*.* /D:1-1-93 /T:12:00

Setting File Date and Time Using the FileFind Command

When you enter the FILEFIND command from DOS or select FileFind from the Norton main menu, the FileFind screen appears (see fig. 6.18).

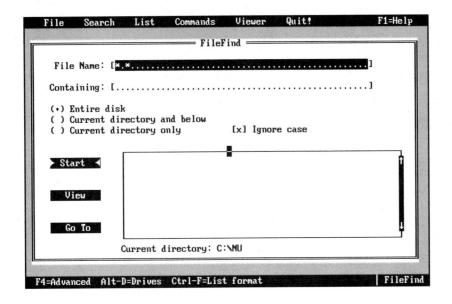

FIG. 6.18.

The FileFind
Screen.

To set the date and time on one or more files, follow these steps:

1. Enter the files to affect in the File Name field. To change all date and time files on drive A to 1-1-93 and 12:00, for example, enter A:*.* in the File Name field. Do not enter anything in the Containing field. Make sure that the Entire Disk option is chosen. If it is not chosen, use the Tab key to highlight that option and press the space bar to lock it in. Or, click on the option with the mouse.

2. Press Enter or click the Start option with your mouse to start the search, which will find all files on drive A and cause their names to appear in the list box on-screen.

3. Select the set Date/Time option from the Commands pull-down menu. To do this, press F10 to activate the menus, use the arrow keys to select the Command menu and the set Date/Time option, and press Enter. Or, select the Commands menu and the Set Date/Time option with the mouse pointer and click once.

4. An option screen similar to the one shown in figure 6.19 appears. The Set Date/Time box enables you to set date and time for one file (the one currently highlighted in the list box) or for all files in the list. Use the Tab key to move the highlight to the option for the entire list and press the space bar to lock in the option. Or, click on the option with the mouse pointer.

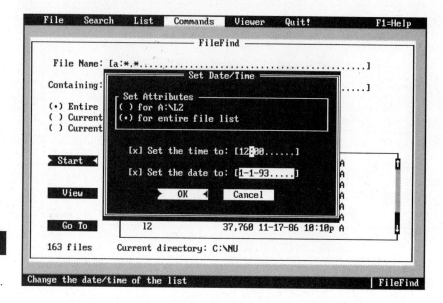

```
                              FileFind
  File Name: [a:*.*....................................................]
  Containing:┌──────────────── Set Date/Time ────────────────┐.....]
             │ ┌─Set Attributes─────────────────────────┐    │
  (•) Entire │ │ ( ) for A:\L2                           │    │
  ( ) Current│ │ (•) for entire file list               │    │
  ( ) Current│ └────────────────────────────────────────┘    │
             │                                                │
  ┌────────┐ │    [x] Set the time to: [12:00......]          │
  │ Start ◄│ │                                                │  A  ↑
  └────────┘ │    [x] Set the date to: [1-1-93.....]          │  A
  ┌────────┐ │       ┌──────────┐    ┌──────────┐             │  A
  │ View   │ │       │ ► OK    ◄│    │ Cancel   │             │  A
  └────────┘ └───────┴──────────┴────┴──────────┴─────────────┘  A
                                                              │  A
  ┌────────┐                                                     A
  │ Go To  │       12          37,760  11-17-86  10:10p  A    ↓
  └────────┘
  163 files       Current directory: C:\NU
```

```
Change the date/time of the list                            │ FileFind
```

FIG. 6.19.

The Set
Date/Time box.

5. Press the Tab key to move to the Set the Time To field and press the space bar to place an X in the selection box. Or, click on this box with the mouse pointer. Press Tab again to place the cursor in the Time box. Enter 12:00.

6. Press the Tab key to move to the Set the Date To field and press the space bar to place an X in the selection box. Or, click on this box with the mouse pointer. Press Tab again to place the cursor in the date box. Enter 1-1-93.

7. Press Enter to choose OK or click on OK with your mouse pointer. The program changes the dates and times according to your selections. Press Esc to end the FileFind program or click on Quit with the mouse pointer.

Locating Files on Disk

There are two Norton commands that enable you to locate files on disk by name. The File Locate (FL) command is designed to be used from the DOS prompt and the FileFind command can be used to locate files interactively.

Finding files on disk is very helpful if you have created a file months ago, and do not remember where you placed it on disk. If you can remember its file name or even a part of the file name, you may be able to locate the file by using the FL or FileFind command. These commands are also helpful for finding duplicates of files on disk or for finding the most recent copy of a file on disk.

Using the File Locate (FL) Command to Locate Files

The File Locate (FL) command is designed to be used from the DOS prompt. The syntax of File Locate is

FL [*filespec*] /*switches*

The available switches for File Locate follow:

Switch	Effect
/A	Searches for files on all drives.
/F[*n*]	Finds the first [*n*] files that match the file specification. The default is 1.
/P	Pauses after each screen.
/T	Searches the directories in the PATH statement only.
/W	Lists files in the wide format on-screen.

To locate all files on all drives that match the file specification *.XYX, for example, you use the command

FL *.XYX /A

Norton then produces a listing of the locations where this file is found.

Using FileFind To Locate a File

When you enter the FileFind command from DOS or choose it from the Norton menu, you see a screen similar to the one in figure 6.18. To locate a file by name on disk, follow these steps:

1. Enter the file name or a part of the file name (using standard DOS global characters * or ?). To find all of the files with an XYX extension, for example, you enter *.XYX in this field. Do not place anything in the Containing field.

2. Select the portion of the disk to search by selecting Entire Disk, Current Directory and Below, or Current Directory Only. To select one of these options, press the Tab key until the option you want is highlighted, and then press the space bar to lock in your option. Or, point to the option with the mouse pointer and click.

3. Press Enter or click the Start option with your mouse to start the search, which will find all files that match the criteria.

4. When the search is finished, a listing of the matching files appears in the file list box.

5. FileFind gives you the option of viewing the contents of a file in the list. Using the up- and down-arrow keys, you can highlight the name of a file. Or, point to the file name with the mouse pointer and click. To view the contents of the file, use the Tab key to highlight the View option and press Enter or point to View with the mouse pointer and click. The contents of the highlighted file will be displayed on-screen. To exit the view, press Esc.

To make a search over multiple drives, you can choose the Select Drives option from the Search pull-down menu and then select the drives to search. A screen such as the one in figure 6.20 appears. Using the Tab key, highlight the drives you want to include in the search and press the space bar to lock them in. Or, point to the drives to search and click. After you make your selections, press the Tab key to highlight the Save or OK option and press Enter. Or, point to the option you want with the mouse and click. Save permanently saves these drives for searching. The OK option only saves these drive specifications for the current run of FileFind. When you perform a search with the Entire Disk option selected, all disks specified here will be searched.

Searching for Information within Files

There are two Norton commands that enable you to search for information within files. The Text Search (TS) command is convenient to use from the DOS prompt and the FileFind command enables you to perform the search interactively.

Performing a text search is helpful when you are looking for a file that contains certain information, but you do not remember the name of the file. You can even perform a search on erased files.

FIG. 6.20.

The Drives to
Search screen.

Locating Information with the Text Search (TS) Command

The Text Search (TS) command enables you to search for text in files anywhere on disk, including erased space. The syntax for the command is

TS [*filespec*] [*string*] [*/switches*]

The *filespec* names the files to be searched, such as *.BAT. If the filespec is missing, all files will be searched. The *string* is the text to be located, such as *ALABAMA*. You want to search for files containing the name of that state. The available *switches* for this command follow:

Switch	Effect
/A	Automates the search. That is, ignores prompts.
/Cn	Begins the search at the cluster specified by *n*.
/CS	Performs a case-sensitive search. Thus, if you specify the search string as *Alan*, it will not find *ALAN*.

Switch	Effect
/D	Searches the entire disk.
/E	Searches only the erased portions of the disk.
/EBCDIC	Specifies that files being searched are in EBCDIC format.
/LOG	Creates output suitable for a log file or printer.
/S	Searches subdirectories also.
/T	Sets the noninteractive summary total.
/WS	Specifies that files being searched are in WordStar format.

To find occurrences of *ALABAMA* in files with a TXT extension, for example, you can use the command

    TS *.TXT ALABAMA

To find all instances of *ALABAMA* in erased space on disk, you can enter the command

    TS *.TXT /E

The command displays the file name or location of a find and asks if you want to continue the search (unless you have used the /A switch). Press Y to continue the search or N to cancel the search.

Locating Information with the FileFind Command

When you enter the FILEFIND command at the DOS prompt or choose FileFind from the Norton main menu, you see a screen similar to the one in figure 6.18.

Using FileFind to locate a file containing specified text is similar to using the command to locate a file, as discussed earlier in "Using FileFind To Locate a File." The two differences are placing a search criteria in the Containing field and specifying whether to ignore case.

The information you place in the Containing field specifies which files appear in the file list box. Only those that match the criteria will be listed. By default, the Ignore Case option is selected. This means that if you search for *QUE*, you will also find *Que*. You can turn off the Ignore

Case option by using the Tab key to highlight the option, and then pressing the space bar to deselect it. Or, point to the option with the mouse pointer and click.

Select the Start option by pressing Tab to highlight it and pressing Enter. Or, point to Start and click the mouse button. The search begins and matching files appear in the list box.

See "Using FileFind To Locate a File," earlier in this chapter, for a discussion of viewing the files in the list box and searching over multiple drives. End FileFind by pressing Esc or clicking on Quit.

Using the File Size (FS) Command

The File Size (FS) command enables you to list the size of a file or the total size of a group of files. For example, you can find out how much room on your disk is taken up by all *.EXE files.

File Size also lists the slack space associated with files. *Slack space* is space within a cluster that is allocated to a file but is not actually used. If a cluster is 512 bytes and a file stored is only 300 bytes long, for example, there are 212 bytes of unused slack space. This space cannot be used by another file, and is thus "wasted" space on disk. The only way you can really control slack space is to control the size of your files so that their size is close to a multiple of the cluster size. This is hard to do. Another way to control slack space is to avoid having many small files by combining them into one large file.

You also can use File Size to determine if there is enough space on a target disk to receive a copy of a group of files. Because the size of clusters differs between hard disks and floppy disks, you cannot tell just by the size of files on your hard disk if they will fit on your floppy disk. A floppy disk may have a 512-byte cluster, for example, while a hard disk may have a 2,048-byte cluster. Thus, the 300-byte file on the floppy disk takes up one cluster (512 bytes), but the same file takes up 2,048 bytes on the hard disk. Even though you may have a group of files that contain more than 360K bytes on your hard disk, they may fit onto a 360K floppy disk. The File Size command will tell you if this is so.

The syntax for the File Size command is

FS [*filespec*][*target drive:*][*/switches*]

The available switches follow:

Switch	Effect
/P	Pauses after each screen.
/S	Includes subdirectories in the file list.
/T	Displays only the total size for the specified files, not each file individually.

To find out the size of all files in the current directory, for example, you use the command

FS *.*

(or just FS)

This also reports the amount of slack space associated with these files.

To find out if there is room for these files to be copied onto drive A, you use the command

FS *.* A:

The command tells you whether there is sufficient space for the files to be copied onto the floppy disk.

Using the Line Print (LP) Command

The Line Print (LP) command enables you to print a text file to the printer. This command is similar to the DOS PRINT command, but it has a number of options not found in PRINT. The syntax for this command is

LP [*filespec*][*output*] [*/switches*]

The output option tells LP where to print the file. The default is PRN. Some common output designations you may use are LPT1, LPT2, COM1, and COM2. The available switches for this command follow:

Switch	Effect
/132	Sets page width at 132 columns.
/80	Sets page width at 80 columns.

Switch	Effect
/B*n*	Sets bottom margin to *n* lines. Default is 3.
/EBCDIC	Tells Line Print that the original file is in EBCDIC format.
/HEADER*n*	Sets type of header where 0 = no header, 1 = header consisting of current date and time on 1 line (default), 2 = current date and time plus file date and time on 2 lines.
/H*n*	Sets page height to *n* lines. Default is 66.
/L*n*	Sets left margin to *n* spaces. Default is 5.
/	Turns page numbering on.
/P*n*	Sets starting page number at *n*. Default is 1.
/PS	Tells Line Print to generate output for a PostScript printer.
/R*n*	Sets right margin to *n* spaces. Default is 5.
/Set:*filespec*	Tells that a Lotus-like printer setup string is in the file specified by the *filespec*.
/S*n*	Sets line spacing to *n* lines. Default is 1.
/TAB*n*	Sets tab spacing to *n* spaces. Default is 8.
/T*n*	Sets top margin to *n* lines. Default is 3.
/W*n*	Sets page width to *n* spaces. Default is 85.
/WS	Tells Line Print that the original file is in WordStar format.

To print the file REPORT.TXT (which was created with WordStar) to the printer, for example, you use the command

    LP REPORT.TXT /WS

Using the Directory Sort (DS) Command

The Directory Sort command enables you to sort one or more directories by name, extension, time, date, or size. You can use the DS command in command-line mode or interactively. The Speedisk command also enables you to sort files. See Chapter 5 for more information.

Sorting files enables you to cause the file names to appear in a particular way when you use a DIR command. This can be useful in finding files that have similar characteristics. If you sort on extension, for example, you can easily locate all EXE files because they will appear together. Also, if you want to look at the names of your most recently changed files, you can sort on date and time. Then, the directory lists all the most recent files at the end of the directory list.

Using Directory Sort Interactively

The syntax for the Directory Sort (DS) command is

> DS *sortkeys* [*directory*] [/S]

The *directory* tells the command which directory to sort. If you do not include a directory, the current directory is assumed. The *sortkeys* tell the command how to sort the files in the directory. The sort keys follow:

Key	Meaning
D	Date
E	Extension
N	Name
S	Size
T	Time

You can include one or more keys in the command line. The sort will progress in the order that the sort keys appear. If you use the keys EN, for example, the sort will be on extension first with names sorted within like extensions. If you place a minus sign after any key, the sort is in reverse order. For example, S sorts by size with smallest to largest listed. The key S- causes the sort to be from largest to smallest.

The /S switch tells the command to sort the files in the current or specified directory and all files in subdirectories.

To sort files in the \MYDIR directory and all subdirectories by Date and Time, for example, you use the command

> DS DT \MYDIR /S

Using Directory Sort in Interactive Mode

If you enter the DS command at the DOS prompt or choose Directory
Sort from the Norton menu, the Directory Sort screen appears (see
fig. 6.21).

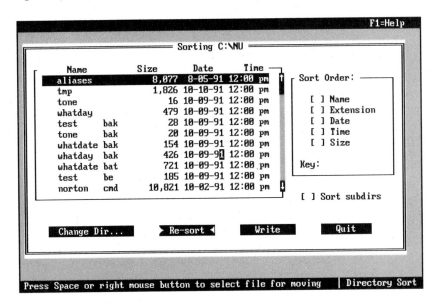

FIG. 6.21.

The Directory
Sort Screen.

On the left portion of this screen is a box containing a list of the files in
the current directory, including their name, size, date, and time.

Manually Rearranging Files

You can manually rearrange the files and directories listed in the box
on the Directory Sort screen by moving a file from one position to another. To move a file using the keyboard keys, follow these steps:

1. Use the arrow keys to point to a file or directory to move. Press
   the space bar to lock in your choice.

2. Use the up- and down-arrow keys to move the selected file or directory to a new location in the list.

3. Press the space bar or Enter to fix the selected file or directory in
   its new location.

To move a file or directory using a mouse, follow these steps:

1. Point to the file you want to move with the mouse pointer.

2. Click and hold down the right mouse button to select the file to move.

3. While still holding down the mouse button, drag the file to a new location in the list. Release the mouse button to fix the file or directory in its new location.

To save this rearrangement to disk, choose the Write option at the bottom of the screen. To select Write, press Tab to move the highlight to the option and press Enter. Or, point to the Write option with the mouse pointer and click. Press Esc or click on Quit to end the program.

Specifying Sort Order

On the right side of the Directory Sort screen is a Sort Order Box. You use this box to specify the sort order of the files. To set the sort order, you must select one or more of the sort items. Use the Tab and arrow keys to point to a sort item, and then press the space bar to lock in your selection. Or, point to a sort item with your mouse pointer and click. Select the items in the order in which you want the sort to take place. To sort by extension first and then name, for example, select Extension first, and then Name. A 1 appears by your first choice, a 2 appears beside the second choice, and so on.

If you want to change the sort order, press the + or - key while your cursor is pointing to the appropriate sort item. A + (plus) or - (minus) appears to the right of the sort item to indicate the sort order. Also, the sort key as you build it appears at the bottom of the Sort Order box.

Using Other Options on the Directory Sort Screen

Below the Sort Order box is a check box named Sort Subdirs. If this is checked, the sort you perform will affect the current directory and any subdirectories. To check this box, press the Tab key to highlight it, and then press the space bar to select it. Or, point to the box with the mouse pointer and click.

To sort a directory other than the one containing the files that appear in the list box, choose the Change Dir option at the bottom of the screen. To select this option, press the Tab key to move the highlight to this option and press Enter. Or, point to the option with the mouse pointer and click. You are prompted to indicate the directory to use.

To sort the file list according to the criteria in the sort box, choose the Re-sort option at the bottom of the screen. To select this option, press the Tab key to move the highlight to this option and press Enter. Or, point to the option with the mouse pointer and click. This causes the files to be sorted according to the criteria in the sort box. However, the files are not sorted permanently on disk.

To cause the sort to be saved to disk so that the files appear in this order when you perform a DIR command, you must choose the Write option at the bottom of the screen. To select this option, press Tab to move the highlight to this option, and then press Enter. Or, point to the option with the mouse pointer and click. You are prompted to indicate the directory to use.

To end the program, press Esc or choose the Quit option at the bottom of the screen.

Chapter Summary

Norton Utilities contains several programs that can jazz up the workings of your computer. You can set colors, graphically manage your directories, find files and text anywhere on disk, place comments on files, time events, and much more. All users have their own ideas about what makes their computers work intuitively for them. With the programs described in this chapter, you have a number of tools to make your computer behave exactly the way you want.

Using Norton Utilities Commands

This chapter lists alphabetically the commands in Norton Utilities Version 6. Use this chapter as a handy reference when you want to learn about or review a command quickly. Commands from the previous versions of Norton Advanced Utilities (4.5 and 5.0) also are listed, with references to the new Version 6 commands that replace the old commands. Each brief command description refers you to the chapter in this book that contains a more complete description of the command.

Several options are used in many of the Norton Utilities 6 commands. In this book, the following conventions apply to the way those options are presented in the command syntax examples:

- Items enclosed in [brackets] are optional.

- For words written in *italic*, substitute the appropriate parameter. To use the DISKREET [*switches*] syntax, for example, you may type

  DISKREET /ON

- The [*d:*] option is a designation for the disk drive name, such as drive A, B, C, or D.

- The [*filespec*] option is a designation for a file specification. Unless noted, this specification can include a path name. The file specification for a file named MYFILE.TXT in the \WP50 directory, for example, is \WP50\MYFILE.TXT. Usually, you can use the asterisk (*) and question mark (?) DOS global file characters (wild cards) in file specifications. For example, *.TXT specifies all files with the TXT extension.

- The [*color*] option refers to a selection of colors. A color designation in a command line, for example, could be WHITE ON BLUE. Using colors is described in Chapter 6.

- A vertical bar (|) between two items, such as ON|OFF means that you can choose one or the other option, but not both at the same time.

- The [/DEBUG] option, when specified, causes the command to display the DOS errorlevel value returned. Some Norton BE commands use this errorlevel for branching control.

Several global switches are available when you use a Norton command from the DOS prompt. You should place these switches on the command line after the command:

Switch	Effect
/BW	Specifies a monochrome display so that the command displays black-and-white rather than color screens.
/G0	Specifies an EGA or a VGA monitor. Produces a graphic mouse pointer if you are using a mouse and causes display boxes to use graphic symbols rather than character-based symbols (for example, uses radio buttons rather than check boxes). To use the /G0 switch with the Disk Tools command, for example, you type DISKTOOL /G0
/G1	Specifies an EGA or a VGA monitor. Disables use of the graphic mouse pointer. Causes display boxes to use graphic symbols, as with /G0.
/LCD	Specifies an LCD (laptop computer display) so that the command uses colors that have been chosen specifically by Norton to appear best on this kind of display.
/NOZOOM	Does not use the zoom-style dialog box.

Batch Enhancer (BE)

Chapter 6

The Batch Enhancer (BE) command consists of a series of subcommands intended to supplement the DOS batch commands. The syntax of the Batch Enhancer command is

> BE *subcommand*

or

> BE *filespec*

If a list of subcommands is stored in a file, you use the second version of the BE command. You also can enter a BE command from the DOS prompt, as in the first version of the BE command. You must include either a subcommand or a filespec command on the BE command line. See Chapter 6 for more information about BE and all its subcommands.

ASK

The BE subcommand ASK waits for a response from the user and stores the response in the DOS errorlevel variable. You usually need to use the DOS IF ERRORLEVEL GOTO LABEL command after ASK. The syntax is

> BE ASK *prompt*[,*keys*][DEFAULT=*key*][TIMEOUT=*n*][ADJUST=*n*][*color*][/DEBUG]

The following command displays the prompt Enter Menu Choice: and waits for your input:

> BE ASK "Enter Menu Choice: ",ABCD,DEFAULT=D,TIMEOUT=60

When you press A, B, C, and so on, the BE ASK command sets the errorlevel code; the first key becomes ERRORLEVEL 1, the second key is ERRORLEVEL 2, and so on. If you do not press a key during the TIMEOUT period of 60 seconds, the DEFAULT option (D) is used.

BEEP

The BE subcommand BEEP creates a tone and uses this syntax:

> BE BEEP [*switches*]

or

BE BEEP [*filespec*][/E]

The switches available for the BEEP subcommand follow:

Switch	Effect
/D*n*	Specifies the duration of a tone, where *n* is in measurements of 1/18 of a second. /D3, for example, specifies that the tone be sounded for 3/18 of a second.
/E	Echoes the text in the file to the screen (when used with a file specification).
/F*n*	Specifies the frequency of a tone, where *n* is cycles per second (Hertz). The switch /F440, for example, plays a tone at 440 cycles per second.
/R*n*	Specifies that the tone repeat *n* times.
/W*n*	Specifies a wait in durations of 1/18 of a second. The switch /W3, for example, causes a wait of 3/18 of a second.

The following command creates a sound at a frequency of 440 Hertz, pauses for 10/18 of a second, and sounds the tone again:

BE BEEP /F440 /R2 /W10

BOX

The BE subcommand BOX draws a box on-screen. The syntax for the BOX subcommand is

BE BOX *top,left,bottom,right*[SINGLE|DOUBLE][*color*]

Descriptions of the BOX parameters follow:

Parameter	Effect
top	Specifies the row number of the upper left corner of the box
left	Specifies the column number of the upper left corner of the box
bottom	Specifies the row number of the lower right corner of the box

Parameter	Effect
right	Specifies the column number of the lower right corner of the box
SINGLE	Produces a box with single lines (default)
DOUBLE	Produces a box with double lines

Remember: Items in uppercase are key words in the command—they appear in the command as written. The parameters in lowercase italics represent some number or option to be placed into the command. For example, *top* = 3, *left* = 2, and so on.

The following command draws a box on-screen with the upper left corner positioned two lines from the top of the screen and 10 columns from the left:

        BE BOX 2,10,20,70 DOUBLE

The lower right corner of the box is 20 lines from the top of the screen and 70 columns from the left. The rectangle drawn uses double lines.

CLS

The BE subcommand CLS is used to clear the screen. Optionally, you may set the screen color. The syntax of the command is

        BE CLS [*color*]

The color selections you can use are described in the BE SA subcommand.

DELAY

The BE subcommand DELAY causes the batch file to delay for a specified length of time. The syntax of the DELAY subcommand is

        BE DELAY [*time*]

where *time* is measured in 1/18 second, or in ticks. The command

        BE DELAY 18

delays the file for one second.

EXIT

The BE subcommand EXIT causes the termination of a Norton script file (not a DOS batch file). You can use this subcommand to stop a script at any point. The subcommand has no options. The syntax is simply

BE EXIT

GOTO

The BE subcommand GOTO enables you to branch the flow of the script to another part of the file. The syntax of the GOTO subcommand is

BE *filespec* [[GOTO] *label*]

where *filespec* is a script file and *label* is a label on its own line and starting in column one in the script file. A label is a statement in the file beginning with a colon (:). An example of a label is

:THISISALABEL

To send the flow of the script to that label, you use this command:

BE *filespec* GOTO THISISALABEL

JUMP

The BE subcommand JUMP enables you to incorporate conditional branching into a script (not for use in a DOS batch file). Unlike GOTO, which always branches to a specified label, JUMP can branch to one of several labels based on the current value of the exit code. The syntax of the JUMP subcommand is

BE JUMP *label1*,[*label2*[,...*labeln*]] [/DEFAULT:*label*]

where *label1* is the name of the label where the flow of the script should be sent if the exit code is 1, *label2* is the name of the label where the flow should be sent if the exit code is 2, and so on. If no label matches the exit code, the flow is sent to the label specified by the /DEFAULT switch. If no label matches the exit code and no default label exists, execution continues with the command following the JUMP command. See the next section on the MONTHDAY command for an example of how to use JUMP.

MONTHDAY

The BE subcommand MONTHDAY returns the day of the month as an exit code, which you then can use in a BE JUMP subcommand or in a DOS IF ERRORLEVEL command. The syntax for the MONTHDAY subcommand is

    BE MONTHDAY [/DEBUG]

The /DEBUG option causes the exit code to be displayed on-screen. To cause a backup to be performed on the first day of the month, for example, you can use the following commands:

    BE MONTHDAY
    BE JUMP BACKUP /DEFAULT:NOBACKUP

Then, on the first of the month, the batch file goes to the label :BACKUP (which contains instructions for performing a backup), and on other days the flow of the script is to the :NOBACKUP label.

PRINTCHAR

The BE subcommand PRINTCHAR prints a character a specified number of times. The syntax of the PRINTCHAR subcommand is

    BE PRINTCHAR *character,repeats* [*color*]

The *character* can be any ASCII character (including extended ASCII), and you can specify any number of *repeats* up to 80. The *color* parameter specifies the color of the text on-screen. See this chapter's discussion of the Screen Attributes (SA) command for more information.

The following command prints the asterisk (*) character 20 times on-screen, all in one line:

    BE PRINTCHAR *,20

REBOOT

The BE subcommand REBOOT enables you to perform a warm boot of the computer. The syntax of this command is

BE REBOOT [/VERIFY]

When the /VERIFY switch is included in the command, you (or another user) are prompted to confirm whether the reboot should take place. You may want to use this command if your batch file (or script file) chooses your AUTOEXEC.BAT or CONFIG.SYS file.

ROWCOL

The BE subcommand ROWCOL places the cursor at a designated location on-screen and optionally displays text at that location. The syntax of the ROWCOL subcommand is

BE ROWCOL *row,col*[,*text*][*color*]

The *row* parameter represents the number of the on-screen row (usually 1 to 25) where you want the cursor and any specified text to appear, and *col* is the number of the on-screen column (usually 1 to 80). If you include a *text* parameter in the command, that text is written to the screen at the designated location. The *color* parameter specifies the color of the text on-screen. See this chapter's discussion of the Screen Attributes (SA) command for more information.

The following command places the cursor 10 lines from the top and five columns from the left of the screen and prints at that location the text specified within the quotes:

BE ROWCOL 10,5,"Make a selection using the cursor keys."

The cursor ends up *after* the printed text, not at (row,col).

Screen Attributes (SA)

The BE subcommand SA sets color attributes for the screen. The syntax of the Screen Attributes (SA) subcommand is

BE SA *main-setting* [*switches*]

or

BE SA [*intensity*][*foreground*][ON *background*][*switches*]

The options for *main-setting* are normal, reverse, or underline. For example,

BE SA NORMAL

is simple and easy to remember. The second version is more complicated, but more powerful. Choices for *intensity* are bright, bold, or blinking. Bright and bold are identical. Choices for *foreground* and *background* colors are white, black, red, magenta, blue, green, cyan, and yellow. The available *switches* include /N and /CLS. /N instructs the SA subcommand not to set border color, and /CLS clears the screen after setting the screen attributes.

The following command causes on-screen characters to appear in bold white on a blue background. When this command is given, it also clears the screen.

BE SA BOLD WHITE ON BLUE/CLS

SHIFTSTATE

The BE subcommand SHIFTSTATE examines the status of the left and right Shift keys, the Alt key, and the Ctrl key (it determines if the key is *shifted* or pressed) and returns an exit code indicating where those keys are in the Shift state. You then can use the exit code to cause the script to branch with the JUMP subcommand or the DOS ERRORLEVEL command. The syntax of the SHIFTSTATE subcommand is

BE SHIFTSTATE [/DEBUG]

The /DEBUG option causes the exit code to be displayed on-screen. Exit codes returned by this command include the following:

Key in Shift State	Returned Code
Right Shift	1
Left Shift	2
Ctrl (left or right)	4
Alt (left or right)	8

You can use the shift state to create several versions of the same command. You can write a script file where BE MYCMD performs one set of commands, for example, but performs another set of commands if it is issued while the Shift, Alt, or Ctrl keys are pressed.

TRIGGER

The BE subcommand TRIGGER halts the execution of a script until a specified time. This command enables you to set up your script so that it stops and then waits until a specified time to continue execution. The syntax of the TRIGGER subcommand is

BE TRIGGER *hh:mm* [AM] [PM]

where *hh:mm* is hours and minutes in military (24-hour clock) time. 14:00 is thus 2:00 p.m. You can use the AM or PM designation on the command line to specify a 12-hour clock time, as in 2:00 PM. In this designation, 12:00 AM is the same as 0:00 (midnight), and 12:00 PM is noon.

You may have a communications program set up, for example, to send data to a long-distance location. You can use the TRIGGER subcommand to tell the program to begin execution early in the morning when telephone rates are lowest. The following command causes the script to pause until 2 o'clock in the morning before continuing:

BE TRIGGER 2:00 AM

WEEKDAY

Similar to the MONTHDAY subcommand, the BE subcommand WEEK-DAY returns the day of the week as an exit code. You can use the WEEKDAY subcommand in a JUMP subcommand or in an IF ERRORLEVEL command. The syntax of the WEEKDAY subcommand is

BE WEEKDAY [/DEBUG]

The /DEBUG option causes the exit code to be displayed on-screen. To cause a backup to be performed on the second day of the week (Monday), for example, you can use the following commands:

BE WEEKDAY
BE JUMP NOBACKUP, BACKUP /DEFAULT:NOBACKUP

On the first day of the week, the command branches to NOBACKUP. On the second day of the week, the batch file goes to the label :BACKUP (which contains instructions for performing a backup), and on other days the flow of the script is to the :NOBACKUP label.

WINDOW

The BE subcommand WINDOW draws a window on-screen, with optional shadow and zoom features. The syntax of the WINDOW subcommand is

BE WINDOW *top,left,bottom,right* [*color*][SHADOW][ZOOM]

Descriptions of the WINDOW parameters follow:

Parameter	Effect
top	Specifies the row number of the upper left corner of the window
left	Specifies the column number of the upper left corner of the window
bottom	Specifies the row number of the lower right corner of the window
right	Specifies the column number of the lower right corner of the window
SHADOW	Adds a shadow to the right and bottom edges of the window
ZOOM	Zooms the window onto the screen—the window starts as a small rectangle and grows to full size

The following command draws a window on-screen with the upper left corner positioned two lines from the top and 10 columns from the left of the screen:

BE WINDOW 2,10,20,70 SHADOW ZOOM

The lower right corner of the window is 20 lines from the top and 70 columns from the left of the screen. The window zooms onto the screen and has a shadow. The main difference between the BOX and WINDOW command is that the BOX command does not overwrite any text on-screen. The WINDOW command blanks out the window, erasing any text on-screen.

Calibrate (CALIBRAT)

Chapter 5

You use the Calibrate command to optimize the speed and reliability of reading and writing information to your hard disk. Calibrate is capable of performing a nondestructive, low-level format, which enables you to check your disk for reliability without destroying the information on disk. You should make sure that any memory-resident programs (TSRs) are not loaded and that only essential device drivers (in your CONFIG.SYS file) are in use when you use this command. The syntax of the Calibrate command is

CALIBRAT [*d:*] [*switches*]

The available switches for the Calibrate command follow:

Switch	Effect
/BATCH	Does not prompt for any input from the user. Returns to DOS when finished.
/BLANK	Blanks the screen during the test.
/NOCOPY	Does not make a duplicate copy of the track being tested.
/NOFORMAT	Performs pattern-testing only and skips the low-level format.
/NOSEEK	Skips the seek tests. Use this switch when you do not want Calibrate to test the head-positioning mechanism of the disk. Usually, you should use Calibrate once without /NOSEEK to test the mechanism. Then, you can include /NOSEEK on subsequent tests.
/PATTERN:*n*	Specifies which testing level (*n*) to use. The parameter *n* can be 0, 5, 40, or 80. The higher the number, the more thorough the test; however, the higher the number, the longer Calibrate takes to test the disk.
/R:*file*	Generates a report and writes it to the file name specified in the switch. You must use the /BATCH switch also when you use /R:*file*.
/RA:*file*	Performs the same function as the /R:*file* switch but appends the information to the file instead of creating a new file.

Switch	Effect
/X:[*d:*][*d:*]	Excludes named drives from the test. For example, /X:DE excludes disks D and E from testing. If your computer has allocated nonexistent drives, you must use this switch to exclude those drives from the tests.

Directory Sort (DS)

Chapter 6

You can use the Directory Sort (DS) command for sorting the names of files on your directory by name, extension, time, date, or size. The syntax of this command is

DS [*sort-keys*] [*pathname*] /S

where *pathname* is the directory to be sorted. If you do not include any sort keys, the program runs in interactive mode. The available sort keys are

Key	Sorts By
N	Name
E	Extension
D	Date
T	Time
S	Size

To sort in name and extension order, for example, type

DS NE

Adding a minus (–) to any sort key reverses the sort order. Thus, –N tells the command to sort by name in reverse alphabetical order. The /S switch tells the command to include subdirectories in the sorting. See this chapter's discussion of the Speed Disk command for more information on sorting directories.

Disk Editor (DISKEDIT)

Chapter 4

Similar to the old Norton Utilities main program, the Disk Editor enables you to view and edit the entire contents of a floppy or hard disk. The Disk Editor is useful when you are not able to recover information by using Norton Disk Doctor II. You must have a good understanding of how disks work, however, to be able to use this program effectively. The syntax of the Disk Editor is

DISKEDIT [*d:*] [*path*] [*filename*] [*switches*]

The available switches for the DISKEDIT command follow:

Switch	Effect
/M	Operates in maintenance mode. This mode enables the program to bypass DOS and look directly at the contents of a disk.
/SKIPHIGH	Does not load into high memory. Use this if you are using a memory manager that is already occupying high DOS memory.
/W	Uses write-able mode. Otherwise, it is in read-only mode, and does not enable you to write information to disk.
/X:[*d:*][*d:*]	Excludes certain drives from absolute sector processing. For example, /X:DE excludes disks D and E from testing. If your computer has allocated nonexistent drives, you must use this switch to exclude those drives.

The Disk Editor is an interactive program that you operate from a menu.

Disk Information (DI)

The Disk Information command in Norton Utilities 4.5 has been integrated into the System Information command in Versions 5.0 and 6.

Disk Monitor (DISKMON)

Chapter 3

The Disk Monitor command helps you protect your information on disk from accidental or unauthorized destruction. Disk Monitor contains three main features:

Disk Protect	Prevents unauthorized use of your files on disk
Disk Light	Places a disk-access light on your monitor so that you can see when your disk is being used
Disk Park	Moves the read/write head on your hard disk to a safe location so that you can move your computer

You should run Disk Monitor interactively (type *diskmon* at the DOS prompt) the first time to choose the type of protection you want (files, system areas, entire disk, and floppy format). Disk Monitor stores those selections in a file named DM.INI. After you have the command set up the way you want it, you can use Disk Monitor and its switches from the DOS prompt. The syntax for using the command from the DOS prompt is

DISKMON [*switches*]

The available switches for the Disk Monitor command follow:

Switch	Effect
/LIGHT+ or /LIGHT–	Turns on (+) or off (–) the Disk Light feature.
/PARK	Parks all drives.
/PROTECT– or /PROTECT+	Turns on (+) or off (–) the protect feature. When this feature is turned on, protection is set to the selections that were stored in DM.INI when you ran the command interactively.
/SKIPHIGH	Does not load into high memory. Use this if you are using a memory manager that is already occupying high DOS memory.
/STATUS	Displays a summary of the Disk Monitor status on-screen.
/UNINSTALL	Uninstalls the Disk Monitor program from memory if that program was the last TSR loaded into memory.

Disk Test (DT)

The Disk Test (DT) command for Norton Utilities 4.5 has been incorporated into the Norton Disk Doctor command for Versions 5.0 and 6.

Disk Tools (DISKTOOL)

Chapter 4

Disk tools are a set of six utilities that contain data-protection and recovery features. These tools enable you to do the following:

- Make a disk bootable
- Recover from DOS's RECOVER
- Revive a defective diskette
- Mark a cluster
- Create a rescue diskette
- Restore with a rescue diskette

The Disk Tools program is primarily designed for interactive use. However, you can select which tool to use and tell the program not to use DOS high memory by including one or more switches on the command line. The versions of the command follow:

DISKTOOL [/MAKEBOOT][/SKIPHIGH]

DISKTOOL [/DOSRECOVER][/SKIPHIGH]

DISKTOOL [/REVIVE][/SKIPHIGH]

DISKTOOL [/MARKCLUSTER][/SKIPHIGH]

DISKTOOL [/SAVERESCUE I /RESTORE][/SKIPHIGH]

A brief description of these switches follows:

Switch	Effect
/DOSRECOVER	Skips the Disk Tools menu and goes right to the Recover from DOS's RECOVER option.
/MAKEBOOT	Skips the Disk Tools menu and goes right to the Make a Disk Bootable option.
/RESTORE	Skips the Disk Tools menu and goes right to the Restore from a Rescue Diskette option.

Switch	Effect
/REVIVE	Skips the Disk Tools menu and goes right to the Revive a Defective Diskette option.
/SAVERESCUE	Skips the Disk Tools menu and goes right to the Create a Rescue Diskette option.
/SKIPHIGH	Does not load into high memory. Use this option if you are using a memory manager that is already using DOS high memory.

Diskreet (DISKREET)

Chapter 3

Diskreet is a program that enables you to protect files or ndisks so that they cannot be accessed by anyone without permission. (The user must know a password to access the protected files.) Files stored by Diskreet are encrypted so that they are unreadable, even by the Disk Editor. An ndisk is an area on your hard disk that operates as if it were a separate disk, and contains encrypted information that is password-protected. In order for the Diskreet program to work, the following line must be in your CONFIG.SYS file:

DEVICE=*path*\DISKREET.SYS

where *path* is the name of the directory where your Norton files are stored. When you boot your computer, this line tells DOS to make the Diskreet driver available for use. The syntax for using Diskreet from the DOS prompt is

DISKREET [*switches*]

The available switches for the Diskreet command follow:

Switch	Effect
/CLOSE	Closes all ndisks
/DECRYPT:*filespec*	Decrypts the specified files
/ENCRYPT:*filespec*	Encrypts the specified files
/HIDE[:*d*]	Hides the specified drive (ndisk)
/OFF	Disables use of the Diskreet driver
/ON	Enables the Diskreet driver
/PASSWORD:*your password*	Specifies password to use for encryption or decryption
/SHOW[:*d*]	Shows the hidden drives (ndisks) being used to store files

Erase Protect

Chapter 3

The Erase Protect (EP) command, called File Save in Version 5.0, moves "deleted" files to a less-used part of the hard disk so that those files remain recoverable for a longer period of time. After the part of the disk that contains a deleted file is used, any deleted files occupying that space become unrecoverable. You usually should include the Erase Protect command in your AUTOEXEC.BAT file so that the command is in effect whenever you delete files.

The Erase Protect command is a memory-resident (TSR) program. The syntax of the Erase Protect command is

EP [*switches*]

The available switches for the Erase Protect command follow:

Switch	Effect
/OFF	Disables the Erase Protect command so that deleted files are not affected. The Erase Protect command remains in memory but does not function unless you turn on the /ON switch again.
/ON	Enables the Erase Protect command to move deleted files to a safe area.
/SKIPHIGH	Does not load into high memory.
/STATUS	Displays the status of the Erase Protect command.
/UNINSTALL	Removes the Erase Protect command from memory if the command was the last memory-resident (TSR) command loaded.

File Attributes (FA)

Chapter 3

The File Attributes (FA) command enables you to display, set, or reset the file attributes archive, hidden, read-only, and system. The syntax of the command is

FA [*filespec*] [*switches*]

The available switches for the FA command follow:

Switch	Effect
/A+	Sets archive attribute on
/A–	Sets archive attribute off
/CLEAR	Removes (clears) all the attributes
/DIR+	Sets hidden directory on
/DIR–	Sets hidden directory off
/HID+	Sets hidden attribute on
/HID–	Sets hidden attribute off
/P	Pauses after each displayed screen
/R+	Sets read-only attribute on
/R–	Sets read-only attribute off
/SYS+	Sets system attribute on
/SYS–	Sets system attribute off
/S	Includes subdirectories when setting attributes
/T	Displays only file and directory totals
/U	Lists all "unusual" files—those that have some attribute set

The following command, for example, sets the read-only attribute to on for all BAT files in the current directory:

FA *.BAT /R+

For more information on setting attributes, see this chapter's discussion of the FileFind command.

File Date (FD)

Chapter 6

The File Date (FD) command enables you to change the date and time stamp on a file. The syntax of the command is

FD [*filespec*] [*switches*]

The available switches for the File Date command follow:

Switch	Effect
/D[:]*date*	Sets date (*mm-dd-yy*)
/P	Pauses after each screen is displayed
/S	Also sets dates on files in subdirectories
/T[:]*time*	Sets time (*hh:mm:ss*)

To set all files on the disk to the date 1-1-94 and the time 12:00, for example, you use the command

FD *.* /D:1-1-94 /T:12:00

For more information on setting time and date on files, see the next section's discussion of the FileFind command.

FileFind (FILEFIND)

Chapters 3 and 6

The FileFind command helps you find files by name in any directory on disk, search for text in files, set file attributes, and set dates and times for files. The FileFind command uses the following syntax:

FILEFIND [*d:*][*filespec*] [*search-text*] [*switches*]

The *filespec* option may include global file characters such as a question mark (?) or an asterisk (*). Some special *filespec* forms and their effects include

.	Searches entire current drive
.*.*	Searches only current directory
:.*	Searches all drives

The switches available for the FileFind command follow:

Switch	Effect
/A[+/−]	Sets or unsets the archive attribute. The plus (+) sets it, and the minus (−) unsets it. If neither + nor − is included, the command lists files that have the archive bit set.
/BATCH	Exits the program automatically and returns to the DOS prompt.
/C	Includes current directory in search.

Switch	Effect
/CLEAR	Clears all file attributes.
/CS	Makes search case-sensitive.
/D[:]*date*	Specifies date to place on the files that match the file specification. The date should be in the format *mm-dd-yy*. (The date format may be different if your computer uses a non-US country code.)
/HID[+|−]	Sets or unsets the hidden attribute. The plus (+) sets it, and the minus sign (−) unsets it. If neither + nor − is included, the command lists files that have the hidden bit set.
/NOW	Sets the time and date to the current system time and date.
/O:*file*	Saves output lists from the command to the file named.
/R[+|−]	Sets or unsets the read-only attribute. The plus (+) sets it, and the minus sign (−) unsets it. If neither + nor − is included, the command lists files that have the read-only bit set.
/S	Includes all subdirectories in search.
/SYS[+|−]	Sets or unsets the system attribute. The plus (+) sets it, and the minus (−) unsets it. If neither + nor − is included, the command lists files that have the system bit set.
/T[:]*time*	Specifies time to place on the files that match the file specification. The time should be in the format HH:MM:SS (military time). (The time format may be different if your computer uses a non-US country code.)
/TARGET:*d*	Determines whether the files specified will fit on the target drive *d*.

The following command sets the date and time to 1-1-93 and noon for all files on the floppy disk in drive A:

    FILEFIND A:*.* /D010193 /T12:00:00

For more information on setting time and date, see this chapter's discussion of the File Date (FD) command.

The following command produces a list of the files stored on drive C that match the *.DRV file specification:

    FILEFIND C:*.DRV

This list reports the file name, size, date, time, and file attributes. For more information on setting file attributes, see this chapter's discussion of the File Attributes (FA) command.

File Fix (FILEFIX)

Chapter 4

You use the File Fix command to diagnose and repair damaged dBASE, Lotus 1-2-3, or Symphony files. File Fix examines the contents of damaged files and attempts to reconstruct the files. Many files can be repaired automatically, but some require intervention by the user to make judgment decisions on how to fix the file. File Fix runs in interactive mode. To begin the program at the DOS prompt, enter the command

    FILEFIX [*filename*]

where *filename* is the name of the file you want to fix.

File Info (FI)

The File Info (FI) command for Norton Utilities 4.5 is not included in Version 5.0 or 6.

File Locate (FL)

Chapter 6

The File Locate (FL) command is similar to the FileFind command, but FL operates only from the DOS prompt and does not include the date-, time-, and attribute-setting functions of the FileFind command. The syntax of File Locate is

    FL [*filespec*] [*switches*]

The available switches for File Locate follow:

Switch	Effect
/A	Searches for files on all drives.
/F[*n*]	Finds the first *n* number of files that match the file specification (default for *n* is 1)

Switch	Effect
/P	Pauses after each screen
/T	Searches the directories in the PATH statement only
/W	Lists files in the wide format on-screen

To locate all files on all drives that match the file specification *.XYX, for example, you use the command

    FL *.XYX /A

File Save

The File Save command in Version 5.0 was renamed Erase Protect in Version 6. See the discussion of Erase Protect in this chapter for information.

File Size (FS)

Chapter 6

The File Size (FS) command enables you to list the size of a file or the total size of a group of files. File Size also lists the slack space. You can use File Size to determine whether a target disk has enough space to receive a copy of a group of files. The syntax of the command is

    FS [*filespec*][*target drive:*][*switches*]

The available switches follow:

Switch	Effect
/P	Pauses after each screen
/S	Includes subdirectories in the file list
/T	Displays only the total size for the specified files, not each file individually

To find out the sizes of all files in the current directory, for example, you use the command

    FS *.*

(You also can use just FS.)

To find out whether you have enough room to copy these files onto disk A, you use the command

FS *.* A:

Format Recover (FR)

The Format Recover (FR) command in Norton Utilities 4.5 has been integrated into the UnFormat command in Versions 5.0 and 6. See the discussion of the UnFormat command for more information.

Image (IMAGE)

Chapter 3

The Image program captures important information about the files on your hard disk and saves that information to a file named IMAGE.DAT. If your disk is formatted accidentally, the information in the IMAGE.DAT file can help the UnFormat program restore your files. To keep the IMAGE.DAT file current, you should place the Image command in your AUTOEXEC.BAT file so that IMAGE.DAT is updated each time you boot your computer. The syntax of the Image command is

IMAGE [*switch*]

The only switch for this command is /NOBACK. This switch instructs the command not to create the backup file IMAGE.BAK.

Line Print (LP)

Chapter 6

The Line Print (LP) command enables you to print a text file to the printer. The syntax of this command is

LP [*filespec*][*output*] [*switches*]

The *output* option tells LP where to print the file. The default is PRN:. Some common output designations you may use are LPT1:, LPT2:, COM1:, and COM2:.

The available switches for this command follow:

Switch	Effect
/80	Sets page width at 80 columns
/132	Sets page width at 132 columns
/B*n*	Sets bottom margin to *n* lines (default is 3)
/EBCDIC	Tells Line Print that the original file is in EBCDIC format
/HEADER*n*	Sets type of header:
	0 = no header
	1 = header consisting of current date and time on line 1 (default)
	2 = current date and time plus file date and time on two lines
/H*n*	Sets page height to *n* lines (default is 66)
/L*n*	Sets left margin to *n* spaces (default is 5)
/N	Turns page numbering on
/P*n*	Sets starting page number at *n* (default is 1)
/PS	Tells Line Print to generate output for a PostScript printer
/R*n*	Sets right margin to *n* spaces (default is 5)
/SET:*filespec*	Tells Line Print that a Lotus-like printer setup string is in the file specified by *filespec*
/S*n*	Sets line spacing to *n* lines (default is 1)
/TAB*n*	Sets tab spacing to *n* spaces (default is 8)
/T*n*	Sets top margin to *n* lines (default is 3)
/W*n*	Sets page width to *n* spaces (default is 85)
/WS	Tells Line Print that the original file is in WordStar format

To print the file REPORT.TXT (which was created with WordStar) to the printer, for example, you use the command

LP REPORT.TXT /WS

List Directories (LD)

The List Directories (LD) command in Norton Utilities 4.5 has been integrated into the Norton Change Directory command in Versions 5.0 and 6.

Norton Cache (NCACHE)

Chapter 5

The Norton Cache program enables you to specify how much random-access memory (RAM) in your computer should be used as a buffer when the computer is reading information from disk. The larger the cache, the faster your disk access will tend to be. To place the Norton Cache program in your AUTOEXEC.BAT file, you can use the following syntax:

>   *path*\NCACHE [*parameters*]

The *path* refers to the directory name where the NCACHE file is stored. To place the program in your CONFIG.SYS file, you can use the following syntax:

>   DEVICE=*path*\NCACHE [*switches*]

The switches available for NCACHE follow:

Switch	Effect
/[–]A	Activates or deactivates caching. Use this switch if you need to deactivate caching in order to run a program in which you do not want caching to be used.
/[–]C	Enables or disables caching of additional information. No new information is cached when this switch is disabled.
/[–]I	Enables or disables IntelliWrites. When on, this switch accelerates disk writes and returns control to the application before the write is finished.
/[–]P	Enables or disables write protection for drives.
/[–]W	Enables or disables write-through caching. When write-through caching is disabled, writes are written directly to the disk, bypassing the cache.

Switch	Effect
/BLOCK=*n*	Sets the size of the cache blocks. The *n* is a number in kilobytes. Use large blocks if you are accessing large files and your disk is unfragmented. Use smaller blocks if you access small files or if your disk is fragmented.
/DELAY=*ss.hh*	Delays writes to the disk in seconds or hundredths of a second (for example, 00.10 is one hundredth of a second). The default is 00.00. Slight writing delays can improve the speed of write-intensive programs.
/DOS=*n* or /DOS=–*n*	Specifies how much DOS (conventional) memory is to be used by the cache. Use this switch only when you do not have any expanded or extended memory. A negative value tells the command to leave that much memory free for other programs to use.
/EXP=*n* or /EXP=–*n*	Specifies how much expanded memory in kilo bytes is to be used by the cache. A negative value tells the command to leave that much memory free for other programs to use. EXP=750, for example, tells the command to use 750K of expanded memory for the disk cache. Any expanded memory used must be LIM 4.0-compatible.
/EXT=*n* or /EXT=–*n*	Specifies how much extended memory in kilobytes is to be used by the cache. A negative value tells the command to leave that much free memory for use by other programs. EXT=256, for example, tells the command to use 256K of extended memory for the cache.
/F	Flushes the cache (empties it). This process causes all writes to disk to be finished.
/G=*n*	Specifies a group sector size (the default is 128). Specify a group size smaller than 128 if you are reading small pieces of information from a random file, such as in a database with small records.
/INI=*filespec*	Indicates where to look for the file that contains installation options. If your installation options are in your \NORTON directory in a file named NCACHE.INI, for example, you use the parameter INI=\NORTON\NCACHE.INI.

Switch	Effect
/INSTALL	Installs the Norton Cache with all default values, including the use of all available expanded and extended memory for the cache. This switch is often the easiest and quickest way to execute the command.
/OPTIMIZE=[S|E|M]	Optimizes for speed, efficiency, or memory.

The S (Speed) option sets the following parameters:

/BLOCK=8K

/DELAY=1.0

/READ=8K

/WRITE=x where x is the largest track (in K) of all tracks being cached

The E (Efficiency) option sets the following parameters:

/BLOCK=s where s is the smallest block size for the current cache size (usually 512K to 1M)

/DELAY=1.0

/READ=8K

/WRITE=8K

The M (Memory) option sets the following parameters:

/BLOCK=8K

/DELAY=0.0

/READ=0 (disables the read-ahead feature)

/WRITE=0 (disables IntelliWrites)

Switch	Effect
/QUICK=ON|OFF	ON displays the DOS prompt even when information is being written to disk. OFF waits until all writes to the disk have finished before displaying the DOS prompt.
/R=Dn	Specifies how many sectors ahead should be read. A specification of R=0 or R=D0 disables read-aheads. R=n causes read-aheads always, and a specification of R=Dn causes read-aheads only when the file being read is not a random file. For n, you can specify a number of sectors from 0 to 15.

Switch	Effect
/READ=*n*	Sets the maximum size (in kilobytes) for read-aheads. For *n*, use a whole number from 8 to 64.
/REPORT=[ON|OFF]	Displays status information (ON) or does not display such information (OFF).
/RESET	Resets the cache statistics, which are viewable on the NCACHE status screen.
/SAVE	Saves current cache settings in the file specified by the /INI switch (or NCACHE.INI).
/STATUS	Displays a number of statistics that enable you to see how effective the cache is working. The higher the ratio, the more effective the cache.
/UNINSTALL	Removes the Norton Cache command from memory. This command does not work unless the Norton Cache program was the last memory-resident (TSR) program loaded into memory.
/USE HMA=YES|NO	Uses the XMS high-memory area to reduce the use of DOS RAM (if set to YES). This option is available only if you have an extended memory manager.
/USEHIGH=YES|NO	Minimizes the use of conventional (low) DOS memory if high memory is available (if set to YES). The default setting is NO.
/WRITE=*n*	Sets maximum size (in kilobytes) for the IntelliWrites buffer. For *n*, use a whole number from 8 to 64.

Norton Change Directory (NCD)

Chapter 6

The Norton Change Directory (NCD) command enables you to manage your directories on disk, to change quickly from directory to directory, and to print a directory tree. NCD gives you more control over directory names than you have with the normal DOS commands. The NCD command is suited particularly for use interactively, but you also can use it from the DOS prompt. In command-line mode, the syntax for the Norton Change Directory (NCD) command can be any of the following:

■ NCD [*dirname*] [*switches*]

■ NCD [*d:*] /V:*label*

■ NCD [*d:*] /l[:*output* [/A[/G[/N]]][/T][/P]

- NCD MD [*dirname*]
- NCD RD [*dirname*]
- NCD SIZE [*dirname*]
- NCD COPY *source destination* [/DELETE]
- NCD GRAFT *source destination* [/NET]
- NCD RMTREE *dirname* [/BATCH]

The *dirname* is the name of the directory you want to change to, make, remove, or display the size of. The source and destination options tell the command the original location of the directory to be copied or grafted (source) and the target location (destination) for the directory.

The available switches for the NCD command follow:

Switch	Effect
/A	Displays the directory tree for all drives except floppies
/BATCH	Skips all prompts and exits to DOS when finished
/G	Displays the directory tree graphically
/L:*output*	Prints the directory tree to the specified output file
/N	Does not write the file TREEINFO.NCD. If you are using NCD on a write-protected disk, you need to use this switch.
/NET	Uses the network method of Copy and Delete to move directories (with the COPY and GRAFT options)
/NG	Displays the tree using non-graphical characters (best when using a printer that does not support graphical characters)
/P	Pauses after each screenful of information is displayed
/R	Updates the file TREEINFO.NCD, which contains information about your directory tree structure
/T	Totals the number and size of all files
/V:*label*	Places a volume label on the disk

Other options for the NCD command follow:

COPY	Copies a directory to a new location. NCD COPY \MYDIR \YOURDIR, for example, copies all files from the directory named \MYDIR to the directory named \YOURDIR. Including /DELETE deletes copied files from their original locations.
GRAFT	Automatically deletes files from the old location.
RMTREE	Removes a directory and all associated files.

The MD and RD versions of the NCD command are similar to the DOS MD and RD commands. You use them to make a new directory or to remove an empty directory. The NCD SIZE command displays the amount of space taken up by the files in the directory.

To use the COPY, GRAFT, and RMTREE options, you first must enable them on the Configure menu, which is accessed from the NCD menu.

To create a directory named \WP50\REPORTS, for example, use the command

    NCD MD \WP50\REPORTS

To use the NCD command to change directories, you type *ncd* plus the name of the directory to which you want to change. To change to the directory \ONE-A\TWO-A\THREE-A\FOUR-A, for example, use the command

    NCD FOUR-A

Norton Control Center (NCC)

Chapter 6

The Norton Control Center (NCC) command enables you to control hardware settings, including display colors, keyboard rates, and clock settings. You can use the Norton Control Center command in command-line or interactive mode. The syntax of the NCC command in command-line mode is

    NCC [*filespec*][*switches*]

The *filespec* variable refers to a file that contains system-information specifications. Before you use this version of the command, you must create this file by using NCC in interactive mode to choose the settings you want and then saving the information to a file.

The available switches for the NCC command follow:

Switch	Effect
/CURSOR	Reads the information in the file named by *filespec* but sets only the cursor size.
/DOSCOLOR	Reads the information in the file named by *filespec* but sets only the previously chosen DOS colors for foreground, background, and border.
/PALETTE	Reads the information in the file named by *filespec* but sets only the palette colors.
/SET	Reads the information in the file named by *filespec* and sets all the parameters.

If you have not created a settings file by running the NCC command in interactive mode, you can set a few options by using certain quick switches, which follow:

Switch	Effect
/25	Places the monitor in 25-line mode (same as /CO80)
/35	Places the monitor in 35-line mode (supported only by EGA monitors)
/40	Places the monitor in 40-line mode (supported only by VGA monitors)
/43	Places the monitor in 43-line mode (supported only by EGA monitors)
/50	Places the monitor in 50-line mode (supported only by VGA monitors)
/BW80	Places the monitor in black-and-white mode with 25 lines and 80 columns
/CO80	Places the monitor in color mode with 25 lines and 80 columns
/FAST	Sets the keyboard rate to its fastest possible value

To set your VGA computer so that 50 lines are displayed on-screen and the keyboard rate is the fastest value, for example, use this command:

    NCC /50/FAST

You also may use the Control Center to set system stopwatches by using the following switches:

Switch	Effect
/C:*comment*	Displays the text string *comment* after you execute the command. Useful for documenting which timer is being reported. If the comment contains any blanks, you must enclose the entire comment in quotes.
/L	Displays time and date on left side of monitor.
/N	Suppresses display of current time and date.
/START:*n*	Begins the stopwatch number *n* where *n* can be a number from 1 to 4.
/STOP:*n*	Stops the stopwatch number *n* where *n* can be a number from 1 to 4.

To access the Norton Control Center interactively, enter the NCC command without using any file specification. The Control Center menu appears, enabling you to choose interactively the same options you can set with switches in the command-line mode.

Norton Disk Doctor (NDD)

Chapter 4

The Norton Disk Doctor (NDD) command finds and corrects, if possible, physical or logical problems on a disk. The syntax of the Norton Disk Doctor command is

NDD [*d:*] [*d:*][*switches*]

The *d:* designations are disk drive names; you can specify more than one. The switches available for the NDD command follow:

Switch	Effect
/C	Tests for bad cylinders on the disk and also tests the partition table, boot record, root directory, and lost clusters (the Complete switch).
/Q	Omits the test for bad cylinders but tests the partition table, boot record, root directory, and lost clusters (the Quick switch).

Switch	Effect
/R:*file*	Outputs to the named file a report about the results of the testing. Use with /Q or /C.
/RA:*file*	Appends the report to the named file instead of making a new file (otherwise, same as /R). Use with /Q or /C.
/REBUILD	Rebuilds the entire disk.
/SKIPHIGH	Does not load into high memory. Include this command if you are using a memory manager that is already occupying DOS high memory.
/UNDELETE	Undeletes a DOS partition that was skipped when a user answered No to the question that asked whether to undelete the partition during a previous run of NDD.
/X:*d*	Excludes drive *d* from examination.

Use Norton Disk Doctor whenever you experience problems in accessing a file or when you get a DOS error message concerning the operation of a disk. NDD is your first line of defense to prevent these problems from getting worse and to solve the problems before any data is lost.

If you enter the NDD command with no switches, you operate in interactive mode. The Disk Doctor menu appears, from which you can choose to diagnose the disk or use common solutions (make a disk bootable, revive a defective disk, or recover from DOS's RECOVER command).

Norton Integrator (NI)

The Norton Integrator (NI) command in Norton Utilities Version 4.5 has been integrated into the NORTON (Norton Utilities Main Menu) command in Versions 5.0 and 6.

Norton Utilities Configuration (NUCONFIG)

Chapter 1

The Norton Utilities Configuration (NUCONFIG) command enables you to make changes in the way the Norton program works. These changes include setting passwords, editing menus, changing video and mouse settings, setting up for Norton Cache, including commands in AUTOEXEC.BAT and CONFIG.SYS, assigning alternate utility names, and uncompressing the program EXE files. From the main Norton menu, you can access these items from the Configuration menu. From the DOS prompt, you can display the Configuration menu by entering the command NUCONFIG.

Norton Utilities Main Menu (NORTON)

Chapter 1

The command NORTON opens the Norton Utilities main menu. From this menu, you can run any of the other Norton Utilities programs. Also, this menu accesses brief help files that describe the purpose and syntax of each utility. To open the Norton Utilities main menu from the DOS prompt, enter the command

    NORTON

Norton Utilities Main Program (NU)

The Norton Utilities main program (the NU command) in Norton Advanced Utilities Version 4.5 has been integrated into the DISKEDIT command in Versions 5.0 and 6.

Quick UnErase (QU)

The Quick UnErase (QU) command in Norton Utilities Version 4.5 has been integrated into the UnErase command in Versions 5.0 and 6.

Safe Format (SFORMAT or FORMAT)

Chapter 3

The Safe Format command prevents you from accidentally formatting a disk that contains important information, and provides some safety checks for those times when you do format a disk. The syntax of the Safe Format command is

SFORMAT [*d:*][*switches*]

You may have renamed the SFORMAT command FORMAT to replace the DOS command. If so, the format for the SFORMAT (FORMAT) command is

FORMAT [*d:*][*switches*]

(SFORMAT.EXE is renamed FORMAT.EXE.) Many of the available switches for the SFORMAT command are similar to the DOS FORMAT switches. These DOS-like switches follow:

Switch	Effect
/1	Formats as single-sided
/4	Formats as 360K (in 1.2M drive)
/8	Formats with eight tracks per sector
/B	Leaves space for system files
/F:*size*	Specifies size of disk in kilobytes (360 or 720) or megabytes (1.2, 1.44, or 2.88) (*size* = 360, 720, 1.2, 1.44, or 2.88)
/N:*n*	Specifies number of sectors per track (*n* = 8, 9, 15, or 18)
/S	Places system files on disk
/T:*n*	Specifies number of tracks (*n* = 40 or 80)
/V:*label*	Places a volume label on disk

The switches unique to Norton's Safe Format command follow:

Switch	Effect
/A	Uses automatic mode (in batch files)
/D	Uses DOS format mode
/Q	Uses quick format mode
/size	Specifies size of disk (*size* = 360, 720, 1.2, 1.44, or 2.88)

To format a disk with system files and place the volume label MYDISK on the disk, for example, use this command:

SFORMAT B:/S/V:MYDISK

You can use the Safe Format command in interactive mode by entering SFORMAT (or FORMAT) with no switches. From the Safe Format menu that appears, you can choose the drive to format, the size of the disk to format, whether to copy system files to the disk, which (if any) volume label to put on the disk, and which format mode to use (safe, quick, or DOS).

Speed Disk (SPEEDISK)

Chapter 5

The Speed Disk command reorganizes your disk so that fragmented files can be unfragmented. Files also may be packed and rearranged to help your disk run at top speed. The syntax of the Speed Disk command is

SPEEDISK [*d:*] [*switches*]

The available switches for the Speed Disk command follow:

Switch	Effect
/B	Reboots after the command finishes.
/F	Performs a full optimization of the disk.
/FD	Performs a full optimization with directories first.
/FF	Performs a full optimization with a file reorder.
/Q	Unfragments free space and fills unused gaps (quick compression).

Switch	Effect
/SD[−]	Sorts file by date. If you include the minus parameter, the sort is from most recent date to oldest date.
/SE[−]	Sorts files by extension. If you include the minus parameter, the sort is in descending alphabetical order.
/SN[−]	Sorts by file name. If you include the minus parameter, the sort is in descending alphabetical order.
/SS[−]	Sorts by file size. If you include the minus parameter, the sort is from largest to smallest.
/U	Unfragments as many files as possible without moving parts of the directory structure. Some damaged files may not be capable of unfragmenting.
/V	Uses verify-after-write data verification. That is, each time information is written to the disk, it is then read from the disk to verify that it was correctly written.

You also can run Speed Disk in interactive mode by typing *speedisk* with switches. In interactive mode, you can choose the preceding options from the Speed Disk menu bar menus. Also, you can choose which files not to move and which files to place first on the disk (nearest track 0).

System Information (SYSINFO)

Chapter 5

The System Information (SYSINFO) command provides information about your computer (computer type, equipment in use, ROM-BIOS information, and so on) and performs tests that enable you to compare your computer's performance to the performance of other computers. The syntax of the System Information command is

SYSINFO [*d:*][*switches*]

The available switches for the System Information command follow:

Switch	Effect
/AUTO:*n*	Operates in automatic mode. The *n* parameter specifies a delay of a certain number of seconds between screens.
/DEMO	Operates in demo mode.
/DI	Produces the Drive Information Summary screen only.
/N	Skips the live memory probe. On some computers, the live memory probe forces you to reboot after the SYSINFO test. Use the /N switch to get around this problem.
/SOUND	Produces a beep between CPU tests.
/SUMMARY	Produces the System Summary screen only.
/TSR	Shows all TSR (terminate-and-stay-resident) programs in memory.

Text Search (TS)

Chapter 6

The Text Search (TS) command enables you to search for text in files anywhere on disk, including erased space. The syntax of the command is

TS [*filespec*] [*string*] [*switches*]

The *filespec* names the files to be searched, such as *.BAT. If this parameter is missing, all files are searched. The *string* is the text to be located in those files, such as ALABAMA.

The available switches for the Text Search command follow:

Switch	Effect
/A	Automates the search and ignores prompts
/C*n*	Begins the search at the cluster specified by *n*
/CS	Performs a case-sensitive search. Thus, if you specify the search string as *Alan*, the command does not find *ALAN*.

Switch	Effect
/D	Searches the entire disk
/E	Searches only the erased portions of the disk
/EBCDIC	Specifies that the files being searched are in the EBCDIC format
/LOG	Creates output suitable for a log file or printer
/S	Searches subdirectories also
/T	Sets the noninteractive summary total
/WS	Specifies that the files being searched are in WordStar format

To find occurrences of ALABAMA in files with a TXT extension, for example, you use the command

TS *.TXT ALABAMA

Time Mark (TM)

The Time Mark (TM) command in Norton Utilities Version 4.5 has been integrated into the Norton Command Center (NCC) in Versions 5.0 and 6.

UnErase (UNERASE)

Chapter 4

The UnErase command enables you to recover erased (deleted) files. You can unerase only files that have not been overwritten by other files. See the description of the Erase Protect command for more information. The syntax of the UnErase command is

UNERASE [*filespec*] [*switches*]

Available switches for the command follow:

Switch	Effect
/IMAGE	Uses the information in the Image file to aid in recovery.
/MIRROR	Uses the information in the Mirror file to aid in recovery. The Mirror file is created by the DOS MIRROR command in DOS Version 5.0.
/NOTRACK	Does not use DOS delete-tracking information to aid in file recovery.

By default, the command uses the most current of the Image or Mirror files and also uses DOS delete-tracking information, if it's available.

You can use the global file characters ? and * to specify which files you want to unerase. The following command, for example, looks for all erased files with the BAK extension:

UNERASE *.BAK

The UnErase command may prompt you to provide the first character of the name of the file to be unerased. Follow the prompts on-screen after entering the command.

UnFormat

Chapter 3

You use the UnFormat command to bring back information on a formatted disk. This command works best if you used the Image (or DOS MIRROR) command to store a copy of the system areas of your disk, or if you formatted the disk by using Safe Format. (See the discussions of the Image and Safe Format commands for more information.) The syntax of the UnFormat command is

UNFORMAT [*d:*]

where *d:* is the name of the disk to unformat. If your hard disk has been formatted, do not copy anything onto the hard disk before attempting to use UnFormat. In this case, you should run the Norton program from a floppy disk. After entering the UnFormat command, follow the instructions on-screen.

Two command-line switches are available for this command. /IMAGE tells the command to use the Image recovery information file. /MIRROR tells the command to use the Mirror recovery information file. If you do not specify to use the Image or Mirror file, UnFormat uses the most recent of the files, if they exist.

Unremove Directory (UD)

The Unremove Directory (UD) command in Norton Utilities Version 4.5 has been integrated into the UnErase command in Versions 5.0 and 6.

Volume Label (VL)

The Volume Label (VL) command in Norton Utilities Version 4.5 has been incorporated into the NCD command in Versions 5.0 and 6.

Wipe Disk

The Wipe Disk command in Norton Utilities Version 4.5 has been integrated into the WipeInfo command in Versions 5.0 and 6.

Wipe File

The Wipe File command in Norton Utilities Version 4.5 has been integrated into the WipeInfo command in Versions 5.0 and 6.

WipeInfo (WIPEINFO)

Chapter 3

The WipeInfo command overwrites information on disk in such a way that the information cannot be recovered. You can use the command to wipe certain files or the entire disk. The syntax of the WipeInfo command is

WIPEINFO *d:*[*disk or file switches*] [*common switches*]

The switches available for the WipeInfo command follow:

Switch	Effect
Disk Switch	
/E	Overwrites only information that is unused or is in erased files—files marked for erasure by the DOS ERASE command but otherwise recoverable.
File Switches	
/K	Also wipes any slack space allocated to a file.
/N	Uses no-wipe mode, which causes the WipeInfo command to behave like the DOS ERASE command. The file is marked as erased, but is not overwritten.
/S	Wipes out files that match *filespec* in subdirectories also.
Common Switches	
/G*n*	Uses a government-standard overwriting procedure. The default for *n* (number of overwrites) is 3. Although the default normally is 0, the /G switch overrides this default. When you include the /G switch, the value written to disk is ASCII value 246.
/R*n*	Overwrites the disk *n* times. The default is 1.
/V*n*	Selects the value that is to be used to overwrite information on the disk. The *n* value can be a number from 0 to 255.

To wipe disk D by using the governmental standard, for example, enter the command

WIPEINFO D:/G

Using
Norton
NDOS

Using NDOS

A file called COMMAND.COM contains the core of the commands used for PC DOS or MS-DOS, the PC's operating system. When you enter a command such as DIR or COPY at the DOS prompt, the COMMAND.COM program interprets that command and causes the computer to perform the request. Norton's NDOS program replaces the normal COMMAND.COM file because NDOS has all of COMMAND.COM's features—and more. By using NDOS, you add a whole new set of "DOS" commands to use.

This chapter explains how to use NDOS commands, under the assumption that you already are familiar with commonly used DOS commands. If you need a refresher course in DOS commands, read Appendix A, "Introduction to DOS."

Installing NDOS

To try out NDOS at any time, begin the program by entering the NDOS command at the DOS prompt. If you like NDOS, you should place the NDOS command in your CONFIG.SYS file so that NDOS activates each time you boot your computer. When NDOS loads, you see the copyright screen. Otherwise, your DOS prompt looks the same as it does under normal DOS. If you use the NDOS command at the DOS prompt to begin NDOS, typing *exit* returns you to the standard COMMAND.COM mode.

You may have installed NDOS as a part of the NORTON install program. If you did not do this, you can install NDOS manually. This brief description, however, covers only a few of the many options that you can use to install NDOS. The simplest way to load NDOS is to place copies of the command NDOS.COM, NDOS.OVL, and KEYSTACK.SYS in the root directory of your computer. Then place the command

    SHELL=C:\NDOS.COM /P

in your CONFIG.SYS file. This command containing the /P switch tells DOS to load NDOS as the primary (/P) command processor. Also include the command

    DEVICE=C:\KEYSTACK.SYS

in the CONFIG.SYS file. You need this command if you want to use the NDOS KEYSTACK command.

You can use numerous options in the NDOS command besides the /P option. These options customize NDOS to your computer (regulate memory usage) and set the size for various options (see also the "SETDOS" section, later in this chapter).

Most users can get by with using only the /P switch in the start-up command. Other start-up options are described in the Norton NDOS Reference Manual, in the section "NDOS Startup Options."

Using NDOS Command Enhancements

Before introducing specific NDOS commands, this chapter describes a number of enhancements that NDOS provides over the normal DOS command usage. These enhancements include on-line help, expanded command-line editing, command recall, more flexible wild-card usage, file descriptions, multiple commands per line, conditional commands, enhanced batch processing, and added redirection options.

Accessing On-Line Help

NDOS provides an on-line help facility for all DOS and NDOS commands. Beginning with DOS 5.0, DOS also has a help feature. To display a brief explanation about a command, enter the command name at the DOS prompt followed by a /? switch. For example, if you enter the command

CLS /?

at the DOS prompt, the information shown in figure 8.1 appears on-screen.

```
C:\NU>cls /?
Clear the video display, optionally to the specified colors.

CLS [[BRIGHT] [BLINK] fg ON bg]

   fg     The foreground color.
   bg     The background color.

The available colors are:

   Black      Blue      Green      Red
   Magenta    Cyan      Yellow     White

CLS clears the display and moves the cursor to the upper left
corner.

C:\NU>
```

FIG. 8.1.

The NDOS Help screen for the CLS command.

You also can get help for NDOS commands not found in DOS. For example, if you enter the command

DELAY /?

at the DOS prompt, the information shown in figure 8.2 appears.

A second way to get help is to press the F1 key to bring up a menu of topics. You then can choose to display information about a particular command.

Another way to get help is to type *help* at the DOS prompt. A Help menu similar to the one in figure 8.3 appears. From this menu, you can choose help topics. Press Esc to end the help procedure.

```
C:\NU>delay /?
Pause for a specified period of time.

DELAY [seconds]

  seconds  Number of seconds to pause.

DELAY by itself pauses processing for one second.

C:\NU>
```

FIG. 8.2.

The NDOS
help screen for
the DELAY
command.

```
For more information on a specific command, type HELP command-name.
APPEND    Allows programs to open data files in specified directories as if
          they were in the current directory.
ASSIGN    Redirects requests for disk operations on one drive to a different
          drive.
ATTRIB    Displays or changes file attributes.
BACKUP    Backs up one or more files from one disk to another.
BREAK     Sets or clears extended CTRL+C checking.
CALL      Calls one batch program from another.
CD        Displays the name of or changes the current directory.
CHCP      Displays or sets the active code page number.
CHDIR     Displays the name of or changes the current directory.
CHKDSK    Checks a disk and displays a status report.
CLS       Clears the screen.
COMMAND   Starts a new instance of the MS-DOS command interpreter.
COMP      Compares the contents of two files or sets of files.
COPY      Copies one or more files to another location.
CTTY      Changes the terminal device used to control your system.
DATE      Displays or sets the date.
DEBUG     Runs Debug, a program testing and editing tool.
DEL       Deletes one or more files.
DIR       Displays a list of files and subdirectories in a directory.
DISKCOMP  Compares the contents of two floppy disks.
---More---
```

FIG. 8.3.

An NDOS
HELP menu.

Using Expanded Command-Line Editing Features

The normal DOS command line has limited editing features. If you type a long command and then notice that something is wrong, you must use the Backspace key to erase much of your command and then re-type the command. With NDOS, you get a basketful of editing options, including the capability to move the cursor around the command line and insert, change, and delete characters. Table 8.1 lists the available editing keys.

Table 8.1 Command Line Editing

Key	Effect
←	Moves cursor one space left.
→	Moves cursor one space right.
↑	Recalls preceding command entered at DOS prompt.
↓	Recalls next command in the commands list.
Ctrl-←	Moves cursor left one word.
Ctrl-→	Moves cursor right one word.
Home	Moves cursor to beginning of line.
Ctrl-Home	Deletes characters from beginning of line to character preceding cursor.
End	Moves cursor to end of line.
Ctrl-End	Deletes characters from cursor to end of line.
Ins	Toggles insert and overwrite modes.
Del	Deletes character at cursor.
Backspace	Deletes character left of cursor.
CR or LF (Carriage Return or Line Feed)	Executes command on command line.
Esc	Erases entire line.
Ctrl-L	Deletes word left of cursor.
Ctrl-R or Ctrl-Backspace	Deletes word right of cursor.

continues

Table 8.1 continued

Key	Effect
Ctrl-D	Deletes current command history entry, erases line, and displays preceding command history entry.
Ctrl-E	Displays last command history entry.
Ctrl-K	Saves current command history list and erases current line.
F1	Begins on-line help procedure.
F3	Repeats preceding command.
F8 or Shift-Tab	Enters a previously used file name displayed by F9 onto the command line.
F9 or Tab and F10	Looks at file name or wild cards left of cursor and replaces file name with first matching file name. Press F9 to replace with next matching name. Press F10 to append file name at cursor.
Alt-255	Normally, if you enter an NDOS line edit command (such as Ctrl-D) on the command line, NDOS performs the function associated with the command. In some cases, however, you may need to include a command character on the command line that you do not want to be seen by NDOS as a command. By pressing Alt-255, and entering the command character (Ctrl-D, for example), NDOS does not respond to Ctrl-D as a command.
	For example, hold down the Alt key and type *255* from the numerical keypad. Release the Alt key and press Ctrl-D. Instead of NDOS recognizing the Ctrl-D as a command, the Ctrl-D character (a diamond) appears on the command line.

Suppose that you want to list a file on-screen with the NDOS LIST command, but all you can remember is that the file has the extension TXT. Enter the command

    LIST *.TXT

and press the F9 key. The first match to *.TXT is placed in the command line instead of *.TXT. If that file is not the one you want, press F9 again, and the next matching file name appears. Keep pressing F9 until the file you want appears. Then press Enter to execute the command.

To recall a previous command, press the up-arrow key. The preceding command entered at the DOS prompt appears, and you can press Enter to execute the command or edit the command with the editing keys. Pressing the up arrow several times recalls commands in sequence, so you can recall a command you entered a number of commands ago. NDOS normally sets aside 1,024 bytes of memory to hold the history commands. You can change this size using the SET command, described in the "SET" section, later in this chapter.

Using Multiple Commands on One Line

With DOS, you can enter only one command per line. With NDOS, you can enter several commands on one line. To enter more than one command on a line, separate each command with a caret (^) character (Shift-6 on most keyboards). For example, to delete all BBB files and then display a directory, enter the following command at the DOS prompt:

ERASE *.BBB^DIR

Using Conditional Commands

NDOS provides a way to execute a second command on a command line based on the outcome of the first command. When a DOS or NDOS command is executed, an exit code in the computer is set. This code explains the result of the command—normally, whether the command succeeds or not. All NDOS commands return an exit code of 0 if successful. If the command is not successful, the exit code is non-0.

If && (two ampersands) separate two commands, the second command is executed only if the first command returns an exit code of 0. If two commands are separated by || (vertical bars, "OR"), the second command is executed only if the first command returns a nonzero exit code.

Suppose that you want to copy the files *.* to the A: disk. If the copy fails, you want the message ERROR IN COPY! to be displayed. You can have this message appear with the command

COPY *.* A: || ECHO ERROR IN COPY!

Using Batch-to-Memory Files

Normally, DOS executes the command in a batch file by reading one line at a time and executing that command before going to the next command. NDOS provides a faster way to execute the commands in a batch file with the batch-to-memory command. This command is designated by a BTM file rather than the command BAT file. The batch-to-memory method of batch file execution is significantly faster than the normal DOS execution.

NDOS batch files also have the advantage of using 128 variables (%0 to %127) instead of the DOS 10 variables (%0 to %9).

To convert a DOS batch file to a batch-to-memory file, use the rename command to change the BAT extension to a BTM extension. To change the batch file named SETUP.BAT to a BTM file, for example, use the command

        RENAME SETUP.BAT SETUP.BTM

Run the BTM file the same way you run a normal BAT file. Entering the command SETUP at the DOS prompt, for example, executes the SETUP.BTM batch file.

Using Executable Extensions

With NDOS, you can specify a meaning to a file extension so that an appropriate program executes when a file with the extension is entered as a command name. Suppose that you have many TXT files that you often want to read on-screen. You can tell NDOS that if you enter the name of a TXT file at the DOS prompt, the name should be viewed with the list command. This command is

        SET .TXT=LIST

If you have a file named MARY.TXT, then entering MARY at the DOS prompt causes the LIST program to execute and display the file MARY.TXT. See the "SET" section, later in this chapter, for more information.

Using I/O Redirection

NDOS uses the standard DOS redirection commands:

        >
        >>
        <
        |

NDOS also adds some new options, however. NDOS has the following redirection commands available:

Command	Effect
< *filename*	Gets input from the file name instead of keyboard.
> *filename*	Sends output of a command into file specified.
>> *filename*	Appends output of a command to file specified.
>! *filename*	Sends output to file, overriding the NDOS NOCLOBBER setting that normally prevents a file from being replaced.
>& *filename*	Sends output and standard error messages to file.
>&> *filename*	Sends only standard error messages to file.
>&! *filename*	Sends output and standard error messages to file, overriding the NDOS NOCLOBBER setting that normally prevents a file from being replaced.
com1 | com2	Uses the output of the command COM1 as the input for the command COM2.
com1 |& com2	Uses the standard output and standard error of COM1 as the input for COM2.

The I/O commands help to redirect information into or from a command. To output the results of the DIR command to the printer (LPT1:), for example, you can use the command

    DIR > LPT1:

To sort the information in a file called LIST.TXT and output the results to a file called SORTED.TXT, you can use the command

    SORT < LIST.TXT > SORTED.TXT

This command tells DOS to use the LIST.TXT file as input into the SORT command and to place the resulting output in the SORTED.TXT file.

These I/O commands also work with NDOS commands. For example, to send the output of the NDOS MEMORY command to the printer, type

    MEMORY>LPT1:

Using Escape Sequences

There are several character sequences that have special meanings in NDOS. These sequences are an Escape character (not the ASCII Esc key) followed by a single letter. The Escape character is produced by pressing Ctrl-X, which appears as an up arrow on-screen. (See "SETDOS," later in this chapter, to change this.) The single letters and their meanings follow:

Escape Command	Meaning
b	backspace
e	ASCII Escape character (ASCII 27)
f	formfeed
n	linefeed
r	carriage return
t	Tab

For example, certain terminals and printers enable you to change characteristics using Escape characters. If your computer has the ANSI.SYS device driver installed (in CONFIG.SYS) and you are using a color monitor, you can set the monitor default color by using ANSI Escape sequences. The command

ECHO ^Xe[1;37;44m

causes your monitor colors to be bright white on blue. The ^X (Ctrl-X) will appear as an up arrow on your screen when you type the command. For more information on ANSI codes, see *Using PC DOS*, from QUE.

Using Norton NDOS Commands

Norton NDOS provides the user with more than 90 commands, some of which are the same as you use in DOS. Some commands are similar to DOS commands but have been enhanced with added features. NDOS also supports many commands supported by the Norton Batch Enhancer (BE) command. More than 50 commands are new NDOS commands.

The following commands supported by NDOS are the same as DOS commands:

BREAK	DATE	TIME
CHCP	EXIT	VER
CTTY	GOTO	VERIFY

Commands similar to DOS commands but enhanced under NDOS follow:

ATTRIB	FOR	REM
CD	IF	REN
CHDIR	MD	RENAME
CLS	MKDIR	RMDIR
COPY	PATH	SET
DEL	PAUSE	SHIFT
DIR	PROMPT	TYPE
ECHO	RD	VOL
ERASE		

The Batch Enhancer commands supported by NDOS are BE followed by these commands:

ASK	MONTHDAY	SHIFTSTATE
BEEP	PRINTCHAR	TRIGGER
BOX	REBOOT	WEEKDAY
CLS	ROWCOL	WINDOW
DELAY	SA	

Chapters 6 and 7 describe the Norton Batch Enhancer commands.

The following sections discuss the enhanced DOS commands and NDOS commands.

Many of the Norton NDOS commands use several options. In this book, the following conventions apply to those options:

■ In the command syntax, items enclosed in [brackets] are optional.

■ For words written in *italic*, substitute the appropriate word. To use the DIR [*switches*] syntax, for example, you may type DIR /W, DIR /P, and so on.

■ The [*d:*] option is a designation for the disk drive name, such as drive A, B, C, or D.

■ The [*filespec*] option is a designation for a file specification. Unless noted, this specification can include a path name. The file specification for a file named MYFILE.TXT in the \WP50 directory, for example, is \WP50\MYFILE.TXT. Usually, you can use DOS global file characters (wild cards)—the asterisk (*) and question mark (?)—in file specifications. For example, *.TXT specifies all files with the TXT extension.

■ The [*color*] option refers to a selection of colors. A color designation can be White on Blue, for example. Chapter 6 describes how to use colors.

The following descriptions of NDOS commands do not cover all the NDOS options that duplicate DOS commands.

?

The NDOS ? command displays a list of available internal NDOS commands. This command has no options; just press ? at the DOS prompt, and a list of the NDOS commands appears on-screen.

ALIAS

With the NDOS ALIAS command, you can create a new command from another command. The syntax of the command is

ALIAS [*switches*] [*name=[value]*]

The available switches for the Alias command follow:

Switch	Effect
/P	Pauses after displaying a screen full of information
/R *filespec*	Tells the command to read an alias list from the file named in the filespec

Suppose that you want to create a new command called DD that performs a DIR /W (wide directory) command. Type the command

ALIAS DD DIR/W

or

ALIAS DD=DIR/W

The equal (=) sign is optional. In this command, the DD is the new name assigned to the value DIR/W. Now, whenever you type the command DD at the DOS prompt, a DIR /W command executes.

ATTRIB

The NDOS ATTRIB command, similar to the DOS ATTRIB command, displays or changes the attribute settings on files. The DOS version of ATTRIB is only available in DOS Versions 3.0 or higher, does not include the /D switch included in the NDOS version, and does not enable you to set hidden or system attributes (until DOS 5.0). The syntax of the command is

ATTRIB [/*switches*] [–|+[AHRS]] *filespec...*

If you enter the command ATTRIB with a path name but without any options, the current attribute settings of the files appear.

The switches available for the ATTRIB command follow:

Switch	Effect
/D	Modifies directory attribute settings and file settings
/S	Modifies the attributes of matching files in subdirectories of the specified directory

The following option settings are available for the ATTRIB command:

Option	Effect
[+|–]A	Sets the archive attribute
[+|–]H	Sets the hidden file attribute
[+|–]R	Sets the read-only attribute
[+|–]S	Sets the system file attribute

For each option, a plus sign (+) sets the attribute and a minus sign (–) unsets the attribute. For example, the command

ATTRIB +RH SECRET.FIL

sets the attribute for the file named SECRET.FIL to read-only and hidden. This command is similar in function to the Norton Utilities FileFind and File Attributes command described in Chapters 6 and 7.

BE

The NDOS BE (Batch Enhancer) commands are similar to the BE commands in Norton Utilities (described in Chapters 6 and 7). The BE commands supported in NDOS follow:

ASK	MONTHDAY	SHIFTSTATE
BEEP	PRINTCHAR	TRIGGER
BOX	REBOOT	WEEKDAY
CLS	ROWCOL	WINDOW
DELAY	SA	

BEEP

The NDOS BEEP command, used to beep the computer's speaker, is similar to the BE BEEP command described in Chapters 6 and 7, but it is an internal NDOS command with a slightly different use. The format of the NDOS BEEP command is

BEEP [*frequency duration*]

where *frequency* is the value in hertz (Hz)—for example, 440 is the rate A—and *duration* is the length of time for the sound in 1/18 second. To sound an A for a half second, for example, you would use the command

BEEP

BREAK

The NDOS BREAK command, similar to the DOS BREAK command, enables, disables, or displays the Break key setting (Ctrl-Break or Ctrl-C). The syntax of the command is

BREAK [ON|OFF]

The OFF option tells DOS to check for a Ctrl-Break (or Ctrl-C) when information is entered into the computer through the keyboard, screen, serial port, or printer. The ON option tells DOS to check for a Ctrl-Break (or Ctrl-C) during any DOS operation. The ON option makes breaking out of a program easier. If the command doesn't include an option, the current status of BREAK is displayed.

CALL

The NDOS CALL command enables you to call one batch file from another batch file. The syntax of the command is

CALL *filespec*

where *filespec* is the name of a batch file. NDOS supports calling batch files of up to eight nested files. For example, within one batch file, to call another batch file called SECOND, you enter the command

CALL SECOND

After the SECOND batch file finishes, control returns to the original batch file.

CANCEL

The NDOS CANCEL command ends a batch file. The syntax of this command is

    CANCEL

No options are available. CANCEL enables you to end a batch file within any nested (called) batch file and return to DOS. For more information, see the "Call" and "Quit" sections.

CD or CHDIR

You use the NDOS CD and CHDIR commands, like the DOS CD and CHDIR commands, to change directories. The NDOS version also displays the name of the current directory. The syntax for the command is

    CD [*d:*][*path*]

where *d:* is the name of the disk drive to access and *path* is the name of the directory. CD changes to the directory designated by the path. The drive is not changed. Entering CD with no option causes the command to display the name of the current directory. As in DOS, entering

    CD\

makes the root directory the default, and entering

    CD..

changes to the parent directory for the current directory. NDOS adds a new feature. Entering

    CD...

changes to the directory one higher than the parent directory. Thus, if you are in the directory \MYDIR\YOURDIR\OURDIR and enter CD..., you change to the \MYDIR directory.

CDD

The NDOS CDD command is similar to the CD command, except that the NDOS CDD command also changes the default drive and directory. The syntax for the command is

    CDD [*d:*][*path*]

If you are in the drive and directory C:\MYDIR, for example, you can enter the command

CDD D:\YOURDIR

to change the default drive to drive D and the default directory to \YOURDIR. CDD otherwise operates just like the NDOS CD command.

CHCP

Like the DOS CHCP command, the NDOS CHCP command displays or changes the current system code page. A *system code page* controls which language character set DOS uses. The CHCP command requires that you have loaded the COUNTRY.SYS information file in the CONFIG.SYS file, run the DOS NLSFUNC (National Language Support) command, and specified code pages with the DOS MODE device CODEPAGE PREPARE = command. (See your DOS manual for information on how to use the NLSFUNC and MODE commands.) The syntax for the command is

CHCP [*nnn*]

where *nnn* is the number of the code page to set. Consult your current DOS manual for a list of the code pages supported by your version of DOS. If you enter the CHCP command without options, the current code page is displayed.

CLS

The NDOS CLS command is similar to the DOS CLS command but also contains the capability to change your monitor's colors. The syntax of the command is

CLS [[BRIGHT][BLINK] *foreground* ON *background*]

Entering CLS with no options clears the screen. The colors available for *foreground* and *background* are black, blue, yellow, green, red, magenta, cyan, yellow, and white. To clear the screen and switch to a bright white foreground with a blue background, for example, use the command

CLS BRIGHT WHITE ON BLUE

The BLINK option makes the entire screen blink in the selected colors. You can use this option to create an eye-catching warning screen in a batch file, for example.

COLOR

The NDOS COLOR command sets the foreground and background colors for your monitor without clearing the screen as CLS does. The syntax for the command is

COLOR [BRIGHT][BLINK] *foreground* ON *background*

The colors available for *foreground* and *background* are black, blue, yellow, green, red, magenta, cyan, yellow, and white. To set your monitor to use white letters on a blue background, for example, use the command

COLOR WHITE ON BLUE

See "SCRPUT," later in this chapter.

COPY

Similar to the DOS COPY command, the NDOS COPY command also enables you to use a list of files to copy. The syntax for the command is

COPY [/*switches*]filespec[+]...[/A][/B] *filespec* [/A][/B]

The available switches for the Copy command follow:

Switch	Effect
/A	Treats file as ASCII text (default).
/B	Treats file as binary.
/M (Modified)	Copies only files with the archive bit set. The archive bit is retained on the copy.
/P	Prompts you to confirm each copy.
/Q (Quiet)	Suppresses display of names of files being copied.
/R (Replace)	Prompts you before overwriting an existing file.
/U (Update)	Copies only files that are newer than the matching target files.
/V	Verifies copy is okay.

You use the /A, /B, and /V switches and the + key with the NDOS Copy command as you use them in the DOS COPY command. In the NDOS version of COPY, you can copy more than one file to a destination. To copy the files *.WKS and *.DBF to the disk in drive A:, for example, use the command

COPY *.WKS *.DBF A:

To copy all files from drive A to drive C and to avoid overwriting any existing files that have the same names on drive C, use the command

COPY /R A:*.* C:

You are prompted to confirm the copy before any file from drive A overwrites a file with the same name on drive C. See "Move," later in this chapter, for more information.

CTTY

The NDOS CTTY command, similar to the DOS CTTY command, changes the default I/O console device—normally, the keyboard and the display screen. The syntax of the command is

CTTY *device*

The possible devices to use include AUX, COM1, COM2, COM3, COM4, and CON (console). To be used by NDOS, the device must support all standard DOS I/O functions, including DOS internal commands (with the exception of the DRAWBOX, DRAWHLINE, LIST, SCREEN, SCRPUT, SELECT, and all the BE commands). To change the CTTY device to a device connected to the first COM port, for example, use the command

CTTY COM1:

Now, the device (normally a terminal) on the COM1 port assumes control of all command input and output for your system.

To change back to the standard use of the keyboard and display, use the command

CTTY CON:

DATE

The NDOS DATE command is similar to the DOS DATE command.

The syntax for the DATE command is

DATE [*mm-dd-yy*]

If you type *date* with no option, you are prompted to enter a new date.

DEL or ERASE

The NDOS DEL (or ERASE) command is similar to the DOS DEL and ERASE commands, but with the NDOS version you can specify a list of files to delete. DEL and ERASE are the same command. The syntax of the command is

DEL [*switches*] *filespec*...

or

ERASE [*switches*] *filespec*...

The available switches for DEL or ERASE follow:

Switch	Effect
/P	Prompts for a confirmation before deleting a file
/Q (Quiet)	Suppresses display of file names being deleted
/Y (Yes)	Prompts when DEL *.* is used
/Z (Zap)	Deletes hidden, system, and read-only files (overrides the NDOS EXCEPT command—see "EXCEPT," later in this chapter)

To erase the files that match the file specifications *.WKS and *.DBF, for example, use the command

ERASE *.WKS *.DBF

or

DEL *.WKS *.DBF

To erase files but be prompted before each delete, use the command

ERASE /P *.WKS *.DBF

or

DEL /P *.WKS *.DBF

DELAY

The NDOS DELAY command causes the computer to pause for a few seconds before resuming operation. This command most often is used in a batch file. The syntax for the command is

DELAY [*seconds*]

To cause the computer to wait 5 seconds before resuming operation, for example, use the command

DELAY 5

DESCRIBE

The NDOS DESCRIBE command creates, modifies, or deletes file and subdirectory descriptions. With the DESCRIBE command, you can place a description on a file or subdirectory so that when you issue a DIR command, the description appears on-screen. The syntax for the command is

DESCRIBE *filespec* ["*description*"]

To add a description to the file MARY.TXT, for example, you can use the command

DESCRIBE MARY.TXT "Mary had a little lamb poem."

Then, when you perform a DIR command, the description appears next to the file name in the directory listing. If you enter the DESCRIBE command with a file name but no description, you are prompted to enter a description. To delete a description, enter a blank description.

For example, to delete the description on MARY.TXT, enter

DESCRIBE MARY.TXT ""

DIR

Like the DOS DIR command, the NDOS DIR command displays file information. Unlike DOS's DIR, the NDOS DIR also displays any descriptions you have defined for file names. With NDOS DIR, you can place more than one file specification on the command line. Also, with NDOS DIR, the file names appear in lowercase, and directory names appear in uppercase, making it easier to tell them apart at a glance. The syntax for the command is

DIR [/A:[*attributes*]][/O[:][*sortorder*]][*switches*][*filespec*]

When you use the /A option, DIR displays only those files that have the requested attribute or attributes set (or not set if a minus sign precedes the attribute name).

The attributes available for the DIR command follow:

Attribute	Meaning
h	Hidden file
r	Read-only file
s	System file
d	Directory
a	Archived file

For example, to list the names of all the read-only files, use the command

DIR /A:r

To list all files that are NOT archived, use the command

DIR /A:–a

With the following *sortorder* options, you can sort the directory list. Placing a minus sign (–) before a sort order causes the sort to be in descending order rather than the default ascending order.

Option	Sort Order
d	Date and time
e	File extension
i	NDOS file description
n	Name
s	Size
g	Lists directories first in the list (default)
u	Unsorted (same as normal DOS DIR)

To list the file in name and extension order, for example, use the command

DIR /O:ne

Other switches available can help you to customize the way the DIR command lists the files. The available switches follow:

Switch	Effect
/1	Displays files in a single-column list
/2	Displays files in a double-column list
/4	Displays files in a four-column list
/A	Displays files with a particular attribute
/B	Suppresses the header line and summary information
/C	Displays file names in uppercase as in the DOS DIR command
/J	Justifies file names as in the DOS DIR command
/K	Suppresses the display of the volume label and path name information
/L	Displays file names in lowercase
/M	Omits the display of total bytes
/N	Resets the DIR command to its default values
/O:n	Displays files in a requested sort order, where n is one of the sort order options
/P	Pauses after each screen of information is displayed
/S	Displays files in the directory and all subdirectories
/T	Displays only the file attributes
/U	Displays only the summary information
/V	Displays the file names sorted vertically rather than horizontally (use with the /2, /4, or /W option)
/W	Displays the files names in wide five-column mode (same as DOS /W)

To display a directory of files with the WKS extension in the MYFILE directory and all of its subdirectories, for example, use the command

DIR \MYFILE*.WKS /S

If you want the DIR command to display files in a certain way all the time, you can set the defaults for the command in your AUTOEXEC.BAT file. To set the command always to display files in sorted order by name (/O:n), for example, use the command

SET DIRCMD=/O:n

where n is one of the sort order options.

DIRS

The NDOS DIRS command displays the current directory stack. The PUSHD and POPD commands, on the other hand, create and recall a directory stack. Suppose that you are in the root directory. When you enter the PUSHD C:\MYDIR command, the C:\ (root) directory is placed in the directory stack and your default directory is changed to \MYDIR. Then enter the command PUSHD C:\TMP; the C\MYDIR directory is placed in the stack, and you are changed to the \TMP directory. If you then enter the command DIRS, the listing

```
C:\MYDIR
C:\
```

is displayed. This listing means that the first (or top) directory in the stack is C:\MYDIR and the previous directory is C:\ (root). See the "POPD" and "PUSHD" sections for more information.

DRAWBOX

The NDOS DRAWBOX command draws a box on-screen. This is similar to, but not the same command as, the Norton BE BOX command. Some differences are that if you draw overlapping boxes using DRAWBOX, the command detects other boxes on-screen and draws appropriate connecting characters when possible. Also, DRAWBOX has a Fill option, which is not available in BE BOX. (BE BOX is discussed in Chapters 6 and 7.) The syntax for DRAWBOX is

DRAWBOX *ulrow ulcol lrrow lrcol style* [BRIGHT] [BLINK] *foreground on background* [FILL *backgroundfill*]

The *ulrow* variable specifies the position of the upper left row of the box. Similarly, the *ulcol*, *lrrow*, and *lrcol* variables specify the upper left column, lower right row, and lower right column. On a standard 25-line-by-80-row screen, the valid rows are 0 to 24 and the valid columns are 0 to 79.

The *style* option refers to the style of box to be drawn. The options follow:

Option	Effect
0	Borderless
1	Single line
2	Double line
3	Single lines on top and bottom, double lines on sides
4	Double lines on top and bottom, single lines on sides

The *foreground*, *background*, and *backgroundfill* variables are colors selected from the options black, blue, green, red, magenta, cyan, yellow, and white.

To draw a single-line box with a bright white foreground and a red background, for example, use the command

DRAWBOX 10 10 20 20 1 BRIGHT WHITE ON RED

DRAWHLINE

With the NDOS DRAWHLINE command, you can draw a horizontal line on-screen. The syntax for the command is

DRAWHLINE *row col len style* [BRIGHT][BLINK] *foreground* on *background*

The *row* and *col* variables specify where the line begins on-screen. The *len* variable specifies the length, and *style* refers to style 1 (single line) or style 2 (double line). The *foreground* and *background* colors are black, blue, green, red, magenta, cyan, yellow, and white.

To draw a single white line with a blue background line across the middle of the screen, for example, use the command

DRAWHLINE 10 0 79 1 WHITE ON BLUE

DRAWVLINE

The NDOS DRAWVLINE command is similar to the DRAWHLINE command, except that DRAWVLINE draws a vertical line on-screen. The syntax for the command is

DRAWVLINE *row col len style* [BRIGHT] [BLINK] *foreground* ON *background*

To draw a single white line with a magenta background down the middle of the screen, for example, use the command

DRAWVLINE 12 0 24 1 WHITE ON MAGENTA

ECHO

The NDOS ECHO command is similar to the DOS ECHO command. The main advantage is that with NDOS, you can use the NDOS redirection symbols (see "Using I/O Redirection") and include multiple commands per line (see "Using Multiple Commands on One Line"). The syntax of the command is

ECHO [ON|OFF|*message*]

In NDOS, the default is ECHO ON for batch files and ECHO OFF for keyboard commands. If you enter ECHO ON at the keyboard, NDOS displays fully parsed and expanded commands (including aliases and variables) before the command is executed. If no arguments are included, ECHO displays its current state (OFF or ON).

For example, look at the following three lines in a batch file:

```
ECHO OFF
REM This is a comment—not displayed
ECHO This is displayed
```

This file causes ECHO to be turned off (first line), which causes the REM (Remark) to *not* be echoed (second line). The third line is displayed on-screen. When entering the ECHO OFF or ECHO ON command, you may precede the command with the @ (at) symbol to suppress the ECHO command from being displayed to the screen. For example, the command

@ECHO OFF

would not be displayed to the screen, but the command

ECHO OFF

would be displayed.

ENDLOCAL

The NDOS ENDLOCAL command restores the computer to a previously saved (with a SETLOCAL command) disk drive, directory, environmental variables, and aliases. This command, which has no options, is useful in a batch file when you temporarily change directories (using the CD command) or disk drives to execute a procedure and you then want to change back to your current settings.

The following example uses the SETLOCAL command to save your current settings. Some changes are made, and then the previous settings are restored by the ENDLOCAL command:

```
SETLOCAL
C:
CD \MYDIR
SET PATH = C:\KWIKSTAT
KS
ENDLOCAL
```

In this example, suppose that your current drive is A and your directory is \. The batch file changes to drive C and the \MYDIR directory, and then executes the SET and KS commands. At this point, if the batch file was ended, your current drive and directory would be C:\MYDIR. However, the ENDLOCAL command automatically switches you back to your original state (captured by the previous SETLOCAL command). Thus, your current drive and directory are set back to A:\. See the "SETLOCAL" section for more information.

ESET

The NDOS ESET command edits environmental variables and aliases. Environmental variables are used to customize how DOS operates. Aliases are substitute names for commands (see "ALIAS," earlier in this chapter). The syntax for the command is

ESET *varname...*

You can list more than one environmental variable in the *varname* list, separating each name with a blank space.

To edit the file search path, for example, enter the command

ESET *path*

The current path is displayed on-screen, and you then can use the NDOS command-line editing commands to edit the path (see table 8.1).

EXCEPT

The NDOS EXCEPT command enables you to perform a command and specify that files that don't match a file specification be used in the command. The syntax for the command is

EXCEPT (*filespec...*) *command*

For example, the DOS command

DIR *.WKS

displays all files with a WKS extension. The command

EXCEPT (*.WKS) DIR

displays all files *except* those with the WKS extension. EXCEPT recognizes all NDOS internal commands, aliases, external commands (including DOS external commands), and batch files. EXCEPT does not work with the DEL or ERASE command if you use the /Z switch on those commands.

EXIT

You use the NDOS EXIT command to return from a secondary command processor. The syntax for the command is

EXIT [*n*]

where *n* is an errorlevel value you have selected to be returned to the calling command processor. If *n* is not included, the errorlevel is the one returned by the last external program. Usually, EXIT is used when a program "shells" temporarily to DOS to enable you to enter a DOS command. Typing *exit* at the DOS prompt returns you to the original program. If you began NDOS from the DOS command line, EXIT ends NDOS and returns you to DOS.

You choose the errorlevel you want. Otherwise, for some Norton commands, the /DEBUG option will display the errorlevel (exit code) returned. In general, 0 means the program exited with no problems and NOT 0 usually means the program ended in error. See the discussion on the BE ASK command in Chapter 6 for more information on using an errorlevel.

FOR

The NDOS FOR command, like the DOS FOR command, repeats several times a command defined by a set of files. The syntax for the command is

FOR *%variable* IN (*set*) [DO] *command*

FOR repeats the command and replaces the variable in the command with the information in the set. Commands recognized by the NDOS FOR command are all internal NDOS commands or aliases, external commands, and batch files. The DOS FOR command requires the variable name to be only one character in length (for example, A) but NDOS allows variable names of up to 80 characters (for example, %variablename). Also, the DO is optional in NDOS, but required in the DOS command.

For example, the command

FOR %a IN (*.DOC *.TXT) DO LP %a

causes all DOC files to be printed with the LP command followed by all TXT files. In other words, this command translates into the two commands:

```
LP *.DOC
LP *.TXT
```

FREE

The NDOS FREE command displays the total disk space available, total bytes used, and total bytes free on disk. The format for the command is

FREE [*d:*]...

To get this information for drives A and C, for example, enter the command

FREE A: C:

If you do not specify a drive, information for the default drive is displayed.

GLOBAL

The NDOS GLOBAL command executes a command in the current directory and its subdirectories. Its syntax is

GLOBAL [*/switches*] *command*

The available switches follow:

Switch	Effect
/I	Ignores nonzero exit codes. Normally, GLOBAL ends if a nonzero exit code is returned.
/Q	Suppresses display of each directory name.

For example, to erase all BK files in the \TEXT directory (assuming that is the current default directory) and all of its subdirectories, use the command

GLOBAL ERASE *.BK

GOSUB

The NDOS GOSUB command calls a subroutine in a batch file. A subroutine in a batch file is a series of commands that begins with a label and ends with the command RETURN. The syntax for the command is

GOSUB *label*

Suppose that you have a subroutine in your batch file with the following commands:

```
:MYSUB
ERASE *.bak
RETURN
```

To execute this subroutine, use the command

GOSUB MYSUB

The command in the subroutine executes, and the flow of the batch file returns to the line following the GOSUB command.

GOTO

Like the DOS GOTO command, the NDOS GOTO command branches the flow of a batch file to a specified label. The syntax of the command is

GOTO *label*

Where a *label* is a standard DOS batch file label, which must begin with a colon (:) on the label line (for example, :ENDBATCH). However, when referenced in the GOTO command line, do not include the colon in the label name. This is standard DOS use for referencing labels.

For example, the command

GOTO ENDBATCH

transfers control of the batch file to the label :ENDBATCH in the batch file. GOTO often is used with the IF command. Suppose that you want to check for the existence of a file and then go to a label depending on whether that file exists. The command

IF EXIST EDIT.EXE GOTO ITSTHERE

causes the flow of the batch file to go to the label :ITSTHERE if the file EDIT.EXE is on disk. If EDIT.EXE does not exist, the flow of the batch file continues with the command following the IF command.

You may use the GOTO statement to exit an IFF block (see the "IF" section, later in this chapter). Note that if you use a GOTO within an IFF block, it must branch entirely outside the block.

HELP

The NDOS HELP command is similar to the DOS (Version 5.0) HELP command. The syntax of the command is

HELP [*topic*] [/*switches*]

Entering HELP with no switches displays a list of topics. From this list you can pick a specific topic for which help is available.

The *switches* for the HELP command follow:

Switch	Effect
/BW	Displays information in black and white
/HERC	Displays information using Hercules Graphics
/G0	Disables the graphic mouse pointer and graphic characters (for EGA or VGA monitors)
/G1	Disables the graphic mouse pointer (for EGA and VGA monitors)
/G2	Disables the use of graphic dialog boxes
/LCD	Displays information using colors appropriate for an LCD (usually a laptop) monitor

To display help on the command HISTORY in black-and-white mode, for example, enter the command

HELP HISTORY /BW

Figure 8.4 illustrates the help screen for the History command. From this screen, you can press N to go to the next topic (commands are in alphabetical order), press P to go to the preceding topic, press T to display a list of topics, or press C to cancel and return to the DOS prompt. You also can use the mouse pointer to select these options.

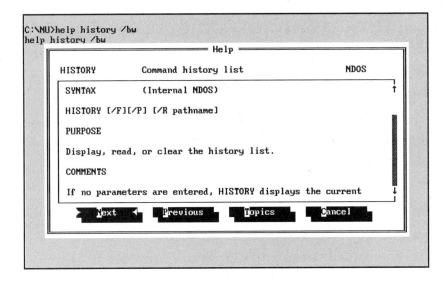

```
C:\NU>help history /bw
help history /bw
                              Help
  HISTORY           Command history list                    NDOS
   SYNTAX              (Internal NDOS)                          ↑
   HISTORY [/F][/P] [/R pathname]
   PURPOSE
   Display, read, or clear the history list.
   COMMENTS
   If no parameters are entered, HISTORY displays the current   ↓
      Next        Previous       Topics        Cancel
```

FIG. 8.4.

Help on the
NDOS History
command.

HISTORY

The NDOS HISTORY command displays, clears, or reads a list of previously entered commands. The syntax of the command is

> HISTORY [/*switches*]

The available *switches* follow:

Switch	Effect
/F (Frees)	Clears the history list
/P	Tells the command to pause after displaying a screenful of information
/R *filespec*	Tells the command to load a command history from the file specified by *filespec*

To save the output of the HISTORY command to a file, use the > redirection option. To save the current history information to a file named HISTORY.TXT, for example, enter the command

> HISTORY > HISTORY.TXT

Entering the HISTORY command with no options causes the command to display the current contents of the history list. Each time you enter a command at the DOS prompt, that command is added to the history list. When the history list gets full (the SETDOS command specifies its size), older commands are dropped to make room for the new commands.

IF

The NDOS IF command, like the DOS IF command, is used in batch processing to transfer the flow of the batch file to a label, depending on a condition. The list of conditions recognized by the NDOS IF command is more extensive than the conditions recognized by the DOS IF command. The syntax of the NDOS IF command is

    IF [NOT] *condition command*

NDOS evaluates the condition. If the condition is true, NDOS executes the command. If the NOT option is used, the command is executed only if the condition is false. The condition can use one of the following forms. (The designation *string* refers to a group of characters.)

Condition	Meaning
string1==*string2* or *string1* EQ *string2*	True if *string1* is equal to *string2*
string1 NE *string2*	True if *string1* is not equal to *string2*
string1 LT *string2*	True if *string1* is less than *string2*
string1 LE *string2*	True if *string1* is less than or equal to *string2*
string1 GT *string2*	True if *string1* is greater than *string2*
string1 GE *string2*	True if *string1* is greater than or equal to *string2*
ERRORLEVEL [*condition*] *n*	Tests error level to the number *n* (use ==, EQ, etc., for *condition*)
EXIST *filespec*	True if file names by *filespec* are found on disk
ISALIAS *aliasname*	True if the specified name is an alias
ISDIR *dirname*	True if the directory named exists

When using EQ, NE, LT, LE, GT, and GE comparisons, IF performs a numeric comparison if both strings begin with numeric digits. The comparison otherwise is an ASCII comparison (but case differences are ignored). For example, the test

    IF "ALAN" LE "BAKER" DIR

performs a DIR command because ALAN is "less than" BAKER—A appears before B in the alphabet. Usually, a variable is used in an IF statement of this sort. If a command line variable %1 is to be compared against "BAKER," for example, the command is

> IF %1 LE "BAKER" DIR

The IF statement also can be used with the NDOS Input command, which enables you to input a variable. For example,

```
:NEXTDIR
INPUT "Enter directory to print or END to End:"
%%CHOICE
IF %%CHOICE == "END" THEN GOTO THATSALL
DIR %%CHOICE >LPT1:
GOTO NEXTDIR
:THATSALL
```

inputs the name of a directory to print. If you enter END, then the procedure stops. Otherwise, the DIR command is performed and the output is sent to the printer (LPT1:).

IFF

The NDOS IFF command, although similar to the IF command, adds an ELSE clause. The syntax of the command is

> IFF [NOT] *condition* THEN *command* ELSE [IFF[NOT]] *condition* THEN *command* ENDIFF

The conditions are the same used in the IF command. NDOS tests the first condition. If that condition is true, the first command is executed. If the first condition is false, the ELSE condition is checked. If the ELSE condition is true, the second command is executed. For example,

```
IF EXIST KS.EXE THEN ^ GOTO ISTHERE ^ ELSE GOTO
NOTTHERE
:ISTHERE
...commands
:NOTTHERE
...commands
```

This example tests to see if the file KS.EXE exists. If the file exists, the flow of the batch file is sent to the label called ISTHERE. If the file KS.EXE does not exist, the flow of the batch file is sent to the label NOTTHERE.

INKEY

The NDOS INKEY command captures a single keystroke as the stroke is entered (usually from the keyboard). You then can assign this input to a variable name. The syntax for this command is

INKEY [/W*n*] [*text*] %%*varname*

The /W*n* switch causes a wait of *n* seconds for an input to be entered. If no keystroke is entered in the specified time, the value of %%varname is unchanged. If you use /W0, then the buffer is checked immediately for a keystroke and returns that value to the %%varname, if a keystroke is present.

The *text* option enables you to display a message on-screen.

The %%*varname* is a variable name where the input is stored. The double % tells NDOS that this is a variable name. (Do not configure %%variable with %variable.) Keystrokes are stored as ASCII values. The uppercase letter A, for example, is 65. Keystrokes that are extended characters are stored in the variable as an @ plus a number. The Home key, for example, is @71.

You can use %%varname in IF statements. For example,

```
INKEY Enter a drive name: %%CHOICE
IF %%CHOICE == "C" THEN GOTO HARDDRIVE
```

In this case, the name of a directory (a single character) is requested. If the value of %%CHOICE is equal to C, then the batch file branches to the label :HARDDRIVE.

INPUT

The NDOS INPUT command enables you to enter a variable. The syntax for this command is

INPUT [/W*n*] [*text*] %%*varname*

The /W*n* switch causes a wait of *n* seconds for an input to be entered. If no keystroke is entered in the specified time, the value of %%*varname* is unchanged. If you use /W0, then the buffer is checked immediately for an entry and returns that value to the %%varname, if a keystroke exists.

The *text* option enables you to display a message on-screen. The %%*varname* parameter indicates a variable %%varname where the input is stored.

INPUT also can be used with an IF command. See the "IF" section for more information.

KEYSTACK

You use the NDOS KEYSTACK command to send keystrokes to a program from a batch file. The syntax for this command is

KEYSTACK ["*text*"][*nn*][@*nn*][!]

The "*text*" is input that is sent as characters to the program. The *nn* values are ASCII codes. For example, 65 sends an uppercase A to the program. The @*nn* values are extended codes.

Suppose that you want to create a batch file that changes one string to another string using the EDLIN editor. (*EDLIN* is an editor provided with DOS. See your DOS manual for more information on EDLIN.) To create such a file (called CHANGE.BAT), use the following commands:

KEYSTACK "1,999R%2" @64 "%3" 13 "Exit" 13
EDLIN %1

Then, suppose you want to change all occurrences (from line 1 to line 999) of the word *lamb* to *sheep* in the ASCII text file MARY.TXT. Use the command

CHANGE MARY.TXT lamb sheep

The KEYSTACK command in the batch file then enters the command (in EDLIN)

1,999RlambF6sheepCR
ExitCR

where F6 is the function key F6 and CR is Enter (carriage return). Notice that the KEYSTACK is defined before the application (EDLIN, in this case) is called. Also, for keystack to work, you must have the device driver KEYSTACK.SYS defined in your CONFIG.SYS file.

LIST

The NDOS LIST command displays a file with forward and backward scrolling. The syntax of the command is

LIST [*switches*][*filespec*]...

The available switches for the LIST command follow:

Switch	Effect
/H	Strips the high bit from each character before displaying it. This process is necessary for displaying some non-ASCII files created by some word processors.
/S	Reads from the standard input rather than from a file. With /S, you can read the output from commands such as DIR as a list file.
/W	Wraps the text at the right margins.

When viewing a file, you can scroll by using the following keys:

Command	Effect
Home	Displays first page of file
End	Displays last page of file
Esc	Exits current file; goes to next file in file specification list (if one exists)
Ctrl-C	Quits list
↑	Scrolls up one line
↓	Scrolls down one line
←	Scrolls left 8 columns
→	Scrolls right 8 columns
Ctrl-←	Scrolls left 40 columns
Ctrl-→	Scrolls right 40 columns
F1	Calls on-line help
F	Prompts and searches for a string
N	Finds next matching string
P	Prints file to LPT1

To examine the file called KS.DOC, for example, enter the command

LIST KS.DOC

To redirect the output of the DIR command to a list, use the command

DIR | *list*/S

LOADBTM

The NDOS LOADBTM command is used in batch files to switch a running batch file from or to the BTM (batch-to-memory) mode. Batch files run faster in BTM mode because all commands are read at once; normal batch files, on the other hand, read a command from disk when needed. The syntax for the command is

LOADBTM [ON|OFF]

For example, placing the command

LOADBTM ON

in your batch file causes the contents of the batch file to be read into memory and executed. The following lines are a small batch file, for example. The LOADBTM command causes the commands beginning with COPY to be read into memory and executed:

```
REM switch to BTM mode
LOADBTM ON
COPY *.* A:
DIR A:
```

LOADBTM ON tells NDOS to read the batch file lines into memory to the end of the batch file or until a LOADBTM OFF command appears.

LOADHIGH or LH

Like the DOS LOADHIGH or LH command, the NDOS LOADHIGH or LH command causes a program to be loaded into high DOS memory. This command can give you more conventional memory and enable you to run larger programs on your computer. You must use DOS 5.0 or higher to use this command; you also must be operating on a 286 or 386 system with suitable software and have the command DOS=UMB in your CONFIG.SYS file.

The syntax for the LOADHIGH command is

LOADHIGH [*filespec*]...

or

LH [*filespec*]...

To load the program MYPROG.COM into high memory, for example, use the command

LOADHIGH MYPROG.COM

If not enough memory is available in the 640K or 1M range to load the program, the program is loaded into conventional memory.

LOG

You use the NDOS LOG command to save a log of the commands entered at the DOS prompt. The syntax for the command is

LOG [/W *filespec* | ON | OFF | *text*]

The /W command causes the command to be stored in the file specified by *filespec*. The ON option tells the command to begin logging commands, whereas OFF turns off the saving of commands. The *text* option enables you to insert a header or other text into the log file. Entering *log* with no options causes the command to report whether the log is on or off. To save a command to a file named MYLOG.TXT, for example, use the command

LOG /W C:\MYLOG.TXT

MD

The NDOS MD (or MKDIR) command operates the same as the DOS MD and MKDIR commands except that with the NDOS version, you can have multiple commands per line. The syntax for the command is

MD [*drive*]*path*...

To create a subdirectory called WP from the root directory, for example, use the command

MD /WP

To create two directories at once (\WP and \KS), use the command

MD \WP^MD \KS

MEMORY

The NDOS MEMORY command, like the DOS MEMORY command, displays the amount of memory available, including total RAM, number of bytes free, total EMS memory and bytes free, XMS memory, size of the total environment and bytes free, size of the alias space and bytes free, and size of the history buffer. No options are available.

MOVE

The NDOS MOVE command moves files to other directories or drives. The syntax, similar to the COPY command syntax, is

MOVE [/*switches*] *filespec... filespec*

The available switches follow:

Switch	Effect
/P	Prompts for confirmation before each move
/Q	Turns off the display of file names as they are moved
/R	Prompts for confirmation before each move that replaces an existing file

To move files with a WKS extension from the C:\MYDIR directory to the D:\YOURDIR directory, for example, use the command

MOVE C:\MYDIR*.WKS D:\YOURDIR

PATH

The NDOS PATH command, similar to the DOS PATH command, tells DOS where to look for executable and batch files when they are not in the current default directory. The main difference in the NDOS version of PATH is that PATH also looks for BTM, COM, EXE, and BAT files. The syntax for the command is

PATH [*path*/[;*path2*]...]

Entering PATH with no options causes the command to display the current path on-screen. Entering PATH with a single semicolon [;] clears the path. To tell NDOS to search the NU, DOS, and KWIKSTAT directories (all on the C: drive) when a command is not in the current directory, use the command

PATH C:\NU;C:\DOS;C:\KWIKSTAT

PAUSE

Like the DOS PAUSE command, the NDOS PAUSE command suspends the processing of a batch program until you press any key (except Ctrl-Break or Ctrl-C). With the NDOS version, you can place more than one command on the command line. The syntax for this command is

PAUSE [*message*]

An example follows:

PAUSE Press a key to continue with this batch file ...

When this command is encountered, the message

```
Press a key to continue with this batch file...
```

appears on-screen, and the batch file does not continue to the next command until a key is pressed. This command often is useful for pausing after displaying information on-screen so that the information does not scroll off the screen before the user has a chance to read the message.

POPD

Use the NDOS POPD command to recall a command from the top of the directory stack. The syntax for this command is

POPD [*]

If the * option is included, the directory stack is cleared.

For more information, see the "PUSHD" section, which describes how to create directory stacks, and the "DIRS" section, which displays the current directory stack.

Suppose that you are in the root directory on drive A. When you enter the PUSHD C:\MYDIR command, the C:\ (root) directory is placed in the directory stack and your default drive and directory change to C:\MYDIR. Then, after you enter the command PUSHD D:\TMP, the C:\MYDIR directory is placed in the stack, and you are changed to the D:\TMP directory and drive. If you enter the command

POPD

you are switched back to the first drive and directory entry on the stack (C:\MYDIR).

PROMPT

The NDOS PROMPT command, similar to the DOS PROMPT command, changes the prompt used by DOS. The syntax of the PROMPT command is

PROMPT [*text*]

Normally, the DOS prompt consists of the current disk name followed by a >. The default prompt if you are logged into drive A, for example, is A>.

The *text* option enables you to specify what appears on the prompt line by listing a series of commands, each preceded by a dollar sign ($). Text that is not a $command is output verbatim. The following $ commands are available:

Command	Meaning
$b	| character.
$c	Open parenthesis (NDOS only).
$d	Current date, WWW MMM DD,YYYY (day of week, month, date, and year). For example, Thu Oct 17, 1991.
$e	Esc character (ASCII 27).
$f	Close parenthesis (NDOS only).
$g	> character.
$h	Backspace character. (You can use this to display characters. For example, dhhhhh$h would cause the last six characters in the date ($d) to be erased from the prompt, so it would appear as Thu Oct 17.)
$l	< character.
$n	Default drive letter.
$P	Current disk and directory in uppercase. (Note: In DOS, $P always displays in uppercase.)
$p	Current disk and directory in lowercase (NDOS only).

continues

Command	Meaning
$q	= character.
$s	Space character.
$t	Current time (by hours, minutes, and seconds).
$v	DOS version number.
$X*d:*	Current disk and directory in uppercase, where *d:* is the drive specification (NDOS only).
$x*d:*	Current disk and directory in lowercase, where *d:* is the drive specification (NDOS only).
$z	Current NDOS nesting level (NDOS only).
$$	Dollar sign.
$_	CR/LF (go to next line).

You cannot find those options marked as NDOS only in the PC DOS or MS-DOS version of the PROMPT command. To cause the prompt to appear as the name of the disk drive and the name of the current directory, for example, use the command

    PROMPT PG

or

    PROMPT xd:

This command causes the DOS prompt when you are on drive C and in the \MYDIR directory to be

    C:\MYDIR>

or

    C:\MYDIR:

PUSHD

The NDOS PUSHD command places a disk drive and directory on the directory stack. The syntax for this command is

    PUSHD [[*d:*]*path*]

For more information, see the "POPD" section, which tells you how to recall a directory stack, and the "DIRS" section, which displays the current directory stack.

Suppose that you are in the root directory on drive A. When you enter the command

> PUSHD C:\MYDIR

the C:\ (root) directory is placed in the directory stack and your default drive and directory changes to C:\MYDIR. Then you enter the command

> PUSHD D:\TMP

which places the D:\MYDIR directory in the stack and changes you to the D:\TMP directory and drive. If you enter the command POPD, you are switched back to the last drive and directory entry (C:\MYDIR).

QUIT

Use the NDOS QUIT command to end the processing of a batch file at any point. No command line options are available. If you quit one batch file that has been called from a previous batch file, you are returned to that previous batch file.

RD or RMDIR

The NDOS RD or RMDIR command, used to remove directories, is similar to the DOS RD or RMDIR command. Unlike the DOS version, however, you can list several directories to delete at once. The syntax for this command is

> RD [*drive:*]*path*...

or

> RMDIR [*drive:*]*path*...

To delete the directories \MYDIR and \YOURDIR, for example, use the command

> RD \MYDIR \YOURDIR

Before removing a directory, you must delete all files in that directory. See the "MD" and "CD" sections for more information.

REM

The NDOS REM command, like the DOS REM command, places a comment in a batch file. For example, the command

REM This is a comment in a batch file

is ignored when the batch file commands are being processed.

Programmers usually use REM lines to document the actions of the batch file for purposes of maintaining the file.

REN or RENAME

The NDOS REN or RENAME command, like the DOS REN or RENAME command, renames a file or subdirectory. The syntax of the command is

REN [*switches*] *filespec... filespec*

or

REN [*switches*] *path... path*

The switches available for the command follow:

Switch	Effect
/P	Prompts to confirm each rename
/Q	Suppresses display of the names of the files as they are being renamed

To rename the file MYFILE.TXT to YOURFILE.TXT, for example, use the command

REN MYFILE.TXT YOURFILE.TXT

Unlike DOS, you can rename files to a different directory (not a different drive). For example, the command

REN \WP\MYFILE.TXT \TMP\YOURFILE.TXT

renames the file in the \WP directory to the \TMP directory. You also can rename directories. For example, the command

REN \MYDIR \YOURDIR

renames the directory \MYDIR to \YOURDIR.

RETURN

The NDOS command RETURN ends a subroutine in a batch file. This command has no command line options. Suppose that you have a sub-routine in your batch file with the following commands:

```
:MYSUB
ERASE *.BAK
RETURN
```

To execute this subroutine, use the command

GOSUB MYSUB

The subroutine is executed up to the command RETURN. The flow of the batch file then returns to the line following the GOSUB command.

SCREEN

The NDOS SCREEN command positions the cursor on-screen and optionally displays a message. The syntax for this command is

SCREEN *row column* [*message*]

For example, to locate the cursor at the 10th row and 4th column and display the message *Here I am*, use the command

SCREEN 10 4 Here I am

SCRPUT

The NDOS SCRPUT command displays text in color. The syntax of the command is

SCRPUT *row column* [BRIGHT] [BLINK] *foreground* ON *background text*

The colors available for foreground and background are black, blue, yellow, green, red, magenta, cyan, yellow, and white. For example, to place the text *This is a message* on-screen with bright white letters and a cyan background 10 rows down from the top and at column 12 from the left, use the command

SCRPUT 10 12 BRIGHT WHITE ON CYAN This is a message

SELECT

The NDOS SELECT command enables you to choose command line file arguments from a full-screen menu by using your arrow keys or the mouse pointer. After you make your selections, the command is executed on the selected files. The syntax for this command is

SELECT [/A:*attributes*][/O:*sortorder*] *command* (*filespec...*)

The /A switch causes files with certain attributes to appear in the select list and the /O switch causes files in the select list to be displayed in a sorted order.

When the /A option is used, SELECT displays only those commands that have the requested attribute or attributes set (or not set if a minus sign precedes the attribute name). The attributes available follow:

Attribute	Designates
h	Hidden file
r	Read-only file
s	System file
d	Directory
a	Archived file

To select to copy to drive A from a list of all archived files, for example, you use the command

SELECT /A:a COPY (*.*) a:\

To select to copy all files that are *not* archived, use /A:–a instead of /A:a.

The *sortorder* options enable you to sort the select list. The following sortorder options are available. Placing a minus (–) before a sort order causes the sort to be in descending order rather than the default ascending order.

Option	Sort Order
d	Date and time
e	File extension
i	NDOS file description
n	Name

Option	Sort Order
s	Size
g	Directories first in the list
u	Unsorted (same as normal DOS DIR)

When you enter the SELECT command, a file list appears on-screen. For example, if you enter the command

SELECT COPY (n*.doc) a:\

you see a screen similar to the one in figure 8.5. Use the up and down cursor-movement keys to move the highlight from line to line. To select a file to be copied, press the space bar (or plus key). Selected files have a small triangle to the left of their names. If a file already is selected, pressing the space bar (or minus key) unselects the file. Pressing the asterisk (*) key selects all files. After you select the files you want to copy, press Enter to initiate the Copy command.

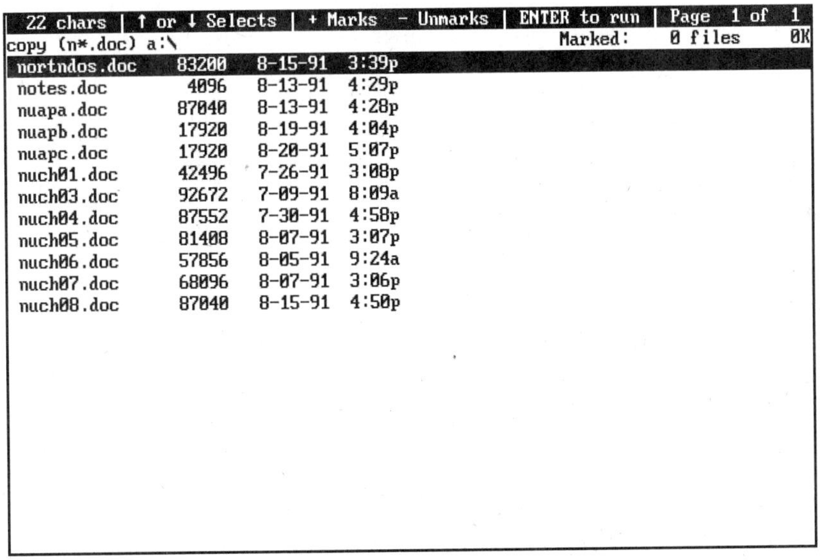

```
  22 chars | ↑ or ↓ Selects |  + Marks  – Unmarks |  ENTER to run | Page  1 of  1
copy (n*.doc) a:\                                Marked:    0 files      0K
 nortndos.doc    83200    8-15-91   3:39p
 notes.doc        4096    8-13-91   4:29p
 nuapa.doc       87040    8-13-91   4:28p
 nuapb.doc       17920    8-19-91   4:04p
 nuapc.doc       17920    8-20-91   5:07p
 nuch01.doc      42496    7-26-91   3:08p
 nuch03.doc      92672    7-09-91   8:09a
 nuch04.doc      87552    7-30-91   4:58p
 nuch05.doc      81408    8-07-91   3:07p
 nuch06.doc      57856    8-05-91   9:24a
 nuch07.doc      68096    8-07-91   3:06p
 nuch08.doc      87040    8-15-91   4:50p
```

FIG. 8.5.

Picking file names from a SELECT command list.

SET

The NDOS SET command, like the DOS SET command, displays, creates, modifies, or deletes environment variables. The syntax of this command is

SET [/P][/R *filespec*...][*variable*[=][*value*]]

The /P option tells the command to pause after displaying a page of entries. The /R *filespec* option tells the command to load a list of environmental variables from the file specified by filespec. To create a file that contains environmental variables, redirect the output of the SET command to a file name. For example, the command

    SET > ENVIRON.LST

creates a file named ENVIRON.LST containing the current environment settings. Then these same settings can be read back by using the /R option.

The command SET with no options lists the current settings to the screen. To add a variable, use the form

    SET *varname=value*

To set the value of the variable MYVAR to the path C:\MYDIR, use the command

    SET MYVAR=C:\MYDIR

To erase the variable MYVAR from the list of variables, use the command

    SET MYVAR

To edit an environment variable, use the NDOS command ESET.

Using the SET command, you can tell NDOS that a file with a particular extension should be used for a particular program. Suppose, for example, that you have many TXT files that you often want to display on-screen to read. You can tell NDOS that if the name of a TXT file is entered at the DOS prompt, the name should be viewed with the list command. See "Using Executable Extensions," earlier in this chapter.

The command to do this procedure is

    SET .TXT=LIST

If you have a file named MARY.TXT, then entering MARY at the DOS prompt causes the LIST program to execute and display the file MARY.TXT.

SETDOS

The NDOS SETDOS command displays or sets the NDOS configuration variables. With this command, you can customize NDOS for your personal use. The syntax of the command is

SETDOS [/*switches*]

The switches available for this command follow:

Switch	Effect
/A*n*	Determines if NDOS tries to use ANSI escape sequences. With /A0, NDOS can determine whether an ANSI driver is installed. /A1 forces NDOS to assume that an ANSI driver is installed. /A2 forces NDOS to assume that an ANSI driver is not installed.
/C*n*	Tells the command what COMPOUND character to use for separating multiple commands on the same line. The default is ^ (caret).
	You cannot use the following characters:
	| < > = , ;
	To use the tilde (~) as the compound character, for example, use the option /C~.
/E*h*	Sets the character to be used as the Escape character (see "Using Escape Sequences," earlier in this chapter). The default is ^X (Ctrl-X), which appears as an up arrow.
	You cannot use the following characters:
	| < > = , ;

Switch	Effect
/F0	Tells the command to turn on file name truncation. (This is the default.) /F1 means use full file names. When truncation is on, a file with a long path may appear in command output with the path \..\.
/H*nnn*	Determines the minimum command size to save to the Norton list. /H0 saves all command lines (default). /H256 disables history saves.
/I	Enables or disables an internal NDOS command. /I–list disables the list command /I+list enables the command.

continues

Switch	Effect
/L*n*	/L0 (default) enables NDOS command-line editing and /L1 reverts to the standard DOS line input.
/M*n*	/M0 (default) sets line editing to overwrite mode. /M1 sets editing to insert mode.
/N*n*	/N0 (default) sets NOCLOBBER to off, which enables files to be overwritten by output redirection (>). /N1 prevents files from being overwritten and requires that a file exist for the >> redirection command to work.
/R	Sets the number of screen rows used by the video display. For example, /R20 sets the rows to 20. This is useful for non-standard monitors with less than 25 lines.
/S	Determines the shape of the NDOS cursor. The format is /S*s*:*e*, where *s* is the starting scan line and *e* is the ending scan line. See Chapter 6 for more information.
/U	/U0 (default) displays file names in commands such as DIR and COPY in lowercase. /U1 displays the file names in uppercase.
/V	/V1 (default) echoes commands from a batch file (verbose). /V0 suppresses command echoing.

To change the compound character to @, for example, use the command

SETDOS /C@

To suppress the display of commands in batch files, use the command

SETDOS /V0

SETLOCAL

The NDOS command SETLOCAL saves the names of the current disk drive, directory, environmental variables, and aliases. The NDOS ENDLOCAL command restores the computer to previously saved names. This command, which has no options, is useful in a batch file when, after you change directory or disk drives temporarily to execute a procedure, you want to change back to your current settings.

The following example uses the SETLOCAL command to save your current settings. Some changes are made in order to run the KS program (which requires the new PATH setting C:\KWIKSTAT). Then, when that program is finished, the previous settings are restored by the ENDLOCAL command:

```
SETLOCAL
C:
CD \MYDIR
SET PATH = C:\KWIKSTAT
KS
ENDLOCAL
```

See the "ENDLOCAL" section for more information.

SHIFT

The NDOS SHIFT command, similar to the DOS SHIFT command, enables you to use more variables in a batch file. Normally in DOS, you can use variables named %0 to %9 (10 variables in all) in a batch file. NDOS supports variables named %0 to %127. Otherwise, SHIFT works the same as the DOS command.

SWAPPING

With the NDOS SWAPPING command, you can display, enable, or disable the NDOS swapping state. The swapping state controls how NDOS swaps its transient portion when other programs run. Setting swapping off usually means that small programs run faster, but the amount of DOS conventional memory temporarily is reduced by as much as 80K. If swapping is on, you have more memory available to run programs.

The syntax for the SWAPPING command is

SWAPPING [ON | OFF]

When you enter SWAPPING with no options, the current swapping state (on or off) is reported. To set swapping on, use the command

SWAPPING ON

To set swapping off, use

SWAPPING OFF

TEE

The NDOS TEE command copies a file to the standard output device (usually the monitor) and meanwhile saves a copy of the output to a file or files. The syntax for the command is

    TEE [/A] *path name...*

The /A switch causes output to be appended to the specified file rather than replacing the file.

TEE often is used to capture the intermediate piped output of a command. To search the file REPORT.TXT for lines containing *CREDIT*, for example, copy the matching lines to C.DAT, sort the lines, and write them to the output file CREDIT.DAT, use the command

    FIND "CREDIT" REPORT.TXT | TEE C.DAT | SORT > CREDIT.DAT

TEXT/ENDTEXT

Use the NDOS TEXT and ENDTEXT commands to display a block of text in a batch file. The syntax for these commands is

```
TEXT
lines of
output text
ENDTEXT
```

For example, the following lines cause the poem *Mary Had a Little Lamb* to be output to the screen from within a batch file:

```
TEXT
Mary had a little lamb
Its fleece was white as snow
And everywhere that Mary went
The lamb was sure to go.
ENDTEXT
```

This method of displaying text is often more convenient than using the ECHO command on every output line.

TIME

Similar to the DOS TIME command, the NDOS TIME command enables you to display or set the current system time. The syntax of the command is

TIME [*hh*[:*mm*[:*ss*]] [A|P]]

To set the system time to 1:30 p.m., for example, enter the command

TIME 1:30 p

or

TIME 13:30

Note that when you do not use the A or P option, the line is in 24-hour format.

TIMER

You use the NDOS TIMER command to turn the NDOS system stopwatch on and off. The syntax of the command is

TIMER [/S]

To start the timer, enter TIMER with no options. To display the current time, leaving the timer running, enter

TIMER/S

When a timer is running, entering the TIMER command with no options turns the timer off. The current clock time and elapsed time then are displayed.

TYPE

The NDOS TYPE command, similar to the DOS TYPE command, displays the contents of a text file on-screen. The DOS version does not have the /L or /P switches. The syntax of the command is

TYPE [/*switch*] *filespec*...

The available switches follow:

Switch	Effect
/L	Precedes each output line with a line number
/P	Pauses after a page of text has been displayed on-screen

To display the contents of the files REPORT.TXT and BUDGET.TXT on-screen and pause at each screen of information, for example, use the command

TYPE /P REPORT.TXT BUDGET.TXT

UNALIAS

The NDOS UNALIAS command removes an alias from the list. The syntax for the command is

UNALIAS *alias*...

or

UNALIAS *

If you use the * version, all aliases are deleted.

You may specify one or more aliases to delete from the list. To delete the aliases D and DDD from the list, for example, use the command

UNALIAS D DDD

See the "ALIAS" section for more information.

UNSET

The NDOS UNSET command removes variables from the environment list. The syntax of the command is

UNSET *name*...

or

UNSET *

If you use the * version, all environment variables are deleted. Use this version with caution.

You may specify one or more names to delete from the environment list. To delete the names MYENV and YOURENV, for example, use the command

    UNSET MYENV YOURENV

See the "SET" section for more information.

VER

The NDOS VER command, like the DOS VER command, displays the current DOS version numbers for NDOS and DOS. The command has no options.

VERIFY

With the NDOS VERIFY command, which is similar to the DOS VERIFY command, you can enable or disable the capability to display the current setting of write verification. DOS uses the verification process to check that no write error has occurred when information is written to disk. The syntax of the command is

    VERIFY [ON | OFF]

If the command is given with no options, the current state of VERIFY is displayed. To enable write verification, enter the command

    VERIFY ON

To disable write verification, enter the command

    VERIFY OFF

The default setting for VERIFY is OFF.

VOL

Similar to the DOS VOL command, the NDOS VOL command is used to display the disk volume label. The syntax for the command is

    VOL [d:]...

Entering VOL with no options displays the volume label for the current disk. You may request the volume label for one or more disks at once. To display the volume label for drives A and C, for example, enter the command

VOL A: C:

Y

The NDOS Y command copies standard input to standard output while copying specified files to standard output. The syntax for the command is

Y *filespec...*

For example, to enter information from the keyboard (standard input), then append the file MARY.TXT to the information, then append to that information a file named HUMPTY.TXT and output the three sources to one file named RHYMES.TXT, use the command

Y MARY.TXT HUMPTY.TXT > RHYMES.TXT

This results in the file RHYMES.TXT which includes

1. Input from keyboard

2. Contents of MARY.TXT

3. Contents of HUMPTY.TXT

When you use the Y command to enter information from the keyboard, you must signal an end to the input by entering a ^Z (Ctrl-Z) and then pressing Enter.

Chapter Summary

The NDOS commands provide you with a much richer operating system than do the normal DOS commands. With NDOS, you retain all the features you are already comfortable with in DOS, you gain more flexibility for the commands you already know, and you gain a whole new repertoire of handy "DOS-like" commands. Some of the handiest benefits of NDOS are its capability to read more than one line on a command line, its extended editing features on the command line, and its capability to enable you to bring up previously entered commands to reexecute.

Using Norton Commander

Norton Commander Basics

Norton Commander 3.0 is a program that enables you to perform a variety of tasks on your computer in a menu-like environment rather than from the standard DOS command line. Instead of having to remember the syntax of the DOS COPY command, for example, you are led through the Commander copy process with a series of menus and prompts.

Commander is not just a substitute for some DOS commands; it also provides you with a number of features that are not found in DOS. You can use Commander, for example, to view the contents of a variety of database, spreadsheet, and word processing files without having to use the respective application programs. Also, Commander enables you to execute several of the Norton Utilities commands, such as those used to display a sorted directory, set file attributes, find files, set an EGA monitor to display more than 25 lines, and more.

One of the main features of Norton Commander is convenience. The program is a bit like an automatic transmission in a car. You can get by with a manual transmission, but an automatic transmission often makes driving the car easier and more pleasurable. In the same way, many of the things that you can do in Commander you can do also in DOS or in Norton Utilities. Commander automates those commands through its menu structure, however, making the "driving" of the computer easier for you. Commander is particularly helpful for beginning users who have not memorized DOS and Norton commands.

This chapter introduces you to the basics of using Norton Commander. The chapter is arranged according to how you normally would use Norton Commander and not necessarily by the order of the options in the on-screen menus. You first learn how to display and access the various Commander menus. Most of the action takes place on the Commander's left and right panels, so the contents of the panels and options for controlling the display of these panels are discussed.

After the preliminary description of how Commander works, the chapter turns to how to manage and manipulate your directories and files; how to look at files from spreadsheets, databases, and word processors; how to use the Commander editor to edit ASCII files; and how to customize Commander to your particular tastes.

Getting To Know the Norton Commander Screen

If you have not installed Norton Commander, refer to the instructions in Appendix C. Then start Commander by typing *nc* at the DOS prompt and pressing Enter. If you want the Commander program to begin each time you boot your computer, include the NC command as the last line in your AUTOEXEC.BAT file. Refer to Appendix A for information on the AUTOEXEC.BAT file.

When you start Norton Commander, you see a screen similar to the one in figure 9.1. Under normal installation, Commander is set up to display initially only a directory panel on the right half of the screen and a function key bar at the bottom of the screen. The screen, however, has four places where you can choose options (or directory or file names): the menu bar, the function key bar, the left panel, and the right panel.

Although only the function key bar and the right panel are visible on the initial screen, you easily can display the menu bar at the top of the screen and the left panel on the left half of the screen. The key combinations for turning on and off the screen components are listed in table 9.1.

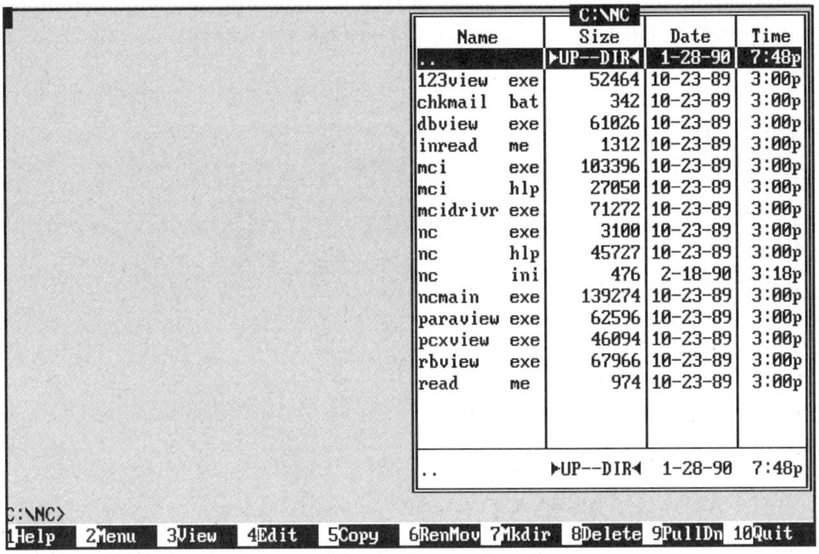

FIG. 9.1.

The opening Norton Commander screen.

Table 9.1 Displaying the Commander Screen Components

Screen Component	Keys To Toggle Display
Menu bar	F9
Function key bar	Ctrl-B
Left panel	Ctrl-F1
Right panel	Ctrl-F2

NOTE In Version 2.0 of Norton Commander, F9 turns on the menu bar but does not turn it off again as F9 does in Version 3.0. In Version 2.0, press Esc to turn off the menu bar.

As discussed in Chapter 2, you can access options in several ways. You can use the point-and-shoot method with the keyboard or the mouse. After a menu appears, you also can press a hot key to choose an option. The hot key usually is the first letter of the option name or the only capitalized letter in the option name. Another method of accessing options is by using control commands. To issue a control command, you hold down the Ctrl key and then press another key. If a control command requires the key combination of Ctrl and the letter C,

for example, the command is shown in this book as Ctrl-C. If a menu
option has an equivalent control command, it appears to the right of
the option name on the menu.

Using the Menu Bar and Its Pull-Down Menus

After you press F9 (PullDn), the menu bar appears at the top of the
Commander screen (see fig. 9.2). (You also can use the mouse to display the menu bar. Just point to the top line of the screen and hold
down the left button.) This menu bar enables you to access five Commander menus: Left, Files, Commands, Options, and Right. When the
menu bar is on, you can use the right- and left-arrow keys (or the
mouse) to point to a menu option. If you press Enter or click the left
mouse button when an option is highlighted, a pull-down menu
appears.

FIG. 9.2.

Displaying the Norton Commander menu bar.

Left	Files	Commands	Options	Right			
				Name	Size	Date	Time
				..	▶UP--DIR◀	1-28-90	7:48p
				123view exe	52464	10-23-89	3:00p
				chkmail bat	342	10-23-89	3:00p
				dbview exe	61026	10-23-89	3:00p
				inread me	1312	10-23-89	3:00p
				mci exe	103396	10-23-89	3:00p
				mci hlp	27050	10-23-89	3:00p
				mcidrivr exe	71272	10-23-89	3:00p
				nc exe	3100	10-23-89	3:00p
				nc hlp	45727	10-23-89	3:00p
				nc ini	476	2-18-90	3:18p
				ncmain exe	139274	10-23-89	3:00p
				paraview exe	62596	10-23-89	3:00p
				pcxview exe	46094	10-23-89	3:00p
				rbview exe	67966	10-23-89	3:00p
				read me	974	10-23-89	3:00p
				..	▶UP--DIR◀	1-28-90	7:48p

C:\NC>

1Help 2Menu 3View 4Edit 5Copy 6RenMov 7Mkdir 8Delete 9PullDn 10Quit

The first four pull-down menus are shown in figures 9.3 through 9.6.
(The Left and Right menus are similar, so the Right menu is not shown
in a figure.) The Left menu controls what you see in the left panel, and
the Right menu controls what you see in the right panel. The Files
menu enables you to choose Commander options that deal with files.

The Commands menu gives you access to a number of disk-management commands similar to some of the Norton Utilities commands. The Options menu enables you to choose various options about how Commander information is displayed on your computer. These menus are described in more detail in subsequent sections of this chapter.

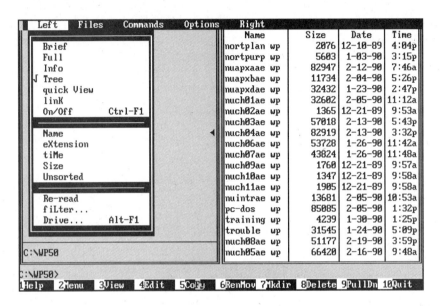

FIG. 9.3.

The Norton Commander Left menu.

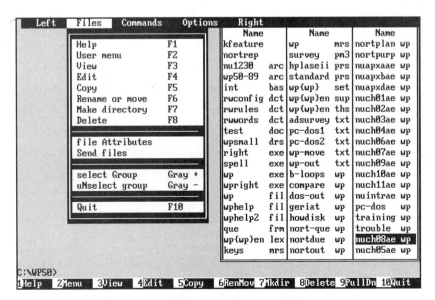

FIG. 9.4.

The Norton Commander Files menu.

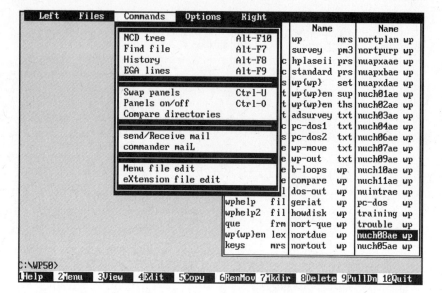

FIG. 9.5.

The Norton
Commander
Commands
menu.

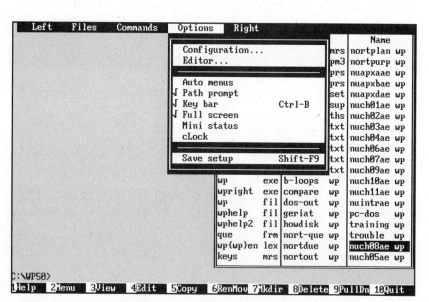

FIG. 9.6.

The Norton
Commander
Options menu.

Using the Function Key Bar

The function key bar appears at the bottom of the screen when the Norton Commander is in operation. If you are using a mouse, you can select one of the function key options by pointing to it with the mouse and clicking the left button. If you are using the keyboard, press the function key that corresponds to the menu number. To choose the Help option (1), for example, press F1. The function keys are described in the following sections.

One of the first function keys you should learn about is F10, which is the Quit key. If you want to end Norton Commander, just press F10. A small dialog box appears in the center of the screen, asking you to verify that you want to quit. To end Commander, press Y, highlight Yes and press Enter, or point to Yes with the mouse and click the left button.

Using the Right and Left Panels

The contents of the right and left panels are controlled by the options on the Right and Left pull-down menus. Depending on your preferences, these panels can contain the following:

- A brief directory of files (names only)
- A full directory of files (including dates, times, and sizes)
- A graphic representation of the directory tree
- Information about the directory and disk
- The displayed contents of a file

When you activate both the left and right panels in Commander by pressing Ctrl-F1 or Ctrl-F2, you see a display like the one in figure 9.7. Usually, once you have activated both panels, the left panel is set up to display the directory tree structure of the disk, and the right panel is set up to display the files belonging to the directory that is selected in the left panel.

You can access information in only one panel at a time. When both panels are displayed, you move from one active panel to the other by pressing the Tab key (or by pointing with the mouse to a panel and clicking the button to activate it). When a panel is activated, you can use the arrow keys to highlight files or directories that you want to access or use in some way.

```
┌═════════════ Tree ═════════════┐┌══════════ C:\WP50 ══════════┐
│ ├─NORTON                       ││  Name     Size    Date    Time │
│ ├─MOUSE1                       ││nortplan wp   2076 12-10-89  4:04p│
│ ├─TYPESET                      ││nortpurp wp   5603  1-03-90  3:15p│
│ ├─LIB                          ││nuapxaae wp  82947  2-12-90  7:46a│
│ ├─BIN                          ││nuapxbae wp  11734  2-04-90  5:26p│
│ ├─DB3                          ││nuapxdae wp  32432  1-23-90  2:47p│
│ ├─FONTS                        ││nuch01ae wp  32602  2-05-90 11:12a│
│ ├─HG                           ││nuch02ae wp   1365 12-21-89  9:53a│
│ ├─KWDISK                       ││nuch03ae wp  57018  2-13-90  5:43p│
│ │WP50         │             ◄  ││nuch04ae wp  82919  2-13-90  3:32p│
│ ├─KW                           ││nuch06ae wp  53728  1-26-90 11:42a│
│ ├─QB                           ││nuch07ae wp  43824  1-26-90 11:48a│
│ ├─PM                           ││nuch09ae wp   1760 12-21-89  9:57a│
│ │  ├─TEMPLATE                  ││nuch10ae wp   1347 12-21-89  9:58a│
│ │  └─GETSTART                  ││nuch11ae wp   1905 12-21-89  9:58a│
│ ├─VENTURA                      ││nuintrae wp  13681  2-05-90 10:53a│
│ ├─CAI                          ││pc-dos   wp  85085  2-05-90  1:32p│
│ ├─FORTRAN                      ││training wp   4239  1-30-90  1:25p│
│ ├─BACK                         ││trouble  wp  31545  1-24-90  5:09p│
│                                ││nuch08ae wp  51177  2-19-90  3:59p│
│C:\WP50                         ││nuch05ae wp  66420  2-16-90  9:48a│
└════════════════════════════════┘└═══════════════════════════════┘
C:\WP50>
 1Help  2Menu  3View  4Edit  5Copy  6RenMov 7Mkdir 8Delete 9PullDn 10Quit
```

FIG. 9.7.

The Norton
Commander
screen with
both panels
activated.

If you want to swap the current left and right panels on-screen, choose
the Swap Panels option from the Commands menu (or press Ctrl-U).
The reasons for swapping panels are purely aesthetic, because you can
perform the same operations regardless of which panel holds the information. Using the Swap Panels option is much quicker, however, than
swapping manually by choosing different options for each panel.

Using the DOS Prompt and the History Option

Notice that the DOS prompt also appears on the Norton Commander
screen, directly above the function key bar. As mentioned previously,
you can use Commander menus to access commands, or you can enter
DOS commands directly from the DOS prompt.

Commander offers another convenient feature for entering DOS commands. If you have entered a DOS command recently and want to
repeat that command, you can use Commander's History option to
review and choose any of the last 15 commands entered at the DOS
prompt. You can access the History option by choosing it from the
Commands menu or by pressing Alt-F8. A panel then appears on-
screen, listing up to 15 commands. You can use the up- and down-
arrow keys or the mouse to point to one of the commands. Press Enter
or click the right mouse button to execute the command.

Controlling the Left and Right Panel Displays

With DOS's DIR command, you can look at the contents of only one directory at a time. When you want to use one of the directory's files in a command such as COPY or RENAME, you must spell out the full file name—and you had better not make any typing mistakes! Using Norton Commander's left and right panels, you can display two directories on-screen—twice as much information as you can with DOS. Also, you can point to and select the files or directories you want to use without worrying about typing them or spelling them correctly. These features are only a few reasons why using Commander's right and left panels is easier than using DOS commands.

Using the Keyboard To Control the Display

As mentioned previously, you press Ctrl-F1 to toggle the left panel on and off and Ctrl-F2 to toggle the right panel on and off. Commander provides several other keyboard commands for controlling the panel display and manipulating the files and directories listed in the panels. These shortcuts are listed in table 9.2.

In addition to the keyboard point-and-shoot method of highlighting with the arrow keys and then pressing Enter to change directories, you can point to a directory name with the mouse and then double-click to change to that directory. You also can change to another directory by typing the following command at the DOS prompt:

> NCD *dirname*

Remember also the shortcut keys Ctrl-PgUp to change to the parent directory and Ctrl-\ to change to the root directory.

At times, you may want to select from a directory panel a number of files at the same time (for example, to copy a group of files with the F5 key). You can select a particular group of files by using the gray + and gray – keys, which usually are located at the right of the keyboard. If you press the gray + key, Commander prompts you to enter all files to include in a selection. You can enter *.TXT, for example, to include all files with a TXT extension. The selected files then appear highlighted in the panel. To exclude files from the list, press the gray – key. You can press the gray – key and then type *b. **, for example, to exclude all files that begin with the letter B. After selecting files, you can use the function key commands to copy, rename, move, or delete these files.

Table 9.2 Using the Keyboard To Control Panel Display

Key	Effect
↑	Scrolls panel information up
↓	Scrolls panel information down
Enter	Changes to a directory if that directory name is highlighted (works like an NCD command); begins a program if a program file name (a BAT, EXE, or COM file, for example) is highlighted; has no effect if any other file name is highlighted.
Ctrl-PgUp	Changes to the parent directory
Ctrl-\	Changes to the root directory
Gray+	Selects a group of files
Gray–	Unselects a group of files
Alt-*file name*	Speed searches for a specified file name
Ins	Selects/unselects file at cursor
Ctrl-Enter	Copies file or directory name to command line
Ctrl-P	Turns inactive panel on or off
Ctrl-O	Turns both panels on or off
Ctrl-U	Switches panels

The Alt-*file name* command enables you to quickly find a file in a directory. Suppose that you are looking for a file named SAMPLING.TXT, for example, and know that its directory contains 200 files. Of course, you can scroll through the entire directory list until you find the file. An easier way, however, is to press Alt-S. A small dialog box appears at the bottom right of the screen. The highlight in the directory panel points to the first file in the list that begins with the letter S. After you press the second letter in the file name, *a*, the highlight moves to the first file name in the directory that begins with *sa*. Usually, by pressing a few letters, you soon locate the file you have in mind. You then can use that file in a command to copy the file, rename it, and so on.

The Ctrl-Enter command enables you to quickly copy the name of a highlighted file to the DOS command area. Suppose that you want to enter the following command at the DOS command prompt:

WP50 FY8990RT.WP5

Instead of typing the whole command (and possibly misspelling the file name), you can highlight the file name in the directory panel. Then type *wp50* and press Ctrl-Enter. The name FY8990RT.WP5 appears on the DOS command line; you have entered the command you wanted.

As mentioned previously, to control exactly what information appears in the panels—and how it appears—you use the options on the Left and Right pull-down menus. The following sections describe these menu options.

Displaying Files in Brief and in Full

The Brief and Full options on the Left and Right menus determine how files are displayed on a panel. The Brief option lists only the file names; the Full option lists the file names with the size, date, and time for each file. Using the Brief option enables you to display more file names at one time. An example of a right panel display with the Brief option selected is shown in figure 9.8. (The right panel in figure 9.7 is in full mode, which is the default mode.) If you have many files in a directory and are interested only in the names, you can use the Brief option to avoid scrolling to find the files you want to access.

```
═══════════ Tree ═══════════    ╔═══ C:\WP50 ═══╗
├─NORTON                         │    Name    │    Name    │    Name    │
├─MOUSE1                         │kfeature    │wp       mrs│nortplan  wp│
├─TYPESET                        │nortrep     │survey   pm3│nortpurp  wp│
├─LIB                            │nu1230   arc│hplaseii prs│nuapxaae  wp│
├─BIN                            │wp50-89  arc│standard prs│nuapxbae  wp│
├─DB3                            │int      bas│wp{wp}   set│nuapxdae  wp│
├─FONTS                          │rwconfig dct│wp{wp}en sup│nuch01ae  wp│
├─HG                             │rwrules  dct│wp{wp}en ths│nuch02ae  wp│
├─KWDISK                         │rwwords  dct│adsurvey txt│nuch03ae  wp│
├│WP50                         ◄ │test     doc│pc-dos1  txt│nuch04ae  wp│
├─KW                             │wpsmall  drs│pc-dos2  txt│nuch06ae  wp│
├─QB                             │right    exe│wp-move  txt│nuch07ae  wp│
├─PM                             │spell    exe│wp-out   txt│nuch09ae  wp│
│  ├─TEMPLATE                    │wp       exe│b-loops   wp│nuch10ae  wp│
│  └─GETSTART                    │wpright  exe│compare   wp│nuch11ae  wp│
├─VENTURA                        │wp       fil│dos-out   wp│nuintrae  wp│
├─CAI                            │wphelp   fil│geriat    wp│pc-dos    wp│
├─FORTRAN                        │wphelp2  fil│howdisk   wp│training  wp│
├─BACK                           │que      frm│nort-que  wp│trouble   wp│
                                 │wp{wp}en lex│nortdue   wp│nuch08ae  wp│
C:\WP50                          │keys     mrs│nortout   wp│nuch05ae  wp│

C:\WP50>
1Help  2Menu  3View  4Edit  5Copy  6RenMov 7Mkdir  8Delete 9PullDn 10Quit
```

FIG. 9.8.

Displaying the right panel in brief mode.

Displaying Summary Information

When you select the Info option from the Left or Right menu, the corresponding left or right panel displays summary information about the current drive, similar to information you would get with the DOS CHKDSK command (see fig. 9.9). The top part of the Info panel tells you the amount of memory available, the disk size and disk space available, the number of files in use, and how much space is taken up by the files.

Note that the bottom part of the Info panel in figure 9.9 includes the message

```
No 'dirinfo' file in this directory
```

In the DIRINFO file, you can place information about or a brief description of the contents of the directory. In the \WP50 directory, for example, you can place the message

This directory contains WordPerfect Version 5.0.

If you want to create such a DIRINFO file for the current directory, press F4 (Edit). A small edit window appears at the bottom of the Info panel. Enter your summary information and press F10 to save the DIRINFO file. Then whenever you display the Info panel for that directory, your description appears at the bottom of the panel.

After you examine the Info panel, you can return the panel to its previous state by pressing Ctrl-L or choosing another panel option from the Left or Right menu.

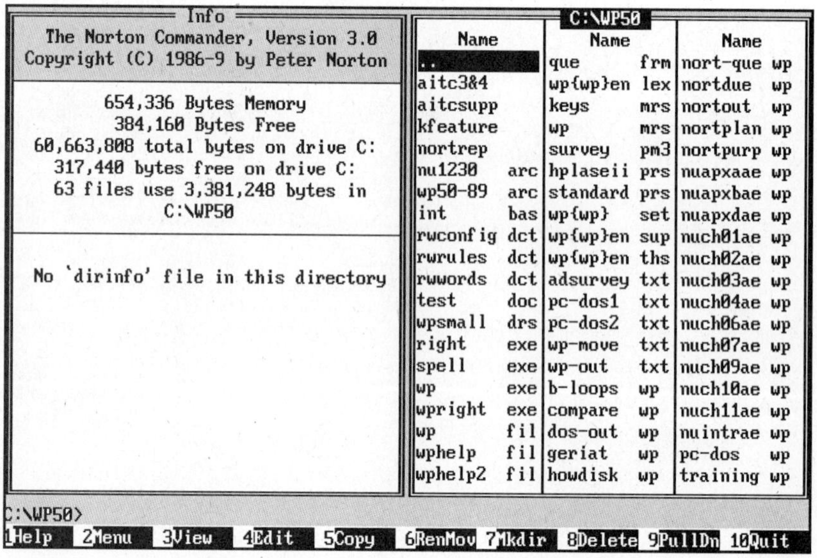

FIG. 9.9.

Displaying the Info panel.

```
═══════ Info ═══════            ══ C:\WP50 ══
   The Norton Commander, Version 3.0     Name          Name              Name
   Copyright (C) 1986-9 by Peter Norton  ..        que      frm  nort-que  wp
                                         aitc3&4   wp{wp}en lex  nortdue   wp
       654,336 Bytes Memory              aitcsupp  keys     mrs  nortout   wp
       384,160 Bytes Free                kfeature  wp       mrs  nortplan  wp
   60,663,808 total bytes on drive C:    nortrep   survey   pm3  nortpurp  wp
     317,440 bytes free on drive C:      nu1230 arc hplaseii prs nuapxaae  wp
     63 files use 3,381,248 bytes in     wp50-89 arc standard prs nuapxbae wp
            C:\WP50                       int    bas wp{wp}    set nuapxdae wp
                                         rwconfig dct wp{wp}en sup nuch01ae wp
                                         rwrules  dct wp{wp}en ths nuch02ae wp
   No 'dirinfo' file in this directory   rwwords  dct adsurvey txt nuch03ae wp
                                         test     doc pc-dos1  txt nuch04ae wp
                                         wpsmall  drs pc-dos2  txt nuch06ae wp
                                         right    exe wp-move  txt nuch07ae wp
                                         spell    exe wp-out   txt nuch09ae wp
                                         wp       exe b-loops  wp  nuch10ae wp
                                         wpright  exe compare  wp  nuch11ae wp
                                         wp       fil dos-out  wp  nuintrae wp
                                         wphelp   fil geriat   wp  pc-dos   wp
                                         wphelp2  fil howdisk  wp  training wp
C:\WP50>
1Help  2Menu  3View  4Edit  5Copy  6RenMov 7Mkdir 8Delete 9PullDn 10Quit
```

The Info option is useful for several reasons. The Bytes Free information tells you how much RAM is available to be used by an application program. Usually a program has a minimum requirement for it to run. You can display the Info panel to check whether you have enough memory to run a particular application program. Commander uses about 13K of memory. Because Commander frees itself from memory when an application program begins and then restarts itself when the program finishes, keep in mind that when you begin an application you have 13K more memory available to you than what is reported in the Info panel. Also, Info tells you how many bytes are free on a disk. This information can be important if you need to copy files to the disk. Displaying the Info panel can save you the trouble of trying to copy files that the disk cannot handle. Also, if you don't know the amount of memory available on your floppy disks, you can get that information from the Total Bytes message.

Displaying a Directory Tree

Choosing the Tree option from the Left or Right menu displays a graphic tree of the disk directory structure, as shown in the left panel of figure 9.8. After you activate a panel containing a directory tree, you can use the up- and down-arrow keys to select a directory as the current directory. (To select a directory in the Tree panel with a mouse, point to the directory name and click the left button.) If the other panel is set up to display file names, that panel displays the file names associated with the selected directory.

Sorting Files

File names displayed in the panels may be listed in a number of sorted orders, according to options on the Left and Right menus. You can list files in order by name, extension, time of creation, or size, or you can choose to have the files listed in unsorted order, which is how they normally would appear in a DOS DIR list. To select a sort option, highlight the Name, Extension, Time, Size, or Unsorted option and press Enter. Alternatively, press the uppercase letter of an option to select it. If you are using a mouse, highlight the option and click either button. After you choose a sort option, a check mark appears to the left of the option in the menu.

Sort orders are helpful if you are trying to locate files by some criterion, such as when they were created or what extension was used. By displaying the files in the appropriate sorted order, you may be able to locate files more quickly.

Filtering Files

The Filter option enables you to select which files are displayed in a panel. When you choose Filter from the Left or Right menu, a dialog box appears in which you can choose the type of files to display. Figure 9.10 shows a Filter dialog box. Your choices include all files, executable files, or a custom list of files. If you choose the Custom option, you then must enter a file specification—using the question mark (?) or asterisk (*) wild-card characters—to describe the files to include. If you want to list only files with the PIX extension, for example, choose the custom list option and enter a *.PIX file specification.

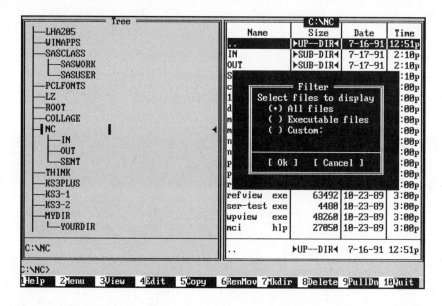

FIG. 9.10.

The Filter dialog box.

Changing Drives

The Drive option on the Left and Right menus enables you to specify which drive should be used for the panel. When you choose this option, a dialog box displays a list of possible drive names. Choose a drive and press Enter, and the panel reflects the change.

Rereading and Updating File Information

The Re-read option on the Left and Right menus makes Commander reread file information from disk and update information in a panel.

The program often performs this operation automatically when a change is made. If you change a disk in a drive or modify a file with a memory-resident program, however, you should choose the Re-read option to make sure that Commander has up-to-date knowledge about the files on disk. Choosing Re-read when the directory tree is activated ensures that Commander has current information about all directories on disk.

Viewing Files

The Left and Right menus' Quick View option displays the contents of a file that is highlighted in the other panel. You can view the contents of files from programs such as Lotus 1-2-3, WordStar, WordPerfect, dBASE III, and others—even if you don't have those application programs. You also can view graphic files that match the Z-Soft PCX standard. The Quick View option is similar to the F3 (View) key (see "Viewing Files with F3," later in this chapter). The Quick View option, however, initially displays only half a screen rather than the full-screen F3 view. Figure 9.11 shows a screen that contains a Quick View panel of a Mosaic Twin spreadsheet file. Notice in the function key bar that the F3 key, which previously had been labeled View, now is called Zoom. When a Quick View panel is displayed, you can press F3 (Zoom) to expand the view from a half-screen panel to the full screen.

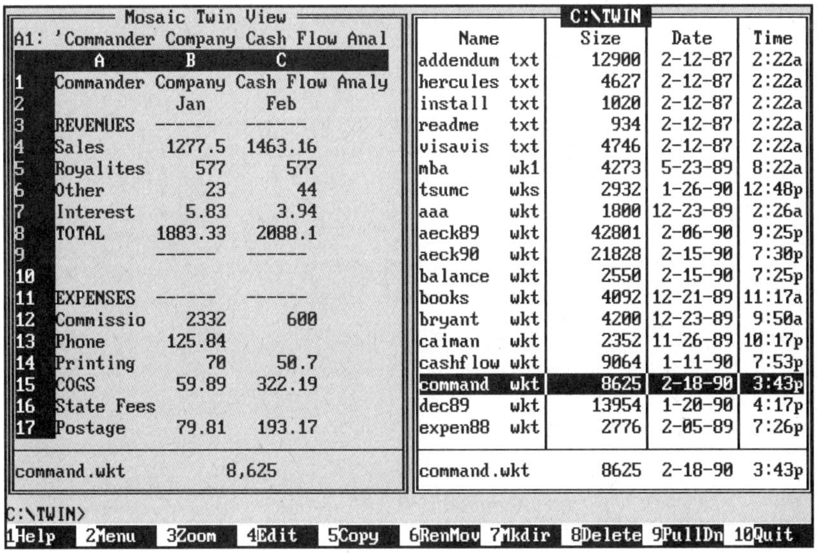

FIG. 9.11.

Using the Quick View option.

Linking Information

The Link option on the Left and Right menus enables you to move information quickly between two computers. The Link option may be handy particularly if you use a laptop computer. To update your desktop computer with information from your laptop (or vice versa), you can use the Link option to copy files back and forth between computers. This option is an advanced feature and is covered in Chapter 10.

Turning the Panels On and Off

The On/Off option on the Left and Right menus toggles the corresponding panel on and off. This option has the same effect as pressing Ctrl-F1 or Ctrl-F2. At times, you may want to see what is "behind" a panel—for example, after you perform a DOS command and information scrolls onto that part of the screen. Norton Commander offers a few other shortcuts for turning panels on and off. Pressing Ctrl-P turns on and off the inactive panel, and Ctrl-O turns on and off both panels.

Managing Your Directories with Norton Commander

Norton Commander enables you to access and manage your directories on disk. Using Commander, you can make new directories by pressing a function key, access a version of the Norton Change Directory (NCD) command similar to the command in Norton Utilities, and compare directories. Table 9.3 summarizes the options used to perform these tasks.

Table 9.3 Commands for Managing Directories

Task	Key	Menu Command
Make directory	F7	Make directory option on File menu
Access NCD program	Alt-F10	NCD Tree option on Commands menu
Compare directories		Compare Directories option on Commands menu

Creating Directories with F7 (Mkdir)

The F7 (Mkdir) key enables you to make a new directory on disk. After you press F7, you are prompted to enter the name of the new directory. Enter the full path name. To make a directory named KWIKSTAT as a subdirectory of the root directory, for example, type the path name *kwikstat*. To make a directory named LETTERS as a subdirectory of the WP directory, type *wp**letters*. When you use the F7 (Mkdir) key, the Norton Commander and Norton Utilities information file TREEINFO.NCD is updated so that the NCD command works properly without having to rescan. (You also can make a directory by using Norton Commander's NCD command and pressing F7; see "Making a Directory with F7," later in this chapter.)

Navigating Directories with the NCD Tree Option

The NCD Tree option is similar to the Norton Utilities Norton Change Directory (NCD) command. Chapter 6 contains a more detailed description of that command. The NCD Tree option enables you to navigate among the directories on disk. This capability becomes more useful as your directory structure grows more complex.

You can choose the NCD Tree option from the Commands menu or by pressing Alt-F10. When you do so, you see a display similar to the one in figure 9.12. After this directory tree is displayed, you can change to a directory simply by moving the highlight to that directory's name and pressing Enter. If you are using a mouse, point to a directory and double-click to change directories. Table 9.4 lists the specific movement keys available on the NCD Tree screen.

Table 9.4 Using Cursor-Movement Keys on the NCD Tree Screen

Key	Effect
↑, ↓, ←, or →	Moves in direction of arrow
PgUp	Moves up tree on page (19 directories at a time)
PgDn	Moves down tree on page (19 directories at a time)
Home	Moves to beginning of tree
End	Moves to end of tree
Gray +	Moves forward one directory entry in the list
Gray −	Moves backward one directory entry in the list

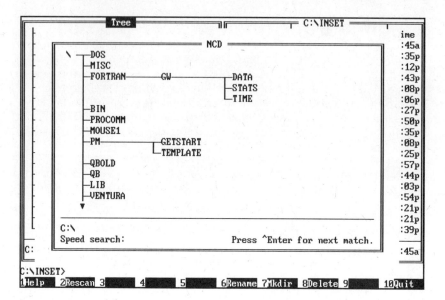

FIG. 9.12.

Displaying a
directory tree.

Other keyboard shortcuts are available when you are working on the
NCD Tree screen. To select a directory, for example, you can just type
its name. You may not have to type the entire directory name for it to
be highlighted. When you begin typing, NCD begins a speed search,
matching the letters you type to the directory names. You need to
type only enough letters to make the name unique. To choose the
\FORTRAN\GW\STATS directory from the tree displayed in figure 9.12,
for example, you need to press only an S at the Speed Search prompt,
because no other directories or subdirectories begin with that letter.
After you press S, the directory name \FORTRAN\GW\STATS is highlighted on-screen. Then press Enter to choose the directory. (If more
than one directory name begins with the letter you press, the first
matching directory in the directory list is highlighted. To search for the
next match, you press Ctrl-Enter.) Table 9.5 summarizes shortcut Commander NCD shortcut commands.

Table 9.5 Using Keyboard Shortcuts on the NCD Tree Screen

Key	Effect
Any letter	Begins speed search to select a directory
Ctrl-Enter	Searches for next match
Enter	Changes directory
F2	Rescans and rebuilds TREEINFO.NCD file
F6	Renames a directory
F7	Makes a directory
F8	Deletes a directory
Esc or F10	Quits NCD

Note that several function keys are listed in table 9.5. These keys are located at the bottom of the NCD Tree display and are described in more detail in the following sections.

Rescanning a Disk with F2

Pressing the F2 (Rescan) key causes NCD to rescan a disk in order to update the directory structure and the TREEINFO.NCD file, which contains the tree structure information. If you make or remove a directory with the DOS MD or RD command rather than the NCD command, for example, the TREEINFO.NCD file becomes out of date. When you rescan to make sure that this file contains current information, the NCD Tree command works faster. The Rescan option has the same function as the Re-read option on the Left and Right menus.

Renaming a Directory with F6

The F6 (Rename) key enables you to rename a directory. DOS has no equivalent feature. To rename a directory, follow these steps:

1. On the NCD Tree screen, highlight the directory to rename.

2. Press F6 (Rename).

3. Type a new name.

4. Press Enter.

Making a Directory with F7

The F7 (Mkdir) key on the NCD Tree screen enables you to make a new directory. First point to the directory that will be the parent directory of the new directory; then press F7, type the new directory name, and press Enter. If you want to create a subdirectory of MISC named TMP, for example, point to MISC on the tree, press F7, and type *tmp*. The result is a directory named \MISC\TMP. To create a subdirectory of the root directory, highlight the \ directory before pressing F7. When you create a directory by using F7, the TREEINFO.NCD file is updated automatically.

The full screen feature that enables you to point to a parent directory using F7 works only with the NCD tree; in other places, pressing F7 causes a dialog box to appear in which you can enter the name of a new directory to make.

Removing a Directory with F8

With the F8 (Delete) key, you can remove a directory. The directory must contain no files or subdirectories. To delete a directory, simply highlight the directory name and press F8. When you delete a directory with this method, the TREEINFO.NCD file is updated automatically.

Using the Compare Directories Option

The Compare Directories option enables you to compare the contents of two directories. Before you use this command, you must display one directory in the right panel and another in the left panel. Then open the Commands menu and choose the Compare Directories option. Any files in one directory having the same name but a more recent date than a file in the other directory are highlighted. This feature can be helpful if you want to compare similar directories. Suppose that you want to make sure that a directory on a floppy has all the latest files from the hard disk directory—you can use the Compare Directories option. You also can use this option to help you make both directories identical by copying unmatching files to the other directory, using the COPY command. (See "Copying Files," later in this chapter.)

Figure 9.13 shows the comparison of two directories named \CAI2DISK on drives A and C. Any files that do not appear in both directories will appear in a different color.

```
┌──────────A:\CAI2DISK─────────┐┌═════════C:\CAI2DISK═════════┐
│  Name     Size    Date   Time││  Name     Size    Date   Time│
│ . .      ▶UP--DIR◀ 7-01-91 4:16p││ . .      ▶UP--DIR◀ 1-19-90 8:51a│
│ !          509   5-20-91 2:05a││ !          509   5-20-91 2:05a│
│ a     img  512   5-20-91 2:05a││ a     img  512   5-20-91 2:05a│
│ apple img  896   5-20-91 2:05a││ apple img  896   5-20-91 2:05a│
│ b     img  640   5-20-91 2:05a││ b     img  640   5-20-91 2:05a│
│ ball  img  256   5-20-91 2:05a││ ball  img  256   5-20-91 2:05a│
│ beetle img 512   5-20-91 2:05a││ beetle img 512   5-20-91 2:05a│
│ c     img  512   5-20-91 2:05a││ c     img  512   5-20-91 2:05a│
│ cai-util exe 79403 5-20-91 2:05a││ cai-util exe 79403 5-20-91 2:05a│
│ cai   exe  89563 5-20-91 2:05a││ cai   exe  89563 5-20-91 2:05a│
│ cai   hlp  6342  5-20-91 2:05a││ cai   hlp  6342  5-20-91 2:05a│
│ caihelp com 4728 5-20-91 2:05a││ caihelp com 4728 5-20-91 2:05a│
│ caipcx com 17885 5-20-91 2:05a││ caipcx com 17885 5-20-91 2:05a│
│ cat   img  768   5-20-91 2:05a││ cat   img  768   5-20-91 2:05a│
│ cat1  img  646   5-20-91 2:05a││ cat1  img  646   5-20-91 2:05a│
│ cat2  img  653   5-20-91 2:05a││ cat2  img  653   5-20-91 2:05a│
│ cat3  img  635   5-20-91 2:05a││ cat3  img  635   5-20-91 2:05a│
│ cat4  img  646   5-20-91 2:05a││ cat4  img  646   5-20-91 2:05a│
│ . .      ▶UP--DIR◀ 7-01-91 4:16p││ . .      ▶UP--DIR◀ 1-19-90 8:51a│
└──────────────────────────────┘└──────────────────────────────┘
 A:\CAI2DISK>
 1Help 2Menu 3View 4Edit 5Copy 6RenMov 7Mkdir 8Delete 9PullDn 10Quit
```

FIG. 9.13.

Comparing
directories.

Managing Your Files with Norton Commander

Along with providing easy management of your directories, Norton Commander enables you to manage your files on disk with options that exceed what you can do with DOS alone. Using Commander, you can copy, rename, move, and delete files. You also can set file attributes and find files on disk. Table 9.6 summarizes the options used to perform these tasks.

Table 9.6 Commands for Managing Files

Task	Function Key	Menu Command
Copy files	F5	Copy option on Files menu
Rename files	F6	Rename or Move option on Files menu
Move files	F6	Rename or Move option on Files menu
Delete files	F8	Delete option on Files menu
Set attributes		File Attributes option on Files menu
Find files	Alt-F7	Find File option on Commands menu

These options are described in the following sections.

Copying Files

You can access the Copy option by pressing F5 (Copy) or by choosing Copy from the Files menu. With the Copy option, you can copy one or more files to another disk or location. This copy procedure is similar to the DOS COPY command. When you use the Commander Copy option, however, you are prompted for the information on which files to copy and where to copy them. You therefore do not have to remember the correct DOS COPY command syntax.

T   I   P   When you are working on a disk with many files, you may want to limit the files that appear on a panel. You can do so by setting the filter to display files that match some file specification. If you are working only with *.EXE files, for example, then set the filter to display only those files. To set the filter, see "Filtering Files," earlier in this chapter.

To copy a file, follow these steps:

1. Display in a panel the files that you want to copy. (Change to the appropriate directory by using the NCD Tree option or by pointing and shooting at the directory name on the other panel that displays the directory tree.)

2. Select the file or files to copy. If you want to copy a single file, highlight that file on the Commander panel. To select multiple files, use the gray + and gray – keys. To highlight one or more files using the mouse, click the right button and drag the mouse pointer over the list of files to highlight.

3. Press F5 or choose Copy from the Files menu. Commander prompts you to specify where to copy the files (see fig. 9.14).

4. Specify the destination. Enter the name of a disk drive such as a:, a path name such as \wp, or a combination such as c:\wp. When specifying the destination, you can press the F10 key to display a tree of the available directories. From this tree, you can highlight the directory to which you want the files copied.

5. After you type or select the destination, press Enter. The copy commences.

Another way to copy files (regardless of the panels displayed) is to press Shift-F5 when your cursor is at the DOS prompt. Commander asks you to enter the specification for the file or files to copy and the destination (see fig. 9.15). You also can press F10 to display a directory tree. From this tree, you can highlight a directory name and then press Enter to select it as the destination. (You also can select with a mouse.)

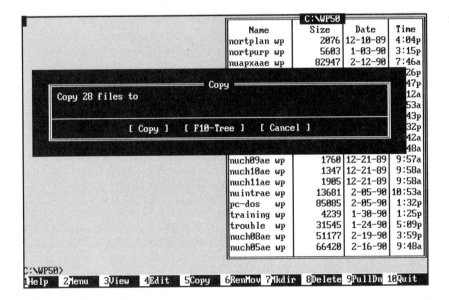

FIG. 9.14.

A message asking you to specify a copy destination.

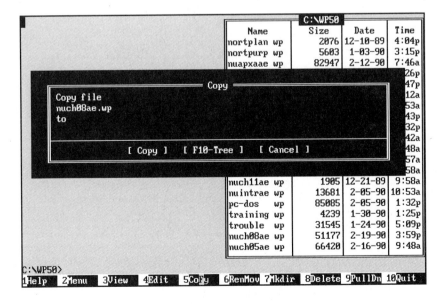

FIG. 9.15.

Using the manual copy process.

Renaming or Moving Files

The Rename or Move option, which you access from the Files menu or by pressing F6 (Rename), enables you to rename one or more files within the same directory or to move one or more files from one location on disk to another location on that disk or another disk. The Rename process works much like the Copy option but simply changes the name of a file within a directory instead of copying the file. You use the Move option to specify a destination other than the current directory. A Move operation copies the file or files to the new destination and erases the original file or files. DOS offers no equivalent MOVE command.

To rename or move a file, follow these steps:

1. Select the file or files to rename or move. If you want to rename or move a single file, highlight that file on the Commander panel. If you want to rename or move multiple files, select those files by using the gray + and gray − keys. To highlight one or more files using the mouse, point to the file name and click the right button. Or, press the right button and drag the mouse pointer over a list of files to highlight.

2. Press F6 or select the Rename or Move option from the Files menu.

3. To rename the selected file or files, specify the destination as a file name or a file specification containing the wild cards * or ?. If you select all files with the WP extension (*.WP), for example, you may type *.bak as the destination. This operation renames all files having the WP extension to files with a BAK extension.

   To move the selected file or files, enter a destination disk or directory different from the current one. You can press F10 to display a tree of the available directories on disk and select the destination by highlighting the directory name. If you enter a destination that is a different directory (or different drive), the selected files are moved to the new location and maintain their original names. If you choose a destination and also include a file specification, the files are moved and renamed. If you select all files with the WP extension in the \WP directory on drive C, for example, and you specify a new destination as A:\WP*.BAK, the files move from the original C:\WP directory to the A:\WP directory and are renamed from WP files to BAK files.

If a file being copied or moved exists already in the target directory, Commander asks

```
Do you wish to write over the old file?
```

You may choose the Overwrite, All, or Skip option. Overwrite
enables you to copy or move the specific file currently being
copied. The All option enables you to use Copy and Move for all
other files to be copied or moved (no more prompting about
overwriting will appear). Skip means that you want to skip this
particular copy or move. To choose an option, press O, A, or S.
Or, point to the option described with the mouse pointer and
click.

To perform a rename or move operation manually, press Shift-F6. Commander prompts you to enter the files to rename or move and the destination. You can press F10 to select a destination directory from the
directory tree.

Deleting Files

The Delete option, which you access from the Files menu or by pressing F8, enables you to delete one or more files. Follow these steps:

1. Select the file or files to delete. To delete a single file, highlight
   that file on the Commander panel. To delete multiple files, select
   those files by using the gray + and gray – keys. To highlight one or
   more files using the mouse, point to the file name and click using
   the right button. Or, press the right button and drag the mouse
   pointer over the list of files to highlight.

2. Press F8 (Delete) or select Delete from the Files menu. A dialog
   box asks

   ```
   Do you wish to delete filename?
   ```

   and gives you Delete and Cancel options (see fig. 9.16). Choose
   the Delete option to delete the files or Cancel to cancel the
   procedure.

To delete files manually, press Shift-F8. Commander prompts you to
enter the file specification of the files to delete. To delete all files with
the BAK extension, for example, type *.bak* and press Enter.

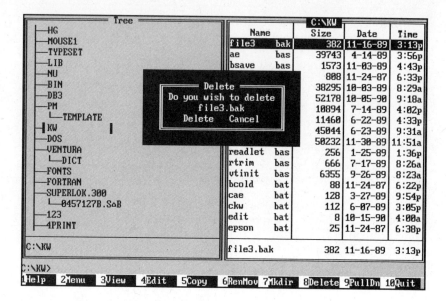

FIG. 9.16.

The Delete
dialog box.

Setting File Attributes

File attributes enable you to set the read-only, archive, hidden, and
system settings for files. These attributes are the same as those described for the Norton Utilities FileFind command. For a more detailed
description of these terms, see Chapter 3. You can set file attributes in
Norton Commander by choosing the File Attributes option from the
Files menu. Follow these steps to set file attributes:

1. Select the file or files for which you want to set attributes. If you
   want to set an attribute for a single file, highlight that file on the
   Commander panel. To set attributes for multiple files, select those
   files by using the gray + and gray – keys. To highlight one or more
   files using the mouse, point to the file name and click using the
   right button. Or, press the right button and drag the mouse
   pointer over the list of files to highlight.

2. Open the Files menu and select the File Attributes option to display the dialog box shown in figure 9.17.

3. Place the cursor in one of the option boxes and press the space
   bar to place an X in the box to select the option. Placing an X in
   the Set column sets the attribute on, and placing an X in the Clear
   column sets the attribute off. If you are using a mouse, point to
   the appropriate option box and click the left button to select. (If
   you choose only one file, the Clear column in the Attributes box
   does not appear—only the Set option appears.)

4. Highlight the Set option at the bottom of the dialog box and press Enter to activate the settings, or choose Cancel to cancel the procedure.

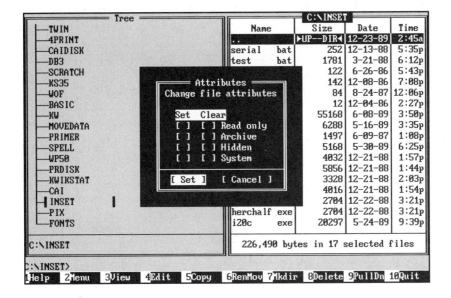

```
═══ Tree ═══                          ╒══ C:\INSET ═══
├─TWIN                      │   Name   │ Size │  Date   │ Time │
├─4PRINT                    │  ..      │▶UP--DIR◀│12-23-89│ 2:45a│
├─CAIDISK                   │serial bat│   252│12-13-88│ 5:35p│
├─DB3                       │test   bat│  1781│ 3-21-88│ 6:12p│
├─SCRATCH                   │          │   122│ 6-26-86│ 5:43p│
├─KS35          ╒══ Attributes ══╕      142│12-08-86│ 7:08p│
├─WOF           │Change file attributes│ 84│ 8-24-87│12:06p│
├─BASIC         │                 │     12│12-04-86│ 2:27p│
├─KW            │ Set  Clear      │  55168│ 6-08-89│ 3:50p│
├─MOVEDATA      │ [ ]  [ ] Read only│ 6288│ 5-16-89│ 3:35p│
├─PRIMER        │ [ ]  [ ] Archive  │ 1497│ 6-09-87│ 1:08p│
├─SPELL         │ [ ]  [ ] Hidden   │ 5168│ 5-30-89│ 6:25p│
├─WP50          │ [ ]  [ ] System   │ 4032│12-21-88│ 1:57p│
├─PRDISK        │                 │  5856│12-21-88│ 1:44p│
├─KWIKSTAT      │ [ Set ]  [ Cancel ]│ 3328│12-21-88│ 2:03p│
├─CAI           ╘═════════════════╛   4016│12-21-88│ 1:54p│
├─INSET         │                 │  2704│12-22-88│ 3:21p│
├─PIX           │herchalf exe│       2704│12-22-88│ 3:21p│
└─FONTS         │i20c     exe│      20297│ 5-24-89│ 9:39p│

C:\INSET                    226,490 bytes in 17 selected files

C:\INSET>
1Help  2Menu  3View  4Edit  5Copy  6RenMov 7Mkdir 8Delete 9PullDn 10Quit
```

FIG. 9.17.

The Attributes
dialog box.

Finding Files

The Commander's Find File option is similar to the FileFind command in Norton Utilities. With Find File, you can locate files on disk by searching for matching file specifications. To find a file or files, follow these steps:

1. Choose the Find File command by selecting it from the Commands menu or by pressing Alt-F7. The prompt

   ```
   File(s) to find:
   ```

   appears.

2. To search for a single file, such as REPORT.90, enter the full file name at the prompt. To search for a group of files, such as all files with the CAI extension, enter a file specification that includes wild cards, such as *.CAI.

3. Press Enter to initiate the search. If a file matching the file specification is found, Commander displays the directory, the file name, the size, and the date and time the file was created. If Commander finds many files matching the specification, it lists them on-screen, grouped in their respective directories.

Figure 9.18 shows a screen that gives the results of a Find File operation for all files matching the specification *.CAI.

To move to the directory containing the file in which you are interested, use the up- and down-arrow keys to highlight the file and then press Enter.

```
┌──────────────── Tree ════════════════╗┌─────────┬C:\WP50──┬─────────┬──────┐
│├─NORTON                              ║│ Name    │ Size    │ Date    │ Time │
│                                      ║│         │         │         │ 5p   │
│              ══════════════ Find File ══════════════════╗        │ 5a   │
│                                                         ┐│ ↑      │ 3p   │
│  \CAI                                                    │        │ 8p   │
│        demo.cai          17,493      12-01-89    1:01a   │        │ 2a   │
│        create.cai        18,598      12-01-89    1:01a   │        │ 9p   │
│        testgra.cai          450      12-01-89    1:01a   │        │ 7p   │
│        quest20.cai       14,588       1-31-90    5:24p   │        │ 9p   │
│                                                          │        │ 6p   │
│  \PROCOMM                                                │        │ 3p   │
│        vendor.cai         1,560       9-12-89    8:42a   │        │ 5a   │
│                                                          │        │ 0a   │
│  \CAI2DISK                                               │        │ 7p   │
│        demo.cai          16,004       1-19-90    9:55a   █│       │ 7p   │
│        create.cai        17,329       1-19-90    9:56a   █│       │ 3p   │
│        testgra.cai          450      12-01-89    1:01a   ↓│       │ 7p   │
│ ────────────────────────────────────────────────────────        │ 4p   │
│  23 files found.                                        │        │ 7p   │
│              Chdir    New search    Quit FF             │        │ 7p   │
│C                                                        ─┘        │ 7p   │
│C:\WP50>
│1Help  2Menu  3View  4Edit  5Copy  6RenMov  7Mkdir  8Delete  9PullDn  10Quit
```

Viewing Files with F3

The F3 (View) function key command is one of the handiest features of Norton Commander. This command enables you to examine the contents of a file without using an application program. To look at a dBASE III database, for example, you normally have to start the dBASE III program, enter a command to get the file you want, and then enter another command to look at the contents of the file. With Commander, however, you simply highlight the file name on-screen and press F3. If you want to manually enter the name of a file to view, press Shift-F3. Commander then prompts you for the name of the file you want to view.

You can use the View option on a number of data-storage file types used by major software programs. See the following lists for compatible programs. Keep in mind that this information is not exhaustive, however, because a number of other programs create files that use the file formats of the popular programs listed. The programs PC-FILE:db from Buttonware and Kwikstat from TexaSoft, for example, create and use dBASE III-type files. Thus, you also can view PC-FILE:db and Kwikstat files with Norton Commander's View option.

Programs Compatible with Commander's View Option

Database Programs

> dBASE II, III, III PLUS, and IV
> dbXL
> FoxBASE
> Microsoft MS Works
> Nantucket Clipper
> Paradox
> R:BASE
> Reflex

Graphics Programs

> All programs that create Z-Soft standard PCX-type (Paintbrush) files

Spreadsheet Programs

> 1-2-3 (Releases 1.x and 2.x)
> Borland Quattro
> Microsoft Excel
> Microsoft Multiplan 4.0
> Microsoft Works
> Mosaic Twin
> Symphony
> VP-Planner Plus
> Words & Figures

Word Processing Programs

> Microsoft Word 4.0 and 5.0
> Microsoft Windows Write
> Microsoft Works
> MultiMate
> XyWrite
> WordPerfect 4.2 and 5.0
> WordStar Pro, WordStar 2000
> All word processors and editors that create ASCII text files

NOTE Your use of the View option with some graphics programs may be restricted according to your monitor's capability to display colors and your computer's memory.

The following sections describe how to use the View option to view databases, spreadsheets, and word processing files.

Viewing Database Files

Norton Commander recognizes common database files for the programs listed in the preceding section. To view the contents of a database file—a dBASE III file, for example—highlight the file name in a panel and press F3 (View). Figure 9.19 shows the screen that is displayed when you select a database file named MAGAZINE.DBF. The information displayed is the first record of the database. Using the up- and down-arrow keys, you can page through the database records and examine them one at a time. Or, you can use the mouse and point to the top or bottom of the screen and hold down the left mouse button to scroll. You cannot change any of the information in the database, however, when using the Commander View option.

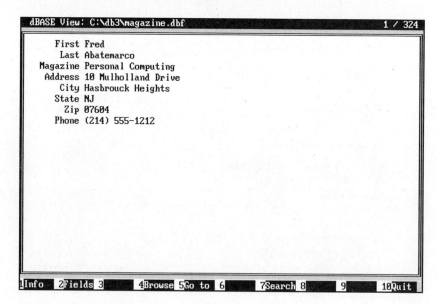

FIG. 9.19.

Using the View option to view a dBASE III database file.

At the top of the view screen, you can see information about which view method is being used to display the contents of a file. Figure 9.19 indicates dBASE View.

The number of the record being viewed and the total number of records in the database appear at the top right of the screen. In figure 9.19, the message 1/324 means that the database contains 324 records, and you are viewing record 1.

Notice also the function key options at the bottom of the dBASE View screen. Table 9.7 lists these function keys and other command and movement keys that you can use when viewing database files.

Table 9.7 Using Keyboard Commands in the Database View

Key	Effect
↑ or Ctrl-E	Goes back one field
↓ or Ctrl-X	Goes forward one field
PgUp or Ctrl-R	Moves up one page or to preceding record
PgDn or Ctrl-C	Moves down one page or to next record
Gray −	Goes to preceding record
Gray +	Goes to next record
Ctrl-Home or Ctrl-PgUp	Goes to first record
Ctrl-End or Ctrl-PgDn	Goes to last record
F1	Displays file information
F2	Displays field information
F4	Browses
F5	Goes to specified record
F7	Searches
Shift-F7	Continues a search
Ctrl-Pause	Stops a search
Esc or F10	Exits view and returns to Commander menu

When you first view a database, a single record is displayed on-screen. If you press F4 (Browse), the display changes to look much like a browse in dBASE, with one record displayed per line. Figure 9.20 shows this display for the MAGAZINE database. Using this method, you can see multiple records at a time. Notice, however, that only the first three fields of the record are displayed. To view the information off the screen to the right, press the right-arrow key until information in the other fields appears. To return to viewing a single record at a time, press F4 again.

Suppose that you want to find information—the phone number of Sam Jones, for example—in a particular record. If you press F7 (Search), a Search dialog box appears where you can enter a *search key* (the text you want to search for). Figure 9.21 shows how you enter the information necessary to search for the name *Jones*. After you enter the search key and press Enter, the first record containing your key in any field appears on-screen. If the record shown is not the one for which you are looking, you can press Shift-F7 to continue the search.

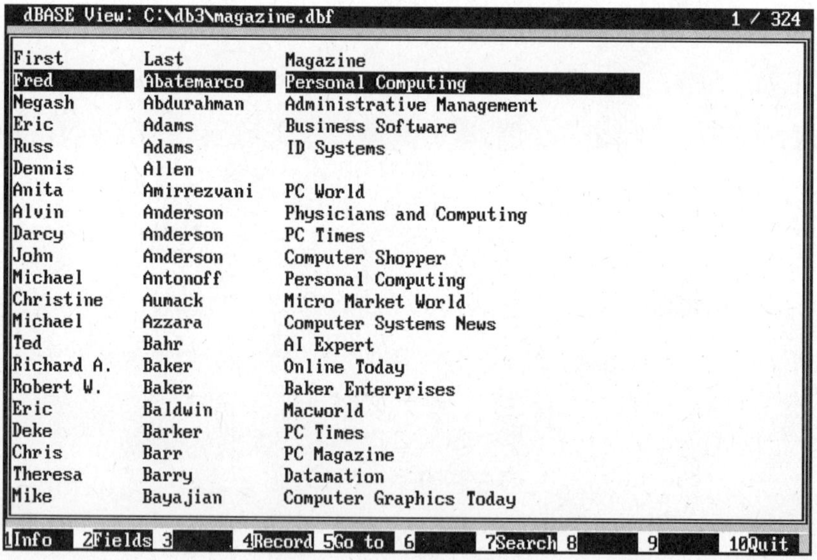

```
 dBASE View: C:\db3\magazine.dbf                            1 / 324
┌─────────────────────────────────────────────────────────────────┐
│First        Last         Magazine                                │
│Fred         Abatemarco   Personal Computing                      │
│Negash       Abdurahman   Administrative Management               │
│Eric         Adams        Business Software                       │
│Russ         Adams        ID Systems                              │
│Dennis       Allen                                                │
│Anita        Amirrezvani  PC World                                │
│Alvin        Anderson     Physicians and Computing                │
│Darcy        Anderson     PC Times                                │
│John         Anderson     Computer Shopper                        │
│Michael      Antonoff     Personal Computing                      │
│Christine    Aumack       Micro Market World                      │
│Michael      Azzara       Computer Systems News                   │
│Ted          Bahr         AI Expert                               │
│Richard A.   Baker        Online Today                            │
│Robert W.    Baker        Baker Enterprises                       │
│Eric         Baldwin      Macworld                                │
│Deke         Barker       PC Times                                │
│Chris        Barr         PC Magazine                             │
│Theresa      Barry        Datamation                              │
│Mike         Bayajian     Computer Graphics Today                 │
└─────────────────────────────────────────────────────────────────┘
 1Info   2Fields 3        4Record 5Go to 6       7Search 8    9      10Quit
```

FIG. 9.20.

Viewing a record from the MAGAZINE database.

If you know the record number of the record you want to view, you can press F5 (Go to). Commander prompts you to enter the record number, and then the program displays that record.

At times, you may need to know the structure of a database. You may be working on a program to merge information from the database, for example, and need to know field names and widths. When you are viewing a database, you can press F2 (Fields) to display the structure of the database, as shown in figure 9.22. The structure gives you information about the field names, types, lengths, and decimals used (if any). When you press the F1 (Info) key, information about the database size, number of fields, and records is displayed.

To exit the view screen and return to the Commander menus, press Esc or F10.

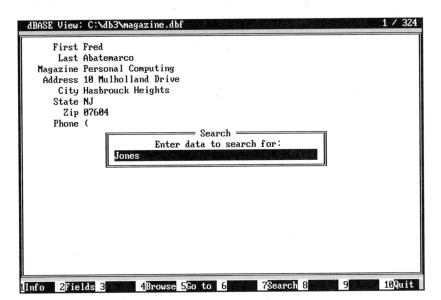

FIG. 9.21.

Searching records for the name *Jones*.

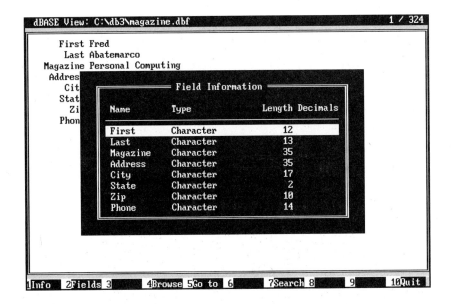

FIG. 9.22.

Using F2 (Fields) to display the structure of a database.

Viewing Spreadsheet Files

Norton Commander recognizes common spreadsheet files for the programs listed in "Viewing Files with F3," earlier in this chapter. To view the contents of a spreadsheet file—a Mosaic Twin file, for example—highlight that file name in a panel and press F3 (View). Figure 9.23 shows the screen displayed after you select the spreadsheet file named COMMAND.WKT. From the WKT extension, Commander knows that the selected file was created by Mosaic Twin, which is a spreadsheet program similar to Lotus 1-2-3.

At the top of the view screen, you can see information about which view method is being used to display the contents of a file. In figure 9.23, the first line indicates `Mosaic Twin View`. The second line of the screen shows the name and contents of the highlighted cell being viewed.

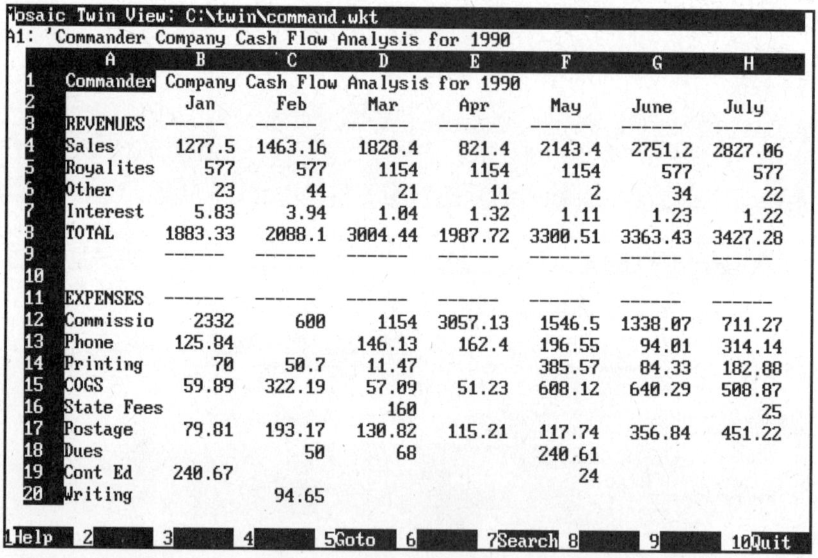

FIG. 9.23.

Using the View option to view a Mosaic Twin spreadsheet file.

```
Mosaic Twin View: C:\twin\command.wkt
A1: 'Commander Company Cash Flow Analysis for 1990
        A         B        C        D        E        F        G        H
 1   Commander Company Cash Flow Analysis for 1990
 2             Jan      Feb      Mar      Apr      May     June     July
 3   REVENUES  ------   ------   ------   ------   ------   ------   ------
 4   Sales     1277.5   1463.16  1828.4   821.4    2143.4   2751.2   2827.06
 5   Royalites  577      577     1154     1154     1154      577      577
 6   Other       23       44       21       11        2       34       22
 7   Interest    5.83     3.94     1.04     1.32     1.11     1.23     1.22
 8   TOTAL     1883.33  2088.1   3004.44  1987.72  3300.51  3363.43  3427.28
 9             ------   ------   ------   ------   ------   ------   ------
10
11   EXPENSES  ------   ------   ------   ------   ------   ------   ------
12   Commissio  2332      600              1154    3057.13  1546.5   1338.07   711.27
13   Phone     125.84            146.13    162.4    196.55    94.01    314.14
14   Printing    70       50.7    11.47                      385.57    84.33    182.88
15   COGS       59.89    322.19   57.09     51.23    608.12   640.29    508.87
16   State Fees                   160                                            25
17   Postage    79.81    193.17  130.82    115.21   117.74   356.84    451.22
18   Dues                 50       68                240.61
19   Cont Ed   240.67                                 24
20   Writing             94.65
1Help    2        3        4       5Goto   6        7Search 8        9       10Quit
```

In this view screen, the F1 (Help) key displays information about cursor movements and the function key commands. The F5 (Go to) option enables you to choose the area of the spreadsheet to display. The F7 (Search) option enables you to search for text within the spreadsheet, and the F10 (Quit) option exits the view and returns you to Commander. Table 9.8 lists these function keys and other command and movement keys that you can use when viewing spreadsheet files.

Table 9.8 Using Keyboard Commands in the Spreadsheet View

Key	Effect
Home	Goes to top left cell
End	Goes to last active cell
← or Ctrl-S	Moves one cell left
→ or Ctrl-D	Moves one cell right
↑ or Ctrl-E	Moves one cell up
↓ or Ctrl-X	Moves one cell down
PgUp or Ctrl-R	Moves one page up
PgDn or Ctrl-D	Moves one page down
Tab or Ctrl-→	Scrolls one page right
Shift-Tab or Ctrl-←	Scrolls one page left
F5	Goes to specified record
F7	Searches
Shift-F7	Continues a search
Esc or F10	Exits view and returns to Commander menu

If you want to search the database for particular information, you can use the F7 (Search) key. If you want to find the label containing the word *Taxes*, for example, you can press F7 and then enter the search word in the View dialog box, as shown in figure 9.24. After you press Enter, the first cell containing a match is highlighted in the spreadsheet. If the label highlighted is not the one for which you are looking, press Shift-F7 to continue the search. If you already know the cell name of the cell you want to view, press the F5 (Go to) key and then enter a cell address (for example, A5 or N50). Press Esc or F10 to exit the view and return to the Commander menus.

Viewing Word Processor Files

Norton Commander recognizes common word processing files for the programs listed in "Viewing Files with F3," earlier in this chapter. To view the contents of a word processing file—a WordPerfect file, for example—highlight that file name in a panel and press F3 (View). A view of a WordPerfect file is shown in figure 9.25.

At the top of the view panel, you can see information about which view method is being used to display the contents of a file. The top line in figure 9.25 indicates WordPerfect View. The top line of the word processing view screen also displays the file name, the current column location of the cursor, the size of the file in bytes, and a percentage that represents the amount of the file that has been paged off the top of the screen.

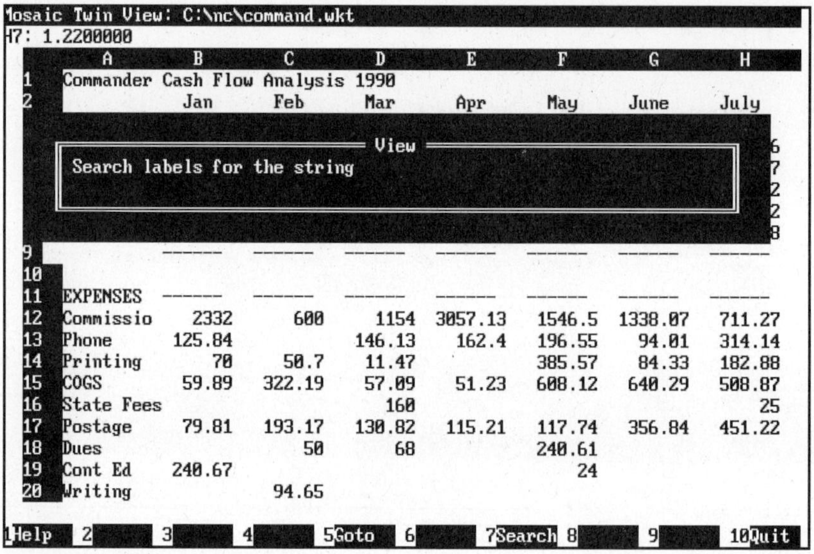

```
Mosaic Twin View: C:\nc\command.wkt
H7: 1.2200000
      A        B       C        D        E       F        G        H
1   Commander Cash Flow Analysis 1990
2             Jan     Feb      Mar      Apr     May      June     July
                              ═══ View ═══                              6
    ┌───────────────────────────────────────────────────────────┐     7
    │ Search labels for the string                               │     2
    │                                                            │     2
    └───────────────────────────────────────────────────────────┘     8
9
10
11  EXPENSES   ──────  ──────   ──────   ──────  ──────   ──────   ──────
12  Commissio  2332     600     1154    3057.13  1546.5  1338.07  711.27
13  Phone     125.84           146.13    162.4   196.55   94.01   314.14
14  Printing    70     50.7     11.47             385.57   84.33  182.88
15  COGS       59.89  322.19    57.09    51.23   608.12   640.29  508.87
16  State Fees                  160                                 25
17  Postage    79.81  193.17   130.82   115.21   117.74   356.84  451.22
18  Dues                50       68               240.61
19  Cont Ed   240.67                                24
20  Writing           94.65
1Help   2      3      4      5Goto  6      7Search 8      9      10Quit
```

FIG. 9.24.

The View dialog box.

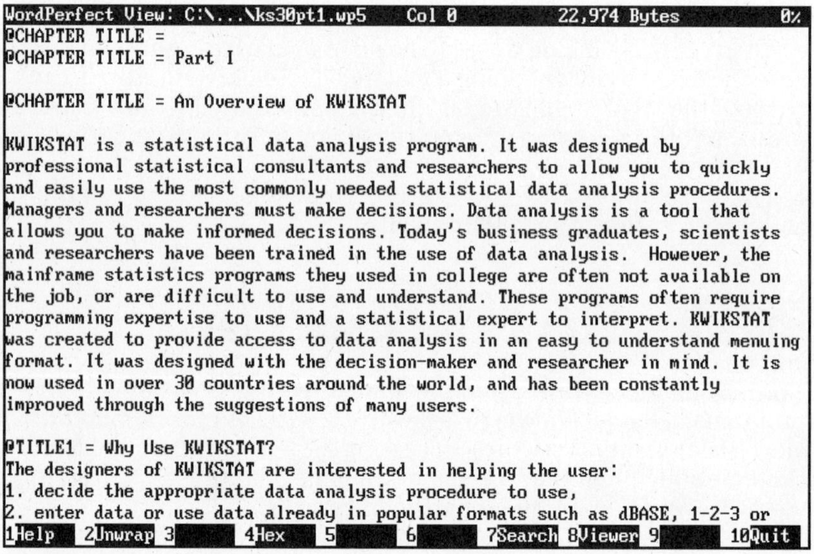

```
WordPerfect View: C:\...\ks30pt1.wp5    Col 0        22,974 Bytes        0%
@CHAPTER TITLE =
@CHAPTER TITLE = Part I

@CHAPTER TITLE = An Overview of KWIKSTAT

KWIKSTAT is a statistical data analysis program. It was designed by
professional statistical consultants and researchers to allow you to quickly
and easily use the most commonly needed statistical data analysis procedures.
Managers and researchers must make decisions. Data analysis is a tool that
allows you to make informed decisions. Today's business graduates, scientists
and researchers have been trained in the use of data analysis.  However, the
mainframe statistics programs they used in college are often not available on
the job, or are difficult to use and understand. These programs often require
programming expertise to use and a statistical expert to interpret. KWIKSTAT
was created to provide access to data analysis in an easy to understand menuing
format. It was designed with the decision-maker and researcher in mind. It is
now used in over 30 countries around the world, and has been constantly
improved through the suggestions of many users.

@TITLE1 = Why Use KWIKSTAT?
The designers of KWIKSTAT are interested in helping the user:
1. decide the appropriate data analysis procedure to use,
2. enter data or use data already in popular formats such as dBASE, 1-2-3 or
1Help   2Unwrap 3      4Hex   5      6      7Search 8Viewer 9      10Quit
```

FIG. 9.25.

Using the View option to view a WordPerfect file.

Table 9.9 lists function keys and other command and movement keys that you can use when viewing word processor files.

Table 9.9 Using Keyboard Commands in the Word Processing View

Key	Effect
↑ or Ctrl-E	Scrolls up
↓ or Ctrl-X	Scrolls down
← or Ctrl-S	Scrolls left
→ or Ctrl-D	Scrolls right
Ctrl-← or Ctrl-A	Scrolls left 40 columns (a half screenful)
Ctrl-→ or Ctrl-F	Scrolls right 40 columns
PgUp or Ctrl-R	Moves one page up
PgDn or Ctrl-C	Moves one page down
Home, Ctrl-Home, or Ctrl-PgUp	Goes to beginning of file
End, Ctrl-End, or Ctrl-PgDn	Goes to end of file
F2	Toggles word wrap on/off
F3	Returns to Quick View panel (available only if the view screen was originally a Quick View panel)
F7	Searches for text
Shift-F7	Continues search
Ctrl-Break or Esc	Stops a search
F8	Selects view type
Esc or F10	Quits

In the WordPerfect View screen, the function key F2 (Unwrap) enables you to toggle the word-wrap feature on and off. When word wrap is on, text that would exceed the right margin is wrapped around to the next line. When word wrap is off, text is permitted to exceed the right margin. You can use the cursor-movement keys to display information past the right margin.

The F4 (Hex) key enables you to examine a file in hexadecimal code. This feature may be useful if you are looking for some special character codes in a file. Sometimes files contain characters that normally are not printable on-screen. These *ghost characters* can cause problems when you try to edit or print the file. If you display the file in hexadecimal format, you can locate these unusual characters and edit them out of your file, using your editor.

When you select a database or spreadsheet file to view, Norton is able to decipher from the extension what kind of file it is. DBF files are dBASE databases, for example, and WKS files are Lotus 1-2-3 spreadsheets. Word processors, however, usually enable you to use any extension when naming your files. Many times, Norton is able to figure out what kind of file you are attempting to display and thus uses the word processor view type the program thinks most appropriate. If Norton is wrong, however, you have to select the view type manually by pressing F8 (View) and then selecting the correct view type. Figure 9.26 shows the Select Viewer dialog box that appears when you press F8.

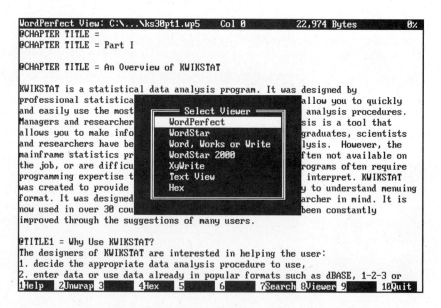

FIG. 9.26.

The Select Viewer dialog box.

Because many word processing documents are long, scrolling through a document to look for a specific piece of information may take time. If you know some key word that is located in or near the paragraph for which you are looking, you can use the F7 (Search) key to help locate the information. Suppose that you are looking for a paragraph about a virus. To find this paragraph, press F7 (Search). A dialog box appears (similar to the ones previously discussed for database and spreadsheet views). Enter the key word *virus* and press Enter. The lines around the first occurrence of *virus* appear on-screen. If this paragraph is not the one for which you are looking, press Shift-F7 to continue the search until you find the right information. To end a search, press Ctrl-Break or Esc.

Press Esc or F10 to exit the view and return to the Commander menus.

Editing ASCII Text Files

In addition to giving you another way to view files, the Edit option from Commander's Files menu (or the F4 key) enables you to edit ASCII text files. You can use this feature to edit files containing up to 25K (about 25,000 characters). The command is ideal if you need to create or modify batch files (such as AUTOEXEC.BAT) or other ASCII text files.

Using the Commander Editor

The Commander editor is a full-screen editor similar to a word processor editor. To use the Commander editor to edit an existing file, highlight the file name in a Commander panel and then press F4 or choose Edit from the Files menu. If you want to enter manually the name of the file to edit, press Shift-F4. Commander then prompts you to enter the file name. Figure 9.27 shows the editor being used to edit the file CONFIG.SYS.

Most of the commands in the editor, particularly the cursor-movement commands, are the same as they would be in any full-screen editor. Several editor commands, however, deserve some added explanation.

You use Ctrl-Q to enter special characters into a file. Suppose that you want to enter the ASCII Esc character in a file as part of a printer code or for some other reason. Normally, if you press Esc, you quit the editor and return to Commander. If you press Ctrl-Q first and then press Esc, however, the Esc character is placed in the file as if you had typed it like any other character.

If the file is long and you want to search for a particular word or phrase, you can press F7 (Search). Commander then prompts you to enter the search word. If the first word found is not the one for which you are looking, press Shift-F7 to repeat the search.

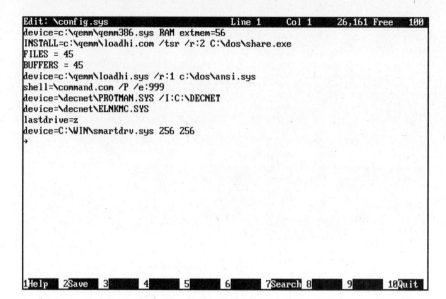

```
Edit: \config.sys                    Line 1      Col 1      26,161 Free    100
device=c:\qemm\qemm386.sys RAM extmem=56
INSTALL=c:\qemm\loadhi.com /tsr /r:2 C:\dos\share.exe
FILES = 45
BUFFERS = 45
device=c:\qemm\loadhi.sys /r:1 c:\dos\ansi.sys
shell=\command.com /P /e:999
device=\decnet\PROTMAN.SYS /I:C:\DECNET
device=\decnet\ELNKMC.SYS
lastdrive=z
device=C:\WIN\smartdrv.sys 256 256
↓




1Help  2Save  3      4      5      6      7Search 8      9      10Quit
```

FIG. 9.27.

Editing the
CONFIG.SYS
file.

To end the editor, press Esc or F10. Remember to save the file before quitting if you want your changes to be saved to disk. Press F2 to save the edited file under the original file name that you chose from the Commander panel. If you want to use a new name, press Shift-F2. Commander then prompts you to enter a new name.

Table 9.10 lists the cursor-movement and editing keys that you can use in the Commander editor.

Using a Substitute Editor

Normally, when you choose an edit option, Commander uses a built-in Norton Commander editor. You may, however, prefer to use your editor if you are familiar and more comfortable with it. You can specify that Commander use a substitute editor of your choice. From the Options menu, choose the Editor option. You then are prompted to choose Built-in (the built-in editor) or External (an external editor). To choose one of the options, use the arrow keys to highlight your choice.

Then press the space bar.

Table 9.10 Using Cursor-Movement and Editing Keys in the Commander Editor

Key	Effect
↑ or Ctrl-E	Scrolls up
↓ or Ctrl-X	Scrolls down
← or Ctrl-S	Scrolls left
→ or Ctrl-D	Scrolls right
Ctrl-← or Ctrl-A	Moves one word left
Ctrl-→ or Ctrl-F	Moves one word right
Home	Goes to beginning of line
End	Goes to end of line
PgUp or Ctrl-R	Moves one page up
PgDn or Ctrl-C	Moves one page down
Ctrl-Home or Ctrl-PgUp	Goes to beginning of file
Ctrl-End or Ctrl-PgDn	Goes to end of file
Backspace	Deletes character to left
Del or Ctrl-G	Deletes character at cursor
Ctrl-Backspace or Ctrl-W	Deletes one word left
Ctrl-T	Deletes one word right
Ctrl-Y	Deletes line
Ctrl-K	Deletes to end of line
Ctrl-Q	Quotes next character. After you press Ctrl-Q, any command you press after that (such as Ctrl-F) causes the character to appear on-screen rather than the command to happen.
F1	Accesses help
F2	Saves file
Shift-F2	Asks for "save as" name
F7	Searches for text
Shift-F7	Continues a search
Esc or F10	Quits editor and returns to Commander
Shift-F10	Saves file and quits editor

If you choose the External option, Commander prompts you to enter the command used to begin the editor. Enter this command followed by an exclamation mark (*!*) if you want to use only a file name when editing, or type *!.!* after the command if you want to use a file name plus an extension. If you are using the WP (WordPerfect) editor in the \WPROC directory, for example, you should enter the following command to indicate that you want the full file name used when editing:

    \WPROC\WP !.!

The path name (\WPROC) is necessary if that is how you must start the editor when you enter the command from the DOS prompt. If you do not specify ! or !.!, Commander uses !.! as a default. Other editors you may use include WordStar, Kwikwrite, PC-Write, and any other editor that can save files in ASCII mode.

Customizing the Norton Commander Screen Display

Norton Commander has several options you can use to customize how the program looks on your screen. You can change the number of lines displayed (if you have an EGA or VGA monitor), for example, thus enabling Commander to display more information per screen. Also, you can control Commander's screen-blanking feature, whether hidden files and directories appear in displayed directories, and other options.

Controlling the Number of Lines On-Screen

The EGA Lines option enables you to set your EGA or VGA monitor to display more than the normal 25 lines per screen. You can access this option by choosing EGA Lines from the Commands menu or by pressing Alt-F9. The command works as a toggle switch. If you have an EGA monitor, choosing the command toggles between the normal 25-line mode and a 43-line mode. If you are using a VGA monitor, you toggle between 25- and 50-line modes. Displaying more information on-screen may simplify your access to files and directories. The only problem with these 43- and 50-line modes is that the characters are smaller than normal and may be more difficult to read—you may need to wear your bifocals!

> **T I P**
>
> If your CONFIG.SYS file in the root directory contains the command line DEVICE=ANSI.SYS, the number of lines that can be displayed on-screen is limited to 25. (See Appendix A for information.) Thus, even if you enter the 43-line EGA mode or 50-line VGA mode, your monitor still displays only 25 lines. You can remove the DEVICE=ANSI.SYS command from the CONFIG.SYS file to enable your monitor to display a larger number of lines per screen. Or, if you are using DOS 4.0 or higher, include the /L switch in the command. Before you decide to remove the ANSI.SYS command, be aware that some programs need it in order to work properly. You need to check your particular applications to determine whether they require ANSI.SYS in order to operate.

Choosing Other Screen Options

The Options menu gives you several other screen options from which to choose. (The Editor option was discussed in "Using a Substitute Editor," earlier in this chapter.) Like the EGA Lines option, these options operate as toggle switches, turning the features off and on. When an option is on, a check mark appears beside the option name in the Options menu. The following options are available on the Options menu:

- *Auto Menus:* This option is an advanced feature that enables you to create custom menus. See Chapter 10 for information.

- *Path Prompt:* Controls whether the DOS prompt includes a path name. If you are in the \WP directory with the Path Prompt option turned off, for example, the DOS prompt (on drive C) is

    C>

    With Path Prompt turned on, the prompt is

    C:\WP>

    Most users prefer the second version of the prompt (which includes the path) because it tells you which directory is being used.

- *Key Bar:* Determines whether the function key bar appears at the bottom of the screen.

- *Full Screen:* Determines whether the right and left panels extend from the top to the bottom of the screen or are only half that size.

432

■ *Mini Status:* Controls the status line at the bottom of each panel. When the Mini Status option is turned on, the status line shows the name, size, date, and time for the highlighted file or directory. If you have made a selection of files, the status line also gives a count of the number of files selected. If the Mini Status option is off, the status line does not appear.

■ *Clock:* Determines whether a clock appears at the upper right corner of the Commander screen. Choosing to have the clock displayed is only a convenience and serves no other purpose.

Another option on the Options menu is Configuration. When you exit Norton Commander, changes in screen options, such as which panels are displayed and how, revert to whatever was in effect when you first started Commander. To save any changes so that they are in effect the next time you use Commander, you must choose to save the setup by selecting the Configuration option from the Options menu and then choosing Auto Save Setup (by default, this is already on). See the next section for more information on using the Configuration option.

Setting Commander Configuration

After you select the Configuration option from the Options menu, you see a dialog box like the one in figure 9.28. Notice that this box has five areas of settings: Screen Colors, Screen Blank Delay, File Panel Options, Tree Panel Options, and Other Options.

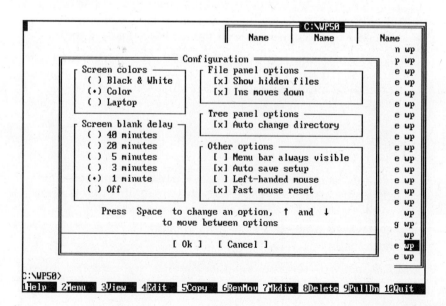

FIG. 9.28.

The Configuration dialog box.

Setting Screen Colors

In the Screen Colors area of the Configuration dialog box, you can tell Commander that you want information displayed on a color monitor, a black-and-white monitor, or a laptop monitor. Select or deselect the type of monitor by using the arrow keys to move the highlight and then pressing the space bar. If you are using a mouse, you can point to the appropriate option and click the left button to select the option.

Setting Screen Blank Delay Options

The Screen Blank Delay options enable you to choose how long Commander waits until automatically blanking out your screen. Blanking out the screen saves your monitor from possible burn-in of an image. (On some screens, if you leave an image on-screen for a long time, a trace of the image remains on-screen like a ghost.) The default time used in Commander before blanking the screen is five minutes.

When Commander blanks out the screen, you see a random pattern of white dots on a black background, resembling stars in the sky. The dots come and go so that you can tell that the computer is working. When the screen is blanked out, you can press any key or move the mouse to bring back the working screen. Commander blanks out the screen only when you are at the DOS prompt—not when you are in a program, such as a word processor. You can choose to turn off the blanking feature or to set the wait from 1 minute to 40 minutes by using the arrow keys to highlight the appropriate option in the Screen Blank Delay area and then pressing the space bar to lock the option into place. If you are using a mouse, point to the option and click the left button.

Setting File Panel Options

In the File Panel Options area of the Configuration dialog box, you indicate whether you want hidden files to appear in directories. You also can choose the meaning of the Ins key when marking files. If you mark the Ins Moves Down option, you can select files from a panel by repeatedly pressing the Ins key. Each time you press Ins, the cursor moves down to the next file. If you do not mark Ins Moves Down, the highlight does not move down to the next file after you press Ins. You instead have to select options with arrow keys and the space bar or with the mouse.

Controlling Automatic Display of Directory Files

The Tree Panel Options area gives you one option: Auto Change Directory. If you turn on this option, you tell Commander that when you highlight a directory in a tree, you want the other panel to display the files contained in the highlighted directory. Select the Auto Change Directory option with the arrow keys and the space bar or with the mouse. This does not affect the NCD command (Alt-F10).

Setting Other Configuration Options

Other options available in the Configuration dialog box include choosing to have the menu bar always visible at the top of the screen (by default it is not visible); automatically saving any changes you make to the configuration during a session (it is on by default); specifying whether you are using a left-handed mouse, which reverses the functions of the left and right buttons (the right mouse is the default); and turning on the fast mouse reset. If the fast mouse reset is on, Commander can return more quickly from a command if you are using a COMPAQ or PS/2 computer with a mouse port. Select options in the Other Options area of the Configuration dialog box with arrow keys and the space bar or with the mouse.

Chapter Summary

This introductory look at Norton Commander showed you how to access the Commander menus and described the meaning of most menu options. You learned how to use Commander as a substitute for DOS commands such as COPY, RENAME, and DEL. Commander also has a Move function to move files, which you cannot do in DOS. The Commander NCD command is an important part of managing the directories on your hard disk. With NCD, you can choose directories from a graphic tree, make new directories, change directories, and remove directories. With NCD, you can rename a directory—something else that DOS cannot do. Using the View file options, you can use Commander to quickly view the contents of a number of word processing, spreadsheet, and database files. You also can use Commander to set screen colors, save your monitor screen by using screen blanking, and more. For information on advanced Norton Commander options, move on to Chapter 10.

Norton Commander Advanced Topics

T he Norton Commander features covered in Chapter 9 are straight-forward commands that you can use without any advanced computer knowledge. Although the topics in this chapter require more knowledge about how a computer works, they also introduce you to some of the more exciting features of Norton Commander. In this chapter, you learn to use menus to customize your computer so that it works the way you think it should work. You learn to shortcut your access to programs so that you can point to files on-screen and have the application program come up immediately. You also discover how to use Commander Mail to send messages by electronic mail (E-Mail) and Commander Link to transfer information quickly from one computer to another.

Creating and Using Menus in Commander

Each person has his or her own particular selection of programs. You may use WordPerfect, Microsoft Excel, and dBASE III, for example. Another person may use PC-FILE, PROCOMM, KWIKSTAT, and 10 other programs. To begin any one of these programs on your computer, you may need to enter several commands. You first may change the directory, then run a preliminary setup program, and then run the actual program, for example. If you use the computer infrequently or have many different directories and programs, you may forget the command sequences for all your programs. You may wish that you had a menu of programs so that you could just choose a program and automatically issue all necessary commands to begin the program. That is exactly what you can do with a Norton Commander user menu.

A *user menu* is a list of items that appears on-screen (like a dialog box) from which you can choose options. A series of commands (usually DOS commands) is associated with each of the options on the user menu. After you choose a menu option, Commander issues these commands in sequence as if they were entered from the DOS prompt, much like a batch file does. Usually, these commands begin a program.

Two kinds of user menus are available: *main* and *local*. You use the same commands to create both menus. The primary physical difference between the menus is the directory in which each menu is stored. The main menu is stored in the \NC directory. Local menus are stored in other directories. The main functional difference between a main menu and a local menu is that local menus usually contain selections that deal with programs in a local directory, whereas a main menu usually contains selections that pertain to programs in a number of different directories.

You activate a user menu by pressing F2 while the Commander program is running and the DOS prompt is on-screen. If a local menu is located in the current directory, that menu appears. If no local menu exists, Commander accesses the main menu from the \NC directory. If no menu is available in either place, you get an error message after you press F2.

Thus, the first (and perhaps the only) menu you usually need to create is the one in the \NC directory—the main menu. If it is the only user menu, you can access it whenever you press F2—from any directory. This setup is the simplest and least complicated. If you want different menus in other subdirectories, however, you need to create local menus. (You can have local menus without having a main menu.)

You may want to have a local menu in a subdirectory that contains a number of programs you want to access.

In your accounting directory, for example, you may want to have a menu of options available to run programs that do posting, end-of-month runs, trial balances, and so on, but you do not want all these options cluttering up the main menu. You therefore may choose the broad topic Accounting from the main menu, which brings up the local menu that has the detailed accounting choices.

Alternatively, because some systems are used by more than one person, you may want to have different menus loading different batch files to start various programs. You can have one batch file that causes WordPerfect to load with a particular data file directory, for example, and another batch file that causes Ventura to call from a particular customer a chapter information file.

Creating User Menus

You create a user menu in Norton Commander by selecting the Menu File Edit option from the Commands menu. You then enter lines of information in a file to tell Commander which selections you want to display in the menu and what should happen when a user chooses any of those menu items. You can place four basic kinds of lines in the menu file:

- *Comment lines* begin with a single quotation mark (`'`). These lines do not influence how the menu looks or functions. Comment lines are optional and are provided only so that you can document what the menu file does. Comments are helpful to other users who may have to change the file in the future, or may be helpful to you if you have to return to the file a year later.

- *Menu items* begin with a single character, called a hot key, followed by a colon (:). To create a menu item called Begin WordPerfect that is chosen when a user presses W, for example, enter this command in the menu file:

    W: Begin WordPerfect

    The W (the hot key) must be in the far left column of the file (flush left). If you enter a noncomment line flush left (any line without a letter and a colon or an apostrophe that is flush left), it becomes a menu item without a hot key. When the menu comes up, the user has to choose the item by highlighting it with the arrow keys and pressing Enter or by pointing and shooting with a mouse.

- *DOS commands* or other commands are listed on the lines following a menu item. These commands must not be flush left. You must indent these commands by placing a tab or one or more blank spaces in front of the text.

- *Blank line separators* should be inserted after each menu item. To create a blank line, press Enter.

To create a typical user menu, follow these steps:

1. Type *nc* and press Enter at the DOS prompt to start Norton Commander (if the program is not running already).

2. Open the Commands menu from the menu bar (see fig. 10.1).

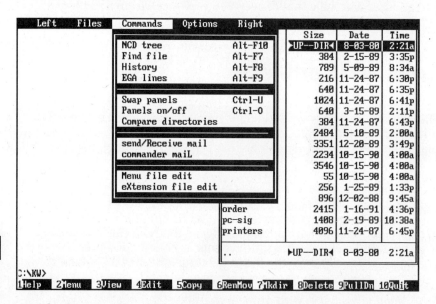

FIG. 10.1.

The Commands menu.

3. Select the Menu File Edit option from the Commands menu.

   A dialog box similar to the one in figure 10.2 appears.

4. You are given the option to create a main menu, a local menu, or to cancel the command. In this example, choose Main. The User Menu edit screen appears (which is really a version of the Commander editor discussed in Chapter 9), with the file named NC.MNU in the \NC directory on-screen and ready for you to edit (see fig. 10.3). (If you choose to edit a local menu in another directory, the edit screen displays the NC.MNU file for you to edit in the specified directory.) Notice the help box at the bottom of the editor screen in figure 10.3. This screen summarizes the file format for creating a user menu.

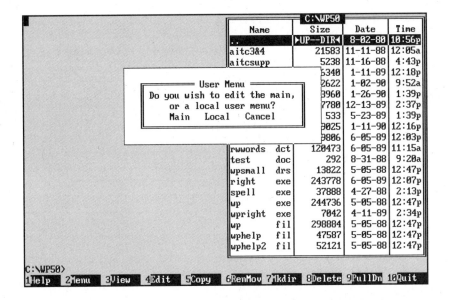

FIG. 10.2.

Creating a user menu.

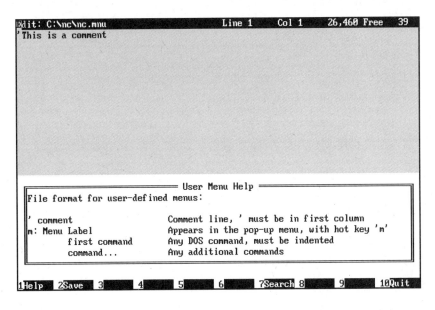

FIG. 10.3.

The User Menu edit screen.

5. In the menu file, enter lines that define your user menu. For example, the lines associated with beginning the WordPerfect program are

    W: Begin WordPerfect
        NCD \WP50
        WP

Note that the menu item line, W: Begin WordPerfect, is flush left in the file, and the other lines are indented. Figure 10.4 shows an example of information entered in the editor to create a menu with three menu selections. Each menu selection begins with a single letter followed by a colon and a brief description of the menu option. Following each menu option are some DOS commands that invoke the appropriate program. The PROCOMM program, for example, begins with two commands. First, the NCD \PROCOMM command changes to the \PROCOMM directory. Then, the PROCOMM command begins the PROCOMM program.

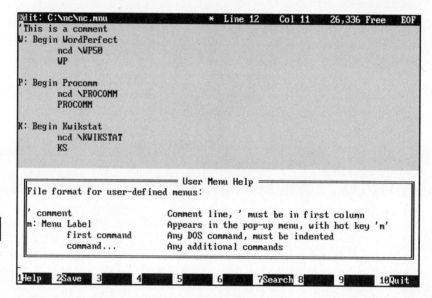

FIG. 10.4.

Menu entries on the User Menu edit screen.

6. Save the menu file by pressing F2 (Save).

7. Quit the menu editor by pressing F10 (Quit).

Invoking User Menus

After you create a menu, you can open it by pressing the F2 (Menu) key from the Norton Commander screen. Remember that if a local menu exists in the current directory, Commander opens that menu. If no local menu exists, Commander opens the main menu located in the \NC directory. Figure 10.5 shows how the menu created in figure 10.4 looks on-screen.

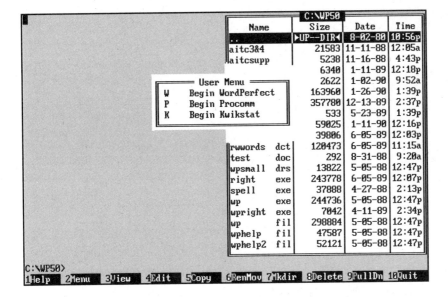

FIG. 10.5.

The menu in
use.

To choose an option on this menu, you can use one of three methods: pressing the option's hot key, highlighting the option and pressing Enter, or double-clicking the option with a mouse. To exit the user menu without choosing an option, press Esc.

Automating Menus

If you are taking advantage of Commander's menu capabilities, you may want to set up the program to display your user menu whenever you start Commander. You may create a series of menus, for example, to help a novice use a variety of application programs. With this design, a user never has to issue a DOS command.

You can automate the user menu system by choosing (turning on) the Auto Menus option from the Options menu. When Auto Menus is turned on (a check mark appears beside it on the menu), the local or main menu (whichever is appropriate to the current directory) opens whenever you begin Commander. Keep in mind, however, that after you or another user ends the menu by pressing Esc or choosing some other menu item, the user menu disappears. You must press F2 to redisplay the menu.

You can design local menus so that they always come back to the main menu, however. For example, the commands that you may use in the main menu to begin WordPerfect could be

```
W: Begin WordPerfect
   NCD \WP50
   WP
   NCD \NC
```

The first line tells the program that the W hot key is associated with the menu item Begin WordPerfect. The second line begins the commands that are used if a user chooses the W option from the menu. This line changes to the \WP50 directory, which contains the WordPerfect program. The third line begins the WordPerfect program. The fourth line changes back to the \NC directory so that the main menu again appears. Thus, after you exit from WordPerfect, the command NCD \NC is issued automatically, which brings you back to the \NC directory and the main menu.

Defining File Extensions in Commander

Another element of Norton Commander that takes some of the work out of accessing application programs is the file-extension feature, which you can use to define meanings for file extensions. After Commander knows the definition of a file extension, you can select any file with that extension from a panel, and Commander begins the appropriate application program necessary to use the file. Recall that a file specification is of the form *filename.ext*, where *ext* is the file extension. If you have defined WP as an extension for WordPerfect, for example, and you then select the file REPORT.WP from a panel, Commander begins WordPerfect with the file REPORT.WP on-screen and ready to edit.

To tell Commander the meanings of various extensions, you must enter information into the file NC.EXT in the \NC directory. To create or edit this file, follow these steps:

1. Open the Commands pull-down menu from the menu bar.

2. Select the Extension option from the Commands menu.

   You see a screen similar to the one in figure 10.6. The help box at the bottom of this screen summarizes the format of an extension command. You now are in the Commander editor.

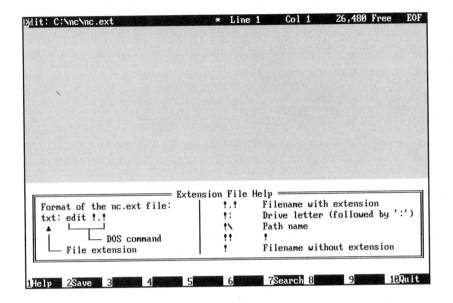

```
Edit: C:\nc\nc.ext              * Line 1    Col 1    26,480 Free    EOF
```

```
══════════════════ Extension File Help ══════════════════
┌──────────────────────────────┬──────────────────────────────────────┐
│ Format of the nc.ext file:   │  !.!     Filename with extension       │
│ txt: edit !.!                │  !:      Drive letter (followed by ':')│
│     ▲   └────┘               │  !\      Path name                     │
│     │      └── DOS command   │  !!      !                             │
│     └── File extension       │  !       Filename without extension    │
└──────────────────────────────┴──────────────────────────────────────┘
```

```
1Help  2Save  3    4    5    6    7Search 8    9    10Quit
```

FIG. 10.6.

Editing the
extension file in
the Commander
editor.

3. For each extension that you want to define, type a line of information, using the following format:

      ext: command !.!

where *ext:* is the extension that you are defining. For example, this
parameter could be DOC: for Microsoft Word files using the DOC extension, FOR: for FORTRAN programs using the FOR extension, and so on.
The second part of the line contains the *command* required to begin the
program associated with the defined file extension. You can include a
path to the command if necessary. The !.! means that the command is
to be followed by a file name with an extension, causing WordPerfect
to load the selected file into the program to begin editing. To tell
Commander to use the command WP from the directory \WP50 to edit
a file with a WP extension, you use the following specification:

      WP: C:\WP50\WP !.!

or

      WP: C:\WP50\WP !.WP

The !.! syntax is a part of Norton Commander's extension definition. It is
similar to DOS's *.* wild-card specification. The use of the !.! specification is a way to define what parameter should be placed on the command line when the program you specify begins. In the preceding
example, you can use !.WP or !.! because both keep the extension WP in
the file specification. The meanings of !.! and related specifications are
detailed in table 10.1.

Table 10.1 Specifying Parameters in the Extension Definition

Specification	Meaning
!.!	File name with extension
!	File name without extension
!:	Drive letter followed by colon
!\	Path name

You must choose the specification in the command line according to what the application program expects in order for the selected file to be accessed. Thus, the specification ! indicates that the file name without an extension is to be placed in the command line. The specification !:!.! means that the drive name and a colon would appear before the file name and extension. If you do not place a !.! or ! specification in the extension definition line, Commander begins the application program but does not automatically access the selected file.

Suppose that you define the specification

CAI: \CAI\CAI !:!\!

Then, if you choose the file DEMO.CAI, the command generated contains the current drive (!:), the current pathname (!\), and the file name without the extension (!). Therefore, if you are in the C:\TMP directory when you choose this file, the DOS command used to start the program will be \CAI\CAI C:\TMP\DEMO.

Figure 10.7 shows an extension file containing a variety of definitions. The first definition is for WordPerfect. The second is to edit files with FOR (FORTRAN) extensions with an editor named Edit, and the third is to begin the CAI program (PC-CAI, a computer-aided instructional program).

After you enter your extension definitions, save them by pressing F2 (Save). End the editor by pressing F10 (Quit). To abandon the edit without saving, press Esc or F10 without first pressing F2.

You then can highlight a file name on a Commander panel and press Enter or double-click to begin using that file in the proper program. To return to this extension file (\NC\NC.EXT) to change, add, or remove any of your definitions, choose the Extension option again from the Commands menu.

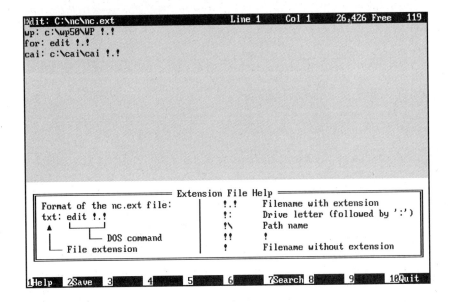

FIG. 10.7.

Extension
specifications.

Using Commander (MCI) Mail

The Commander menu and extension features enable you to access
information easily on your computer. Commander Mail enables you to
send and receive information to and from other computers through the
MCI electronic network. Specifically, the options you have with MCI
Mail include the following:

■ *Sending and receiving electronic mail (E-mail). Electronic mail* is a
message that is sent electronically from one user's computer to
one or more other computers. You write a message on your computer and send the message to someone who has an MCI account.
You also can send ASCII text files as electronic mail. The message
is routed electronically to the specified electronic address
(the recipient's computer), and the recipient can then read the
message.

■ *Sending a letter through Commander Mail to the MCI network and
having that letter printed on paper and mailed to a designated
address.* You write the letter on your computer and send it and the
address to the MCI network. MCI prints the letter and puts it in
the mail.

■ *Sending information to a fax machine through MCI Mail.* You create a letter on your computer and send the letter to the MCI network with a fax number. MCI then sends the letter to the appropriate fax machine.

■ *Sending messages to other electronic mail services, such as CompuServe and Telemail X.400.* This feature is useful if you want to send electronic mail to someone who is not an MCI subscriber but is a subscriber on CompuServe or Telemail.

MCI Mail is a convenient way to communicate quickly. It is particularly well-suited for members of an organization or colleagues who live in diverse places. Messages can be sent at the convenience of the sender and received at the convenience of the recipient. Also, messages arrive much faster than they do by express mail and have the clarity of a letter as opposed to the possible misinterpretations that characterize voice messages. Using MCI Mail, salespeople can send orders to the home office at the end of each day, and journalists can communicate with their offices and send messages and stories quickly. The possibilities for improved communications are endless.

Using Commander's MCI interface rather than MCI's interface (which you can use if you dial MCI) means that you do not have to use a communications program (such as PROCOMM, Crosstalk, and so on), you can do all the work of preparing and reading communications off-line (which saves phone connect time), and you can use the Commander's simple pull-down user interface.

Reviewing the Requirements for Using MCI Mail

As mentioned in Chapter 2, you need an MCI account and some computer hardware to use MCI Mail. To get an MCI account, call (800) 444-6245. MCI will assign you a user name and a password, which you will receive by mail within several days.

You also need to have a modem hookup on your computer. Generally, personal computers have two kinds of modem hookups: internal and external. An *internal modem* fits inside your computer in one of the expansion slots. An *external modem* is connected to a communication port on your computer with a serial cable.

With an internal modem, all you see from the outside are phone jacks on the back of the computer. One of these jacks is labeled *To Line*. To hook your modem into the phone system, you must run a phone line from the To Line jack in the back of the computer to the phone wall jack. Usually, another jack in the back of the computer is called *To Phone*. You can use this jack to hook up a normal telephone. Figure 10.8 illustrates this hookup.

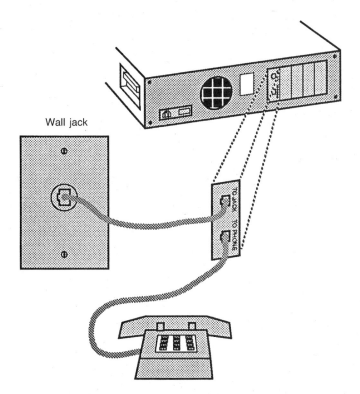

Wall jack

FIG. 10.8.

Hooking up an internal modem.

An external modem is hooked into your computer through a serial port—usually the COM1 or COM2 port. Your COM port is usually a 25-pin (RS-232) connector, as shown in figure 10.9. IBM AT-type machines use a 9-pin connector. A cable is attached to the COM port on the back of the computer and is also attached to the modem. A phone line then is hooked into the modem (in the To Line jack) from the phone wall plug. Optionally, you can have a regular phone hooked into the modem's To Phone jack. This hookup is shown in figure 10.10.

Serial Connectors

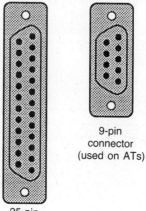

9-pin
connector
(used on ATs)

25-pin
RS-232 connector

FIG. 10.9.

25-pin and
9-pin serial
connectors.

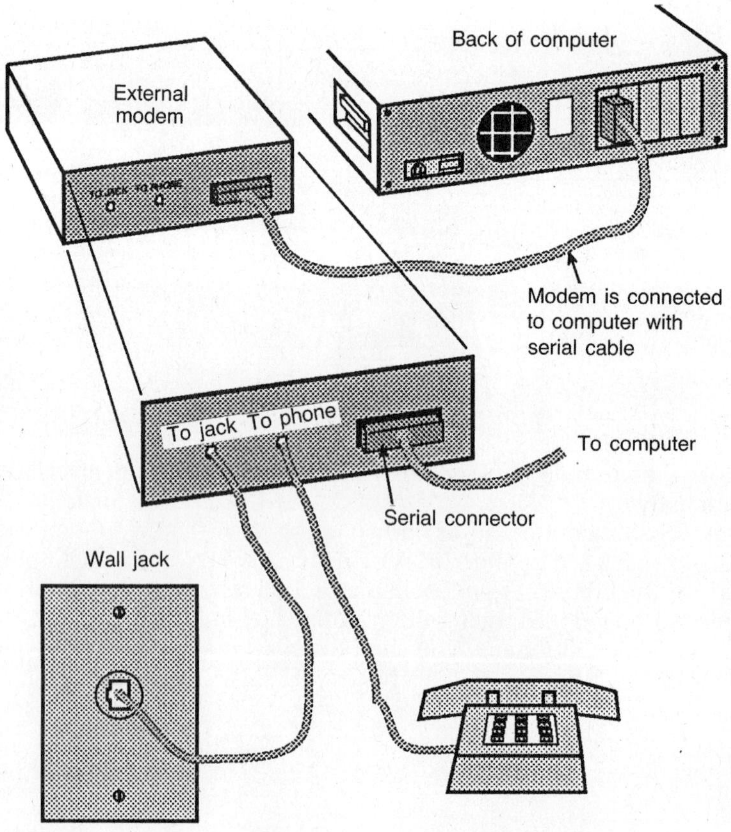

Back of computer

External
modem

Modem is connected
to computer with
serial cable

To jack To phone

To computer

Serial connector

Wall jack

FIG. 10.10.

Hooking up
an external
modem.

MCI supports modems using speeds of 300, 1200, and 2400 baud. The *baud rate* is the speed at which your computer modem transmits and receives information. Although a baud rate of 300 is slow, 1200 and 2400 baud are acceptable. Speeds of up to 9600 baud will soon be commonplace.

T I P

If you do not have a modem, here are some tips on what to look for. The faster the speed of the modem, the more quickly you can send and receive messages over the phone lines. The quicker the communication, the shorter the phone call and (usually) the less the cost to access services like MCI. (You are charged for the time connected.) Probably the most commonly used modems today are 2400 baud. If you are on a tight budget, however, you can buy a 1200 baud modem for less than $100. Using a slow, 300-baud modem is not a good idea.

Also, you need to get a Hayes-compatible modem. Modems are operated through a command language (similar to how a PC DOS computer is operated through DOS commands). Hayes-compatible modems use the AT command set, which is what Norton Commander is set up to use when talking to a modem.

The advantage of using an internal modem is that it does not need to use your communication port, which you may want to use for something else. Using an internal modem makes changing from computer to computer difficult, however, because you have to take your computer apart to remove the modem. An external modem has an important advantage in that you can easily switch it and use it on more than one computer by simply unplugging the cable from one computer and plugging it into another. The disadvantage of the external modem is that it takes up more room on your desk. Other than these convenience considerations, the internal and external modems operate the same way.

As soon as your computer is set up with a modem and you have an MCI account, you can start sending messages.

Setting up Commander Mail To Communicate with MCI Mail

To set up Commander Mail, open the Commands menu from the menu bar and choose the Commander Mail option. The first time you choose Commander Mail, you see a screen like the one in figure 10.11. This screen tells you that you must go through a setup procedure before you can use Commander Mail. You need to have your MCI account information handy. If you do not want to set up Commander Mail at this time (if you do not have your account number yet), press Esc to end this option. Otherwise, press Enter to proceed with the setup.

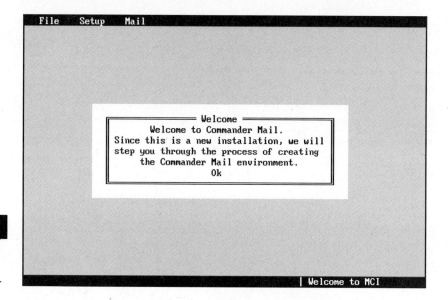

FIG. 10.11.

The Commander Mail setup message.

Adding, Deleting, and Modifying Accounts

If you proceed with the Commander Mail setup, the first item you see is the Account 1 dialog box (see fig. 10.12). In this box, you enter information about your MCI account. First you must enter your MCI account name, which is often the first letter of your first name followed by your full last name. No blanks are included in the MCI account name. After entering your name, enter your password and MCI ID. These pieces of information are all contained in the Welcome to MCI Mail kit that you receive in the mail after you subscribe.

After you finish entering your account information, indicate whether you want to receive mail. Check Yes (press Y) to be able to send *and* receive MCI electronic mail, or select No (press N) if you do not want to receive mail and plan to use MCI Mail only to send information. (Or, click on Y or N with the mouse pointer.) Choose Yes at the bottom of the screen to confirm the information for this account. The MCI Account List box appears. If more than one person with MCI accounts will be using Commander Mail on this machine, you can add additional accounts by choosing the Add option. If you need to change or remove one of the accounts after you enter it, highlight the account and choose the Modify option to make changes or the Delete option to remove the account. When you finish making additions, modifications, or deletions, choose OK to save the list.

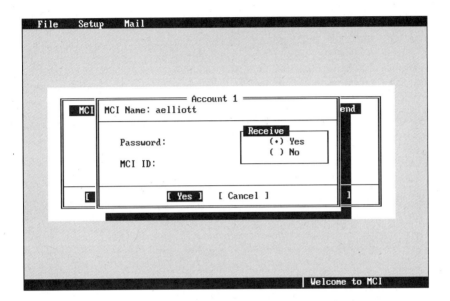

FIG. 10.12.

Setting up an MCI account.

After you finish entering your account information, the MCI Account List screen appears again (see fig. 10.13). This time the screen contains information about your account. Highlight your MCI name and choose the Use option to tell Commander Mail to charge your account for messages being sent. Commander will use this account for all future uses of MCI mail unless you choose another account. If you enter only one account, that account is highlighted and will be the one you use.

Specifying Directories for Message Storage

During the setup procedure, the next dialog box that appears indicates the directories where MCI messages will be stored (see fig. 10.14). The default directories are \NC\OUT, \NC\IN, and \NC\SENT. The OUT directory stores outgoing mail, the IN directory stores incoming mail, and the SENT directory stores copies of messages you have sent

already. You can type new names for these directories or accept
the defaults. To enter new names, use the arrow keys to highlight the
directory to change, type a new directory name, and press Enter. When
the directory names are as you want them, choose the Yes option in
the dialog box. To choose Yes, you can press Y, press Tab to move the
highlight to Yes and then press Enter, or point to Yes with your mouse
and click.

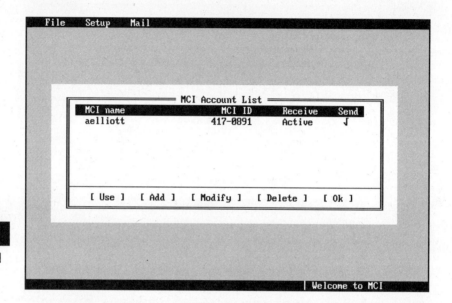

FIG. 10.13.

The completed
MCI Account
List screen.

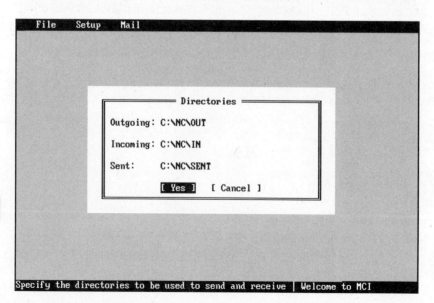

FIG. 10.14.

Accepting or
modifying the
outgoing,
incoming, and
sent directories.

Specifying Your Modem Setup

You must next tell Commander Mail about your modem setup.
Figure 10.15 shows the Modem dialog box. The Port setting indicates
which serial port is being used for your modem. If you have only one
serial port on your machine, you are usually using COM1. If you have
two serial ports, you need to check your system's documentation to
determine which port you are using. Usually, the COM1 port is any
built-in port on your computer and the COM2 port is a port added with
an expansion card.

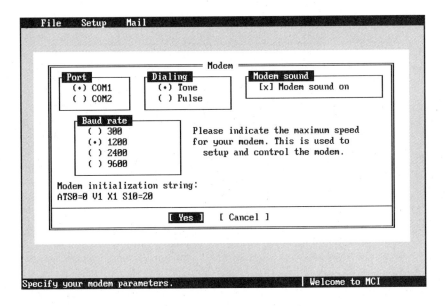

FIG. 10.15.

Specifying the
modem
parameters.

The Dialing option indicates whether your telephone exchange uses
tone or pulse dialing. Some older exchanges use only pulse dialing. If
you can use phones with only rotary dials, your exchange supports
only pulse dialing. If you are able to use a phone with a touch-tone
numeric pad, your exchange supports tone dialing. If you do not know
whether your telephone exchange supports tone dialing, call your
telephone operator.

The Modem Sound option indicates whether you want to hear the
dialing process as it is taking place. (If your modem does not have a
speaker, you will not hear the dialing even if you check this option.)
The advantage of hearing the dialing process is that you can tell if the
call is going through properly. If you have a speaker modem but you do
not hear the dialing taking place, it may mean that you have selected

the wrong COM port. You can easily hear if something interferes with the connection (such as a busy signal). If you cannot hear the dialing process, you must wait for a message from the computer before you know whether the connection has been made properly. Usually, this takes less than 30 seconds.

The Baud Rate option indicates the speed that you are using. For the fastest communication, choose the highest baud rate your modem can support—up to 2400 baud. The baud rates supported by your modem should be listed in your modem documentation. Commander has a 9600 baud option; however, as of the print time of this book, MCI does not support this speed.

Note the Modem Initialization String field at the bottom of the Modem dialog box. The *modem initialization string* is a code set by Commander Mail for using your modem. The code in figure 10.15 is for a Hayes-compatible modem, which is the most common type of modem. If you are using a Hayes-compatible modem, you do not have to know which initialization string to use. Commander Mail supplies the necessary code. Unless you are a sophisticated user who likes to try different ways of doing things, you should never have to change this code. If you are using a non-Hayes-compatible modem, you need to check your documentation for the proper initialization string.

After you choose all proper options on the Modem dialog box, choose Yes to save these parameters.

Specifying the Phone Number

The next setup dialog box asks for the phone number to be used to communicate with MCI Mail (see fig. 10.16). Your Welcome to MCI Mail information kit contains the phone numbers you can use:

(800) 234-6245 for 300- and 1200-baud modems

(800) 456-6245 for up to 2400-baud modems

If you are using a 300- or 1200-baud modem, use the first number. If you are using a 2400-baud modem, use the second number. Type the appropriate number in the Phone Number dialog box. The Prefix entry is any number or series of numbers that you must type to get an outside line. In many businesses, this prefix is 9. After you enter the phone number and any necessary prefix, choose Yes to save this information.

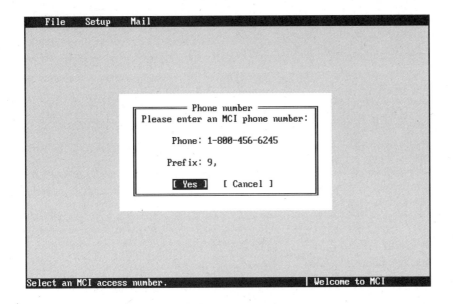

FIG. 10.16.

Specifying the
MCI phone
number.

At this point, the Commander Mail setup program begins creating the directories you specified in the Directories dialog box. A New Directory dialog box appears in sequence for each of the three new directories—IN, OUT, and SEND (or another three directories if you changed the names). Figure 10.17 shows the New Directory dialog box that asks whether you want Commander to create the \NC\IN directory. Choose the Mkdir option to make these directories on your hard disk. (To choose Mkdir, press M, use the arrow keys to highlight Mkdir and then press Enter, or point to Mkdir with a mouse and click once.) If you cancel the creation of a directory, MCI Mail returns you to the DOS prompt. If you try to run MCI Mail, you are prompted again to make the directories needed. You will not be able to run MCI Mail until these directories exist.

At this point, you have reached the end of the setup procedure. A dialog box appears with the following message:

```
Commander Mail has now created the parameter file,
MCI.INI, required to run the communications driver,
MCIDRIVR.EXE.
```

This message tells you that the choices you selected in the setup procedure are stored in the file MCI.INI and that the program now is ready to begin communications.

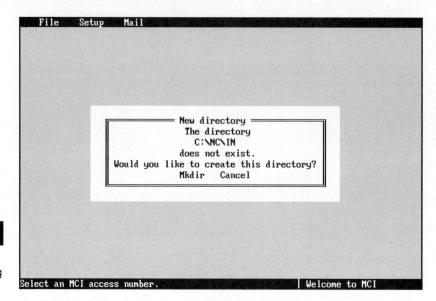

```
    File    Setup    Mail




                 ╔══════ New directory ══════╗
                 ║       The directory       ║
                 ║         C:\NC\IN          ║
                 ║      does not exist.      ║
                 ║ Would you like to create this directory? ║
                 ║       Mkdir    Cancel     ║
                 ╚═══════════════════════════╝




  Select an MCI access number.              │ Welcome to MCI
```

FIG. 10.17.

Making the IN
directory during
setup.

Beginning a Mail Session

After you set up the MCI Mail parameters, a screen like the one in
figure 10.18 appears after you choose the Commander Mail option from
the Commands menu. The In Box screen holds any messages that have
been received and are waiting to be read. The first time you use
Commander Mail, no messages appear on this screen.

Notice the Commander Mail menu bar at the top of the screen. Three
pull-down menus are available: File, Setup, and Mail. To move your
cursor to this menu bar, press F9 or point to the menu bar with the
mouse. Use the arrow keys to point to a menu and then press Enter to
display the menu (or point with a mouse and click).

Getting Help

The first menu is the File menu (see fig. 10.19). It contains three
options: Help, About MCI, and Quit. You can activate the first option
(Help) also by pressing the F1 key. The Help option provides brief information about how to use various parts of Commander Mail. The About
MCI option lists phone numbers for MCI phone support and the MCI
support mailbox. The Quit option ends your Commander Mail session.

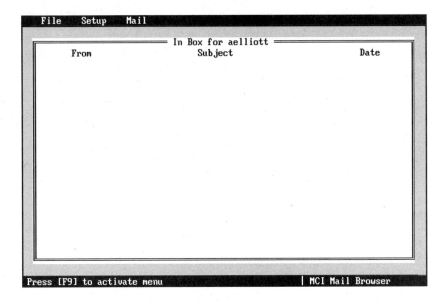

FIG. 10.18.

The In Box
screen.

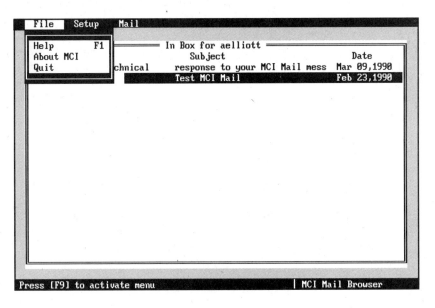

FIG. 10.19.

Commander
Mail's File
menu.

Establishing Communications Settings

The second menu is the Setup menu (see fig. 10.20). It contains six options: Address Book, MCI Accounts, Schedule, Phone, Modem, and Directories. The following sections discuss each of these options.

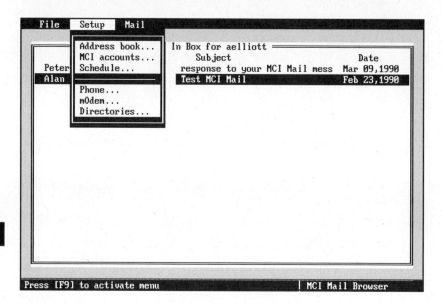

Commander Mail's Setup menu.

Adding Addresses to the MCI Address Book

The Address Book option enables you to create a list of addresses of people to whom you plan to send messages. After you choose this option, you see the MCI Address Book dialog box. Figure 10.21 shows an address book that contains only one address.

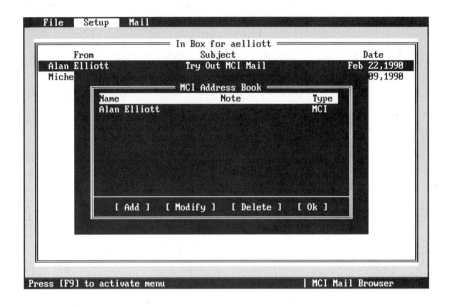

FIG. 10.21.

The MCI
Address Book
dialog box.

At the bottom of the box are four options:

Option	Effect
Add	Adds a name to the address book
Modify	Changes the highlighted address
Delete	Deletes the highlighted address
OK	Exits the Address Book dialog box and returns you to the Setup menu

After you choose to add an address to the address book, you see the Address Type dialog box (see fig. 10.22).

In this box, you must choose how to send the message to this address. You have five options:

    MCI Instant
    Paper Mail
    FAX
    Telex
    External Mail System

If you will be sending messages to the same person, but using different methods (MCI or a fax, for example), you must enter an address for each way that you want to send the messages.

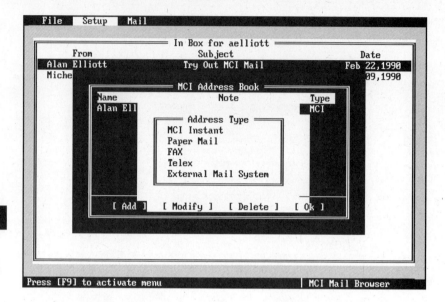

FIG. 10.22.

Indicating
address type
for an Address
Book entry.

If you choose MCI Instant, you see the MCI Subscriber Address dialog
box (see fig. 10.23). In this box, you enter the information about the
MCI account to which the message will be sent. You must know the MCI
user name or the MCI account number for this address. If you know one
but are unsure about the other, just enter the one you know. The information you put in the Name, Note, Location, and Organization fields
appears on the electronic message you send. The highlighted area next
to each part of the address indicates how many characters you can
enter for that address component. After you enter information in the
Name field, press Enter to move to the next field. You also may use the
arrow keys to move from field to field.

If your recipient is not an MCI account holder, you can choose Paper
Mail in the Address Type dialog box. You may want to use MCI Paper
Mail rather than send the letter yourself for several reasons. You may
like the important-looking, telegram-like style of MCI letters. You may
find this method easier than writing and printing the letter yourself.
Also, if you are away from your office, you may want to write and send
letters directly from your computer—from a hotel room, a conference,
or anywhere that you can plug your computer into a phone plug. After
you choose the Paper Mail option, Commander prompts you to enter
information for the following fields:

> Name
> Note
> Country
> Title/Company
> Addr.Line1

Addr.Line2
City
State
ZipCode

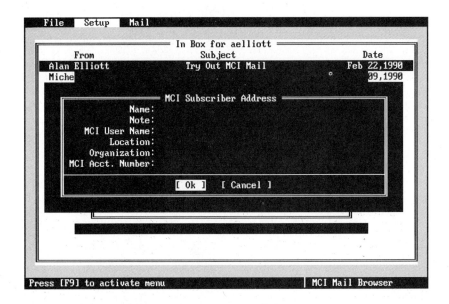

FIG. 10.23.

Entering an
MCI subscriber
address.

Type information for each field and press Enter to move to the next field. Use the arrow keys to move from field to field if you need to make any corrections. The information you enter is used to address the letter that MCI then sends by regular mail. For a paper address, you must include a name and address. The Note, Addr Line 2, and Title/Company fields are optional. Move the highlight to the OK option and press Enter (or select OK with the mouse) to end the entry process.

If you want to send your message to a fax machine, you can choose the Fax option in the Address Type dialog box. For this option, you are asked to enter information for the following fields:

Name
Note
Phone #
Retry

You *must* include a name and phone number, but the Note and Retry fields are optional. In the Retry field, you can enter the number of hours that MCI should keep trying to send the message if it cannot get through. The default is 4 hours. You can enter a number between .5 and 12 hours. If you cannot reach the fax number (it may be busy, for example), MCI continues to try to send the fax for the length of time specified in the Retry field. After MCI has sent the fax successfully or has exhausted all attempts (for example, time expires), you receive an electronic mail message from MCI telling you whether it was successful in sending the fax.

If you want to send a message to a Telex address, choose Telex from the Address Type dialog box. Then supply information for the following fields:

> Name
> Note
> Country
> Telex Number
> Answerback

The Name and Telex Number fields are required. If you leave the Country field blank, Commander Mail uses USA as the default. Do not use the Answerback field unless you know your recipient's answerback code. (*Answerback* is a verification code used by some Telex subscribers as a safety feature.)

 NOTE You also can receive Telex messages through MCI Mail. Your telex number is 650 plus your MCI ID number. If your MCI ID is 123-4567, for example, then your Telex number is 6501234567. Messages sent by Telex appear in your MCI Commander Mail In Box as electronic messages.

To send a message to a person on an electronic mail service other than MCI, you must choose External Mail System as the address type. You then are asked to supply information for the following fields:

> Name
> Note
> Mailsystem
> MBX Info 1
> MBX Info 2
> MBX Info 3

The Name, Mailsystem, and MBX Info 1 fields are required. The Mailsystem field contains the name of the electronic mail service, such as CompuServe. (No other mail systems are currently supported.) The MBX Info 1 field contains the ID number for that service, such as 12345,789. The MBX Info 2 and 3 fields are reserved for future use. MCI periodically adds new services that it can reach. Your correspondence from MCI will explain any future uses for these fields.

After you add addresses to your address book, they appear in the MCI Address Book dialog box when you create a message. You then can highlight an address and select it to be used as the recipient of the message.

Editing and Deleting Addresses

Eventually, you probably will need to modify or delete some addresses. To modify an address, open the Setup menu and choose the Address Book option. Highlight the address to be modified and then choose the Modify option. The address appears, and you can use the arrow keys to move from field to field, making necessary corrections to the address. Select OK to save the modification.

To delete an address, choose the Address Book option from the Setup menu. Highlight the address to be deleted and choose the Delete option. Then select OK to save the change.

Specifying MCI Accounts

The MCI Accounts option on the Setup menu enables you to choose which account should be used to send messages. You can add new accounts, modify current accounts, or delete accounts. This procedure is the same as when you added your first account during the setup procedure.

A person's name or other information may change, for example. To modify an account after you complete the initial setup, choose the MCI Accounts option from the Setup menu. The account list appears on-screen. You then can highlight the account to change and choose the Modify option. Commander Mail displays the information on-screen so that you can edit it. Press Esc when you finish modifying the account. Choose OK to save the modified account list.

Deleting an existing account is similar to modifying one. To delete an account, choose the MCI Accounts option from the Setup menu. When the account list appears, highlight the account to delete and choose the Delete option. Then choose OK.

Setting Up MCI Mail To Run Automatically

The Schedule option on the Setup menu enables you to specify when and if Commander Mail automatically calls MCI. You can set up Commander Mail to send and receive messages unattended during the night when rates are lower, for example. Any received messages are on your computer when you come to work the next day. You may have a number of salespeople sending in orders daily. You can set up Commander Mail to call MCI several times during the day to collect messages being sent in—and to send your salespeople confirmations that their orders were received.

After you choose the Schedule option, a Schedule dialog box like the one in figure 10.24 appears. You have two choices—to use MCI Mail on demand or on a schedule. Using MCI on demand means that you manually choose when to contact MCI Mail. If you choose the Use Schedule Below option, MCI Mail initiates calls at the times specified. To specify times to initiate an MCI call, type up to eight times in the dialog box at the designated locations. Then choose Yes to close the Schedule box and return to the Setup menu.

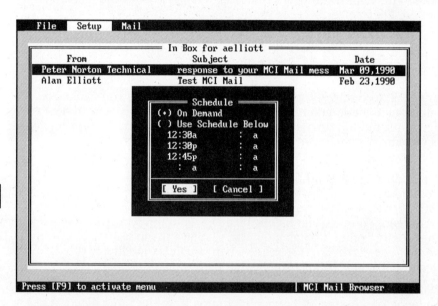

FIG. 10.24.

Completing the Schedule dialog box for automatic communications.

For Commander Mail to operate in automatic mode, you must begin the MCIDRIVR program from the DOS prompt. After you set up the times in the Schedule dialog box for Commander to call MCI Mail, load the MCIDRIVR program by entering the following command at the DOS prompt:

MCIDRIVR

After you enter this command, the Commander MCI Mail program becomes a background program and you are returned to the DOS prompt where you can run other programs. Even if you are using another program at the time, Commander Mail initiates a call at the scheduled times, sends all messages you have in your Out Box, and receives any messages that are waiting for you.

When you enter the MCIDRIVR command at the DOS prompt, you have several switches to choose from that control features of this program. Table 10.2 lists the switches available for the MCIDRIVR command.

Table 10.2 Switches for the MCIDRIVR Command

Switch	Effect
/A	Aborts the current communications session.
/D	Leaves the MCIDRIVR in memory but disables it (turns it off temporarily).
/E	Enables the driver. You use this switch if the MCIDRIVR program is in memory but is disabled.
/N	Initiates a session. The program immediately dials the MCI phone number and sends and receives messages. The command MCIDRIVR/N, for example, begins an MCI session immediately, even if it was not in the schedule.
/S	Sets the status. Sets the DOS errorlevel to 0 if the driver is waiting for a scheduled event, or sets errorlevel to 1 if the driver is in a communications session. You can use this switch in a batch program. For more information, see Chapter 6.
/X	Exits (terminates) the current session and removes the driver from memory.

Changing the MCI Phone Number

The Phone option on the Setup menu enables you to change the MCI phone number and prefix used in calling MCI Mail. MCI will contact you if the number you use to access MCI services changes. The dialog box displayed by the Phone option is the same dialog box that you used in the initial setup procedure to specify the MCI phone number.

Changing Modem Settings

The Modem option on the Setup menu enables you to change the settings for your modem, which you may need to do if you install a different modem. Your new modem may run at a different speed than your original modem, for example. The modem settings include communications port, tone or pulse dialing, modem sound, baud rate, and initialization string. The dialog box displayed by the Modem option is the same dialog box that you used in the initial setup procedure to specify modem settings.

Changing Message Directories

The Directories option on the Setup menu enables you to change the names of the directories that you use to store outgoing messages, incoming messages, and sent messages. Remember that these directories usually are set as \NC\OUT, \NC\IN, and \NC\SENT in the setup procedure. You may want to change directories, for example, from drive C to another disk if drive C is getting full and cannot store all the messages being received.

Managing Messages

You use the Mail menu from the Commander Mail menu bar to manage your incoming and outgoing messages (see fig. 10.25). The four basic tasks that you perform from this menu are creating, sending, receiving, and reading messages.

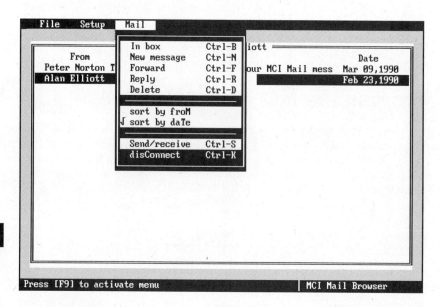

FIG. 10.25.

Commander Mail's Mail menu.

To mail an electronic message, follow these three basic steps:

1. Choose the New Message option from the Mail menu and select the destination of your message from your MCI Address Book.

2. Write the message using the Commander editor and save it to disk.

3. Send the message by choosing the Send/Receive option.

This sequence is one you will probably follow most often when using the Mail menu. The following sections discuss how to use these and other options on the Mail menu to manage your incoming and outgoing mail messages.

Creating Messages

After you choose the New Message option from the Mail menu, you see a screen similar to the one in figure 10.26. At the top of the screen, you enter information that tells MCI where to send the message. These fields are To, CC (carbon copy), Subject, Attach, and Handling. The To field is the only required field. To enter information in the To field, make sure that the field is highlighted and then press Enter to display the Edit Send List dialog box (see fig. 10.27).

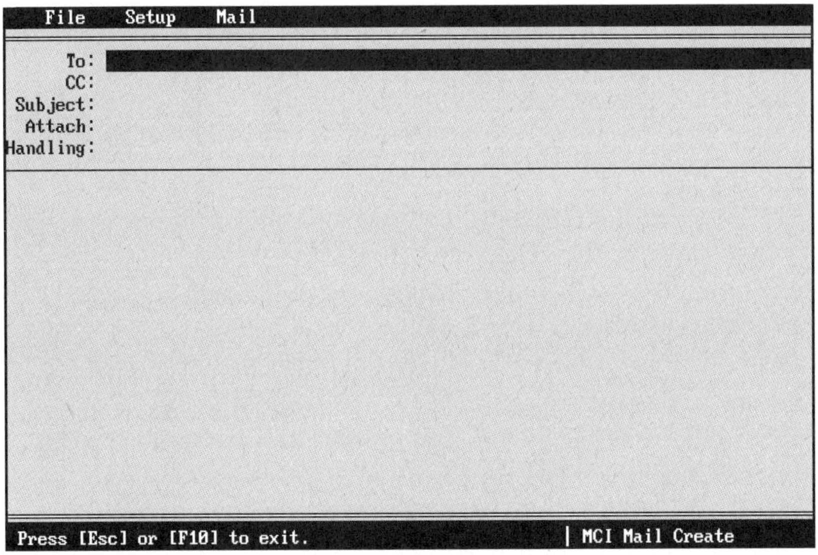

```
   File    Setup    Mail
      To:
      CC:
 Subject:
  Attach:
Handling:




Press [Esc] or [F10] to exit.          | MCI Mail Create
```

FIG. 10.26.

Creating a message.

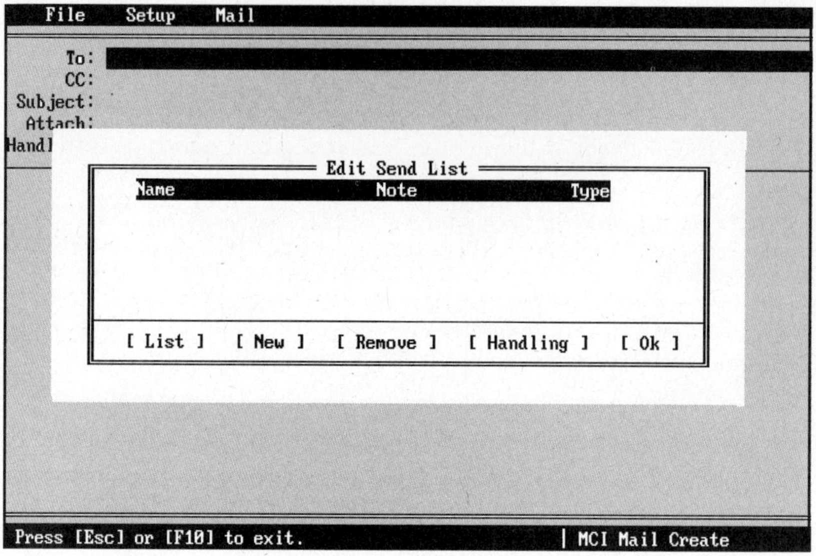

FIG. 10.27.

Specifying
message
recipients.

The Edit Send List dialog box creates a list of names to whom your message should be sent. Choose the List option to display the list of names in your address book (see fig. 10.28). You can choose an address from this list to indicate where to send your message. To choose an address, use the up- and down-arrow keys to highlight the address. Then choose Select by pressing S, using the right- and left-arrow keys to highlight Select and pressing Enter, or pointing to Select with the mouse and clicking. You are returned to the Edit Send List dialog box, and the name you highlighted appears in the box. Choose List and repeat this process for as many addresses as you want to select. Notice the Add option in the Address Book dialog box. You can add a new address to your Address Book by choosing this option. The Cancel option cancels the Address Book and returns you to the Edit Send List dialog box without adding any names.

If you choose the New option in the Edit Send List dialog box, you can enter all of the information needed to send a message. You are asked whether you want to add this name to your address book. The Remove option enables you to delete a name from the list. The Handling option enables you to choose several ways of handling your message. After you choose the Handling option, a dialog box appears where you can enter one of four options:

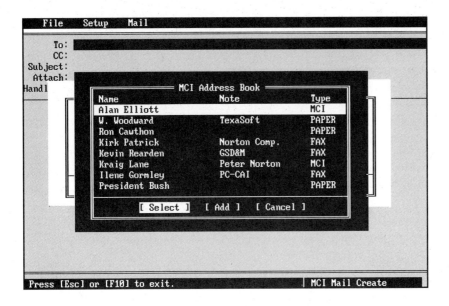

FIG. 10.28.

The Address
Book.

Option	Effect
Receipt	Indicates that you want to receive a receipt verifying that the recipient has received the message.
4hour	Specifies priority delivery of the message.
Charge	Specifies a charging code. This code can be anything you want, because it is for your internal use only. The code, however, cannot contain any blank spaces. (You choose Charge and then type a code.)
Alert	Notifies the recipient by telephone that an MCI message has been sent. You must supply the recipient's phone number.

After you list all the names in the Edit Send List dialog box where you
want to send this message, choose OK.

You can select names for the CC field of the New Message screen in the
same way you select names for the To field. You can type any information in the Subject field. The Attach field is used to specify the name of
a file to include with the message. This file must be an ASCII text file.
If you want to include the file named SALES.TXT from the C:\REPORT
directory, for example, type the following line in the Attach field:

C:\REPORT\SALES.TXT

You use the Handling option to specify the same handling for all recipients in the send list. When you choose a Handling option for this message, it is in effect for all addresses in the list. You cannot specify the Alert option on one address, for example, and not on another in the same message.

After you enter in the New Message screen all the information about where to send the message, type the actual message in the bottom half of the screen. In this screen, you are using the Commander editor, which uses all the keystroke commands mentioned in Chapter 9. After you type the message, press F10. You are given the option to save the message or to end without saving. The message is saved to your \NC\OUT directory and waits there to be sent.

Sending and Receiving Messages

After you create a message, you need to connect to the MCI network to send and receive messages. Choosing the Send/Receive option from the Mail menu instructs Commander Mail to begin a communications session. A communications session performs the following tasks:

1. Calls the MCI Mail service.

2. Sends any messages you have in the Out Box.

3. Receives messages from MCI and puts them in your In Box.

If you use the Schedule feature to have Commander Mail automatically send and receive mail, it performs this entire Send/Receive procedure without any human intervention. When you manually choose the Send/Receive option, you see the Send/Receive MCI Mail screen, from which you can monitor the progress of the communication to MCI Mail and the sending and receiving of messages. The box in the upper left corner lists six activities that will be taking place:

> Initializing
> Dial Service
> Get into MCI
> Send Mail
> Receive Mail
> Terminate Session

While each of these activities is taking place, a dot blinks to the left of the item. As the session completes each one of the activities, a check mark appears next to the item. The *initializing* process is when your computer establishes contact with your modem. The *dial service* activity is when the MCI phone number is being called. If your modem has a speaker and you have chosen to hear the sound, you should hear the dialing. Note that the lower left box also displays information about what is happening. This includes messages about your modem setup—the baud rate or the MCI name of the phone number being dialed, for example. While you are connected to MCI, the message

    Connected to MCI

appears. When the session is over, the message

    Hanging Up

appears, and then a message stating the length of the session appears. Boxes on the right side of the screen give you information about the progress of the session. The Total Session box is a bar graph that shows you how much of the session has gone by. The Current Activity graph shows the progress of some activity such as sending or receiving messages. The MCI and Commander Activity areas display messages such as

    Wait, Receive, and Send

which give the status of the modem activity.

After connecting to MCI, Commander Mail sends your account name and password to MCI. If these names are correct, you are logged onto MCI. After you log in, any messages in your Out Box (the \NC\OUT directory) are sent, and any messages from MCI that are waiting to be received are placed in your In Box (the \NC\IN directory). Then the session is terminated.

The Sent and Received messages in the lower left corner of the screen tell you how many messages were sent and how many were received. The time spent logged onto MCI is displayed in the Current Timer area of the screen. When the session is over, you can go to your In Box to examine any messages.

Reading Messages

You use the In Box option on the Mail menu to examine incoming messages. Figure 10.29 shows an In Box screen containing messages to be read. To look at a message in this list, highlight it and press Enter. If you are using a mouse, point to the message and double-click the left button. The message then appears on-screen. If it is too long to fit, you can use the PgUp and PgDn keys to see more of the message (see fig. 10.30). Press Esc to exit the message and return to the In Box.

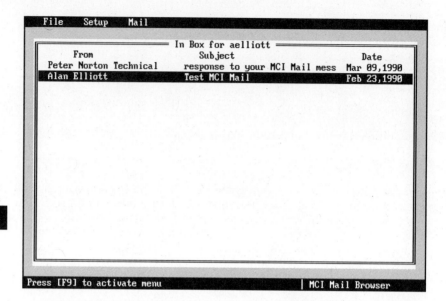

FIG. 10.29.

An In Box
screen
containing
two messages.

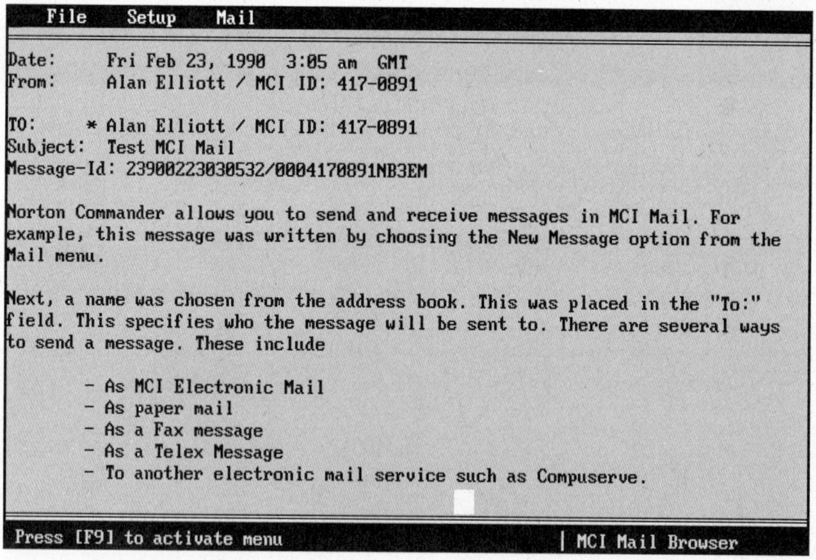

FIG. 10.30.

Viewing a
message.

Using Other MCI Mail Options

In addition to creating, sending, receiving, and reading messages, other tasks are necessary to manage your electronic mail. These tasks include forwarding, replying to, deleting, sorting, and printing messages, as well as disconnecting. Options for these functions—with the exception of printing—also are found on the Mail menu.

Forwarding Messages

If you choose the Forward option from the Mail menu, you can select a message in your In Box and forward it to a person in your address list. This option enables you to send to a third party a message you have received from someone else.

Replying To Messages

The Reply option on the Mail menu enables you to choose a message from your In Box and reply to that message. When you choose to reply, the To field in the message editor is completed with the name of the person who sent you the message. Type a message, and it is stored in the Out Box to be sent the next time you use the Send/Receive option.

Deleting Messages

Choosing the Delete option from the Mail menu enables you to delete a message that is in your In Box. You should periodically delete these messages to free up space on your hard disk. Another way to delete messages from the In box is to move those files to another directory. You can use the Commander Move command (F6), for example, to move all files in the directory \NC\IN (which is your In box) to another directory.

Sorting Messages

Commander Mail sorts the messages in your In Box by the name of the sender or by the date. Choose Sort by From or Sort by Date from the Mail menu to designate the sorting method you prefer. A check mark appears next to the option that is in effect. If you typically only have a handful of messages in your In Box, either sort will do, because you easily can see all the message names on one screen.

Printing Mail Messages

One option that is not directly provided by Commander Mail is a feature to print a message. Because the messages are ASCII text files, however, you can print messages from your IN, OUT, or SENT directory by using DOS PRINT. To print the message in the In Box named ELLIOTT.U00, for example, you can use the following command at the DOS prompt:

    PRINT \NC\IN\ELLIOTT.U00

Disconnecting Communications

During an MCI Send/Receive session, you may want to cancel the communications before they are completed. You can do so by opening the Mail menu and choosing the Disconnect option. You can press Esc or Ctrl-K to end the session. For example, you may begin a session, realize that the messages being sent are wrong, and then want to cancel the session quickly.

Using Commander Link

Commander Link enables you to link two local computers and copy or move files from one computer to the next. It also enables you to rename or delete files on either computer. Link may come in handy if you are upgrading from one computer to another and want to copy your old files to a new computer. The feature also can be helpful if you use a desktop computer and a laptop. In many cases, laptops use 3 1/2-inch diskettes and desktop computers use 5 1/4-inch diskettes. Commander Link enables you to access files from the laptop without copying the file to a middle computer that has 3 1/2- and 5 1/4-inch drives.

Commander Link has two requirements:

1. Your two computers must be attached by a serial null-modem cable connected to the COM1 or COM2 port on each computer.

2. Norton Commander must be running on both computers.

You can buy null-modem cables from most computer supply stores. A null modem is not like the modem that you use to connect your computer to the phone system because it does not actually modulate or demodulate the communication signal. It simply feeds the signal from one computer to the next. Basically, a null modem is a serial cable with some of the wires crossed. These cables cost about the same as a normal serial cable. After you attach the null-modem cable to the serial ports of both computers and start Norton Commander on both computers, you are ready to use Commander Link. Figure 10.31 shows how the null-modem cable is connected to two computers.

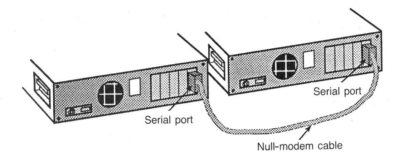

FIG. 10.31.

The null-modem cable connected to two computers.

To begin Commander Link, choose the Link option from the Left or Right pull-down menu (see fig. 10.32). A dialog box like the one in figure 10.33 appears. Note that the Mode options include Master and Slave. One computer must be designated as the master, and the other as the slave. All commands are then given from the master machine. Using your arrow keys, highlight the Master or Slave option for each computer and press the space bar. A dot between the parentheses indicates the selected option.

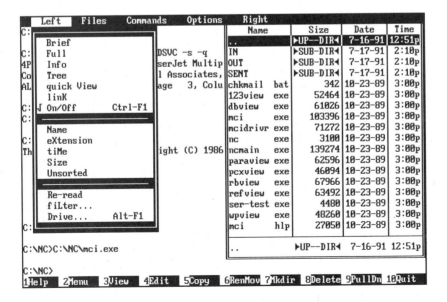

FIG. 10.32.

The Left pull-down menu showing the Link option.

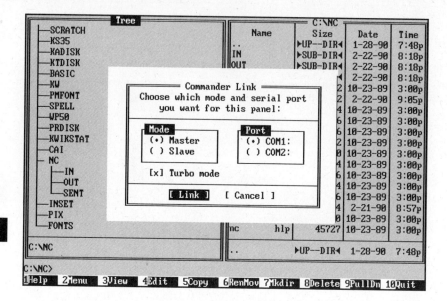

	Tree			C:\NC		
		Name	Size	Date	Time
SCRATCH			▶UP--DIR◀	1-28-90	7:48p
KS35		..			
KADISK		IN	▶SUB-DIR◀	2-22-90	8:18p
KTDISK		OUT	▶SUB-DIR◀	2-22-90	8:18p
BASIC				2-22-90	8:18p

Commander Link
Choose which mode and serial port
you want for this panel:

Mode
(•) Master
( ) Slave

Port
(•) COM1:
( ) COM2:

[x] Turbo mode

[Link]   [Cancel]

FIG. 10.33.

The Com-
mander Link
dialog box.

C:\NC
C:\NC>
1Help 2Menu 3View 4Edit 5Copy 6RenMov 7Mkdir 8Delete 9PullDn 10Quit

The Port options are COM1 and COM2. For each computer, choose the Port option that corresponds to the serial port where you have attached the cable. The Turbo Mode option maximizes the speed of the communications between master and slave computers. If you have trouble communicating, turn off this option on both computers and try again.

To begin the link procedure, choose the Link option at the bottom of the Commander Link dialog box. You then can access files in the slave machine or the master machine by using the Copy, Rename/Move, and Delete options on the master machine. You cannot use DOS commands to access files across the link.

After you set up the link on the master and slave machines, you see panels similar to the ones in figure 10.34. In this example, the left panel reports the directory of the slave machine. Notice that the directory indicator at the top of the panel reads Link:C:\KWIKSTAT. This message indicates that the slave (linked) machine is set to the C:\KWIKSTAT directory. The master machine's directory is on the right panel and is set at C:\NC. Using the menu bar (for the left panel, in this example), you can change the directory listing of the slave machine to a full or brief listing. Because of the way the Link program operates, none of the other settings work for the slave machine. The keyboard on the slave machine does not respond when the machine is set to slave mode.

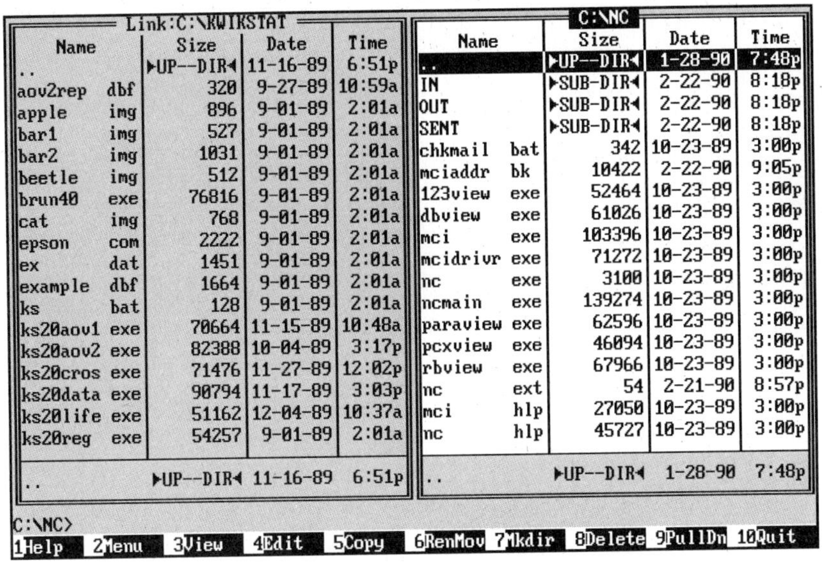

```
 ══════ Link:C:\KWIKSTAT ══════          ╔═══ C:\NC ════════════════════╗
   Name     │ Size │ Date │ Time │    Name      │ Size │ Date │ Time
            │▶UP--DIR◀ 11-16-89 6:51p│  ..        │▶UP--DIR◀ 1-28-90  7:48p
 ..         │         │         │       │ IN       │▶SUB-DIR◀ 2-22-90  8:18p
 aov2rep dbf│    320  9-27-89 10:59a│   OUT       │▶SUB-DIR◀ 2-22-90  8:18p
 apple   img│    896  9-01-89  2:01a│   SENT      │▶SUB-DIR◀ 2-22-90  8:18p
 bar1    img│    527  9-01-89  2:01a│   chkmail bat│    342 10-23-89  3:00p
 bar2    img│   1031  9-01-89  2:01a│   mciaddr bk │  10422  2-22-90  9:05p
 beetle  img│    512  9-01-89  2:01a│   123view exe│  52464 10-23-89  3:00p
 brun40  exe│  76816  9-01-89  2:01a│   dbview  exe│  61026 10-23-89  3:00p
 cat     img│    768  9-01-89  2:01a│   mci     exe│ 103396 10-23-89  3:00p
 epson   com│   2222  9-01-89  2:01a│   mcidrivr exe│ 71272 10-23-89  3:00p
 ex      dat│   1451  9-01-89  2:01a│   nc      exe│   3100 10-23-89  3:00p
 example dbf│   1664  9-01-89  2:01a│   ncmain  exe│ 139274 10-23-89  3:00p
 ks      bat│    128  9-01-89  2:01a│   paraview exe│ 62596 10-23-89  3:00p
 ks20aov1 exe│ 70664 11-15-89 10:48a│  pcxview exe│  46094 10-23-89  3:00p
 ks20aov2 exe│ 82388 10-04-89  3:17p│  rbview  exe│  67966 10-23-89  3:00p
 ks20cros exe│ 71476 11-27-89 12:02p│  nc      ext│     54  2-21-90  8:57p
 ks20data exe│ 98794 11-17-89  3:03p│  mci     hlp│  27050 10-23-89  3:00p
 ks20life exe│ 51162 12-04-89 10:37a│  nc      hlp│  45727 10-23-89  3:00p
 ks20reg  exe│ 54257  9-01-89  2:01a│
 ..         │▶UP--DIR◀ 11-16-89  6:51p│ ..        │▶UP--DIR◀ 1-28-90  7:48p
 C:\NC>
 1Help  2Menu  3View  4Edit  5Copy  6RenMov  7Mkdir  8Delete  9PullDn  10Quit
```

FIG. 10.34.

Panels showing master and slave directories.

You also can change directories on either machine. If the slave machine is set to a subdirectory, for example, such as C:\KWIKSTAT in figure 10.34, choose the .. name at the top of the directory list to switch to the root directory of the slave machine. From there, you can point to and choose another directory on the slave machine. You can choose a directory on the master machine in the same way.

You can copy files to or from the master and the slave and you can delete or rename files on the master or the slave machine. Where the files are copied, moved from, deleted, or renamed is determined by which panel you are operating in. If you are operating from the link panel, which represents the linked (slave) machine, then deleting a file deletes a file on the slave machine. If you delete a file on the nonlink panel, you are deleting a file on the master machine. Because Commander makes it so easy to delete files, you need to be careful when you delete. Basically, think of the link panel as being just another directory, although it happens to be on another machine.

In Commander Link, you use the Norton Commander Copy, Rename/Move, and Delete commands in essentially the same way you always do—just as if you were using two directories on the same hard disk. (See Chapter 9 for more information.)

To copy files from the slave machine to the master machine, follow these steps:

1. Select the file or files to copy.

   If you want to copy a single file, highlight that file on the Commander panel. You may have to change directories on the link (slave) panel to locate the file.

   If you want to copy multiple files, move your cursor to the slave directory panel and press the gray + key. You then are prompted to specify files to include. Enter a file name or a file specification, which can include the asterisk (*) or question mark (?) wild-card characters, and press Enter. The selected files appear highlighted. (Also, you can press the gray – key to select files to exclude.)

   You can add files to the select list by highlighting the file name and pressing the Ins key. Or, press the right mouse button and drag the pointer across a number of files to select.

2. Press F5 (Copy). Commander prompts you to specify where to copy the files to the master machine.

3. Select the destination.

   A default destination often appears on-screen. To accept that destination, press Enter. Otherwise, enter the name of a disk drive such as A:, a path name such as \WP, or a combination such as C:\WP. When specifying the destination, you can press F10 to display a tree of the available directories on the master machine. From this tree, you can highlight the directory to which you want to copy the files.

4. Press Enter, and the copy commences.

5. End the link by choosing the Link option from the master machine's Right or Left menu. This step disables the link and returns the master and slave machines to normal operation.

To give you an idea of how quickly operations can occur in linked machines, a test copy of a 90,794-byte file took only 18.27 seconds. In other words, the file was copied at about 5,000 bytes per second.

Chapter Summary

This chapter covered advanced Norton Commander features. These capabilities generally take a little more time to learn and use, but they provide some of the more exciting aspects of the program. The menu options enable you to customize Commander menus to fit your particular needs. The communications options—Mail and Link—enable you to communicate around the world or to the computer on the next desktop. In all, Norton Commander provides a number of powerful features with which you can make better use of your computer resources.

Using Norton Backup

PART

V

OUTLINE

Protecting Your Information
with Norton Backup

Protecting Your Information with Norton Backup

T he Norton Backup program enables you to copy information quickly from your hard disk to a number of floppy disks. You use this procedure to make a backup copy of the information on your hard disk so that you can recover the information that was lost because of mechanical failure, an accident, or sabotage. Although Norton Utilities also provides ways of recovering erased files and formatted hard disks, it cannot recover data from a mechanically damaged disk. The Norton Backup program is a separate program that you can purchase; it is not a part of Norton Utilities or Commander.

If you have not installed Norton Backup, refer to the installation instructions in Appendix C.

If your computer is jolted or dropped, the read/write head in your hard disk may scratch the surface of the magnetic platter. When this happens, you may be unable to read information from the disk. Also, with the proliferation of computer viruses these days, the information on your hard disk could be erased or compromised by a malicious software program. More commonly, you may accidentally erase files on your disk, overwrite files with erroneous information, or format your disk. Keeping backups of your hard disk is an easy way to protect your information from these kinds of dangers.

The Norton Backup program is a perfect complement to the protection given by Norton Utilities. If you already have learned how to use Utilities or Commander, you will adapt easily to Norton Backup's menu interface. As with Norton Utilities and Norton Commander, you can use a mouse or the arrows on the cursor keypad to choose options with the easy-to-use point-and-shoot menu access.

Norton Backup also is easy to use from a conceptual viewpoint. With very little experience, you can learn how to use the program to perform basic backups of your system. With a little more experience, you can use Backup's advanced features. Norton Backup also has some advantages over the DOS BACKUP and RESTORE commands.

To run the DOS BACKUP command, you must enter the command from the DOS prompt and carefully include a list of switches and parameters describing your backup. With Norton Backup, however, you make your choices through menu selections. You also have more control in selecting which files to back up and in automating the backup process than you do with DOS's BACKUP command.

This chapter describes how to use Norton Backup to back up your hard disk and to restore information to your hard disk when you need it. Before you learn the specifics of using Norton Backup, you should develop a backup strategy. This process is covered in the next section. The "Performing a Basic Backup and Restoring Information to Your Hard Disk" section, later in this chapter, covers how to use Norton Backup to perform a simple and quick backup of your system by using the Norton Backup menus. The "Using Advanced Features of Norton Backup" section covers options on how to customize the backup procedure and how to implement a consistent organization-wide backup process. The "Automating Norton Backup" section describes methods of programming the backup procedures so that you can back up with a minimum number of keystrokes.

Creating and Implementing a Backup Strategy

To use any backup program effectively, you need a backup strategy. Many people are not sure how often they should back up. This is a difficult question to answer in a book, because the frequency of backups will vary with each person. The amount of backups depends mainly on the value of your information. If you use your computer for playing games and using programs that do not store information (such as communications programs, entertainment programs, and so on), you do not need to back up very often—the information on your computer does not change often, so there is little value in having more than one backup copy. If you are a stockbroker and keep valuable financial information on daily sales and commissions, however, you will probably want to back up every day. A good rule of thumb is that you should back up if the effort of doing so is less than the pain of redoing the original work.

A backup strategy is presented in this chapter that will meet the needs of most business situations in which people must back up some information weekly. If you need to back up more than this, make the backup time frames shorter. If this plan asks you to back up too much for your situation, make the time frames longer.

One of the important parts of a backup strategy to keep in mind is that you are protecting your data from a variety of disasters—not just a hard disk crash. Accordingly, your strategy should include a provision for off-site storage of your information. Therefore, many situations call for a backup procedure that creates more than one version of the backup. For example, use the following strategy:

1. Perform a backup of your computer and keep it at home or in another building. You can use this backup in the event of a disaster that destroys your computer and office. Perform this backup once a month.

2. Perform another backup and keep this copy in your office. You will use this backup if your computer disk is damaged or if you lose files on disk, but your computer still is functioning properly. Perform this backup once a week or more.

3. If needed, you can make daily backups of only those files that have been changed or created since the last backup. This is called an *incremental backup*. (You can then use Incremental Copy to restore files without relying on the full backup.)

Again, the frequency of your backup should be geared toward how much information you are willing to lose—a day, a week, or a month.

Another part of the backup strategy deals with selecting which files to back up. You usually do not need to back up all files on your hard disk. If you lose your hard disk files and still have your master copy of your WordPerfect program disks, for example, you can reinstall that program from the original disks—you do not need a backup copy. Usually, backups should concentrate on files that contain information you use or files that would be hard to reinstall or recreate. Norton Backup enables you to select which kinds of files not to back up. Therefore, you can save a lot of time by not backing up EXE and COM files that you can reinstall easily from original program disks.

Also, for your daily or weekly backups, you do not have to back up all files each time. Norton Backup enables you to perform an incremental backup, which backs up only files that changed since the last backup. Therefore, if you are performing daily backups, you may want to perform your full backup on Friday, and incremental backups on Monday through Thursday.

A backup program will do you little good unless you use it regularly—do not wait until disaster strikes before deciding to implement a backup strategy. Norton Backup makes the backup chore easy and efficient.

Performing a Basic Backup and Restoring Information to Your Hard Disk

To begin the Norton Backup program to back up or restore files, you enter the command

NBACKUP

from the DOS prompt.

Figure 11.1 shows the Norton Backup main menu. This menu contains four options: Backup, Restore, Configure, and Quit. Select one of these options by using the arrow keys to highlight an option and then pressing Enter. If you are using a mouse, you can point to the option you want and click the left mouse button.

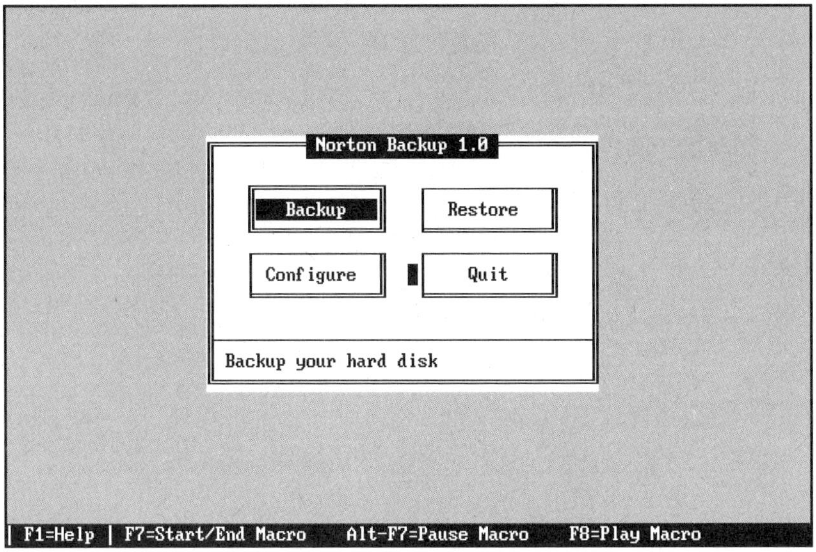

```
┌─────────── Norton Backup 1.0 ───────────┐
│                                          │
│   ┌───────────┐      ┌───────────┐       │
│   │  Backup   │      │  Restore  │       │
│   └───────────┘      └───────────┘       │
│                                          │
│   ┌───────────┐  ▌   ┌───────────┐       │
│   │ Configure │      │   Quit    │       │
│   └───────────┘      └───────────┘       │
│                                          │
├──────────────────────────────────────────┤
│   Backup your hard disk                  │
└──────────────────────────────────────────┘
```

| F1=Help | F7=Start/End Macro   Alt-F7=Pause Macro   F8=Play Macro

FIG. 11.1.

The Norton
Backup main
menu.

You use the Configure option to change your configuration that was set originally when you installed Norton Backup. The Quit option ends the Norton Backup program and returns you to the DOS prompt. The Backup and Restore options are discussed in "Using Advanced Restore Features" and "Automating Norton Backup," later in this chapter.

In this chapter, you learn how to perform a backup and restore by using Norton Backup's basic options. After you are comfortable with the basics of using Norton Backup, you may want to use some advanced options that enable you to automate the backup process.

Backing Up Your Entire Hard Disk

After you choose the Backup option from the Norton Backup main menu, you see a menu similar to the one in figure 11.2. Notice that one letter in each option name is highlighted. To select one of the options, you can press the highlighted hot key (for example, the T key to select Backup To), use the arrow keys to highlight your choice and press Enter, or point to the option with the mouse and click the left mouse button once.

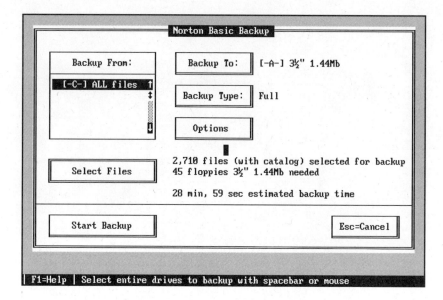

FIG. 11.2.

The Norton
Basic Backup
menu.

To perform a backup of your hard disk to floppy disks, you must be
sure that the Backup From and Backup To settings are correct. The
Backup From setting should be the name of your hard disk. Usually,
this is drive C. If you have more than one hard disk, you need to use the
arrow keys (or a mouse) to select the hard disk to back up from. Similarly, you need to make sure that the Backup To selection is set to the
floppy disk on which you want to store the information. Usually, this
selection is set to drive A. If you have other floppy disk drives and want
to back up to one of them, select the Backup To option. A list of the
available disks appears from which you can choose the disk to back up
to (see fig. 11.3).

The default backup type is Full. This type backs up all selected files on
the Backup From drive to the Backup To drive. The next section discusses how to change the default backup and how to select which files
to back up. For information on the other options, see "Using Backup
Options," later in this chapter.

To the right of the Select Files option on the Norton Basic Backup
screen is a description of the number of files scheduled to be backed
up and an estimate of the number of disks needed to perform that
backup. You do not need to format these disks because the Norton
Backup procedure performs a format as the backup is in progress.
Norton Backup also provides an estimate of the time required to perform the backup.

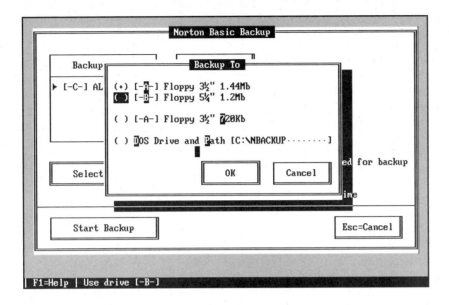

```
┌─────────────────────────────────────────────────────┐
│            ═══ Norton Basic Backup ═══               │
│  ┌─Backup───────┐ ┌──── Backup To ────┐              │
│  │              │ │                   │              │
│  │► [-C-] AL     │ (•) [-A-] Floppy 3½" 1.44Mb        │
│  │              │ (•) [-B-] Floppy 5¼" 1.2Mb          │
│  │              │                                     │
│  │              │ ( ) [-A-] Floppy 3½" 720Kb          │
│  │              │                                     │
│  │              │ ( ) DOS Drive and Path [C:\NBACKUP·······] │
│  │              │                                   │  │
│  │              │                          ed for backup │
│  │ Select       │  ┌────────┐  ┌─────────┐            │
│  │              │  │   OK   │  │ Cancel  │       ine   │
│  └──────────────┘  └────────┘  └─────────┘            │
│                                                       │
│  ┌──────────────┐                    ┌─────────────┐  │
│  │ Start Backup │                    │  Esc=Cancel │  │
│  └──────────────┘                    └─────────────┘  │
│                                                       │
│ F1=Help │ Use drive [-B-]                             │
└─────────────────────────────────────────────────────┘
```

FIG. 11.3.

The Backup To
dialog box.

> **T I P**
>
> It is very important to match your diskette size with the disk drive
> you are using for backup. Do not try to use a 5 1/4-inch, 360K dis-
> kette, for example, in a drive meant for a 5 1/4-inch, 1.2M diskette.
> Similarly, do not use a 3 1/2-inch, 720K diskette in a 3 1/2-inch, 1.44M
> drive.

At the bottom of the Norton Basic Backup screen are the choices Start
Backup and Esc=Cancel. If you decide to cancel this backup, press Esc.
To begin the backup, select the Start Backup option.

When you begin the backup procedure, you see a screen similar to the
one shown in figure 11.4. The top left of the screen contains a diagram
of the directories on your hard disk, and the top right of the screen
displays the files in the highlighted directory. As the backup continues,
you see the progress being made as the highlight moves down the directory tree.

At the bottom right of the screen is a set of statistics and information
about the backup. As the backup progresses, information about the
number of disks used and the estimated and actual time for the backup
is displayed.

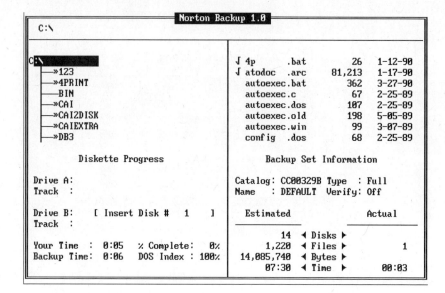

FIG. 11.4.

The Norton
Backup screen.

During most of the backup, you will be watching the information at the bottom left of the screen. Notice in figure 11.4 that the prompt Insert Disk #1 is highlighted (it will probably be blinking on your screen). After you insert a disk, the backup begins and a small bar shows the progress of the backup to that disk. When the first disk is full, the message Insert Disk #2 appears. The disk light on your disk drive will not go out; this is to keep the motor running, which prevents the time lost when the motor has to stop and restart. Take out Disk #1 (your first backup disk) and insert Disk #2 (your second backup disk) into the drive. Each time a disk is full, a message appears to insert the next disk. This continues until the backup is finished. You must plan to stay at your computer during the backup process so that you can change disks as soon as you are prompted. The DOS field reports the efficiency of the backup, where 100% is at maximum efficiency.

NOTE   Be sure to label properly each diskette with its backup number. You will need to know the number of each backup disk when you restore files from the diskettes back to the hard disk.

Backing Up Selected Files

Norton Backup enables you to select which files to back up. In the
Basic Backup screen in figure 11.2, notice the Select Files option.
Choose this option to tell Norton Backup which files you want to back
up. After you choose Select Files, you see the Select Backup Files
screen (see fig. 11.5). This screen is divided into two parts. The left
part shows the directory structure on your hard disk. Directories with
names preceded by a chevron (») contain files that you have selected
to back up. If an arrow precedes a directory name, all files in that directory are selected to be backed up.

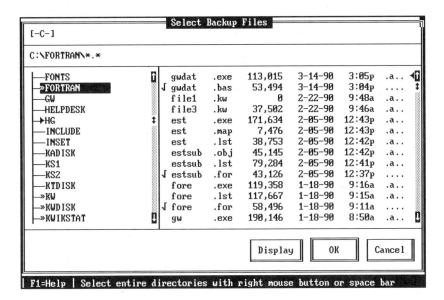

FIG. 11.5.

The Select
Backup Files
screen.

The highlighted directory has its file names displayed on the right side
of the Select Backup Files screen (in fig. 11.5, this is the FORTRAN
directory). File names that are preceded by a check mark (✓) are
selected for backup. File names that are preceded by a period (.) or a
blank are excluded from the backup. You can select entire directories
(including all files) or individual files to back up.

Selecting and Deselecting Entire Directories To Back Up

To select all of the files in a directory to be backed up, highlight a directory name on the left side of the screen. If your cursor is not on the left side of the screen, press the left-arrow key or point to the directory with a mouse and click the left button. After you select a directory, you can press the space bar to select or deselect the files in that directory. After you select the files for backup, the file names are preceded by a check mark. When you deselect the files, the file names are preceded by a period or a blank.

Selecting and Deselecting Groups of Files

It is common to want to select or deselect files containing the same extension. You may want to deselect all files with the EXE extension, for example. To do this, follow these steps:

1. Choose the Display option from the Select Backup Files screen. To select this option, press Tab until the Display option is highlighted and then press Enter, point to Display with your mouse and click the left button once, or press D. A dialog box appears similar to the one in figure 11.6. In this box, you indicate which files to display on the right side of the Select Backup Files screen. You can choose to display the files *.EXE, for example.

   Now, when you point to a directory name on the left side of the screen, only EXE files will appear on the right side.

2. Press the space bar to deselect or select all EXE files in that directory.

You can be in any directory when you specify certain files to select. After you specify that only EXE files should be displayed, they will be the only files displayed, regardless of which directory you move to. To change this display specification, you must return to the Display option and change your selection criteria.

You can go through this process several times to eliminate other kinds of files that you do not want to back up, such as COM, OBJ, and LIB files—files that you can restore from master program disks.

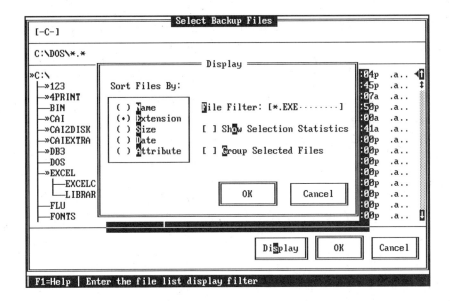

FIG. 11.6.

The Display
dialog box.

Selecting and Deselecting Individual Files

There may be individual files that you want to select or deselect after
you have selected or deselected entire directories or types of files. To
select or deselect a file, highlight the directory containing the file on
the left side of the Select Backup Files screen. Use the right-arrow key
to move your cursor to the right side of the screen. Point to the file to
be selected or deselected and press the space bar. When the file is
checked, it will be backed up (selected); otherwise, the file will not be
backed up (deselected).

Performing a Backup with the Selected Files

After you select files for backup, the backup process is the same as for
a full backup, as described in "Backing Up Your Entire Hard Disk," earlier in this chapter. From the Norton Basic Backup menu, choose the
Start Backup option and follow the prompts on-screen.

Performing Incremental Backups and Copies

If you perform backups on a regular basis, there usually is no need to perform a full backup each time. You can save on the amount of time you spend doing backups by performing incremental backups.

Suppose that you perform a backup every day. On Friday, you could perform a full backup (and take it home during the weekend). Then, on Monday through Thursday you could perform incremental backups—backing up only the files that have changed that day.

Performing incremental backups means that you will be backing up updated copies of files that you backed up on Monday. This means that you will have a growing stack of diskettes containing the backup of your hard disk. This why you want to start over every Friday with a full backup to consolidate the file changes made during the week—this cuts down on duplicated files and on the number of diskettes used. Also, when you decide to restore a file, finding the right file becomes more of a problem if you have multiple copies of it backed up.

Your computer (or, more specifically, DOS) keeps track of which files have been backed up. The archive attribute is set when a file is backed up. This archive attribute (or flag) is an On/Off switch that is stored by DOS with the file name. The archive attribute tells DOS whether a file has been backed up. When you alter a file or create a new file, DOS unsets the archive attribute. When you perform an incremental backup, DOS looks for the files that do not have the archive attribute set, and it backs up only those files. Then, DOS sets the archive attribute for these new files as they are backed up. When you perform your next incremental backup, only new or changed files since the last incremental backup are backed up. (See Chapter 3 for more information on archive flags.)

To perform an incremental backup, choose the Backup Type option from the Norton Basic Backup screen. You see a dialog box like the one in figure 11.7. From this Backup Type box, choose the Incremental option by pressing I to select Incremental or by pointing with your mouse between the parentheses before Incremental and clicking.

After you select the incremental type backup, the backup process is the same as for a full backup (see "Backing Up Your Entire Hard Disk," earlier in this chapter). From the Norton Basic Backup menu, choose the Start Backup option and follow the prompts on-screen.

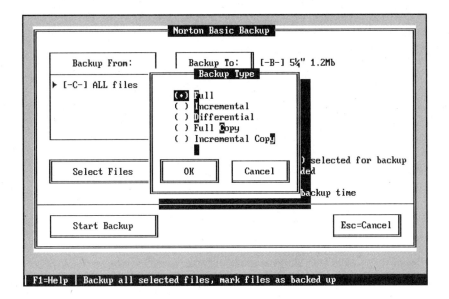

```
┌─────────────────────── Norton Basic Backup ───────────────────────┐
│                                                                    │
│  ┌──────────────────┐  ┌─────────────┐                             │
│  │   Backup From:   │  │ Backup To:  │  [-B-] 5¼" 1.2Mb            │
│  └──────────────────┘  └─ Backup Type ─────────┐                   │
│  ▶ [-C-] ALL files        (•) Full             │                   │
│                           ( ) Incremental       │                   │
│                           ( ) Differential      │                   │
│                           ( ) Full Copy         │                   │
│                           ( ) Incremental Copy  │                   │
│                                                 │                   │
│  ┌──────────────────┐  ┌────────┐  ┌─────────┐  ) selected for backup
│  │   Select Files   │  │   OK   │  │ Cancel  │  ded                 │
│  └──────────────────┘  └────────┘  └─────────┘                      │
│                                                 backup time         │
│  ┌──────────────────┐                        ┌───────────┐          │
│  │   Start Backup   │                        │ Esc=Cancel│          │
│  └──────────────────┘                        └───────────┘          │
└────────────────────────────────────────────────────────────────────┘
 F1=Help │ Backup all selected files, mark files as backed up
```

FIG. 11.7.

The Backup Type dialog box.

Using Other Backup Types

The Backup Type dialog box contains several other selections. The Full option and Incremental options are discussed earlier in the chapter.

The Differential option is similar to the Incremental option—it backs up files that you changed or created since the last backup—but it does *not* set the archive attribute on a file like the Incremental option. When you perform a differential backup, therefore, your computer keeps no record of the backup. There may be occasions when you want to back up changed files, but you do not want to set the archive attribute. You may use Backup to copy files from one computer to another, for example. In this case, you do not want the copy to count as a backup.

The Full Copy option is similar to the Full option, but it does *not* set the archive attribute like a regular full backup does. You may want to perform a full backup without disturbing your normal backup procedure, which relies on the archive attributes being set for incremental backups. You may want to use Backup to copy the contents of the entire hard disk to a new computer, for example. Because this backup does not fit into your normal daily, weekly, or monthly backup scheme, however, you do not want this backup to set the archive attributes and disturb your normal backup set of disks.

The Incremental Copy option enables you to perform a backup of selected files that you changed or created since the last backup *without* setting the archive attributes. This option provides you with a complete set of backup disks for these files—not just "add-on" disks for the full backup. (A normal incremental backup creates disks that depend on a previous full copy to be restored. You can use Incremental Copy to restore files without relying on a previous full backup.) The Incremental Copy option enables you to restore these files to another disk more easily. You can use this procedure to transfer files to another computer without interfering with your normal incremental backup procedure.

Using Backup Options

There is one selection remaining on the Norton Basic Backup screen to be discussed—Options. This selection enables you to select backup options (see fig. 11.8).

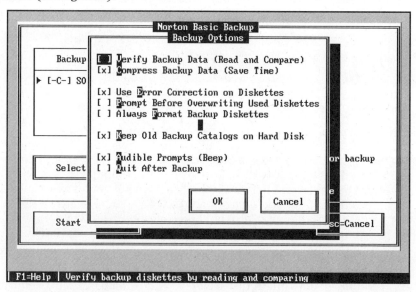

In the Backup Options dialog box, an item is selected if an X appears to its left. Use the arrow keys to point to a selection, and use the space bar to place an X or remove an X from the selection (or point between the brackets in front of an option with the mouse and click the left button). You can select the following options from the Backup Options dialog box:

■ *Verify Backup Data (Read and Compare):* Double-checks information as it is written to disk. This option slows down the backup process, but gives you more assurance that the backup is correct. Usually, you should not have to use this option. If your disk drives are old or have had read and write problems in the past, however, you may want to choose this option as an added measure of protection.

■ *Compress Backup Data (Save Time):* Compresses the data written to disk so that more information can be written to each disk. This means that you will be able to use fewer disks. When the Compress selection is off, backup will be faster, but it will take more diskettes. You usually will want to choose this option.

■ *Use Error Correction on Diskettes:* Provides additional checking of the information as it is written and read to and from the backup disks. If your data is very critical, you may want to use this extra measure of safety. Also, you may use the Verify Backup option to verify that the information written to disk matches the original files exactly. Use this option as a special safety feature of Norton Backup.

■ *Prompt Before Overwriting Used Diskettes:* Causes Norton Backup to prompt you before writing information to a previously used diskette. This could save you from accidentally writing over important information. It also may slow down the backup process.

■ *Always Format Backup Diskettes:* Causes Norton Backup to format disks as the backup is taking place. You may want to use this option if the disks you are using for backup were formatted on an older version of DOS.

■ *Keep Old Backup Catalogs on Hard Disk:* Causes Norton Backup to keep old backup catalogs (containing backup information) each time you perform a backup. Otherwise, when you perform a full backup, the old catalogs are deleted. You may want to select not to keep old catalogs in order to conserve disk space.

■ *Audible Prompts (Beep):* Determines whether a beep sounds when Norton Backup prompts you to change disks and issues warnings.

■ *Quit After Backup:* Determines whether Norton Backup returns to the Backup menu or to DOS after it performs the backup.

Restoring Backed-Up Files

You may never have to use your backup disks to restore files. When disaster strikes, however, those backup disks suddenly become very valuable. You may restore one file from your backup diskettes to your hard disk, a selected number of files, or all files.

The restore process is managed from the Norton Basic Restore screen, as shown in figure 11.9. To display this screen, choose the Restore option from the Norton Backup main menu. Before choosing the Start Restore option from the Norton Basic Restore screen, you need to check several options—Restore From, Catalog, Options, and Select Files.

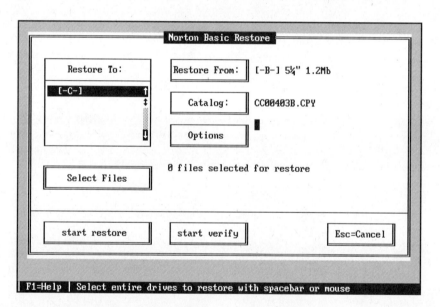

FIG. 11.9.

The Norton Basic Restore menu.

Choosing Restore From

You chose the Restore To setting during the configuration process when you installed Norton Backup. The Restore From selection also will reflect what you chose during installation. If you need to use another disk drive to restore the disks, you can select the Restore From option and change the setting.

Choosing the Restore Catalog

Each time you perform a restore, Norton Backup keeps a copy of the catalog of files restored. After you select the Catalog option from the Norton Basic Restore menu, you see the Select Catalog dialog box (see fig. 11.10). Notice the list of catalog files in the middle of the box. A catalog of each backup is kept on your hard disk and on the last diskette of the backup floppy diskettes. Because you may have multiple backups (one day old, one week old, and so on), you must choose from this list of catalogs that will be used to perform the restore.

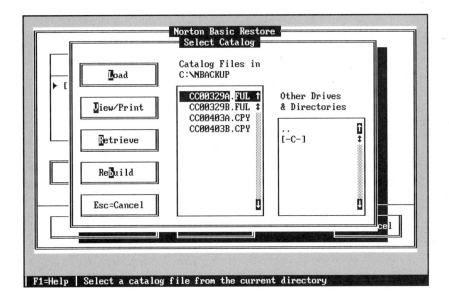

FIG. 11.10.

The Select Catalog dialog box.

From the Select Catalog dialog box you can view or print the contents of a catalog by highlighting its name in the center of the screen and choosing View/Print. You use the Retrieve option to retrieve a catalog from the last floppy of a backup. If you are restoring to a machine or hard disk that did not create that backup, for example, you must retrieve the catalog. You use the Rebuild command to rebuild a catalog if the last disk of a backup has been damaged. After you indicate which catalog to use, choose the Load option, which loads that catalog and returns you to the Restore menu. The Other Drives & Directories box enables you to search for catalog files in locations other than the current catalog files list box. You can search the other drives list by pressing Tab to move your cursor to that box, and then use the up- and down-arrow keys to select a drive or directory to search.

Selecting Restore Options

When you choose Options from the Norton Basic Restore box, you see a screen similar to the one in figure 11.11. Skip the Options menu if you do not want to set any of these options by pressing Esc or by pointing to Cancel with your mouse and clicking.

FIG. 11.11.

The Restore Options dialog box.

The Verify Restore Data option on the Restore Options menu causes Norton Backup to double-check the contents of the file after it is copied to the hard disk. This option slows down the restore, but may be advisable if you have had any difficulties in performing a successful restore.

The Prompt options cause Norton Backup to prompt you before overwriting existing directories or files or before creating new files on disk. Choosing these options drastically increases the amount of interaction you will have during the restore process but may be necessary if there is a possibility that the restore will overwrite valuable information on your hard disk. If you are restoring files that may overwrite important existing files, you should use Prompt Before Overwriting Existing Files as a precautionary measure.

Restore usually will not restore empty directories unless you choose the Restore Empty Directories option. You may turn off audible prompts by deselecting the Audible Prompts option. After you select all of the options you want by placing an X to the left of the option name, choose OK to close this dialog box and return to the Basic Backup menu. If you choose Cancel instead of OK, all options return to their previous states and you return to the Basic Backup menu. Selecting Quit After Restore causes the program to return to DOS when the restore is finished.

Selecting Files To Restore

After you choose the Select Files option from the Norton Basic Restore menu, you see the Select Restore Files screen (see fig. 11.12). This screen is similar to the Select Backup Files screen. You choose files to restore the same way that you choose files to back up. When you choose a file to restore, a check mark appears beside the file name (like the one next to the file BIG.DBF in figure 11.12). You can choose to restore one file, several files, an entire directory, or all directories.

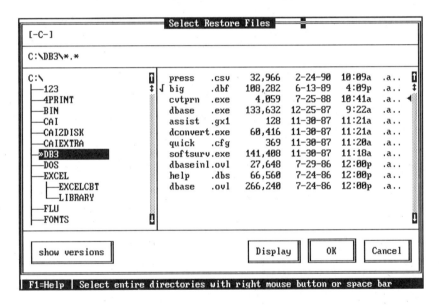

	Select Restore Files	
[-C-]		
C:\DB3*.*		

```
C:\                    press    .csv      32,966   2-24-90  10:09a  .a..
├─123               √ big      .dbf     108,282   6-13-89   4:09p  .a..
├─4PRINT              cvtprn   .exe       4,059   7-25-88  10:41a  .a..
├─BIN                 dbase    .exe     133,632  12-25-87   9:22a  .a..
├─CAI                 assist   .gx1         128  11-30-87  11:21a  .a..
├─CAI2DISK            dconvert .exe      60,416  11-30-87  11:21a  .a..
├─CAIEXTRA            quick    .cfg         369  11-30-87  11:20a  .a..
»DB3                  softsurv .exe     141,408  11-30-87  11:18a  .a..
├─DOS                 dbaseinl .ovl      27,648   7-29-86  12:00p  .a..
├─EXCEL               help     .dbs      66,560   7-24-86  12:00p  .a..
│  ├─EXCELCBT         dbase    .ovl     266,240   7-24-86  12:00p  .a..
│  └─LIBRARY
├─FLU
├─FONTS
```

```
  show versions              Display    OK    Cancel
```

F1=Help │ Select entire directories with right mouse button or space bar

FIG. 11.12.

The Select Restore Files screen.

If you choose files to restore that already may be on disk, you may want to choose one or more of the prompt selections in the Options menu (see the preceding section).

The Show Versions option on the Select Restore Files screen enables you to see information about several versions of a file. You may have incrementally backed up the file called SALES.DBF every day, for example. In this case, the backup diskettes would contain several versions of this file. To choose the proper version to restore, highlight the file name on-screen and select the Show Versions option, which displays the versions with the date and time they were created. From this list, select the proper version to restore. The Display option enables you to look at a list of the files selected for backup. The Cancel option exits the screen and returns you to the Basic Restore menu.

After you make your selections for which files to restore, choose the OK option to return to the Norton Basic Restore menu.

Starting the Restore

After you select which files to restore, select the Start Restore option from the Norton Basic Restore menu. A screen similar to the one in figure 11.13 appears. An Alert box prompts you to insert a diskette into the disk drive. Place the proper diskette into the drive and choose Continue. Follow the prompts on-screen to complete the restore process.

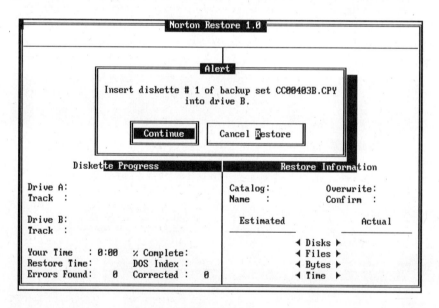

FIG. 11.13.

The Alert dialog box.

What can you do if your hard disk and your Norton Backup program are destroyed? If you are restoring your files to a new or reformatted hard disk, follow these steps:

T I P

1. Install the Norton Backup program to the new or reformatted hard disk.

2. Insert the last diskette of your most recent backup (or the backup you want to use to restore your files) into your disk drive.

3. Begin the backup by typing *nbackup* and choosing Restore from the Norton Backup main menu.

4. The Norton Basic Restore screen appears. Make sure that the Restore From option refers to the drive where your backup diskette is located.

5. Choose the Catalog option from the Norton Basic Restore screen, and then choose the Retrieve option from the Select Catalog menu. This step accesses catalog information that Norton uses to restore files. Choose the latest catalog file and press Esc to exit this option.

6. Select all files to be restored.

7. Insert Disk 1 of the backup disks into the disk drive, choose Start Restore from the Norton Basic Restore screen, and follow the prompts on-screen.

Verifying That a Restore Is Possible

Even with all of the checks and double-checks, a set of backup disks may become unusable. This damage could be from environmental factors such as magnetism, heat, or cold. Disks also can become unusable because of the deterioration of the magnetic surface on the diskette.

You can check a set of backup disks by performing a verify immediately after creating the disks or any time in the future. You begin a verify just like you begin a restore. The only difference is that instead of choosing the Start Restore option on the Norton Basic Restore menu, you choose Start Verify. A Verify is similar to a Restore, but it does not actually restore the files to the disk; it examines the files to see if they can be restored.

You should perform a verify on the first backup that you create on your computer to ensure that everything is okay. If you are going to use a set of diskettes to move information from one computer to another—you may want to take the diskettes to your new home on the coast, for example—you should verify that the backup disks are okay before taking them to your new location. Otherwise, you may be disappointed.

Some companies run a periodic check of a disaster-recovery plan. For example, what happens if your office burns down? Can you recover your data? You can simulate the recovery of your computer information by performing a verify on your backup disks. Performing a quarterly simulation is a good test of the integrity of your backup plan, as well as a test of the disks. After you perform the simulation, ask yourself if you are satisfied with the amount of information that you would be able to recover after a disaster.

Using Advanced Features of Norton Backup

Performing a backup and restore using advanced features is similar to performing a basic backup and restore. The main difference is that Norton enables you to set up prescribed backup procedures and additional backup and restore options by using the advanced features. Follow these steps:

1. Choose the Configure selection from the Norton Backup main menu.

   The Norton Backup Configuration menu appears, enabling you to set the program level, mouse characteristics, type of video display, and other settings related to your computer (see fig. 11.14).

2. Select the Program Level option from the Configuration menu. Use the arrow keys to highlight the Program Level option in the Norton Backup Configuration box and press Enter. Or, point to the Program Level option with a mouse and click. The Program options are Basic, Advanced, and Preset. Select Advanced and then select OK to return to the Configuration menu.

3. Save the new configuration by choosing the Save Configuration option from the Norton Backup Configuration box. Exit the Configuration menu by choosing OK.

The following information describes how to perform a backup using the advanced backup options. Because many of these options are the same as in a basic backup, only the advanced options are emphasized.

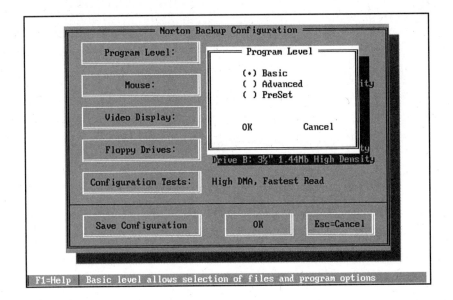

FIG. 11.14.

The Norton
Backup
Configuration
dialog box.

Using the Advanced Backup Menu

After you choose the advanced program level for the Norton Backup
configuration and then choose OK, choose the Backup option from
the main menu. The Norton Advanced Backup menu appears (see
fig. 11.15). Notice that this menu is similar to the Basic Backup menu
except for the addition of the Setup File option at the top left of the
screen. Creating and using setup files is discussed in "Creating and
Using Setup Files," later in this chapter.

Using Advanced Select Files Options

After you choose Select Files from the Advanced Backup screen, the
Select Backup Files screen appears (see fig. 11.16). Notice the addition
of the options Include, Exclude, and Special at the bottom left of the
screen. These options are not available in the Basic Backup program
level. The Include and Exclude options enable you to include or exclude
groups of files to be backed up.

If you choose the Include option, the Include Files dialog box appears
(see fig. 11.17). To include files, enter the appropriate path for the
directory at the path prompt and a global file specification at the file
prompt. Type *.exe* to match all files with an EXE extension, for example. If you mark the Include All Subdirectories option with an X,
all matching files in subdirectories also are included. Each time you

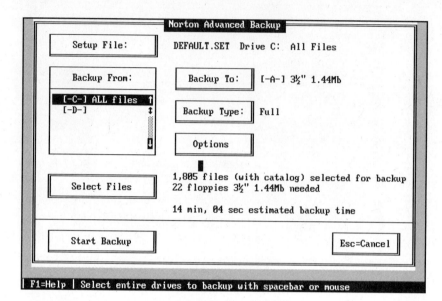

FIG. 11.15.

The Norton
Advanced
Backup menu.

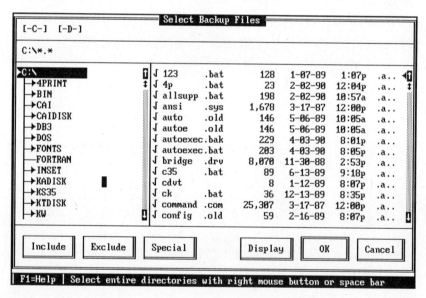

FIG. 11.16.

The Advanced
Select Backup
Files menu.

indicate an Include Files specification and choose OK, that specification is added to a list, and the Include Files screen reverts to the state shown in figure 11.17. You now can enter another specification to include on the list. You can list a number of file specifications to include, such as *.EXE, *.COM, *.TXT, and so on.

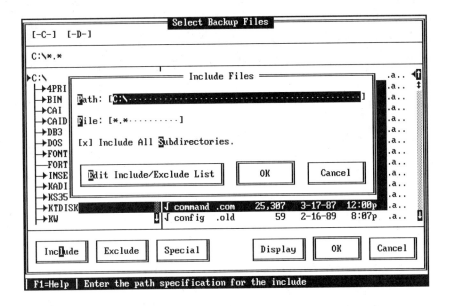

FIG. 11.17.

The Include
Files dialog
box.

To view the list of included and excluded files, choose the Edit
Include/Exclude List option from the Include Files dialog box. The
Edit Include/Exclude List screen appears (see fig. 11.18). By using
the up- and down-arrow keys to highlight one of the items on the list,
you then can choose to edit the item, delete it from the list, or copy
it by choosing one of the options at the bottom of the dialog screen.
Choose OK when your list of included and excluded files is complete.

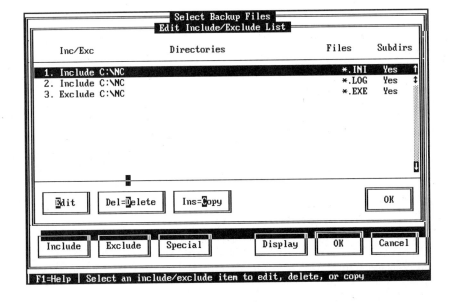

FIG. 11.18.

The Edit
Include/Exclude
List screen.

Another option on the Select Backup Files screen is the Special option (figure 11.19 shows the Special Selections dialog box). This option enables you to select a date range of files to back up. After you choose the Date Range option from the Special Selections menu, you are prompted to enter a beginning and ending date. The date range 1-1-91 to 12-31-91, for example, backs up only files created in 1991.

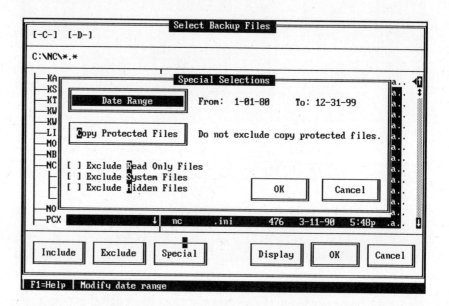

FIG. 11.19.

The Special Selections dialog box.

You also can select options to exclude the following:

- Read-only files
- System files
- Hidden files

Using arrow keys and the space bar or a mouse, place an X in the selection box in front of the file types to exclude from backup. If you choose the Copy Protected Files option on the Special Selections menu, you are prompted to enter a list of copy-protected files to exclude from backup.

Selecting Advanced Backup Options

After you choose Options from the Norton Advanced Backup screen, you are presented with a different set of options than when using the basic backup procedure. The Backup Options box for advanced backup is shown in figure 11.20.

```
╔═══════════════════════════════════════════════════════════╗
║              Norton Advanced Backup                        ║
║                  Backup Options                            ║
║                                                            ║
║   ┌──────────────────────┐                                 ║
║   │ Data Verification:   │ Off       [ ] Proprietary Diskette Format
║   └──────────────────────┘           [ ] Always Format Diskettes
║                                                            ║
║   ┌──────────────────────┐           [x] Use Error Correction
║   │ Data Compression:    │ Save Time                       ║
║   └──────────────────────┘           [x] Keep Old Backup Catalogs
║                                                            ║
║   ┌──────────────────────┐           [ ] Quit After Backup ║
║   │ Overwrite Warning:   │ Off                             ║
║   └──────────────────────┘                                 ║
║                                                            ║
║   ┌──────────────────────┐                                 ║
║   │ Full Backup Cycle:   │ No Cycle                        ║
║   └──────────────────────┘                                 ║
║                                                            ║
║   ┌──────────────────────┐           ┌────────┐ ┌────────┐ ║
║   │ Audible Prompts:     │ Low       │   OK   │ │ Cancel │ ║
║   └──────────────────────┘           └────────┘ └────────┘ ║
╚═══════════════════════════════════════════════════════════╝
  F1=Help │ Select how much verification to use
```

FIG. 11.20.

The Advanced Backup options box.

The Data Verification option causes the backup procedure to verify the data more thoroughly as it is written to the backup disks. Norton Backup compares the backup file to the original file to verify that the backup copy is exactly the same as the original. This option slows down the backup procedure, but a slower backup may be worth protecting very important data.

You can choose from three options with the Data Compression option:

- *Save Time:* Does little compression, but is quicker and uses more diskettes.

- *Save Disks (low):* Does more compression and takes fewer disks, but is slower than the Save Time option.

- *Save Disks (high):* Performs maximum compression and takes the fewest disks, but is slow.

If you set the Overwrite Warning option to On, you are prompted each time before the program overwrites backup diskettes that already contain data.

The Full Backup Cycle option enables you to specify the number of days between full backups. If you set this cycle to 7, for example, when you attempt to do a partial backup on the seventh day, a message appears explaining that you should be doing a full backup. You may set the cycle to any number of days between 0 and 999. You may set the Audible Prompts option to Off, Low, or High.

Other selections on the Backup Options screen are listed on the right half of the screen. If you select Proprietary Diskette Format, Norton uses a special technique of formatting the disk that is faster and stores more information about the file to disk than the normal DOS format. If you select Always Format Diskettes, the backup procedure formats each backup disk as information is written to the disk, even if the disk already has been formatted. This is a safety check to make sure that the disk does not contain any bad sectors, but it may slow down the backup process.

When you choose User Error Correction, Norton writes additional information to each disk that can be used by Norton to recover damaged disks, but it takes up more space on the disk. If you select Keep Old Backup Catalogs, Norton does not delete accumulated catalogs from previous backups. If you are overwriting old backup disks for a new backup, you probably do not want to keep the old catalogs.

The Quit After Backup option causes Norton Backup to return to the DOS prompt after it finishes a backup. You generally use this when you are running the backup from a batch process (see "Automating Norton Backup," later in this chapter).

Creating and Using Setup Files

You use setup files to capture all of the backup settings and selections you have made for a backup so that you will not have to repeat that process. You can give each setup selection a name so that you can choose the backup setup from the Setup File option on the Norton Advanced Backup menu. You may have a Weekend setup that backs up the entire disk, for example, which is what you want to do on Fridays. Another setup may be called Weekday, which is an incremental backup that you want to perform on Monday through Thursday.

To create a setup file, fill in the fields for the options described in the Advanced Backup menu: Backup To, Backup From, Backup Type, Options, and Select Files. Then, choose the Setup File option. A dialog box similar to the one in figure 11.21 appears. On this screen, name the setup file and enter a description containing up to 24 characters (press Tab or Shift-Tab to get to these fields, or point and click with a mouse). After you enter a new name and description for the setup, choose the Save option.

After you have several setup files defined, you can choose the Setup File option from the Advanced Backup menu and choose the kind of backup to perform. The current selection will be displayed on the Advanced Backup menu next to the Setup File option.

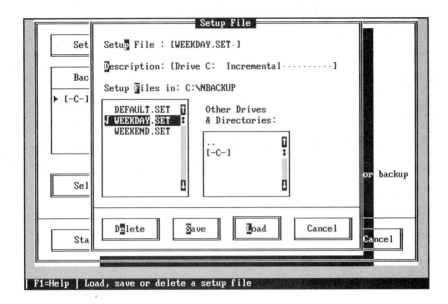

FIG. 11.21.

The Setup File dialog box.

If you are in charge of backups in an organization, you can make standard setup files and distribute them to the entire organization— to each person owning and using Norton Backup. This distribution would enable unsophisticated users to perform backups without having to understand all of the procedures for setting options and selecting files. Simply copy the SET and SLT files, which are created when you save a setup to each computer using Norton Backup. This makes that setup available on each person's computer. You also can include some backup automation to make the backup even more easy to perform. These techniques are discussed in "Automating Norton Backup," later in this chapter.

T I P

Using Advanced Restore Features

The Advanced Restore procedure is similar to the Basic Restore process (see "Restoring Backed-Up Files," earlier in this chapter), with the addition of a few options. These options include the Setup File option and different Restore options.

Using a setup file option in an advanced restore enables you to capture and then reuse the settings that you want to use in a restore operation. You create and select setup files by using the same process described in "Using Advanced Select Files Options." The Advanced Restore screen has a different set of restore options than the Basic Restore screen. The Advanced Restore Options screen is shown in figure 11.22. Some of these options are the same as on the Basic Restore screen. Those that are different are described here.

```
╔══════════════ Norton Advanced Restore ══════════════╗
║                    Restore Options                   ║
║                                                      ║
║  ┌────────────────────┐                              ║
║  │ Data Verification: │ Off          [ ] Restore Empty Dirs    ║
║  └────────────────────┘                              ║
║                                      [ ] Restore To Other Drive ║
║     ┌─────────────────┐                              ║
║     │ Restore Prompts:│ Off          [ ] Restore To Other Dir  ║
║     └─────────────────┘                              ║
║                                      [ ] Quit After Restore     ║
║       ┌────────────────┐                             ║
║       │ Overwrite Files:│ Older Files Only           ║
║       └────────────────┘                             ║
║        ┌──────────────┐                              ║
║        │ Archive Flag:│ Do not change                ║
║        └──────────────┘                              ║
║       ┌────────────────┐                             ║
║       │ Audible Prompts:│ Low                        ║
║       └────────────────┘                             ║
║                                  ┌──────┐  ┌────────┐ ║
║                                  │  OK  │  │ Cancel │ ║
║                                  └──────┘  └────────┘ ║
╚══════════════════════════════════════════════════════╝
 F1=Help │ Select how much verification to use
```

FIG. 11.22.

The Advanced
Restore options.

After you select the Data Verification option, a dialog box appears from which you can choose one of several methods of verification:

- *Off:* Provides no verification, but offers the fastest speed when restoring files.

- *Sample Only:* Verifies every eighth track of data.

- *Read Only:* Reads the data after it has been written.

- *Read and Compare:* Reads the data and compares it to the data on the backup diskette. Requires the most amount of time, but provides the highest amount of safety.

The Restore Prompts option, when on, causes the program to prompt you before it restores a new directory or creates a new file on the target drive. Using prompts can slow the restore process considerably, but they provide a greater amount of safety.

You can choose from three settings for the Overwrite Files option:

- *Never Overwrite Files:* Prevents the accidental overwriting of files already on disk. Choose this option if you do not want restored files to replace same-named files already on disk.

- *Always Overwrite:* Causes the restore to copy all files specified by the Restore selection, even if it overwrites a same-named file already on disk.

- *Overwrite Older Files:* Causes the restore to overwrite only files with a date that is older than the one from the backup files. The default setting is to overwrite older files only.

These options do not affect files being restored that do not have same-named files already on disk.

You can set the Archive Flag option to Do Not Change, Mark as Backed Up, or Marked as Not Backed Up. The archive flag is normally set to Do Not Change. This means that if a file to be restored sees the same file already on disk, it will not change its archive flag as a result of the restore. The Mark as Backed Up option turns off all archive flags on restored files, and the Mark as Not Backed Up option turns on the archive flag for all files restored. Usually, the default Do Not Change is the best, but there may be special circumstances—such as restoring to a new machine—when you want to have more control over the setting of the archive flag. Of course, you also can use the Norton Utilities FA command to set the archive flag (see Chapter 3).

You can set Audible Prompts to Off, Low, or High.

There are several other selections on the right side of the Restore Options screen. The Restore Empty Dirs option, if selected, enables the restore process to recreate empty directories that may have been backed up.

The Restore To Other Drive and Restore To Other Dir options enable you to redirect where the restored files will go. If you select one of these options, a dialog box appears where you can define the destination of the restore.

All other options and procedures on the Advanced Restore screen are the same as on the Basic Restore screen. To continue with the restore process, set all options according to your needs and choose the Begin Restore option from the Advanced Restore main menu.

Automating Norton Backup

If you always perform the same type of backup, using the same options, you can automate the backup procedure so that you can begin a backup with just a few keystrokes. You can automate the backup process by using macros or the DOS prompt command level options.

Using Macros To Capture and Replay Commands

You can think of a *macro* as a tape recorder—it records your keystrokes and plays them back again. You can use a macro to capture a series of keystrokes that choose certain backup or restore procedures. Then, when you want to repeat the same process later, you can replay the macro.

Before creating a macro, plan carefully which keystrokes you will need. Also, after you create a macro, test it before using it regularly. You cannot use the mouse when recording a macro. The macro you make will be associated with the setup file currently in use. Therefore, make sure that you first choose the correct setup file.

To begin the recording process, press F7. The message Recording appears at the lower left corner of the screen. As you progress through your keystrokes, you will be simulating a backup or restore—not actually performing one. Therefore, instead of pressing Enter and the space bar to select certain options, use the following simulation keys:

Press	To Simulate
Ctrl-Enter	Enter
Ins	On
Del	Off

When you select files to be included or excluded in a backup, use Ins to select and Del to deselect—not the space bar. Whenever you would press Enter, use Ctrl-Enter instead.

To stop recording, press F7 again. To play back your recording, press F8. Always check your macro before distributing it to other users. Because this macro is associated with a setup file, it will be available whenever you use that setup file. You even can begin a macro from the DOS prompt, as described in the next section.

You can use a macro to automate the backup procedure for a user who is uncomfortable dealing with these kinds of tasks. Record a backup session so that users can repeat the same backup with a batch file command, as described in the next section.

Using Batch Files To Automate Backup

Another method of automating the backup and restore process is by including commands on the DOS command line. To begin the NBACKUP program and automatically use the WEEKEND setup file, for example, enter the following command at the DOS prompt:

NBACKUP WEEKEND

If there is a macro associated with the WEEKEND setup file, you can cause the macro to begin by using the DOS command

NBACKUP @WEEKEND

You can enter these commands at the DOS prompt or as a line in a batch file. If you created a macro for the weekend backup process, therefore, you can create a batch file named WEEKEND.BAT, which contains commands such as these:

```
echo off
echo This is a batch file for Weekend backups
cd\nbackup
nbackup @weekend
cd\
echo ——————The backup is finished——————
```

Then, the user just enters the command

WEEKEND

at the DOS prompt to begin the backup process.

Chapter Summary

You can use Norton Backup at two levels of sophistication: basic and advanced. The basic backup procedures enable you to perform backups without having to be concerned about choosing many options. On the other hand, you also can use Norton Backup in advanced mode, which enables you to select from a wide variety of backup options. If you are setting up a controlled backup process for yourself or an organization, Norton Backup has features that enable you to automate the backup process so that you can perform sophisticated backups and restores with a minimum amount of user intervention.

Introduction to DOS

DOS, which stands for disk operating system, is a software program that manages the resources of your computer. On the IBM personal computer, this operating program is called PC DOS. IBM-compatible computers use a nearly equivalent DOS called MS-DOS, which stands for Microsoft DOS. Microsoft is the company that designed DOS for the IBM family of personal computers.

In everyday events—banking, filing, and checking your coat—items are stored and retrieved. Information is just one more thing that needs to be stored somewhere so that it can be retrieved later. Because the computer deals mainly with information, having a "manager" that puts information somewhere and then later retrieves it makes sense. On the computer, DOS is the manager, and you are the one that makes requests about what to do with the information stored on the computer.

For DOS to understand what you want it to do, you have to speak its language. This appendix introduces the basic concepts and commands—the language—of DOS. If you are a computer beginner, read this entire appendix before using the book, because the book frequently references DOS commands and concepts. If you are familiar with some parts of DOS, you may not need to read the entire appendix. Instead, you can study only the topics that you want to learn more about and those that will be helpful to you while using this book (and your computer). The topics covered in this appendix include the following:

- Learning how DOS works
- Reviewing commonly used DOS commands
- Managing a hard disk by using DOS commands
- Using batch and system files
- Using DOS to back up information on your hard disk
- Using DOS 5

Understanding How DOS Works

Before learning what specific tasks DOS can do, you must first understand how DOS works. Before you can do that, however, you must understand the concept of computer files. You can relate computer files to paper files that are used in the workplace. You undoubtedly are familiar with manila folders in a file cabinet. Each folder contains information about some person, item, contract, and so on. Computer files operate under the same idea. Like a physical file, a computer file contains information. This information may be your resume, your monthly budget, an economics report, or a software program. Rather than physical pieces of paper, you have electronically stored information on the disk.

Somehow, the computer needs to keep track of all the files on disk. Also, a facility is needed for making copies of files, erasing files, and performing other managerial functions concerning the resources of the computer. DOS manages these resources under the direction of you, the computer operator.

This appendix begins with a summary of the changes DOS has undergone since its inception. You then learn how DOS gets your computer going, how to name and use DOS files, and how to issue DOS commands.

Reviewing the Evolution of DOS

When the IBM PC was first introduced in October 1981, it operated under the PC DOS operating system, Version 1.0. Since that time, PC DOS has undergone several changes, and newer versions have been released. Because you are likely to find several versions in use in any business or university, knowing some of the differences among the various versions is helpful. Some earlier versions of PC DOS are not fully compatible with the newer versions.

The primary reason for continually changing DOS is so that it can support new storage devices introduced on new versions of the PC. Usually, these changes have to do with advancements in disk storage. When the PC was first introduced, it supported only single-sided diskettes—disks that stored information on only one side. When double-sided disks were introduced, a new version of DOS was required, and DOS Version 1.1 was released. Along with supporting new disk devices, new versions of DOS also have improved and changed some other features, such as support for new kinds of monitors and other peripherals.

The various changes in PC DOS are outlined in table A.1. Changes in DOS are typically considered upwardly compatible. That is, new versions of DOS usually are able to read information from disks created with old versions of DOS—but not always. A major change was made in DOS 2.0, for example, in the way information is stored on disk. The result is that a diskette formatted with DOS 2.0 cannot be read on a machine that uses DOS 1.1 or DOS 1.0. Also, because hard disks were first supported with Version 2.0 of DOS, the Norton Utilities programs covered in this book are based on the assumption that you are operating with DOS Version 2.0 or higher.

Booting Your Computer

The computer hardware by itself does not "know" how to do many tasks. What it can do is match patterns of 0s and 1s and use those patterns to follow commands that programmers have stored in the computer's memory. Because the computer knows so little, a way is needed to "teach" it quickly what to do. That teaching process occurs when the computer is booted.

Within the PC, a small amount of information always is present in the ROM (read-only memory). This memory contains the BIOS (basic input-output system) and some other diagnostic and language programs. This memory does not contain DOS.

Table A.1 Versions of PC DOS

Version	Primary Feature(s)
1.0	Supports single-sided diskettes (160K)
1.1	Supports double-sided diskettes (320K)
2.0	Supports hard disks and a subdirectory file structure (double-sided disks, now 360K)
2.1	Supports the half-height diskettes on the IBM PCjr
3.0	Supports the 1.2M floppy and other new functions of the IBM PC AT
3.1	Supports networking
3.2	Supports 720K 3 1/2-inch floppy diskettes, laptop computers, and networking
3.3	Supports 1.44M 3 1/2-inch floppy diskettes and the PS/2 series of computers
4.0	Features pull-down menus and supports drive use past the previous 32M limit
5.0	Supports 2.88M 3 1/2-inch floppy diskettes, provides better memory management, and adds some data recovery features

How then, can the computer operate? When you turn on the computer, it has only the most primitive instructions. The computer knows enough, however, to look for DOS on a disk in the disk drive. The computer "pulls itself" to life by reading its instructions from the DOS program on disk. In computer jargon, loading DOS into memory is called *booting* the machine, which comes from the old saying *pulling yourself up by your own bootstraps*. This booting process occurs whenever you turn on the computer.

After you load DOS into memory from your diskette or hard disk, the computer can perform many management functions. Most of these functions are ways of accessing and manipulating information on disk.

At times, you may need to reboot the computer. A program bug, for example, may cause the computer to freeze, so that it will not respond to program commands anymore. Your only chance for recovery may be to reboot. One obvious way to reboot is to turn off the machine and then turn it back on. This process is called a *cold boot*. Electronic equipment, however, is particularly sensitive to being turned on and off. The computer's electronics stabilize when the power is turned on.

Many times, if an electronic component is going to fail, it does so after you first turn it on—when it gets the initial burst of power.

Because of this danger of failure, the system gives you a built-in way to restart the computer without turning off the power. This method of rebooting is called a *warm boot*. To perform a warm boot, hold down the Ctrl and Alt keys and press Del. Hold down all three keys for a second, let up on all keys, and the computer reboots. Some computers have restart buttons that also perform warm boots. Using Norton Utilities, you can enter the command BE REBOOT to cause the computer to perform a warm boot.

After you boot your computer properly, you are ready to store and use information.

Naming and Using DOS Files

As mentioned previously, files stored on a computer are like manila folders stored in a file cabinet. Some identifying name usually is written on each folder's tab. If the folder contains the budget for May 1991, for example, the tab may say *BUDGET MAY 91*. If the folder contains a copy of the annual report, the tab may say *ANNUAL REPORT*. The name on the tab gives a short description of the contents of the file.

Also, you usually do not place folders in file drawers at random. All the Budget files may be in one drawer and all the Report files may be in another drawer. In fact, you may reserve an entire file cabinet for reports, while another cabinet may contain only financial information. You should name and organize files on the computer in the same way.

Specifying File Names

Just like the name tab on a paper folder, each computer file has a name (called a *file name*). A file name should briefly describe the contents of the file. Your resume may be named RESUME, for example, and the May 1991 budget may be named BUDMAY91. When you create related files, select names that are similar. If you are writing a three-part paper, for example, you may want to create three separate files named PART1, PART2, and PART3. If you are collecting monthly data, you may want to name the files containing the information MAY91, JUNE91, and JULY91.

Although you usually create files from applications rather than from DOS, the file names you use must obey DOS guidelines. A DOS file name can contain up to eight characters, including all letters (upper- and lowercase) and numbers, but it cannot contain spaces or the following punctuation marks:

. ' \ / [ ] : | < > + = ; * ? ,

Some programs enable you to use a space in a file name, but not on the DOS level, so you should avoid using spaces.

Using File Extensions

In the case of computer files, the name includes a second part, called the *extension*, which you can use to specify the type of file—whether it is a word processing file, a database file, a letter, or a budget. You can include up to three characters in the extension, which you separate from the file name by a period (.). You can name the resume file you create with the WordPerfect word processor RESUME.WP, for example, or you can name the letter you write concerning a certain project PROJECT.LET. This extended form of the name is called the *file specification*, or *filespec* for short. You also may include a drive name in your file specification such as drive C or drive A—for example, C:MYFILE.DOC or C:\MYFILE.DOC.

DOS and other software programs commonly follow certain conventions in the use of file extensions, because extensions often tell the computer what kind of information is in the computer file. Files on disk that contain DOS commands usually end with the extension COM. BASIC language programs end with the extension BAS. Application programs also use certain extensions. Lotus 1-2-3 files, for example, may end in WKS or WK1. Table A.2 lists some of the common extensions. You need to be aware of the extensions that DOS uses so that you can choose your own extensions without conflicting with these predefined extensions.

Using Global File Characters

One major reason for selecting similar names for related files is that you then have the ability to manipulate those files simultaneously as a group. If the files are named similarly, DOS (and Norton) commands enable you to refer to more than one file by using wild cards or global file characters. These global file characters are the asterisk (*) and the question mark (?). Like a wild card in a poker game, you can substitute the * and ? for any characters—the asterisk for any number of characters, and the question mark for any one character.

Table A.2 Common Extensions

Extension	Use
BAS	BASIC language program
BAT	Batch command file (a type of DOS file)
BMT	Norton batch-to-memory file
COM	Command program (DOS command)
DBF	dBASE database file
EXE	Executable program (software)
PRN	Lotus print-to-disk file
SYS	File containing system information
TXT	Text file (standard ASCII)
WKS	Lotus 1-2-3 spreadsheet file

If you want to copy all your data files from one disk to another, for example, you must tell DOS which files to copy. Suppose that your files are named JAN, FEB, MAR, and so on, through DEC. To copy all 12 of these files would require 12 commands, each specifying one file to copy. If you named the files JAN.DAT, FEB.DAT, MAR.DAT, and so on through DEC.DAT, however, you could copy all the files by using the single file specification *.DAT. This specifies files with the extension DAT, regardless of the file name. In this case, you are using the DAT extension to remind the user that these files contain data.

Because the ? wild card replaces only one character, the specification ???.DAT substitutes for up to three characters in a file name. This file specification selects J.DAT, JA.DAT, and JAN.DAT, but not JANU.DAT or JANUARY.DAT. The wild card specification *.* matches all files—all file names and all extensions. This appendix gives you specific examples of using wild cards as it introduces DOS commands. Wild cards also are used extensively in Norton commands. Norton's NDOS provides more flexible use of wild cards. See Chapter 8, "Using NDOS," for more information.

Issuing DOS Commands

DOS, in the form of PC DOS and MS-DOS—the common disk operating systems for the IBM and compatible family of computers—is similar to a language. DOS performs management functions on the PC, but not until you instruct it to do so. You, the user, are the one who typically gives those instructions in the form of a DOS command. A DOS command usually is a word (often a verb) that tells DOS what you want it to do. Sometimes the command is followed by one or more words that clarify which task the command is to perform. These words, or *parameters*, are called *options* or *switches*.

The command CLS (Clear Screen), for example, tells DOS to blank out the screen. The CLS command requires no other parameters. On the other hand, the command COPY requires that you also specify what to copy. Therefore, you must include additional information in the command.

When the DOS prompt is visible on the computer screen, the operating system is waiting for you to type a DOS command or the name of an executable program. The DOS prompt usually is a letter (A, B, C, and so on) followed by the > symbol. The following prompt, for example, means that DOS is waiting for instructions and that drive A is the logged-on drive or the default drive:

    A>

If DOS needs to look on disk for some information, it automatically looks on the default drive unless you direct the system to look elsewhere. If you are using a hard disk system, the default drive is usually C, and the prompt is

    C>

This prompt specifies that you are logged onto drive C. To change drives, type the drive letter followed by a colon and then press Enter.

DOS consists of a number of commands, which are categorized into two types: *internal* and *external* commands. Internal DOS commands are copied into the computer's memory when DOS is loaded as you boot the computer. These commands stay in memory until you turn off the computer, and you may use the commands whenever the DOS prompt appears on-screen. Internal commands covered in this appendix include ATTRIB, CD, CLS, COPY, DEL, DIR, ERASE, FIND, MD, PATH, PROMPT, RD, RENAME, and TYPE.

If you stored every DOS command in memory, however, not enough memory would be left for application programs. Some DOS commands, therefore, are not copied onto the computer's memory at boot time but are stored on disk in a file until they are needed. These external DOS commands on disk usually are identified by the COM extension. The FORMAT command, for example, is stored on the DOS diskette as the file FORMAT.COM. If you use an external command, it must be available on disk. After you enter the FORMAT command, for example, DOS looks on the default (logged-on) disk to find the file FORMAT.COM. If the file is not found, the following message appears on-screen:

```
Bad command or file name
```

This error message tells you that the command you requested was not found on disk. External commands covered in this appendix include BACKUP, CHKDSK, DISKCOPY, FORMAT, PRINT, RECOVER, RESTORE, and TREE. See "Working with Directory Path Names," later in this appendix, to learn how to access external DOS commands.

Norton commands are much like DOS external commands. Each command constitutes a program that resides on disk until you enter the command name at the DOS prompt. Then the program is entered into memory and run.

To enter a DOS command, type it at the DOS prompt and press Enter. To use the DIR command to display a list of the files located in the default directory, for example, type

DIR

and press Enter. To command DOS to display a directory of a disk other than the default disk, you must add more information to the DIR command. To display a directory of the files on the diskette in drive A, for example, use this command:

DIR A:

Reviewing Commonly Used DOS Commands

Although dozens of DOS commands are available, this introduction to DOS is limited to the commonly used commands that you refer to or may need in order to understand the information in this book. This appendix covers selected options and switches for each command. For a more complete list of command parameters, consult your DOS manual or *Using MS-DOS 5* (published by Que).

NOTE In the syntax descriptions of the DOS commands, items enclosed in [brackets] are options. Items that appear in *italics* are command variables. You should replace the *filespec* variable with a real file specification when you enter the command at the DOS prompt.

ATTRIB

The ATTRIB command lists or sets the *read-only* and *archive attributes* of files. You cannot write to, change, or erase a file that is read-only. The read-only attribute protects the file from accidental or unauthorized change. The archive attribute indicates whether the file has been backed up. The archive attribute is used for some backup procedures. The ATTRIB command is available on DOS Version 3.0 or higher. The syntax of the command is

ATTRIB [+/–R][+/–A]*filespec*[/S]

A +R sets the file or files indicated in the *filespec* to read-only. A –R turns off the read-only attribute. A +A sets files to archive (archive is set to On), and a –A turns off the archive attribute. When you back up a file by using a backup procedure, the archive attribute setting is switched off, indicating to the system that the file has been backed up.

If you use the /S switch, the files in all subdirectories that match the *filespec* also are affected. If you do not use the +/–R or +/–A option, ATTRIB lists file names that match the *filespec* and reports the current archive and read-only settings for those files. Norton's NDOS provides an ATTRIB command with additional features beyond the DOS ATTRIB command (see Chapter 8 for more information).

CHKDSK

The CHKDSK command enables you to examine a diskette or hard disk to determine how much space is being used and whether the disk has any problems. CHKDSK, for example, may detect such problems as lost clusters in files on disk. CHKDSK summarizes the amount of available memory on disk and also reports the amount of RAM available to the computer. CHKDSK is an external DOS command, and uses this syntax:

CHKDSK [*d:*][/F]

where *d:* specifies the diskette or hard disk to check. To check the disk in drive B, for example, use this command:

CHKDSK B:

The /F switch tells CHKDSK to attempt to fix any problems found with the file allocation table. If you do not use the /F switch, CHKDSK still tells you how much space would be fixed if the /F switch had been used, but it does not fix the problems. A better approach than using

CHKDSK is to use the Norton Disk Doctor (NDD) to find and solve these kinds of disk problems. For more information on NDD, see Chapter 4.

CLS

The CLS command clears the screen. No options or switches are available. The syntax is simply

    CLS

Norton's NDOS provides a CLS command with additional features beyond the DOS CLS command (see Chapter 8 for more information).

COPY

The COPY command is one of the most powerful and frequently used DOS commands. COPY copies one or more files to another disk or to the same disk under a new name. The syntax is

    COPY [*d:*]*filespec* [*d:*][*filespec*]

A more easily remembered syntax is

    COPY *source destination*

To copy the file named REPORT.TXT from the current default disk (A) to disk C, for example, use this command:

    COPY REPORT.TXT C:REPORT.TXT

The source in this command is the file REPORT.TXT, and the destination is C:REPORT.TXT. Note that you do not have to specify a drive letter if the file is on the default drive. Also, you can omit the name of the destination file if it is the same as the source file. Therefore, the following command from the A> prompt performs the same copy performed by the preceding command:

    COPY REPORT.TXT C:

The source file does not have to be on the default drive. You can copy files located on a drive other than the default to another drive simply by including the drive specification in both the source and destination file names. You also can change the name of a file during a copy.

Suppose that the default drive is C and you want to copy a file from drive A to drive B and rename the file at the same time. Use this command:

COPY A:REPORT.TXT B:RPT.TXT

Another way to use the COPY command is to copy a file on the same disk to a different file name. To make a duplicate copy of the file REPORT.TXT and call the duplicate copy REPORT.DUP, for example, you can use this command:

COPY REPORT.TXT REPORT.DUP

Attempting to copy a file to itself results in an error. The following command produces an error message:

COPY REPORT.TXT REPORT.TXT

You also can copy multiple files simultaneously, using the global file characters. To copy all your DAT files from the default drive C to drive A, for example, use this command:

COPY *.DAT A:

Norton's NDOS provides a COPY command with additional features beyond the DOS COPY command (see Chapter 8).

DIR

The DIR command displays names of files on disk, file sizes, and dates and times the files were created. The syntax of the DIR command is

DIR [*d:*][*filespec*] [/P][/W]

The minimum version of the command is

DIR

The DIR command gives you a list of all the files contained on the default drive.

To list files located on another drive, specify the drive letter. To obtain a listing of files on drive B, for example, use this command:

DIR B:

If you include a file specification in the command, DIR lists only those files that match the specification. To view a directory of only the files with DAT extensions, for example, use this command:

    DIR *.DAT

To list all files beginning with the letter R, type

    DIR R*.*

The switches in the DIR command are /P and /W. The /P switch instructs DOS to pause after a screenful of file names is displayed. If more than 22 file names are contained in a directory, the names usually scroll off screen during a directory listing. With the /P switch, the first 22 files are listed, and the following message appears at the bottom of the screen:

    Strike a key when ready...

After you press a key, the next 22 files are displayed. This process continues until all files are listed.

The /W switch stands for *wide listing*. In this version of the list, only the file names appear, with several file names listed on each line. This format enables you to display more file names on one screen.

You can combine the DIR command's options and switches. The following command, for example, lists all the files on drive B with a DAT extension, in wide format:

    DIR B:*.DAT /W

Norton's NDOS provides a DIR command with additional features beyond the DOS DIR command (see Chapter 8).

DISKCOPY

Many times you may want to make an exact copy of a diskette. In fact, when you get new software, you always should copy all the original disks and then use copies rather than originals in your work. You use the DISKCOPY command to copy the contents of an entire diskette from one disk to another of equal size. The syntax is

    DISKCOPY *d1: d2:*

where *d1:* is the source diskette and *d2:* is the destination diskette. To copy the disk in drive A to the disk in drive B, for example, use the command

DISKCOPY A: B:

If the destination disk is not formatted, the DISKCOPY procedure formats the disk. DISKCOPY makes an exact copy of a diskette. Therefore, if the source or destination diskette contains any bad sectors, the DISKCOPY procedure may not work. Also, both source and destination diskettes must be of the same size. You cannot use the DISKCOPY command to copy from the hard disk to a floppy, for example, because the hard disk is a different size than the floppy diskette.

If you are using a system with only one floppy disk drive, you still can perform a DISKCOPY procedure. From the A> prompt, use this command:

DISKCOPY A: B:

DOS prompts you to insert the source diskette into the drive; then the system prompts you to place the destination diskette in the drive. You may have to swap diskettes several times during each DISKCOPY procedure.

ERASE and DEL

The ERASE and DEL commands remove files from the disk. These commands are identical and use the same syntax:

ERASE [*d:*][*filespec*]

or

DEL [*d:*][*filespec*]

Paying attention to what is on your disk and how much space you have used is essential. A common problem when using a computer is running out of space on disk. The ERASE and DEL commands are available to remove unneeded files from disk and to free up that space for use by other files. You can use these commands, like most DOS commands, on a single file or on multiple files, using the global file characters. To erase the single file named REQUEST.LET, for example, type

ERASE REQUEST.LET

or

    DEL REQUEST.LET

To erase all files with the extension DAT, use

    ERASE *.DAT

To erase all files, use

    ERASE *.*

After you enter the ERASE command, DOS prompts you with the question

    Are you sure (Y/N)?

DOS is offering you a chance to change your mind before it erases everything on your disk. Press Y and Enter to continue with the erase, or press N and Enter to cancel the procedure.

WARNING: Be very sure that you know what you are doing when you enter the ERASE command. Check to make sure that you are logged on to the correct disk drive and directory. (If you accidentally erase a file, however, you may be able to recover it with the Norton Quick UnErase command. See Chapter 4 for more information.)

Norton's NDOS provides ERASE and DEL commands with additional features beyond the DOS ERASE and DEL commands. See Chapter 8 for more information.

FDISK

The FDISK command prepares your hard disk (fixed disk) to be formatted. Usually you need to execute this command only once—when you first get a new computer. Occasionally, you may need to start over by using the FDISK command again. The FDISK command begins a program that prompts you with questions about how you want to set up your hard disk.

> **WARNING:** If you use FDISK on a hard disk, all information on that disk may be lost. Use FDISK only when you are sure you want to start from scratch on the disk. Refer to your DOS manual for details. If you are not an experienced user, do not use FDISK until you verify with an experienced user that it is the correct command to use.

FIND

The FIND command (also called a *filter*) searches for a string of characters within a file or files and lists each line in the file that contains text matching the string. The FIND command can help you look for a file that contains particular information. The syntax of the FIND command is

FIND *string* [*filespec*] [*filespec*] [*filespec*]...

To determine whether the string *1990 REPORT* is in the files REPORT.1, REPORT.2, and REPORT.3, for example, use this command:

FIND "1990 REPORT" REPORT.1 REPORT.2 REPORT.3

The results of a find may look like this:

```
---------REPORT.1
---------REPORT.2
THE 1990 REPORT ON SILVER PRICES
---------REPORT.3
```

In this example, the phrase *1990 REPORT* was found only in the file named REPORT.2. The line that contains the phrase is listed below the name of the file being searched. The other files had no finds associated with them.

The Norton's Text Search (TS) and FileFind commands are a powerful alternative to the DOS FIND command. See Chapter 6 for more information.

FORMAT

The FORMAT command prepares diskettes (and hard disks) for use. After you purchase diskettes, you cannot simply put them into the disk drive and use them. You first must format them. Formatting specifies how information is to be stored on disk. The FORMAT procedure also analyzes the entire disk for any defective tracks and prepares the disk to accept DOS files. The syntax of the FORMAT command is

FORMAT [*d:*][/*switches*]

Suppose that you are using a computer with a hard disk drive and you are logged on to drive C. The simplest command to format a new diskette in drive A is

FORMAT A:

After you enter the FORMAT command, DOS responds with the message

```
Insert new diskette for drive A:
and strike ENTER when ready:
```

This prompt gives you a chance to back out of the command if you discover that you do not want to format that diskette. If you want to cancel the command at this point, press Ctrl-Break.

WARNING: You can destroy all information on a diskette or hard disk drive by using the FORMAT command incorrectly. If you do not enter the name of the drive to format, for example, the FORMAT command uses the default drive. Thus, if you enter the following command from the C> prompt, DOS assumes that you want to format the hard disk drive C:

FORMAT

Be careful not to do this (unless you want to erase everything on your hard disk)!

The FORMAT command has a number of switches. Only the two most common ones—/V and /S—are described here. The /V switch enables you to give a *volume name* (the name, or label, of the disk displayed in a DIR command output) to the disk being formatted. To format a disk on drive A and give it a volume label, use this command:

FORMAT A:/V

DOS prompts you with the message

```
Volume label (11 characters, ENTER for none)?
```

You then can type your volume name at the prompt (you can use up to 11 characters). You may want to name your diskettes as a way of uniquely identifying them.

The /S switch causes the FORMAT procedure to create a system disk—one that contains the files necessary to boot the computer. To format the disk in drive A with a label and the system files, type

FORMAT A:/S/V

The Norton Safe Format (SFORMAT) command is a safer, faster alternative to the DOS FORMAT command. Also, the Norton UnFormat command enables you to unformat a formatted hard disk, with some restrictions. For more information, see Chapters 3 and 4. DOS Version 5.0 also contains an UNFORMAT command. Also beginning with DOS 5.0, the DOS format of a floppy disk is similar to the Norton Safe Format in that it is possible to unformat the disk. If you are using a DOS version prior to DOS 5.0, it is impossible to recover a formatted floppy disk formatted with the DOS version of FORMAT.

PRINT

The PRINT command enables you to print the contents of a text file to the printer. The syntax is

PRINT [*d:*]*filespec* [/T]

To print a file in drive B called EXAMPLE.TXT to the line printer, for example, enter the command

PRINT B:EXAMPLE.TXT

The computer responds with the prompt

```
Name of list device(PRN):
```

Press Enter to print the file to the standard print device (PRN=Printer), or enter another device name such as LPT1 or LPT2 (parallel ports), or COM1 or COM2 (serial ports).

You can queue several files to print at once by entering several PRINT commands; DOS remembers each of the files and prints them in the order of the PRINT commands. If you decide that you want to stop the print job, reenter the command with the /T switch. To terminate the current print job, for example, enter the command

PRINT /T

This command terminates all print jobs in the print queue. A cancellation message is displayed, the page in the printer is advanced to the top of the form, and the printer's buzzer sounds. See Chapter 7 for a description of the Norton Line Print (LP) command.

RECOVER

The RECOVER command recovers files that have been damaged in some way. You can misuse this command easily, so you should consider using the Disk Tools command instead. For more information, see Chapter 4.

RENAME and REN

The RENAME (or REN) command changes the name of a file on disk. Suppose that you save a file named REPORT with your word processor, but you misspell the file name by typing *repotr*. When you are back in DOS, the easiest way to correct the problem is with the RENAME command. The syntax of the RENAME command is

RENAME [*d:*]*filespec1 filespec2*

Notice that the command REN is an acceptable abbreviation of the RENAME command. Basically, the RENAME command has the following form:

RENAME *oldname newname*

where *oldname* is the current name of a file, and *newname* is the name you want the file to have. You must include a space between the oldname and newname specifications. To rename the file REQUEST.LET as REQUEST.TXT, for example, use this command:

RENAME REQUEST.LET REQUEST.TXT

You can use wild-card characters to rename a group of related files. To rename the files JAN.DAT, FEB.DAT, and so on, through DEC.DAT on drive A to the new names JAN.OLD, FEB.OLD, and so on, through DEC.OLD, use this command from the A> prompt:

RENAME *.DAT *.OLD

You cannot rename a file to a file name that currently exists on that disk. If you try this, you see the error message

```
Duplicate file name
```

or

```
File not found
```

Also, note that RENAME is not a COPY command, which means that you cannot rename a file from one disk drive to another. The following command, for example, does not work:

RENAME A:REQUEST.LET B:REQUEST.LET

If you attempt to use this command, the error message

```
Invalid parameter
```

appears. Norton's NDOS provides RENAME and REN commands with additional features beyond the DOS RENAME and REN commands. See Chapter 8 for more information.

SYS

The SYS command transfers system files from a bootable disk to another disk. The syntax of the SYS command is

SYS *d:*

where *d:* is the drive name of the disk where you want to place the system files.

The SYS command does not transfer the file COMMAND.COM to the destination disk. You can use the regular COPY command to copy the COMMAND.COM file to the disk. See the FORMAT/S command in the "FORMAT" section, earlier in this chapter, for more information.

The system files are hidden files. You cannot access them by using the normal COPY command, nor do they appear when you issue a DIR command. You must place the system files at a certain spot on disk, so unless you formatted a disk using the /B switch, SYS cannot transfer a copy of the system files to the disk. The Norton Disk Doctor's Disk Tools' Make a Disk Bootable option, however, enables you to transfer system files to a disk that has not been prepared to accept them.

TYPE

The TYPE command prints the contents of a file to the screen. The syntax of the TYPE command is

TYPE [*d:*]*filespec*

To display the contents of the EXAMPLE.TXT file located on drive B, for example, use the command

TYPE B:EXAMPLE.TXT

The file to be printed should be a text file. If you attempt to use TYPE to print the contents of a file that is not an ASCII file, the result probably will be a series of meaningless characters on-screen.

Norton's NDOS provides a TYPE command with additional features beyond the DOS TYPE command (see Chapter 8).

Managing Your Hard Disk

Most microcomputers being sold today include a hard disk storage device. A *hard disk* (also called a *fixed disk*) is a permanent disk that usually is housed in the computer and is capable of storing many times the amount of information that a single floppy diskette can hold. The size of most hard disks is measured in megabytes (M), or millions of bytes. A 30M hard disk can store 30 million characters of information.

Using a computer with a hard disk creates several challenges. The fact that a hard disk can store more information can be an advantage as well as a disadvantage. A hard disk relieves you from having to keep up with a mile-high stack of floppy diskettes, but it requires more planned organization. Managing more than 1,000 files stored on a hard disk can be a huge task. When you enter a DIR command, the information could take several minutes to scroll by.

You can solve this dilemma by dividing the hard disk into several directories, each of which contains related information. One directory may contain all DOS files. Another directory may contain word processing files. Yet another directory may contain database files. Each directory functions almost like a separate diskette.

DOS has a particular way to set up directories. When you format a disk (including a floppy diskette), the format procedure automatically creates one directory, called the *root directory*. You can create other directories to branch off the root, thus building a directory tree. You must choose which directories to create, and you must develop the philosophy behind the structure. Figure A.1 shows one possible directory tree. This tree is organized by task. The top directory is the original or root directory. Branching off are directories (or subdirectories) that contain the task-oriented partitions of DOS, Word Processing, Database, and Spreadsheet.

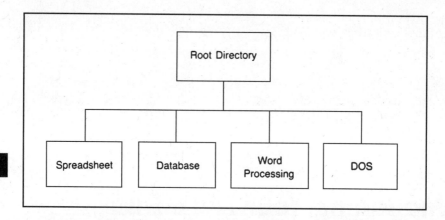

FIG. A.1.

A directory
structure.

Creating directories according to a planned directory tree can be helpful and can make your work more efficient. You can move from branch to branch according to the tasks you want to complete. If you are doing word processing, for example, you can move to the word processing directory, which gives you access to all your word processing files. Working from this directory also separates you from the unrelated files in other directories. If you are in the word processing directory and enter the command DIR, for example, you get a list of files in that directory only.

How do you create a directory? How do you move from one directory to another? How do you get rid of a directory? These questions are answered by a series of DOS commands, which enable you to create, use, and remove directories as needed:

Command Name	Abbreviation	Effect
MKDIR	MD	Makes a directory
CHDIR	CD	Changes directories
RMDIR	RD	Removes a directory

Before learning how to use the DOS commands to manage your hard disk, you should understand how the names of the directories are related to file specifications. You can use the Norton Utilities and Norton Commander NCD (Norton Change Directory) program instead of the DOS commands. This program provides a graphic interface to make creating, changing, and removing directories more intuitive. It also has additional capabilities, such as renaming directories.

Working with Directory Path Names

Each directory has a name. The root directory always is designated as the \ directory, but you assign your own names to the directories you create to branch off the root directory. A directory name can include up to eight characters (see "Specifying Files Names," earlier in this appendix, for more information on restrictions that apply to file names).

When referring to a directory name, most people use the entire path name. A directory's path name describes the path DOS can take through the directory tree structure to find the directory. The WP directory branching off the root directory usually is referred to as \WP. The directory named LETTERS branching off the WP directory is specified by the path name \WP\LETTERS. Thus, a backslash (\ ) is used for two purposes:

- The first backslash (\ ) specifies the root directory.

- A backslash (\ ) also separates the names of subdirectories.

A directory path becomes a part of the file specification of any file in that directory. The path appears between the drive specification and the file name and always contains a beginning and an ending backslash. In general, a complete file specification consists of the following:

   d:\path\filename.ext

which represents a drive name, a path, a file name, a period, and an extension.

The complete file specification for a file named MYFILE.TXT on drive C in the \WP directory, for example, would be

   C:\WP\MYFILE.TXT

Norton's NCD command provides additional features beyond the DOS MD, CD, and RD commands. See Chapter 6 for more information.

Creating New Directories

You use the DOS MKDIR command, often abbreviated as MD, to make a new directory. The syntax of the command is

MD *path*

or

MKDIR *path*

The following command creates a directory named \WP on drive C:

MD \WP

The new \WP directory branches directly off the root directory. To make a directory named LETTERS that branches off \WP, use this command:

MD \WP\LETTERS

Changing Directories

Every hard disk has one or more directories, beginning with the root directory. The CHDIR command (or CD, in its abbreviated form) changes from the current directory to another directory on the same disk drive. While in a particular directory, you can enter commands such as DIR or RENAME that apply only to the files in the current directory. The syntax of the CD command is

CD *path*

or

CHDIR *path*

To change to the directory named \WP, enter the command

CD \WP

To go back to your root directory, enter the command

CD \

Using the CD command, you can move from any directory to any other directory by entering the command and the complete path of the directory to which you want to change.

Another version of the CD command is

CD..

This command takes you to the next directory up in the tree structure. Suppose that you are in the directory \WP\LETTERS. Typing *cd..* will change you to the \WP directory.

Removing Empty Directories

Sometimes you need to remove a directory from the hard disk to make room for other, more important files. You use the RMDIR (RD) command for that purpose. You cannot remove a directory that contains any user files, however, so you must erase or move all files in the directory first. The syntax of the Remove Directory command is

RD *path*

or

RMDIR *path*

To remove the directory named \MYDIR, for example, use this command:

RD \MYDIR

Listing Directories

When your hard disk contains a number of directories, you may want to view a list of which directories are available. The DOS command to perform that task is TREE. The TREE command displays a listing of all the directories on the specified drive. The syntax is

TREE [*d:*]

To see which directories are on your entire disk, enter the command

TREE

Beginning with DOS Version 4.0, the TREE command creates a graphic display of directory names, making it easier for you to see the structure and paths.

Giving Paths to Programs

At this point, you are undoubtedly familiar with the concept of the path as part of a file specification. PATH also is a DOS command. The PATH command tells DOS where to look for programs that are not in the current directory. Many application programs require you to know how to create or modify a PATH command. The syntax for the PATH command is

PATH [*path*];[*path*];[*path*]...

The TREE command, for example, requires that the file TREE.COM be on disk. Under normal circumstances, if you enter TREE in the \\WP directory, you get the message

```
Bad command or file name
```

because the TREE.COM command file is not in the \\WP directory and DOS cannot find and execute the command. To avoid having to keep copies of all programs in all directories or always typing full path names, you can tell the computer where to find programs when they are requested in a directory in which they do not reside. This function is the responsibility of the PATH command.

The PATH command gives the computer a priority list of directories for searching for executable program files. The PATH command causes DOS to search for only three kinds of executable files: COM (command), EXE (program), and BAT (batch) files.

A common directory setup includes a directory named \\DOS. The \\DOS directory generally contains all the DOS files, including all external DOS commands. You also may have a \\NORTON directory that contains all the Norton commands. The PATH command

PATH C:\\;C:\\DOS;C:\\NORTON

tells DOS that if a command is given in any directory and the command is not found in that directory, DOS should look first in the root directory (specified in the PATH command as C:\\). If the command is not found there, DOS should look in the next directory listed in the PATH command—the C:\\DOS directory. Finally, if the command still has not been found, DOS should look in the C:\\NORTON directory. When the command TREE is given in the \\WP directory, therefore, the command file TREE.COM is found in the \\DOS directory, and the command is successful. Notice that each directory name in the PATH command is separated from the preceding directory name by a semicolon (;).

When a PATH command is given, it remains in effect until you reboot the computer or turn it off. Therefore, you usually enter the command only once each time you boot the computer. As you learn in this appendix's description of the AUTOEXEC.BAT file, you can automate the entry of the PATH command.

Controlling the DOS Prompt

When switching from directory to directory, you often may have difficulty keeping track of which directory you are in. One way to solve this problem is to customize the DOS prompt, which is normally C> on a hard disk, by using the PROMPT command. The syntax of this command is

   PROMPT [*prompt commands*]

The various prompt commands are listed in table A.3. Each command must be preceded by a dollar sign ($). Any text following the PROMPT command that is not preceded by a $ is displayed literally.

Table A.3 PROMPT $ Commands

Command	Displays
_ (underscore)	Carriage return, line feed
B	|
D	The system date
E	The Escape character
G	>
H	The Backspace character
L	<
N	The default drive letter
P	The current path
Q	=
T	The system time
V	The version of DOS

Entering the DOS command

PROMPT PG

causes the DOS prompt to include the path as a part of the prompt. The $P is the prompt command for the path, and the $G is the prompt command for the greater than sign. Thus, the prompt (while you are in the root directory) becomes

C:\>

The \ between the C: and the > tells you that you are in the root directory. If you enter the command CD \DOS, the prompt becomes

C:\DOS>

This prompt indicates that you are in the DOS directory.

The PROMPT command offers a variety of ways to customize the DOS prompt. You can display any text by including it in the PROMPT command without a preceding $. You can use a command like this to display a unique prompt:

PROMPT This computer belongs to Bill!$_$P$G

The text *This computer belongs to Bill!* is output literally. The $_ command (a dollar sign and an underscore) tells PROMPT to perform a carriage return and a line feed, which means that the cursor moves to the next line. On the next line is the prompt specified by the PG prompt commands. Thus, when you are logged on to the root directory, this prompt appears:

```
This Computer Belongs to Bill!
C:\>
```

Norton's NDOS provides a PROMPT command with additional features beyond the DOS PROMPT command. See Chapter 8 for more information.

Using Batch and System Files

A BAT file extension indicates that a file is a batch file—a file containing several DOS commands that you want to execute in a particular order. A system file often is designated by the SYS extension. A common system file that you need to know about is CONFIG.SYS, which tells the computer certain information about how to operate.

Creating Batch Files

If you have a series of DOS commands that you perform repetitively, you can create a file that contains those commands and have DOS execute all the commands in sequence. Suppose that you often use these two commands:

    CLS
    DIR/W

These commands clear the screen and perform a directory command in wide mode. You can place these two commands in a file, such as one named WIDE.BAT. Then, rather than remembering exactly how to type these commands each time you need them, you can type the batch file command *wide*. With this command, you tell DOS to execute the two commands contained in the batch file WIDE.BAT.

You have several ways to create this kind of file. The most common method is to use a file editor. A simple file editor named EDLIN is included as a part of DOS. Most word processing programs also have the capability to create batch files. DOS 5.0 contains an editor named EDIT that is a full-screen editor with mouse support.

An optional way to create a batch file without using a text editor follows:

1. Enter the following command, which tells DOS that you will be entering (copying) information from the CONSOLE and that the information is to be placed in the file named WIDE.BAT:

       COPY CON WIDE.BAT

2. Enter the commands that you want to include in the batch file. You may want to enter these commands, for example:

       CLS
       DIR/W

   Note that you see no DOS prompt.

3. End this procedure by pressing the F6 function key or Ctrl-Z. The lines you typed now are stored in the file called WIDE.BAT.

Creating an AUTOEXEC.BAT File

DOS looks for a special batch file called AUTOEXEC.BAT each time you boot the computer. If you want a series of commands to execute each time you boot the computer, you should place them in the AUTOEXEC.BAT file. If you always want the PATH and PROMPT commands to be activated when the computer is booted, for example, you can create an AUTOEXEC.BAT file containing these commands in the same way you created the WIDE.BAT file earlier. Then, whenever you boot your computer, your path is set up, and your prompt is customized automatically. These two commands frequently are included in the AUTOEXEC.BAT file.

Creating a CONFIG.SYS File

Another file that DOS looks for each time you boot the computer is CONFIG.SYS. Like the AUTOEXEC.BAT file, CONFIG.SYS is not a required file. If you do have a CONFIG.SYS file in your root directory, however, DOS looks in the file to see how you want the computer configured. You rarely have to decide for yourself what goes into the CONFIG.SYS file, because the software you install usually has instructions about its requirements for the file. DOS, for example, usually enables software to communicate with eight files at once on disk. This number sounds like a great many files, but some complicated programs such as dBASE III need more access to the disk than what DOS usually provides. Therefore, the dBASE III installation manual tells you to place the following lines in your CONFIG.SYS file:

    FILES = 20
    BUFFERS = 15

These commands allow more files and more disk buffers (*reserved portions of RAM that temporarily hold data that is to be written to disk*) than would usually be available. These lines are the two most common settings in the CONFIG.SYS file. Other items that you can set in this file include the following:

Item	Effect
COUNTRY	Specifies which country you are in (this has to do with how dates are displayed, for example).
DEVICE	Specifies certain kinds of input and output devices such as monitors, plotters, memory disks, and so on.
LASTDRIVE	Specifies the maximum number of disk drives on your computer (normal setting is E).

> **CAUTION:** Unless directed to set or change the information in CONFIG.SYS by your program documentation, you should only change or add to this file under the guidance of someone familiar with its use. For more information, see *Using PC DOS* from Que.

You can create the CONFIG.SYS file with a word processor (using text file mode), the Edlin editor, the Norton Commander editor (F4), or the COPY CON command, as described for batch files. The Norton NUCONFIG command also enables you to add or remove drivers and program commands to the CONFIG.SYS and AUTOEXEC.BAT files.

Remember that DOS executes the AUTOEXEC.BAT and CONFIG.SYS files at boot time. If you change one of these files, you then must reboot the computer to have DOS act on the information in the files.

Using DOS To Back Up Your Hard Disk

Another important feature of DOS is its capability to back up the information on your hard disk.

You easily can destroy data on a diskette or hard disk. In fact, sometime during your use of the computer, you are likely to lose some data. If you are careful, you will experience such a loss only rarely, and if you have a backup procedure, you should be able to recover from the loss with a minimum of grief. Although Norton Utilities can help you recover information in a number of ways, keeping backup copies of your work still is a good idea.

One of the simplest ways to back up your information is to make multiple copies of everything you do. If you are writing a paper, for example, be sure to keep at least two copies, each on a separate disk. If your original copy is on a hard disk, copy the file to a floppy each time you finish working on the file.

Also, save your work often. Never work on a document for hours without making copies. If the electricity goes off or the computer has problems, you easily can lose an entire day's work. How often you should save your work is determined by how much time you are willing to lose. If you do not mind potentially losing a few hours' worth of work, save and back up your work (just files you are working on—not the entire disk) every few hours, or at least once a day.

Besides backing up a single file (which you can do easily with the COPY command), you also can take advantage of a DOS procedure for backing up an entire hard disk: the BACKUP command.

Using BACKUP

The most common way to back up a hard disk is to copy it to floppy diskettes. The DOS BACKUP command enables you to copy files from the hard disk to any number of floppy diskettes. You can copy the entire disk or just portions of it to diskettes. You may need 30 or more diskettes to back up an entire disk. The syntax of the BACKUP command is

BACKUP *source destination* [/*switches*]

The simplest form of the BACKUP command is

BACKUP C: A:

This command tells DOS to back up all files on drive C to floppy diskettes in drive A. After you issue the command, the computer prompts you to insert Disk #1 into drive A. Information is copied to the diskette until it is full, and then you are prompted to insert Disk #2 into the drive. This procedure is repeated until all the files are backed up onto the diskettes. Note, however, that this form of the command backs up only the files from the currently active directory.

If you are using DOS Version 3.2 or earlier, all backup diskettes first must be formatted. Unfortunately, this requirement means that you must have some idea of how many diskettes you will need for the backup. To back up a 10M hard disk to 360K floppy diskettes, you need 28 diskettes (10,000,000/360,000=27.7). Starting with DOS 3.3, you do not need to format diskettes to use for backup. The procedure formats the disks during the backup (if you used the /F switch).

You usually have no reason to back up copies of executable programs from the hard disk, because you should have those programs on their original floppy diskettes, which you could reload in a crisis. What you do want to back up are the files containing your work. To back up specific files, you can enter the names of those files by using global file characters. Suppose that you name all your data files with a DAT extension, and you want to back up all those files. Use this command:

BACKUP C:*.DAT A:

This command backs up DAT files only in the active subdirectory. To back up all directories, make sure that your file specification begins with the root directory (\) and add the /S switch to the command, as in

    BACKUP C:*.DAT A:/S

To back up all files in all directories and all subdirectories, use this command:

    BACKUP C:\ A:/S

The switches available for the DOS BACKUP command follow:

Switch	Effect
/A	Adds more files to a set of already backed-up files
/D:mm-dd-yy	Backs up all files modified on or after a specified date
/F	Tells Backup to format disks used in the backup if they have not been formatted
/M	Backs up files that have been modified since the last backup
/S	Backs up all subdirectories, starting with the specified or current directory
/T:time	Backs up all files modified at or after the specified time (hh:mm:ss)

Using RESTORE

If you need to use one or more of the files that you have backed up with the DOS BACKUP command, you must use the RESTORE command to copy these files from the backup diskettes back to the hard disk. The syntax of this command is

    RESTORE *source destination* [*/switches*]

An example of the RESTORE command is

    RESTORE A: C:/S

This command restores all files from floppies in disk A (source) to the fixed disk C (destination), including all subdirectories (/S). Other options for the RESTORE command are listed in your DOS manual. One that is particularly helpful is the /P or PROMPT switch. When you use this switch, the computer prompts you before restoring a file and enables you to choose the files to restore.

Creating a Disaster Recovery Plan

You should set up a procedure to back up your hard disk—or portions of it—regularly. Here is an example of a good procedure:

1. After initially loading your hard disk, back up the entire hard disk twice.

2. Back up the entire disk daily, using the /M and /A switches.

3. Back up the entire disk once a week. Place the weekly backup in a secure area, away from the office, or have someone take the backup diskettes home.

This procedure results in two backups: one weekly backup stored away from the office in case of an emergency (such as a fire or flood), and one "working" backup at the office to be used daily.

Keep a copy of this book and the Norton Utilities program handy in case a disk accidentally is formatted. See Chapters 3 and 4 on how to prepare for and recover from a potential disk-related disaster.

Because backups take up so much diskette space, you should keep your hard disk clear of unneeded files. Unneeded files on a disk can clutter the directories, limit the amount of disk space for other uses, and prolong the backup procedure. Another good idea, along with the backup procedure, is to set aside time once a week to erase any unneeded files from the hard disk, or to copy them to floppies on a semi-permanent basis.

Alternatives to the BACKUP command are available. Commercially available programs such as Norton Backup and Fastback provide a quicker way to back up your hard disk. The Norton Backup program is described in Chapter 11. Also, backup devices such as tape drives and optical disk drives enable you to back up an entire hard disk to a single tape or disk in a few minutes.

Using DOS 5.0

DOS 5.0 is the latest version of DOS on the market at the time of this writing. Although the commands described in this brief introduction to DOS are still in DOS 5.0, the new version contains some additional features that relate to data protection and recovery.

DOS 5.0 contains the commands UNDELETE and UNFORMAT, which are similar to Norton's UnErase and UnFormat commands. These Norton and DOS commands are compared in Appendix B.

Also, DOS 5.0 contains a program called MIRROR, similar to Norton's IMAGE program which saves information about your FAT, directory, and system information to help in format and file recovery. In fact, Norton programs will use information in the DOS MIRROR file, if it is available, to help with the recovery of files or in unformatting a disk. If you use the Norton IMAGE program, you do not need to use the DOS MIRROR program.

Also, the DOS 5.0 FORMAT command now formats diskettes in a way similar to Norton's Safe Format command. Instead of wiping out all information on disk (which is what happens with FORMAT DOS Version 4.0 and earlier), DOS 5.0 FORMAT, in its default mode, only clears the directory and FAT—which enables you to use the UNFORMAT command to recover the diskette if needed.

Another important feature of DOS 5.0 is its use of RAM memory. In many cases, using DOS 5.0 can free up a significant amount of conventional memory, which gives programs more operational space.

DOS 5.0 also provides a replacement for the out-dated EDLIN line editor. The new Edit program is a full-screen editor, which behaves much like a word processor.

Comparing DOS and Norton Utilities Commands

This appendix contains an alphabetical list of frequently used DOS commands and their descriptions. Each DOS command is compared with a similar Norton Utilities command. In most cases, the Norton commands have advantages over the DOS commands. These advantages are described briefly, and examples of DOS commands and the corresponding Norton commands are given. For more information on the available options and switches for each Norton command, consult the alphabetical list of Norton Utilities commands in Chapter 7. Also, NDOS commands that are similar to DOS commands are not listed here. You will find a list of NDOS commands in Chapter 8, "Using NDOS."

ATTRIB versus FileFind and File Attributes

ATTRIB displays or sets read-only and archive attributes for a file. DOS Version 5.0 also enables you to set the system and hidden attributes.

To set files to read-only, enter the command

    ATTRIB +R *.TXT

To display the current attributes for all *.TXT files, enter the command

    ATTRIB *.TXT

FileFind and File Attributes (FA) enables you to set all four attributes, including read-only, archive, hidden, and system. The FA command also can display a directory of files and attributes. It can clear all attributes at once with the /CLEAR switch.

To set all files with the *.TXT extension to read-only (including files in subdirectories), enter the command

    FA *.TXT /R+

Using the FileFind command, you can set attributes interactively from menu options.

The FileFind and FA commands are described in Chapters 3 and 7.

CHDIR or CD versus Norton Change Directory

CHDIR (CD) enables you to change to another directory.

To change to the \WP\LETTERS directory, enter the command

    CD \WP\LETTERS

Norton Change Directory (NCD) enables you to use only a partial name (when it is unique) to change directories. You can use the NCD command in command-line mode or in interactive mode. In interactive mode, you can switch to a directory by moving the cursor to the directory name displayed in a tree diagram.

To change to the directory named \WP\LETTERS, enter the command

NCD LET

The NCD command is discussed in Chapters 6 and 7.

CHKDSK versus Norton Disk Doctor

CHKDSK enables you to check your disk for errors within the file allocation table (file fragmentation or lost clusters, for example) and the DOS directory and report the status.

To test a disk and attempt to fix any logical problems in the directory or file allocation table, enter the command

CHKDSK A:/F

Norton Disk Doctor (NDD) performs a more thorough check of the disk than CHKDSK. NDD searches the disk for bad sectors and attempts to correct both physical and logical problems. You also can use NDD in interactive mode.

To test the partition table, boot record, root directory, and lost clusters, enter the command

NDD/QUICK

The NDD command is discussed in Chapters 4 and 7.

DATE versus Norton Control Center

The DOS DATE command enables you to set the system date for your computer. This often will not change the *internal clock* (which keeps track of date and time even when the computer is turned off) in the counter, however, so when you reboot, you may have to reset the date again. To permanently reset the date, you must use the Setup command on some computers.

To reset the date, type

DATE 10-24-91

The Norton Control Center (NCC) Time and Date option enables you to reset the system date. For many computers, this also will reset the internal clock.

The NCC command is discussed in Chapters 6 and 7.

DEL or ERASE versus WipeInfo

DEL or ERASE deletes one or more files.

To delete files with the BAT extension in the default directory, enter the command

DEL *.BAT

 You can unerase these files with the Norton UnErase command.

WipeInfo erases files so that they cannot be recovered—not even by Norton UnErase operations. Optionally, WipeInfo can mimic the DOS ERASE command to erase files so that they can be unerased. WipeInfo has the advantage of being able to erase files across subdirectories.

To wipe out all files with the BAT extension in the current directory and all subdirectories, enter the command

WIPEINFO *.BAT/S

The WipeInfo command is discussed in Chapters 3 and 7.

DIR versus FileFind and File Attributes

DIR lists selected file names to the screen.

To display all files with the BAT extension, for example, enter the command

DIR *.BAT

FileFind enables you to display selected file names in a list box, within a directory, or on the entire hard disk. File Attributes (FA) can list a directory of files including their file attributes, which are not listed with the DIR command.

To list all files on the disk that match the specification, including those in subdirectories, enter the command

FA *.BAT

FIND versus FileFind and Text Search

FIND enables you to find and report the existence of specified text in selected files. You must explicitly list all the files you want to be searched; you cannot use global characters in the search file names.

To list to the screen any lines in the REPORT.DOC file that contain the string *text*, type

FIND "text" REPORT.DOC

FileFind enables you to search files in subdirectories and to search erased spaces on the disk for the specified search string. You can make a search case-sensitive. *Erased space* is information on disk that was once the information in a file. When a file is erased, only the reference to the file is actually deleted. The actual contents of the file remain on disk in "erased space" until it is overwritten by another file.

To search all files having the DOC extension in the current directory and subdirectories or the character string specified by *text*, enter the command

FILEFIND

The FileFind interactive search screen appears. You then can enter the criteria for your search. Specify to search *.DOC in the search entry area, and choose to search the entire disk, the current directory, or the current directory and the subdirectories of that directory. Then, choose the Start option on the menu, and the search begins. After FileFind locates files that contain the desired text, you can select a file from the list and choose to view its contents.

The Text Search (TS) command enables you to perform a text search from the DOS prompt. To search for the word *DEFICIT* in all files on disk that match *.RPT, you would enter

TS *.RPT "DEFICIT" /S

The searching capabilities of FileFind and TS are described in Chapters 6 and 7.

FORMAT versus Safe Format

FORMAT prepares a disk to store files.

To format and place a volume label on the disk in drive A, enter the command

FORMAT A:/V

Beginning with Version 5.0, the default method of formatting a diskette for the DOS FORMAT command is similar to the Norton Safe Format option.

Safe Format (SFORMAT) formats disks. The Safe Format command has several safety features not available in the DOS FORMAT command. Safe Format saves format information in case the format is an accident, for example. This feature enables you to unformat the disk with the Norton Utilities UnFormat command. Safe Format provides several format modes, including Safe Format, the normal DOS FORMAT, and a quick format. The quick format mode simply places a new system area on an already formatted disk—effectively erasing all records pertaining to directory and file locations on disk. You also can run Safe Format in interactive mode and choose options from menus rather than remembering command-line switches.

To format and place the label MYDISK on the disk in drive A, enter the command

SFORMAT A: /V:MYDISK

Safe Format is described in Chapters 3 and 7.

MIRROR versus Image

The DOS MIRROR command saves information about the files on disk to support the use of the DOS UNDELETE and UNFORMAT programs. Usually, you place the MIRROR command in your AUTOEXEC.BAT file so that a copy of the file information is saved each time you boot your computer. MIRROR is available in DOS, beginning with Version 5.0.

The Norton Image program is similar to the MIRROR command. For use in DOS recovery commands, the Image program is preferable to the MIRROR command. It saves information about the files on your disk and is used to support the Norton UnErase and UnFormat commands. The Norton UnErase and UnFormat commands will use MIRROR information if IMAGE information is missing and MIRROR information is available. Usually, you place the Image command in your

AUTOEXEC.BAT file so that a copy of the file information is saved each time you boot your computer.

The Image command is discussed in Chapters 3 and 7.

MKDIR or MD versus Norton Change Directory

MKDIR (MD) makes a directory.

To make a subdirectory named LETTERS in the WP directory, enter the command

MD \WP\LETTERS

Norton Change Directory (NCD), when used with the MD option, makes a directory. This command also updates the NCD directory file, which gives you quicker access to directories when you later use the NCD command in interactive mode. In interactive mode, you can add a directory by "pointing" to the directory name on-screen and pressing F7 (Mkdir). Also, the NCD command has a Rename option, which enables you to rename a directory. DOS has no equivalent command.

To make a subdirectory named LETTERS in the WP directory and update the NCD directory file, enter the command

NCD MD \WP\LETTERS

The NCD command is discussed in Chapters 6 and 7.

MODE versus Norton Command Center

MODE specifies communications port settings (among other features).

To set up the communication port number 1 as 1200 baud, for example, type

MODE COM1 BAUD=1200

or

MODE COM1:1200

Norton Command Center (NCC), when used with the Serial Ports option, enables you to set up the parameters of a serial port interactively by choosing options from a menu.

The NCC command is discussed in Chapter 6 and 7.

PRINT versus Line Print

The DOS PRINT command prints the contents of an ASCII file to the printer or other output device. To print the file MYSTUFF.TXT, for example, you can use the command

    PRINT MYSTUFF.TXT

The Norton Line Print (LP) command includes options not available in PRINT. You can choose to include line numbers in the printout, to include a header, to print files from WordStar files, and so on. To print the file MYSTUFF.TXT and include line numbers, type

    LP MYSTUFF.TXT /N

The Line Print command is discussed in Chapters 6 and 7.

RECOVER versus Disk Tools

RECOVER tries to reclaim disks or files with defective sectors.

> **WARNING:** The RECOVER command is dangerous because the slightest misuse can be devastating. Files often are renamed to machine-generated names, and perfectly good files can be lost easily. Do not use this command unless you know exactly what you are doing.

Norton's Disk Tools, when used with RECOVER, attempts to reclaim files and directories that have been renamed and removed by the DOS RECOVER command. Rather than use RECOVER to reclaim files, use the NDD command in interactive mode and choose the Diagnose option or Disk Tools' Revive a Defective Diskette option.

Chapters 4 and 7 discuss Disk Tools.

RMDIR or RD versus Norton Change Directory

RMDIR or RD removes a directory.

To remove the \WP directory, enter the command

    RD \WP

Norton Change Directory (NCD), when used with the RD option, removes a directory. This command also updates the NCD directory file. You can run NCD in interactive mode, where you can remove a directory by pointing to the directory name on a graphic tree and pressing F8 (Delete).

To remove the \WP directory, enter the command

    NCD RD \WP

The NCD command is discussed in Chapters 6 and 7.

SYS versus Disk Tools

SYS places system files (but not the COMMAND.COM file) on disk, if the disk was prepared to receive system files when it was formatted originally.

To place the system files on drive C, enter the command

    SYS C:

Disk Tools, when used with the Make a Disk Bootable option, places the system files on a disk even if it was not prepared to do so when it was formatted. This option also copies the COMMAND.COM file to the disk to make it bootable.

Chapters 4 and 7 discuss Disk Tools.

TIME versus Norton Control Center

TIME enables you to set the system time on your computer. For many versions of the PC, however, the DOS time setting does not reset the internal clock, so when you reboot, your time setting may have gone away. To set the internal clock, you may have to use the Setup command.

To set the system time, type

        TIME 10:40

Norton Control Center's (NCC's) Date and Time option enables you to set the system time. For many computers, this also sets the internal clock.

The NCC command is discussed in Chapters 6 and 7.

TREE versus Norton Change Directory

TREE displays information about directories on disk. Beginning with DOS 4.0, this command displays directories in a graphic tree structure.

To display directory names for the entire disk, enter the command

        TREE \

Be sure to include the space between TREE and \.

Norton Change Directory (NCD), in interactive mode, displays directories in a tree structure and enables you to point to directory names on-screen and choose to add, rename, delete, or change the directories.

The NCD command is discussed in Chapters 6 and 7.

UNDELETE versus UnErase

The DOS UNDELETE command restores a previously deleted file. If you used ERASE or DEL to delete the file named MYFILE.WKS, for example, you can use

> UNDELETE *.WKS

to search for all files with a *.WKS extension. You then are prompted to enter the first letter of the name of each deleted file found. The UNDELETE command is available beginning with DOS 5.0.

The Norton UnErase command is similar to UNDELETE. UnErase presents you with a list of possible files to delete and lists the likelihood of UnErase's success (poor, fair, good, excellent). You may view the contents of a file before undeleting it. Also, Norton contains a manual unerase feature that enables you to piece together an erased file that cannot be unerased automatically. The Norton UnErase command uses information in MIRROR or Image files to assist in recovering files.

The UnErase command is discussed in Chapters 4 and 7.

UNFORMAT versus UnFormat and Disk Tools

DOS UNFORMAT enables you to restore a formatted disk or a disk that has been restructured by the DOS RECOVER command. UNFORMAT uses information from the MIRROR file created when the DOS MIRROR command was run last. To unformat the disk in drive C, for example, you enter the command

> UNFORMAT C:

The DOS UNFORMAT command is available beginning in DOS version 5.0.

The Norton UnFormat command also enables you to restore a formatted disk. It can use information in the DOS MIRROR file or the Norton Image file to restore a hard disk. Norton UnFormat can also unformat a disk when this information is not present; however, files in the root directory will be lost and directories under the root will be named DIR0, DIR1, and so on. You can use the Norton Disk Tools command to recover from the DOS RECOVER command.

The UnFormat command is discussed in Chapters 3 and 7 and the Disk Tools command is discussed in Chapters 4 and 7.

VOL versus Norton Change Directory

VOL displays the volume label for a disk.

To display the name given to the diskette in drive B when it was formatted, enter the command

VOL B:

The Norton Change Directory (NCD) command enables you to change a volume label. In interactive mode, the option is on the Disk pull-down menu.

The NCD Command is discussed in Chapters 6 and 7.

Installing Norton Programs

This appendix covers installation procedures for Norton Utilities 6, Norton Commander 3.0, and Norton Backup 1.1. You learn how to install these programs on a hard disk-based system. Installation also includes the creation of an emergency floppy disk.

Installing Norton Utilities 6

Norton Utilities Version 6 comes with four 5 1/4-inch diskettes: two 1.2M program diskettes and two 360K emergency diskettes or four 3 1/2-inch, 720K diskettes. You will use the diskettes appropriate for your computer. If your floppy disk A is a 720K or 1.44M, 3 1/2-inch disk drive, use the 3 1/2-inch diskettes. If your disk A is a 1.2M disk drive, use the 5 1/4-inch diskettes.

The full Norton Utilities 6 program takes about 2.8M of disk space. Because one of Norton Utilities' primary functions is to enable you to manage your hard disk better, you probably will not install the full system on a floppy disk machine. Therefore, these installation instructions assume that you will be installing the full program on a hard disk.

To install Norton Utilities 6 on your hard disk, follow these steps:

1. Turn on your computer and boot it in the usual way. End any programs that are started automatically (such as a menu), so that you are at the DOS prompt (usually a C> prompt on a hard disk).

2. Insert the Norton Utilities installation disk into drive A.

3. Change the DOS prompt to drive A by entering the command

   A:

   Your prompt should be A> or A:>, or an equivalent prompt.

T   I   P

Many times after a manual is printed, errors are found in the manual or there is some new information that you need to know. On the installation disk, the file READ.ME contains last-minute notes about the program.

You can print the READ.ME file with the command

   COPY READ.ME LPT1:

This command assumes that you have a printer installed on printer port 1. If you do not have a printer, use the type command to examine this file on-screen. Type

   TYPE READ.ME

to examine the contents of the READ.ME file. You also can examine this file by using the Norton Commander Editor or View option; you can use your word processor to view the contents of the file; or you can use the Norton Utilities LP program to print the file once you have installed the program.

4. To begin the installation procedure for Norton Utilities, enter the command

   INSTALL

   The first screen that appears prompts you to choose display colors for the installation. The options are Black & White or Color.

5. Use the up- and down-arrow keys to select the option that matches your monitor and press Enter or point to the option with the mouse and click once.

   Following the color choice screen, the installation program scans for a previous version of the software on your hard disk. If you have an old copy on your disk, the installation program will default to that directory to install the new version. Otherwise, the installation directory will be \NU. (You will be able to specifically choose the directory to install to later.)

   Following the scan for an old version, the next screen displays a warning. This screen warns you not to install the utilities if your disk has been formatted accidentally or if you want to unerase some files that are still on your hard disk. You need to perform these commands from a floppy disk.

6. To cancel the installation procedure, press R from the warning screen to return to DOS. Or, point to the Return to DOS box with your mouse pointer and click. To continue with installation, press Enter. Alternatively, point to the OK box with the mouse and click.

   The next screen that appears gives you a summary of how the installation process will take place (see fig. C.1).

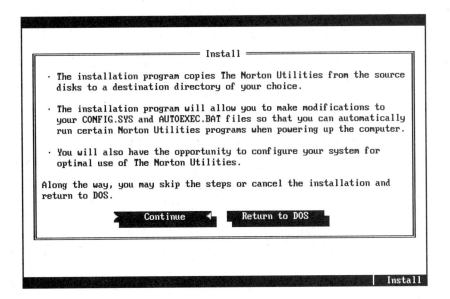

FIG. C.1.

The Norton Utilities Install screen.

The installation procedure does the following:

■ Copies Norton Utilities files to your hard disk.

■ Enables you to place certain Norton Utilities commands in your AUTOEXEC.BAT and CONFIG.SYS files.

■ Enables you to set the configuration of your computer (screen colors, mouse, graphics).

7. Select Continue by pressing Enter or clicking on Continue with the mouse pointer.

You see the Install dialog box shown in figure C.2. From this screen, you can choose the directory in which the program will be installed.

8. If you want to accept the default location, press Enter to continue the installation. You may change the destination by pressing the Backspace key to delete the C:\NU location on-screen, and enter a new location. After specifying the directory name, press Enter to continue. If there is an old version in this directory, it will be deleted before the new version is installed.

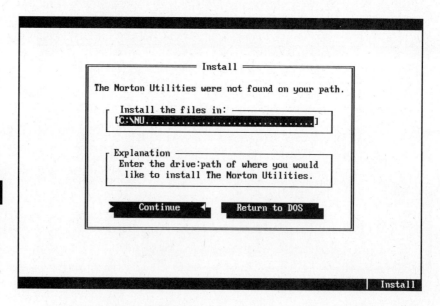

FIG. C.2.

Using the Norton Utilities menu to choose the disk drive and directory to install to.

The Install Program Files dialog box appears, from which you can choose what portions of the program you want to install (see fig. C.3). A check appears to the left of every option that is selected to be installed.

9. Use the up- and down-arrow keys or your mouse to move from option to option. Press the space bar to select or deselect options (or use your mouse). The amount of space that would still be available on your disk (in this case 983K) and the amount of space that will be taken if the selected files are installed (in this case, 2,598K) are displayed. Unless you do not have space to install the entire program, you probably will want to accept the full installation. After you make your selection, press Enter to begin the installation or point to the Install option with your mouse and click.

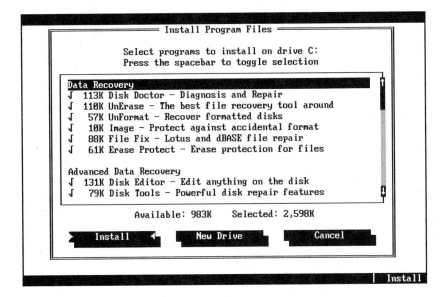

FIG. C.3.

Selecting the programs to install.

The installation program begins copying files from the installation disk. You are prompted to change disks during the installation process. At one point in the installation, you are prompted to insert the Emergency Disk into drive A. This disk contains a portion of the Utility programs that you may need if your hard disk is formatted accidently or has other problems that make it unusable (see fig. C.4).

10. Insert the appropriate disks as prompted.

11. After all files are copied to disk, you are given options on configuring the program for your computer. The options are Easy and Advanced. Use the up- and down-arrow keys to highlight Easy or Advanced and press Enter. Or, point with the mouse pointer to the option you want and click. If you choose the Easy option, the installation program updates your PATH command to include

the appropriate path to access the program and places the IMAGE command in your AUTOEXEC.BAT file. If you choose the Advanced option, you can set program options including setting passwords and installing drivers in the CONFIG.SYS file.

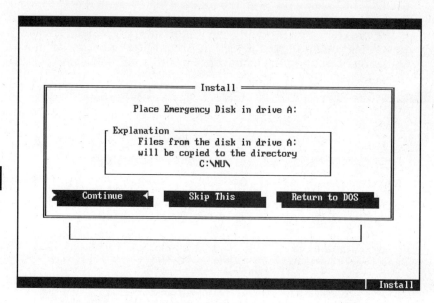

FIG. C.4.

A message telling you to insert the Emergency disk into the installation drive.

Whether you choose Easy or Advanced, the configuration options may be set or reset at any time by choosing the Configuration menu from the main Norton Utilities menu. A description of how to set these options is covered in Chapter 1.

After you finish installation, you are prompted to reboot your computer, to go to the Norton Utilities Directory, or to Return to DOS (see fig. C.5).

12. Reboot your computer to make sure that all changes to the AUTOEXEC.BAT and CONFIG.SYS files are placed into effect.

To begin the program, type *norton* at the DOS prompt. Be sure to keep your emergency disk in a safe place in case you need it to recover information on your hard disk. Also, keep the original installation diskettes in a safe place in case you need to reload the program.

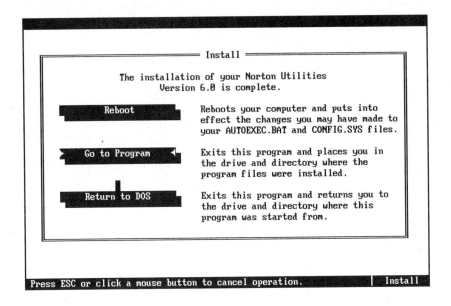

FIG. C.5.

Choosing how
to end the
installation
process.

Installing Norton Commander 3.0

The Norton Commander 3.0 package comes with two 5 1/4-inch, 360K diskettes and one 3 1/2-inch, 720K diskette. Obviously, you need to use the diskettes appropriate to your computer. If your drive A is a 720K or a 1.44M, 3 1/2-inch disk drive, use the 3 1/2-inch diskette. If your drive A is a 360K or a 1.2M disk drive, use the 5 1/4-inch diskettes.

Norton Commander takes about 850 bytes of disk space. Because one of the Commander's primary functions is to enable you to manage your hard disk better, you probably will not install the program on a floppy-based machine. Therefore, these installation instructions assume that you are installing Norton Commander on a hard disk system.

To install Norton Commander 3.0, follow these steps:

1. Turn on your computer and boot it normally. Exit any programs that are started automatically (such as a menu) so that you are at the DOS prompt (usually a C prompt on a hard disk).

2. Change the DOS prompt to drive A by entering the command

    A:

Your prompt should be A>, A:\>, or an equivalent prompt.

3. Insert the installation disk into drive A.

For 5 1/4-inch drives, insert the first 5 1/4-inch Commander disk (Disk #1) into drive A.

For 3 1/2-inch drives, insert the 3 1/2-inch Commander disk into drive A.

T   I   P   After a manual is printed, errors often are found in the manual, or some new information is discovered that you need to know. Commander has two files on disk that contain this type of information. The file INREAD.ME contains helpful information about what to do if the installation process does not work. The file READ.ME contains last-minute notes about the program. You can print these files with this command:

COPY *.ME LPT1:

This command assumes that you have a printer installed on printer port 1. If you do not have a printer, use the TYPE command to examine these files on-screen. To examine the contents of the INREAD.ME file, enter

TYPE INREAD.ME

To examine the contents of the READ.ME file, enter

TYPE READ.ME

---

4. To begin the installation process, type the following command and press Enter:

INSTALL

You first are prompted to

```
Select drive to install Norton Commander from
```

A list of drives is given, such as A, B, and so on.

5. Type the letter of the drive containing the installation disk.

You see a screen similar to the one in figure C.6, which summarizes the installation process.

At the bottom of the screen are two options: OK and Return to DOS. OK is highlighted.

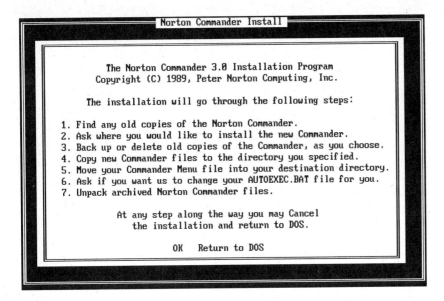

FIG. C.6.

The Norton
Commander
Install screen.

6. To continue with installation, press Enter. To return to DOS, press R.

   The Install program next looks at your disk to see whether a current copy of Norton Commander is installed in a directory named \NC. If you have an old copy, you are given a chance to delete the old copy or back it up to some other location on disk.

7. If you have an old copy of Norton Commander, you will be prompted to choose one of three options: Overwrite, Back Up, or Return to DOS. Use the arrow keys to point to the option you prefer and press the space bar to lock in your choice. Or, point to the option with the mouse pointer and click.

   The Overwrite option writes the new version to the old directory, overwriting the old version. The Back Up option causes the installation program to write the old files to a backup directory named NC.BAK. The Return to DOS option cancels installation. After you choose an option, press Enter or click on OK to continue with the installation.

   You then are asked to enter the name of the disk and directory to which Commander should be copied (see fig. C.7). The default location for Commander to be installed is C:\NC.

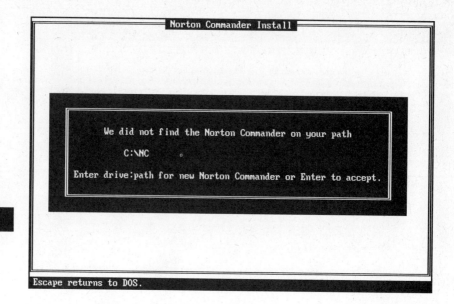

FIG. C.7.

Specifying
the Norton
Commander
directory.

8. If you accept this location, press Enter to continue the installation. You can change the destination by pressing the Backspace key to delete the destination and entering a new location.

The installation program prompts you once more before the copy begins—to give you a chance to return to DOS and cancel installation.

9. To continue with installation, press Enter to accept the highlighted OK option. To return to DOS, cancelling the installation, press the right-arrow key to highlight the Return to DOS option, and press Enter. Or, click on the option you want with the mouse pointer.

The Install program asks whether you want the path to the Commander directory placed in the PATH statement of your AUTOEXEC.BAT file (see fig. C.8).

10. If you are installing Commander for the first time, choose OK. If you already have a path to the Commander's directory, you can press S to skip this part of the installation.

After all the files are copied to disk, the installation is complete. To begin Norton Commander, you enter the following command at the DOS prompt:

NC

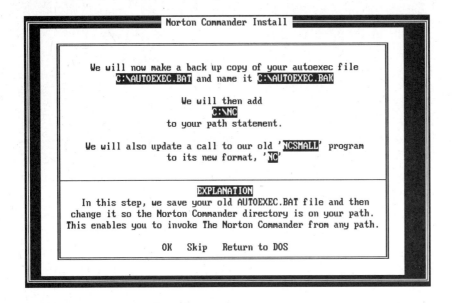

```
╔══════════════ Norton Commander Install ══════════════╗
║                                                       ║
║  ┌─────────────────────────────────────────────────┐ ║
║  │   We will now make a back up copy of your autoexec file │
║  │   C:\AUTOEXEC.BAT and name it C:\AUTOEXEC.BAK    │ ║
║  │                                                   │ ║
║  │              We will then add                     │ ║
║  │                    C:\NC                           │ ║
║  │          to your path statement.                  │ ║
║  │                                                   │ ║
║  │   We will also update a call to our old 'NCSMALL' program │
║  │          to its new format, 'NC'                  │ ║
║  │                                                   │ ║
║  ├─────────────────────────────────────────────────┤ ║
║  │                  EXPLANATION                       │ ║
║  │   In this step, we save your old AUTOEXEC.BAT file and then │
║  │  change it so the Norton Commander directory is on your path. │
║  │  This enables you to invoke The Norton Commander from any path. │
║  │                                                   │ ║
║  │          OK    Skip    Return to DOS              │ ║
║  └─────────────────────────────────────────────────┘ ║
║                                                       ║
╚═══════════════════════════════════════════════════════╝
```

FIG. C.8.

The Norton
Commander
Install
AUTOEXEC.BAT
prompt.

If you want Commander to run each time you boot your computer, you can place the NC command as the last line in your AUTOEXEC.BAT file. See Appendix A for an explanation of the AUTOEXEC.BAT file and how to edit it.

Installing Norton Backup 1.1

The Norton Backup 1.1 program comes with a 3 1/2-inch diskette and two 5 1/4-inch diskettes. If you are using a computer with a 3 1/2-inch disk (720K or 1.44M) drive, you will use the single 3 1/2-inch diskette to install the program. If you are using a computer with a 5 1/4-inch disk (360K or 1.2M) drive, you will use both 5 1/4-inch diskettes to install the program.

The Backup program requires that you have two blank diskettes to test the program. Therefore, be sure you have these handy when you begin the installation. If you have 3 1/2-inch and 5 1/4-inch disk drives, you can use either size for the test.

The Norton Backup installation program performs several tasks:

- Copies necessary files to your hard disk.
- Modifies your AUTOEXEC.BAT file to place the Norton Backup directory in your PATH command.

■ Examines your computer setup to determine which disks your computer contains and which disks may be used as backups.

■ Runs several tests on your computer to determine the most efficient way to perform the backup. These tests deal with the speed of your computer and your disks.

To install Norton Backup, follow these steps:

1. Insert Disk #1 (or the single 3 1/2-inch diskette) into drive A.

2. Make the DOS default drive A by entering the command

    A:

3. From the DOS prompt, enter the command

    INSTALL

    The Install program asks you a series of questions about your computer. Usually, the best choice is to choose the default settings offered, unless you have a reason to change them. You may change settings later from the Norton Backup program.

4. Choose the default settings or make changes as necessary.

After you choose your basic options, the installation procedure runs a series of tests. You will need two blank diskettes to complete these tests. Follow the instructions on-screen, which prompt you to place the disks in the disk drive at certain times during the test. If your computer fails either of these tests, Norton Backup attempts to reset its options to compensate for the problem. You will be informed as to the results of the test. If your computer fails certain tests, the backup program will still work, but it will not be able to back up at its highest speed.

After you install Norton Backup, it is a good idea to back up all or a portion of your hard disk, and then restore it to verify that the program is installed and is working correctly.

After Norton Backup has been installed, begin the program by entering the command

    NBACKUP

at the DOS prompt.

Dealing with Disk-Related Problems

Norton Utilities Version 6 provides a number of commands that help you fix disk problems that cannot be solved with DOS commands alone. Many disk problems are caused by bad spots developing on the magnetic surface of a disk. The magnetic signal on the disk gradually weakens until DOS cannot read the information. Other problems are caused by a disk getting almost full and files becoming so fragmented that DOS loses track of critical information. If these problems begin to appear, you may experience difficulties, ranging from the inability to read one file to the inability to access your entire hard disk.

The first part of this appendix describes some common problems and suggests how you can use Norton Utilities commands to diagnose and solve these problems. Sometimes, however, a disk may be irreparable with these methods. You may have to perform a low-level format on the hard disk, which is explained later in this appendix. (See "You Need To Perform a Low-Level Format of a Hard Disk," later in this appendix, for more information.)

Another problem is computer sabotage. The information on your computer may be damaged by a computer virus or by the deliberate act of an individual. For information on handling these types of problems, see "You Need To Deal with Viruses and Sabotage," later in this appendix. For suggestions on how to respond to common DOS error messages, see the final section, "Responding to DOS Error Messages."

Diagnosing and Fixing Disk Problems

This section presents several common disk problems and gives you suggestions for solving them with Norton Utilities and other commands.

Your Computer No Longer Boots from the Hard Disk

If your computer has booted from the hard disk in the past but now will not, you must boot from a floppy diskette in drive A, using a disk that contains DOS. Make sure that the disk contains the same version of DOS that is on the hard disk.

One situation that can cause this problem is if you no longer have the correct COMMAND.COM file in your hard disk root directory. After you boot your computer, examine your hard disk's root directory to determine whether it contains the correct COMMAND.COM—you should be able to tell from its date. If it does not match the date and size on the original DOS disk, copy the correct COMMAND.COM onto the hard disk and try booting again.

If the COMMAND.COM file is okay, your system files may have become corrupted. You can use the DOS SYS command to transfer a fresh copy of the system files to the hard disk. Better yet, use the Norton Disk Tool's Make a Disk Bootable option. This option places COMMAND.COM and the system files on your disk. If this approach does not work, your hard disk may be damaged physically—take it in for repair.

You should keep a floppy disk handy that contains the files necessary to boot your computer in case your computer becomes unbootable from the hard disk. This floppy disk should be formatted with the system (/S FORMAT option); it should contain the DOS programs FDISK and DEBUG; and it should contain the Norton programs Disk Tools, Norton Disk Doctor, and the files AUTOEXEC.BAT and CONFIG.SYS. Also include any device drivers (mouse driver, plotter, and so on).

T I P

Your Hard Disk Cannot Be Formatted as a System Disk

The hard disk, like a floppy diskette, uses track 0 to store system information. If that track is bad on a hard disk, the DOS FORMAT command will not create a bootable hard disk. Several possibilities exist for recovering from this problem. After booting from a floppy diskette in drive A, use the Norton Disk Doctor to diagnose the hard disk and attempt to fix the problem. If that approach does not work, you may need to perform a low-level format of the disk. If the disk contains valuable information, you need to use a nondestructive program such as HFORMAT or Spinrite, or Norton's Calibrate command. See "You Need To Perform a Low-Level Format of a Hard Disk," later in this appendix, for more information.

You Get Errors Trying To Copy a Diskette with DISKCOPY

If you use the DOS DISKCOPY command to copy a disk, you may get read errors or write errors, or both. Read errors are associated with reading information from the source disk. Write errors are associated with writing information to the destination disk. If a bad or unreadable spot exists on the source disk, it causes the read error. Similarly, if a bad or unreadable spot exists on the destination disk, it causes a write error. If you get a write error, change to another destination diskette.

The read error is of most concern because it occurs on the disk that contains the original information. If you get a read error, examine the source disk by using Norton Disk Doctor II. NDD will tell you if the read error is in an area that contains a file. If this type of problem is found on disk, NDD will attempt to correct the problem by moving the file to another, safer part of the disk.

You Need To Perform a Low-Level Format of a Hard Disk

When hard disks are manufactured, they contain random magnetic information. To make the disk usable, the manufacturer of the hard disk drive or disk controller performs a low-level format on the hard disk. This format is much more thorough than the procedure performed by DOS FORMAT. A low-level format prepares the surface of the hard disk to receive a DOS format and checks the surface to detect bad spots.

Occasionally, a working hard disk develops problems that cannot be corrected except by a low-level disk format. Some machines have low-level format programs built into their ROM software. Using the DOS DEBUG program, you can tell the program to begin operating. This low-level format usually is a completely destructive format, however, and other, nondestructive low-level format programs are available. Some examples of nondestructive, low-level format programs are HFORMAT (part of HTEST from Paul Mace Software), SpinRite from Gibson Research, and the Calibrate program in Norton Utilities 6. By using one of these low-level format procedures, you may be able to recover some information from the disk.

> **WARNING:** Do not perform a low-level format of your disk unless you are an experienced computer user. Before performing the low-level format described here, try the low-level (nondestructive) format described in Chapter 5.

To use the machine's built-in program to perform a low-level format (which is destructive to data on the disk), follow these instructions:

1. Boot the computer, using the original DOS disk in drive A.

2. Begin the DEBUG program, which is located on the DOS disk, by typing the command *debug*.

3. A - prompt should appear on-screen. At this prompt, enter the message G=C800:5 and press Enter. If nothing happens within a minute or two, your machine probably does not have a built-in low-level format program. You must reboot the computer and use a program such as HFORMAT.

4. If a low-level format program does exist in ROM, another prompt appears. At this prompt, enter an interleave number, which controls your hard disk access time. The interleave determines how much information is read from the disk on each pass. You should choose an interleave number from 3 to 6. On most AT-type computers, enter an interleave of 3. On most PC- or XT-type computers, enter an interleave of 6. If your PC-type computer is a turbo, you may be able to choose a lower interleave than 6 and therefore make your disk access faster. If you choose a suboptimum interleave, however, your disk access will be too slow. If, after performing the low-level format and some tests (such as the System Information SYSINFO command), you feel that your disk access is too slow, try a higher interleave number. Running the Calibrate command will give you the best interleave ratio for your disk. Using Calibrate, you can change the interleave without having to redo the destructive low-level format.

The low-level format may take several hours to perform. After it finishes, you need to run the DOS FDISK command before formatting the disk.

You Need To Deal with Viruses and Sabotage

At some time, you may become the unfortunate victim of deliberate computer-information destruction. Someone may sabotage your information by destroying, changing, or erasing information on your computer disk. Or, your computer may become infected by some type of computer virus program. Virus programs have been known to come from normal commercial software (rarely), from pirated software, and from demos that appear in the mail. Some virus programs are nondestructive and simply give you a message (and a scare). Other virus programs may attempt to destroy all data on your disk.

You can take a few precautions to lessen your chance of being sabotaged. First, load software only from reputable sources, and limit others' access to your computer. Also, set the attributes on important files to read-only. These files should at least include the COMMAND.COM, AUTOEXEC.BAT, and CONFIG.SYS files in your root directory. Compare the size of your copy of COMMAND.COM on your hard disk to the copy on your original DOS diskette. If the sizes differ, your COMMAND.COM may be infected.

Another important step in being prepared for data destruction is having current backups of your computer's information. You particularly may want to keep a backup disk of the files in your root directory. Also, keep a current copy of your original DOS disk and a copy of Norton Utilities handy.

Virus programs continue to get more complicated and destructive. Depending on the nature of the attack, you may not be able to recover any information. If your computer's disk has been compromised by a virus or sabotage, however, Norton Utilities offers some hope of recovery. The following paragraphs offer possible solutions to various problems arising from virus programs or sabotage.

Your Files Have Been Erased

Use the Norton UnErase command to recover erased files. Do this before you write new information to your disk.

Your Files and Directories Have Been Erased

Use the Norton UnErase command to recover each directory and any associated files that have been erased.

Your System Files Have Been Altered

Virus programs often attempt to change the COMMAND.COM file or other system files. If you suspect a virus, compare the date and time of the COMMAND.COM file in your hard disk's root directory with the original (or backup) copy of COMMAND.COM. If you notice any difference, replace the infected file on the hard disk.

To replace not only COMMAND.COM but also the other system files, boot your computer from a copy of your original DOS disk in drive A. Use the Norton Disk Tools' Make a Disk Bootable option to copy a fresh version of the system to the hard disk. If your problem was caused by a virus program, examine your hard disk to find and remove that program. Until you are sure that you have corrected the problem, quarantine all files from this computer and the floppy you used to reboot the computer—do not distribute any files (particularly program files) from the computer or floppy to any other computer.

Your AUTOEXEC.BAT File Has Been Altered

If you discover that your AUTOEXEC.BAT file has been changed, try to determine when and why the change was made. Some software installation programs change this file and the CONFIG.SYS file as part of the installation process. Some virus programs, however, may change the AUTOEXEC.BAT file in order to run a destructive program or a *counter program* that will eventually release a destructive virus. A counter program counts the number of times your computer is booted or a program is run, and then activates on a preset count. You should examine your AUTOEXEC.BAT and CONFIG.SYS files and understand the reason for each command. If you notice a suspicious command, replace the old AUTOEXEC.BAT with your backup copy, or delete the unknown command. If AUTOEXEC.BAT calls an unknown program, determine where the program is and what it does. Remove the program from your computer if you do not know its purpose. A well-publicized virus that was sent to hundreds of persons in the guise of a demo program used a command in the AUTOEXEC.BAT file to trigger its main counting mechanism.

A Hidden File or Directory Appears on Your Hard Disk

Some legitimate programs create hidden files or directories on disk as part of a file-protection scheme. Some virus programs, however, also create hidden files and directories in which destructive programs may reside. Using the Norton Control Center (NCC) command, you can see any hidden directories that reside on your disk. If you notice one directory that looks suspicious, investigate. Also, using the Norton FileFind command, you can discover any hidden files on disk. Again, if you do not know why the files are there, investigate to find out whether a legitimate program placed them there or whether they were created from an unknown source. If you suspect sabotage, be sure to keep copies of all important files on backup disks until you are sure that the danger is past.

Your Hard Disk Has Been Erased

If your hard disk looks like it has been erased completely or formatted, you have several options:

■ Boot your computer from the original DOS disk and then use the Norton UnErase command to see whether any directories and files can be saved. Some attacks have been known to rename files and directories. You may have to examine recovered information file-by-file to determine what the information is.

■ If the disk was formatted, you can try to unformat the disk by using the UnFormat command. If you recently ran the Image command, the recovery will be easier.

■ Virus attacks are becoming smarter and more destructive. Having backups of your files is important because some attacks completely destroy data. For these problems, recovering your information from backup diskettes is the only solution.

Responding to DOS Error Messages

This section contains information about what to do if you encounter DOS error messages. Not all possible DOS error messages are covered, but the ones mentioned represent the most commonly seen disk-oriented messages.

Abort, Retry, Ignore, Fail?

This message may appear if you attempt to read or write something to a disk, printer, or another device. If a disk is bad or not properly in the disk drive, for example, DOS displays this error message. You have four choices for responding to the prompt: press A to abort, R to retry, I to ignore, or F to fail. The meanings of these options follow:

Option	Effect
Abort	Cancels the procedure
Retry	Tries the procedure again
Ignore	Ignores the error and proceeds
	During a copy, for example, Ignore tells the copy to continue, but the resulting file may have missing information that could not be copied correctly.
Fail	Skips the problem, and DOS tries to continue with the procedure

If the problem is the incapability to access a disk drive, you may be prompted to enter a new current disk drive name. (Fail is similar to Ignore.)

The message

```
Abort, Retry, Ignore, Fail?
```

may appear for disk- or other device-related problems.

Disk-Related Problems and Solutions

Sometimes if you choose Retry, DOS can read or write to the disk on the second or third try. Even if this approach works, however, you may need to correct the problem by running the Norton Disk Doctor (NDD) to fix files or Speed Disk to unfragment files.

If the problem is with a floppy diskette, verify that your disk is properly in the disk drive. Make sure that the disk is not upside down, for example, and that the disk drive door is shut.

Sometimes the magnetic media in the disk jacket gets stuck because of a jacket flaw or because the media is out of alignment. Remove the diskette from the drive and tap the disk on its side to attempt to loosen it, being careful not to touch the magnetic media. Place the disk back in the drive and try again.

You should be sure that the disk is formatted and that it is formatted so that it can be read on the disk drive you are using. If you are using a 360K drive, for example, and have inserted a disk originally formatted as a 1.2M disk, it cannot be read in that drive.

If you cannot readily solve the problem, choose the Abort option and examine the disk by using the Norton System Information (SYSINFO) or NDD command.

If you are convinced that the disk is formatted properly for this drive, but DOS is still having trouble reading a file, try to correct the problem by using the Norton Disk Doctor (NDD) command.

Problems Caused by Other Devices

Make sure that your printer is turned on and that it is on-line. Correct any problems and select Retry. Also make sure that a cable is attached properly to the device. Correct any problems and select Retry.

DOS may be trying to communicate with some other device that is not turned on or is not attached properly. If so, choose Abort by pressing A and correct the problem.

If DOS is attempting to communicate through a COM port, make sure that it is set up correctly. You can use the DOS MODE command or the Norton Control Center (NCC) to set up a communications (serial) port. Abort the current procedure and fix the problem.

Access Denied

This message may appear if you attempt to change (write to) a file that has its attribute setting as read-only. You can change this setting with the DOS ATTRIB command or with the Norton FileFind command. Make sure that you want to change this file before removing the read-only status.

Access denied also may appear if you attempt to use a subdirectory as a file, such as trying to edit the subdirectory.

Bad Command or File Name

This message appears if you enter a command at the DOS prompt that DOS does not recognize—for example, if you misspell the command. If you see this message, first check your spelling.

Another possibility is that you entered a correct command but were not in the proper directory or did not have your PATH command set up to find the command in its directory. Correct your PATH command (usually in your AUTOEXEC.BAT file), or change directories by using the DOS CD command or the Norton Change Directory (NCD) command.

Bad or Missing Command Interpreter

This message usually appears if the file COMMAND.COM is not on the boot disk or if DOS has a problem reading this file. If you attempted to boot from a floppy diskette, perhaps it was not a boot disk. If you were booting from a hard disk, you need to correct the problem by rebooting from drive A with a correct version of DOS and then fixing the problem on your hard disk. You may have to copy COMMAND.COM back to the hard disk's root directory. If your hard disk still has problems, you may need to use the Norton Disk Doctor (NDD).

Cannot Find System Files

This message appears if DOS cannot find the hidden system files required to boot the computer. You cannot make a disk bootable simply by placing the COMMAND.COM file on it. You must use the DOS SYS command or Norton Disk Tools' Make a Diskette Bootable option to place these hidden files on a disk.

Cannot Read File Allocation Table

This message may occur if you use the DOS RECOVER command. Rather than use this DOS command, use the Norton Disk Doctor (NDD) to attempt to recover damaged files. If you already have used RECOVER, use Norton Disk Tools to recover from the RECOVER command.

Data Error

This message usually means that a disk has a bad spot and DOS is trying to read or write to that spot. You can attempt to locate and correct this problem by using the Norton Disk Doctor (NDD) command.

Drive Not Ready Reading/Writing Device

This message can occur if the drive door is not fully closed. Check to see that your diskette is inserted properly in the drive and that the drive door is fully closed. The problem also may be caused by a defective drive. If so, you need to get a qualified technician to correct the problem.

Error in Loading Operating System

This message may appear if DOS is unable to find the proper system information while attempting to boot the system. Turn off your computer and try again. You may need to boot the computer from a DOS diskette in drive A and then correct the problem by writing a fresh copy of the system files to disk by using the DOS SYS command. Alternatively, use the Norton Disk Tools' Make a Diskette Bootable option to correct the problem.

Error Writing Fixed Disk

This message may be caused by DOS's incapability to write system start-up information to a disk. Use the Norton Disk Doctor (NDD) command to analyze and correct the problem. If the problem persists, attempt to copy as much information from this disk as possible. You may need to boot from a floppy diskette in drive A. You also may need to perform a low-level format of the disk. See "You Need To Perform a Low-Level Format of a Hard Disk," earlier in this appendix.

Error Writing Partition Table

This message may appear during the FORMAT procedure and may be caused by a hardware problem or a physically damaged disk. Probably, the boot record at the beginning of the disk cannot be read or written to. A possible solution is to reformat the boot record. You can use Norton Disk Doctor (NDD) to attempt to fix your disk and recover information. However, you may need to replace your disk, get a technician to correct the hardware problem, or perform a low-level format on your disk. For more information, see "You Need To Perform a Low-Level Format of a Hard Disk."

File Allocation Table Bad

If this message appears, somehow DOS has lost information about where files are stored. This information normally is kept in the file allocation table (FAT). Two (usually identical) copies of the FAT usually reside on disk. By using the Norton Disk Doctor's Diagnose Disk option, you may be able to recover information from the duplicate FAT.

File Cannot Be Copied to Itself

This message occurs if you omit a required destination when using the COPY command. For example, the command

    COPY MYFILE.TXT

produces this error message because DOS does not enable the file, if it exists, to be written to itself.

File Creation Error

This message occurs if DOS is unable to write a file to a directory. The directory or disk may be full. Use the DIR command to list files and see how much space is available on disk. If the directory or disk is full, you can delete unnecessary files to make room for the file. This error message also can occur if you attempt to write to a read-only file. If you want to write to a file that has the read-only attribute set, you need to change the file's attribute (use the DOS ATTRIB command or Norton's FileFind command) or save the file under another name.

Also, the disk may be physically damaged, and DOS may have tried to write the file to a bad spot on the disk. You can verify whether there are bad spots on the disk by running the Norton NDD command. NDD will mark bad spots so that they will not be used to store files.

File Not Found

You get this message if you attempt to access a file that is not in the current directory or is not in the directory of the specified path. You may have misspelled the file name or included an incorrect path. You can use the FileFind command to locate the file in another directory. If you still get this message, the file space on the disk may be damaged. You then should try to reclaim the file with Norton Disk Doctor's Diagnose Disk option.

General Failure

This message is displayed if DOS cannot figure out why a problem has occurred. In this case, you may have to do your own fishing for the culprit. If you are attempting to access a disk in a drive, you may want to make sure that the disk is readable. For example, are you attempting to access a 1.2M, 5 1/4-inch disk in a 360K drive or a 1.44M, 3 1/2-inch disk in a 720K drive? Also, check to see that your diskette is inserted correctly in the disk drive and that the disk drive door is closed all the way. The problem also can be caused by a damaged disk or disk drive. Try the disk in another disk drive or use Norton Disk Doctor to attempt to read the diskette.

Incorrect DOS Version

This message occurs if you attempt to use a DOS external command from a version of DOS other than the one under which the machine was booted—for example, you attempt to use the PRINT command (PRINT.COM) for DOS 3.3 when the machine was booted with DOS 4.0. You should make sure that all your DOS commands on disk are from the same version of DOS. To find out which version of DOS you are using, enter the VER command at the DOS prompt.

Incorrect (or Invalid) Number of Parameters

This message appears if you enter a DOS command with the wrong number of parameters. Check your DOS command syntax and reenter the command.

Insufficient Disk Space

This message appears if you attempt to write a file to a disk that is full or does not have enough free space to hold the file. To correct the problem, erase unneeded files and retry. You also can use the FileFind command to see whether there is enough space on a destination disk to receive one or more files.

Invalid Drive Specification (or Invalid Drive or File Name)

This message appears if you use a drive specification that does not exist. If you use drive D in a DOS command when you have no drive D, for example, DOS gives you this error message.

Invalid Partition Table

This message occurs if DOS attempts to boot the computer from your hard disk and finds something wrong with the computer's partition information. This information should be on your disk at track 0. If this area is bad, you can use Norton Disk Doctor from Disk Tools to diagnose and recover the information for you.

Invalid Path, Not Directory, or Directory Not Empty

This message appears if you attempt to remove a directory that contains files or that does not exist. If you want to remove an existing directory, you first must erase all files and subdirectories contained in that directory.

Memory Allocation Error

This message appears if a program you are running overwrites the area in the computer's memory that stores important DOS information, or if not enough memory is available to load portions of DOS. This command may freeze your computer and cause you to have to reboot. A possible solution to this problem is to lower the number of buffers and/or device drivers specified in your CONFIG.SYS file or to remove some memory-resident (stay-resident, pop-up) programs.

Missing Operating System

You get this message if DOS attempts to boot the computer from a disk that the system thinks is a bootable disk, but some or all of the system information is missing. To correct the problem, you can reformat the disk with DOS (copy all files first) or use the Norton Disk Doctor's Make a Diskette Bootable option. With Norton, none of the files on disk are removed, so you do not have to back up the disk first.

No Room for System on Destination Disk

This message occurs if you attempt to use the DOS SYS command to place a copy of the system files on a disk, but the disk has not been prepared during the format procedure to receive those files. To make the disk bootable with DOS, you should copy all files from the disk and then reformat the disk with the /S option. The Norton Disk Doctor's Make a Diskette Bootable option can create a bootable disk without destroying files, even on a disk that was not formatted to be a system disk.

Non-System Disk

This message occurs if you attempt to boot from a disk that does not contain the full DOS system or that has damaged system disks. If you are using a hard disk system, make sure that you do not have a disk in drive A, because the computer then attempts to boot from that disk. If your disk should be bootable but is not, you can attempt to fix the disk by using Norton Disk Doctor's Make a Diskette Bootable option.

Not Ready

This message appears if DOS attempts to read or write information to a device and cannot. This problem may occur because the disk drive door or knob is not closed completely, the disk is not formatted, the printer is not turned on or is not on-line, or another device is not ready to receive information. Investigate, correct the problem, and try again.

If a drive becomes overheated, it may produce the Not ready message. Check to see whether the computer is getting proper ventilation. (You may need to vacuum the vents around the edges of the computer.) Also, if your computer has an exhaust fan, make sure that it is working properly. Turn off the computer and let the disk cool down. If the problem continues, see a technician for further diagnosis.

Probable Non-DOS Disk

This message occurs during a CHKDSK command if DOS has problems reading the FAT or the disk media descriptor. This problem may occur particularly on a hard disk larger than 32M that is partitioned into several drives. You usually can fix the problem by running the Norton Disk Doctor's Diagnose A Disk procedure.

Read Fault Error

This message appears if DOS is unable to read information from a disk. The disk may be seated improperly in the drive, or the drive door may not be closed properly. You also probably will get the message

    Abort, Retry, Ignore, Fail?

Abort the procedure and reseat the disk. To reseat the disk, take the diskette out of the drive and tap the disk on its side to loosen it up. On a 5 1/4-inch disk, you can carefully place two fingers in the center hole and move the disk in the cover to loosen the disk. Place the diskette back into the drive and close the drive door. If other disks work in the drive, but this one cannot be read, try the Norton Disk Tools' Revive a Defective Diskette option.

Required Parameter Missing

This message occurs if you enter a DOS command with an invalid number of parameters. Check your DOS command syntax and reenter the command.

Sector Not Found

This message may occur as a result of DOS attempting to read or write something to a disk when the sector on the disk cannot be accessed. You also probably will see the message

```
Abort, Retry, Ignore, Fail?
```

Abort the current command by pressing A and then Enter.

If the problem occurs with a floppy diskette, try to read the information in another drive. Copy all the files you can from the disk. Use the Norton Disk Doctor to find and mark bad spots on the disk. Also try the Norton Disk Tools' Revive a Defective Diskette option. Reformat the floppy or discard it.

If the problem occurs with a hard disk, use the Norton Disk Doctor command to find and mark the bad sectors. If the problem persists on the hard disk, you need to back up all possible files and then perform a low-level format on the disk. For more information, see "You Need To Perform a Low-Level Format of a Hard Disk," earlier in the appendix.

Seek Error

This message appears if DOS is unable to find the track on disk that is needed to read or write information to the disk. You also get the message

```
Abort, Retry, Ignore, Fail?
```

Choose to abort the process by pressing A and then Enter.

If this message appears while you are trying to access a floppy diskette, take the disk out, tap it on its side, and reinsert it correctly into the drive. If the problem continues, attempt to fix the problem with Norton Disk Tools' Revive a Defective Diskette option. Copy all possible information from the disk and then discard the disk or reformat and reuse it.

If the problem occurs when you are trying to access a hard disk, attempt to copy as much information off the disk as possible. You may try to use the Norton Disk Edit command to edit the bad sectors back to health. After you have recovered as much information as possible, perform a low-level format on the hard disk. For more information, see "You Need To Perform a Low-Level Format of a Hard Disk," earlier in the appendix.

Too Many Parameters

This message occurs if you enter a DOS command with an invalid number of parameters. Check your DOS command syntax and reenter the command.

Top Level Process Aborted, Cannot Continue

This message appears if a DOS command failed when trying to access the disk. Reboot and run the Norton Disk Doctor (NDD) procedure to locate and attempt to fix any bad sectors.

Write Protect Error

This message may appear if you attempt to write information to a disk that is write-protected. On a 5 1/4-inch diskette, you set write protection by placing a piece of tape over the notch on the side of the diskette. A 3 1/2-inch diskette is write-protected when you move the write-protect tab so that an open hole appears in the corner of the disk. Before removing write protection, make sure that you want to change information on the disk.

Symbols

A

B

M

O

Q

Find It Fast With Que's Quick References!

Que's Quick References are the compact, easy-to-use guides to essential application information. Written for all users, Quick References include vital command information under easy-to-find alphabetical listings. Quick References are a must for anyone who needs command information fast!

Free Catalog!

Mail us this registration form today, and we'll send you a free catalog featuring Que's complete line of best-selling books.

Name of Book _____

Name _____

Title _____

Phone (___) _____

Company _____

Address _____

City _____

State _____ ZIP _____

Please check the appropriate answers:

1. Where did you buy your Que book?
   - ☐ Bookstore (name: _____)
   - ☐ Computer store (name: _____)
   - ☐ Catalog (name: _____)
   - ☐ Direct from Que
   - ☐ Other: _____

2. How many computer books do you buy a year?
   - ☐ 1 or less
   - ☐ 2-5
   - ☐ 6-10
   - ☐ More than 10

3. How many Que books do you own?
   - ☐ 1
   - ☐ 2-5
   - ☐ 6-10
   - ☐ More than 10

4. How long have you been using this software?
   - ☐ Less than 6 months
   - ☐ 6 months to 1 year
   - ☐ 1-3 years
   - ☐ More than 3 years

5. What influenced your purchase of this Que book?
   - ☐ Personal recommendation
   - ☐ Advertisement
   - ☐ In-store display
   - ☐ Price
   - ☐ Que catalog
   - ☐ Que mailing
   - ☐ Que's reputation
   - ☐ Other: _____

6. How would you rate the overall content of the book?
   - ☐ Very good
   - ☐ Good
   - ☐ Satisfactory
   - ☐ Poor

7. What do you like *best* about this Que book?
   _____
   _____

8. What do you like *least* about this Que book?
   _____
   _____

9. Did you buy this book with your personal funds?
   - ☐ Yes   ☐ No

10. Please feel free to list any other comments you may have about this Que book.
   _____
   _____
   _____

QUE

Order Your Que Books Today!

Name _____

Title _____

Company _____

City _____

State _____ ZIP _____

Phone No. (___) _____

Method of Payment:

Check ☐ (Please enclose in envelope.)

Charge My: VISA ☐   MasterCard ☐

American Express ☐

Charge # _____

Expiration Date _____

Order No.	Title	Qty.	Price	Total

You can **FAX** your order to **1-317-573-2583.** Or call **1-800-428-5331, ext. ORDR** to order direct.

Please add $2.50 per title for shipping and handling.

Subtotal _____

Shipping & Handling _____

Total _____

QUE

BUSINESS REPLY MAIL

First Class Permit No. 9918   Indianapolis, IN

Postage will be paid by addressee

que®

11711 N. College
Carmel, IN 46032

BUSINESS REPLY MAIL
First Class Permit No. 9918   Indianapolis, IN

Postage will be paid by addressee

que®

11711 N. College
Carmel, IN 46032